Research Series on the Chinese Dream and China's Development Path

Drawing on a large body of empirical studies done over the last two decades, this Series provides its readers with in-depth analyses of the past and present and forecasts for the future course of China's development. It contains the latest research results made by members of the Chinese Academy of Social Sciences. This series is an invaluable companion to every researcher who is trying to gain a deeper understanding of the development model, path and experience unique to China. Thanks to the adoption of Socialism with Chinese characteristics, and the implementation of comprehensive reform and opening-up, China has made tremendous achievements in areas such as political reform, economic development, and social construction, and is making great strides towards the realization of the Chinese dream of national rejuvenation. In addition to presenting a detailed account of many of these achievements, the authors also discuss what lessons other countries can learn from China's experience.

Wen Xian

Chinese Food Security Strategy

The Ever-Normal Granary in History and Beyond

Translated by Wei Zhu

SSAP

Springer

Wen Xian
Department of Economics
Shaanxi Normal University
Xi'an, China

Translated by
Wei Zhu
School of Foreign Languages
South-central Minzu University
Wuhan, China

ISSN 2363-6866 ISSN 2363-6874 (electronic)
Research Series on the Chinese Dream and China's Development Path
ISBN 978-981-95-7963-1 ISBN 978-981-95-7964-8 (eBook)
https://doi.org/10.1007/978-981-95-7964-8

This book is published with financial support of the Chinese Fund for the Humanities and Social Sciences.

Jointly published with Social Sciences Academic Press

This Springer imprint is published by the registered company Springer Nature Singapore Pte Ltd.
The registered company address is: 152 Beach Road, #21-01/04 Gateway East, Singapore 189721, Singapore

Sponsored by "Chinese Fund for the Humanities and Social Sciences" (22WJLB002)

Where uncertainty doth reign,
The Ever-Normal Granary shall remain.

Author's Preface

Historically, China has been a predominantly agrarian country, with a long-standing tradition of storing grain as a safeguard against famine. The Ever-Normal Granary represents a typical institutional form of such grain reservation. A substantial high-quality research achievements has already been accumulated both in China and abroad on the Ever-Normal Granary. Building on this foundation, the present book seeks to make a marginal yet meaningful contribution, which may be summarized in two main respects. First, in terms of its analytical framework, the book attempts to move beyond a single, linear narrative of Chinese history. It aims to construct a "coordinate system" bridging history and economics, ancient and modern, as well as China and the West, in order to explore the repeated "transcendence" of this ancient institution across time and space. Second, at the level of economic thought and economic philosophy, the book addresses the question: Why was the Ever-Normal Granary necessary? It seeks to interpret the Chinese economic wisdom embedded in this institution, namely the "Doctrine of the Mean", and further to investigate the underlying moderation in contemporary Chinese economic theory and institutional practice.

In the view of ancient Chinese thinkers, the "ever-normal" socio-economic development requires both effective government intervention and the spontaneous regulation of the market. The economic principles later articulated by Adam Smith as the "invisible hand" and by John Maynard Keynes as the "visible hand" had, in fact, already been clearly expounded in the pre-Qin text *Guanzi*. For example, the chapter "Maintaining Restraint" of *Guanzi* vividly illustrates the idea of the "invisible hand": "Indeed, it is the nature of men that whenever they see profit, they cannot help chasing after it, and whenever they see harm, they cannot help running away... Indeed, those who are skilled in government control the presence of wealth so that the people are naturally content. Without pushing them, they go; without pulling them, they come. Without trouble or worry, the people enrich themselves. It is like a bird sitting on its eggs: there is neither shape nor sound, but the young suddenly appear quite complete."[1] The idea advanced in the *Guanzi* that "extravagance in spending" (*chimi*, increased fiscal spending) can be used as a policy instrument

[1] Guanzi. 1998. *Political, Economic, and Philosophical Essays from Early China*, vol.2. trans. W. Allyn Rickett. Princeton: Princeton University Press. p. 220.

to achieve "full employment," constitutes one of the central themes of the present study.

Today, China's pursuit of high-quality economic development is attracting increasing global attention. The country is successfully stepping on a distinctive path toward Chinese-style modernization, and the underlying intellectual and cultural logic behind this trajectory has become a subject of growing interest and reflection. While this book takes the Ever-Normal Granary as its point of departure, it ultimately arrives at the principle of "maintaining balance through the mean". If this argument holds, the author cautiously hope that this way of telling a "Chinese story" may, to some extent, help readers better understand the continuity of Chinese economic thinking across time, as well as its creative application in different historical contexts. It may also shed light on the close connection between China's present-day development and success and its long-standing historical and cultural traditions, especially its economic heritage. From *Guanzi*, a text dating back more than two thousand years ago, we can discern the remarkable yet still insufficiently recognized achievements of ancient Chinese thinkers in the realm of economic thought.

The English edition of this book has been revised, supplemented, and refined on the basis of the original Chinese edition. Its publication has benefited from the support of the "Chinese Fund for the Humanities and Social Sciences." The initiation and implementation of the project have received strong support from Professor Zhang Yaguang of the School of Economics at Peking University and Research Fellow Jiang Hong of the Max Weber Institute of Sociology at Heidelberg University. The translation has been undertaken by Associate Professor Zhu Wei of the School of Foreign Languages at South-Central Minzu University, who has devoted tremendous effort to this work. Hereby I would like to express my sincere gratitude for their generous assistance and dedicated contributions. During the publication process, Editor Gao Jing of Social Sciences Academic Press (China) was responsible for coordination among all parties, while Ms. Emily Zhang of Springer undertook the English editing and proofreading. I would also like to extend my heartfelt thanks to them for their meticulous and conscientious work.

Wen Xian

Contents

About the Author

Wen Xian is a professor in the Department of Economics at the International Business School of Shaanxi Normal University. His primary research focuses on theoretical economics, with specific areas of interest including economic history (history of economic thought and economic history), as well as comparative economics, macroeconomics and development economics. He pays particular attention to the comparison and integration of Chinese and Western economic traditions, as well as the construction of a discourse system for Chinese economics.

About the Translator

Wei Zhu is an associate professor in the School of Foreign languages, South-central Minzu University. Her research interest includes translation studies and translation technology.

Chapter 1
Introduction: Intertwined History and Economy

Heaven's Way—to supply who wants
By taking from the have-mores—
Is not the Way of men
Who take from those in need
To serve those who have more.
Who will use the surplus to serve this world below?
None but men of the Way.
—Laozi (Spring and Autumn Period)[1]

Passing the danger with joy,
Carry out restriction in the proper position.
From the central and correct place,
His advance is without limitation.
When Heaven and Earth regulate their restriction,
Then the four seasons complete their functions.
When restriction is put into regulation,
Then resources will not be exhausted
And people will not be hurt.
—I Ching (Book of Changes)[2]

1.1 Orientation of Study

Since the reform and opening-up in the late 1970s, especially since the entry of the twenty-first century, with its tremendous economic achievements and increasing contributions to and positive impacts on the world, China has examined itself with

[1] Laozi. 2001. *Dao De Jing: The Book of the Way*. trans. Moss Roberts. Berkeley, Los Angeles and London: University of California Press. p.181.

[2] Huang, Alfred. 1998. *The Complete I Ching*. Vermont: Inner Traditions. pp. 465–466.

W. Xian, *Chinese Food Security Strategy*, Research Series on the Chinese Dream and China's Development Path,
https://doi.org/10.1007/978-981-95-7964-8_1

greater confidence. The "Chinese Road", "Chinese Model" and "Chinese Solution", along with their underlying historical and cultural traditions, have attracted worldwide attention. As we advance into the new era, it has become an inevitable yet urgent topic for in-depth and systematic study to explore and uncover the modern value of China's economic traditions based on the practical needs of its economic development, and to construct a discourse system of economics with Chinese characteristics.[3] The discussion in this book unfolds against such a backdrop, specifically stemming from the following questions.

Over two thousand years ago, China had already established a vast and unified country in which the government managed a large population. In the traditional agricultural society, what policies were implemented to stabilize economic and social development, and create brilliant agricultural civilizations in ancient world history? Especially when agricultural production fluctuated greatly due to climate change and disasters, what policies did the state adopt to address the economic volatility triggered by these agricultural production fluctuations? If such questions can be further distilled into the following one: what are the thoughts, systems and practical paths that Chinese employed to maintain economic stability and development in ancient China? Then another question arises: Do these economic traditions have any connection with modern economics, especially macroeconomic theories and policies? If so, can we further uncover the value of Chinese economic traditions through theoretical analysis and comparative studies across different eras, cultures, and economic forms, thereby serving the development of contemporary China?

These interrelated questions are obviously worth exploring in depth due to their theoretical and practical significance. However, putting them together would create a vast system of problems, making it difficult to delve into comprehensively. Nevertheless, by selecting an appropriate research topic to connect and integrate them, we can use this as a starting point to interweave the "longitude" of history and the "latitude" of economics, making some meaningful explorations from a minor perspective, thereby discovering the potential connections between traditional, modern and future development of China.

Based on the above considerations, this study focuses on "the Ever-normal Granary".[4] We find that the vast economic system in ancient China, rooted in the

[3] In the field of economics, the construction of a discourse system for economics with Chinese characteristics has become a significant topic in frontier exploration. For relevant analysis, please refer to the following article: Xie, Fuzhan. 2019. Accelerating the construction of a discipline system, academic system, and discourse system for philosophy and social sciences with Chinese Characteristics. *Chinese Social Science.* (5): 4–22. Only through inheritance can development be achieved, and only by turning to the traditions can innovation be made. Undoubtedly, exploration of Chinese millennium-long economic tradition from the perspective of economic history will play a pivotal role in construction of the system.

[4] "Ever- Normal Granary" (*changping cang*), more exactly translated as "granary [for maintaining] constant [price] stability", were in imperial times created with the aim to control grain prices. After bad harvests, grain stored in the granaries was thrown (*tiao*) on the local market to keep the price low, while in years of bumper harvests, grain was taken out of the local market and stored (*di*) for coming years. The system originated in the regional state of Wei during the Warring States period

small-scale peasant economy, has the inherent demand for "macro-stability" and "macro-control". In line with this, Chinese governments of various dynasties gradually explored and developed a set of economic management system, whose functions in organizing, coordinating and allocating resources cannot be underestimated. Among them, the Ever-normal Granary created by Geng Shouchang in the Western Han dynasty (206 B.C.-24 A.D.) was particularly noteworthy for its mechanism of *pingdi* (increased-price purchase) and *pingtiao* (reduced-price sales). Specifically, during times of low grain prices, grains were purchased at guaranteed prices and stored at granaries to prevent farmers from suffering losses brought by low prices. Conversely, during times of high grain prices, grains stored at the granaries were sold at restricted prices to prevent populace from suffering of losses due to high prices, thereby implementing buffering regulation on grain supply and demand as well as prices. A review of ancient Chinese history reveals that Ever-normal Granary system was an important option in the "menu" of the economic systems and policies during the periods of unified rule following the Han dynasty. Moreover, in establishing the Ever-normal Granary system, people of various dynasties discussed and summarized the experiences of previous dynasties, highlighting its importance for the stability of the economy and the sustenance of the people. Therefore, the "layer-upon-layer accumulation" of the Ever-normal Granary thus became a distinctive "economic tradition" of ancient Chinese agricultural society. Through continuous exploration, improvement, and development, this system reached maturity and completeness during the Qing dynasty. In the 1930s, this system even became the model for agricultural reform in the United States during the Great Depression.[5] Thus, the Ever-normal Granary provides an excellent sample for our research. The evolution and development of this economic tradition between ancient and modern time, as well as between the East and the West, can serve as a typical case to help us answer the series of questions posed above.

In the process of economic and social changes, ancient Chinese economic thoughts, systems, policies, and practices interacted and influenced each other, forming an intrinsically correlational system that spans from economic philosophy to economic theory and then to practical applications. If we were to give this an overall label, "economic tradition" would be quite appropriate. Thus, the "economic tradition" of the Ever-normal Granary as a grain reserve system, also encompasses the basic elements of thoughts, systems, policies and practices. It should be noted that economic thoughts not only encompass the systematic reflections on economic practices but also involve the important modes of economic thinking (such as economic philosophy embodying worldviews and methodologies). Then, how did the ancient Chinese develop the tradition of the Ever-normal Granary based on their

(476–221 BC), where Counsellor Li Kui invented the so-called *pingdi* system, which worked in the way just described. A similar method was applied by Fan Li and is described in the book Guanzi. They were given the name *changing cang* because they balanced out (*ping*) price fluctuations over long periods (*chang*).

[5] Li Chaomin has conducted systematic studies on this issue. Please refer to the discussions hereinafter.

fundamental modes of thinking? This is another significant question that this research aims to address. Furthermore, if we remove the word "granary" from the term and elevate "ever-normal" to a more general discussion of economic stability, our research will further involve the evolution from the ancient ever-normal tradition to the contemporary path of the socialist economic system with Chinese characteristics. This will encompass richer and deeper theoretical explorations as well as policy discussions of practical significance.

1.2 Academic Review, New Clues, and New Perspectives

The Ever-normal Granary involves various economic systems and policies in ancient China, including agricultural administration, fiscal policy, grain administration, warehousing administration and famine administration (*huangzheng*), etc., to which Ancient Chinese people attached great importance to. Summarizing historical experience, formulating policies, and putting them into practice are crucial reasons why relevant historical materials have been recorded, sorted out, analyzed, summarized and handed down through generations. Among them, Treatise on Food and Money (*shi huo zhi*) in the official histories of various dynasties, historical books on institutions and regulation,[6] historical documents on famine administration (*huangzheng*)[7]and warehousing administration,[8] as well as various local gazetteers and personal collected works, all contain relatively concentrated records on this topic.

[6]Examples include the following: *Tongdian* ("Comprehensive Institutions", an encyclopedia compiled in the Tang dynasty (618–907) by the prominent scholar-official Du You (735–812), which includes a survey of the social, political and cultural institutions of Chinese history and serves as a longstanding model for the compilation of Chinese encyclopedias), *Song Huiyao Jigao* ("Song Government Manuscript Compendium", a Qing dynasty collection of Song dynasty writings on Song government, edited by Xu Song and others who extracted the manuscripts in part from the Ming dynasty *Yongle Encyclopedia* (1408), which contains a large quantity of Imperial edicts and decrees as well as memorials and other documents relating to institutional mechanisms of the Song dynasty), *Qingchao Wenxian Tongkao* ("Comprehensive Textual Research of Historical Documents of Qing Dynasty", a 300-volume officially compiled historical record of institutional regulations of the Qing dynasty compiled by Zhang Tingyu and others, which documents the laws and regulations from the founding year of the Qing dynasty in 1616 to the 50th year of Emperor Qianlong's reign in 1785).

[7]Jiuhuang Huomin Shu ("*A Book on Relieving Famine and Reviving the People*"), written by Dong Wei in the Southern Song dynasty (1127–1279), is the first monograph on famine administration (*huangzheng*). Since then, books on famine administration have continuously emerged, with the Qing dynasty producing the most. Many of these books are included in the 12-volume collections: Li, Wenhai, et al. ed. 2010.*Collections of Chinese Books on Famine Administration*. Tianjin: Tianjin Ancient Books Publishing House.

[8]Examples include *Changpingcang Kao* ("Study of the Ever-normal Granary"), *Yicang Kao* ("Study of the Charity Granary") and *Shecang Kao* ("Study of the Community Granary") written by Yu Sen, an official in Qing dynasty. in Li, Wenhai et al. ed. 2010. *Collections of Chinese Books on Famine Administration*, vol.2. Tianjin: Tianjin Ancient Books Publishing House.

The large-scale establishment of Ever-Normal Granaries reached its zenith during the Qing dynasty. Researches on ancient Chinese grain administration, warehouse administration, and famine administration in the Republic of China period (1912–1949) addressed Ever-Normal Granaries of various dynasties to varying degrees. Scholars conducted pioneering explorations into the origin, functions, operational mechanisms, and development and evolution of Ever-Normal Granaries from different perspectives such as grain and agriculture systems, famine relief policies, warehousing systems, and their impact on the world.[9] Among them, Deng Yunte's work "A History of Famine Relief in China", with its study of famine administration (*huangzheng*), provides an important perspective for subsequent researches on Ever-Normal Granaries. Meanwhile, Shen Wenfu's work "On the Ever-normal Granary Policy throughout History and around the World" opens up new paths for research of the modern transformation of Ever-normal Granary with its great foresight.

Since the 1980s, Ever-normal Granary gradually became a researched topic of sustained interest in academic circles. Zhang Gong's comprehensive review of the storage system of the Tang dynasty, including the Ever-normal Granary, provided significant inspiration and guidance for subsequent research, prompting scholars to explore this topic from various perspectives.[10] Building on previous researches, studies from the 1990s to the present have mostly focused on important historical stages of the development of Ever-normal Granary, often narrowing their attention to specific dynasties or periods. Although there has been little focus on "comprehensive study of historical documents" (*tongkao*)[11] that connect various eras, research

[9] For more information, see: Yu, Shude. 1921. Preventive measures against agricultural famines in ancient China - Ever-Normal Granaries, Charity Granaries and Community Granaries (Part 1). Eastern Miscellany. 18 (14): 18–30; Yu, Shude. 1921. Preventive measures against agricultural famines in ancient China - Ever-Normal Granaries, Charity Granaries and Community Granaries (Part 2). Eastern Miscellany. 18(15): 17–33; Lin, Puchu. 1930. A study of granaries. *New Life,* 3(9): 76–88; Lang, Xiaoqing. 1933. *A History of Food Supply in China.* Beijing: Commercial Press; Feng, Liutang. 1934. *A History of Food Policy in Ancient China.* Beijing: Commercial Press; Deng, Yunte. 1937. *A History of Famine Relief in China.* Beijing: Commercial Press; Wen, Yibo. 1943. *A History of Grain Administration in China.* Chongqing: Cheng Chung Book Company; Huang, Boxuan. 1944. The Origin and Nature of Ever-Normal Granaries. *Economic Forum,* 2(2): 47–54; Shen, Wenfu. 1944. On the Ever-normal Granary policy advocated by Wallace in the United States. *Economic Forum.* 2(7–8): 21–26; Shen, Wenfu. 1945. On the Ever-normal Granary policy throughout history and around the world. *Eastern Miscellany.* 41(6): 20–30; Yu, Youyu. 1948. *A Study of China's Warehousing System.* Shanghai: Cheng Chung Book Company; etc.

[10] See: Zhang, Gong. 1986. *A Preliminary Study of Granary System in the Tang Dynasty.* Beijing: Zhonghua Book Company; Xu, Jianqing. 1987. Examining the accumulation in China's feudal society and its role in social reproduction from the perspective of granary storage. *Researches in Chinese Economic History. (3): 31–48*; Chen, Chunsheng. 1989. On the Ever-normal Granary in Guangdong during the Qing Dynasty. *Journal of Chinese Historical Studies.* (3): 66–79; Liu, Qiugen. 1989. The operation of the Ever-normal Granary in the Tang and Song Dynasties and the implementation of the Green Sprouts Act. *Journal of Hebei University (Philosophy and Social Sciences).* (4): 16–20.

[11] Liu Jiapeng's exploration of grain reserve ideas throughout history covers the development and evolution of the Ever-normal Granary system throughout ancient history. See: Liu, Jiapeng. 2010.

on Ever-normal Granary of specific periods, especially of the Song and Qing dynasties, has made significant progress. These studies cover a wide range of aspects about Ever-normal Granary, such as its establishment and evolution, roles and functions, operational mechanisms, institutional safeguards, performance evaluations, spatial layouts, regional cases, storage technologies, institutional changes and their evaluations, the relationship between Ever-normal Granary and other types of granaries, as well as its rise and fall, and its advantages and disadvantages.

Through various methods such as historical data excavation, combination of qualitative and quantitative analysis, and comparative studies across dynasties, the academic community has gained an increasingly in-depth and comprehensive understanding of the Ever-normal Granary in important periods of Chinese history from diverse perspectives such as famine administration (*huangzheng*) history, granary administration history, agricultural history, fiscal history, institutional history, social history, intellectual history, regional history, historical geography, management history and price history. They have made the following achievements:

Firstly, the roles, functions, and effects of the Ever-normal Granary in various periods in traditional agricultural socioeconomic management, social governance (typically in famine relief administration), and other fields have been gradually unveiled.[12]

Secondly, by putting the Ever-normal Granary within the entire granary system, researchers have explored the intrinsic connections between the Ever-normal Granary and other types of granaries, recognizing that the latter increasingly played the role of "stabilizing prices" throughout history, hence the gradual development of a mutually complementary and coordinated relationship among various granaries.[13]

The Evolution of Thoughts on Grain Reserve Regulation System in Ancient China. Beijing: Economic Press China.

[12] See: Niu, Jingzhong. 1991. The social functions of the Ever-normal Granary and Community Granary in the Qing dynasty. *Journal of Inner Mongolia University (Humanities and Social Sciences)*. 22(1): 45–51; Tian, Hua.1992. Research on the Ever-normal Granary in the Jin dynasty. *Agricultural Archaeology*. 9(1): 256–261; Zhang, Yan. 1993. A preliminary study on the Ever-normal Granary system in the Qing dynasty. *The Qing History Journal*. (4): 28–39; Liu, Cuirong. 2005. Review of the stability function of the Qing dynasty warehousing system. in *Economic Pulse*. ed. Chen, Guodong et al. Beijing: Encyclopedia of China Publishing House. pp. 340–341; Wang, Wendong. 2006. A comparative study of the Green Sprouts Act in the Song dynasty and the Ever-normal Granary system in the Tang and Song Dynasties. *Researches in Chinese Economic History*. (3):29–36; Wei, Tian'an. 2007. Some issues concerning the Ever-normal Granary system. in *The Song History Research Forum*. ed. Jiang, Xidong et al.vol.8. Hebei University Press; Kong, Xiangjun. 2009. Research on Ever-normal Granary in the Two Song Dynasties. *Journal of Nanjing Agricultural University (Social Sciences)*. 9(4):102–108; Murong, Hao. 2004. Exploring Ever-normal Granary in the Han dynasty. *Inner Mongolia Social Science*. 35(3): 77–79.

[13] See: Zhang, Yan. 1998. On the relationship between Ever-Normal Granaries and relevant granaries in the Qing dynasty. *The Journal of Chinese Social and Economic History*. (4): 52–58; Zhang, Wen. 2001. Prevention of disasters - storage system. in *Study of Social Relief in the Song Dynasty*. Chongqing: Southwest Normal University Press; Li, Huarui. 2012. The development and changes of the disaster relief storage system in the Song dynasty. In *Jinan Historical Science*. ed. Ma, Mingda. Guilin: Guangxi Normal University Press.vol.7, pp.497–531.

Thirdly, a new research orientation has emerged, which is based on multi-dimensional examinations of economic and social systems. The analytical methods and historical materials have continuously expanded, with increasing attention being paid to regional economic and local societal perspectives, as well as micro-level case studies of granaries. Regional economics, local social perspectives, and micro-level case studies of granaries have received increasing attention. Utilizing local gazetteers, granary records, credit records of granary operations and other materials, scholars have further conducted empirical study of the management of the Ever-normal Granary, which led to their understanding of the specific operational conditions.[14]

Fourthly, the influence of national will, governance capacity and political trends on the establishment, development, management of the Ever-normal Granary—along with its advantages, disadvantages, and performance—has been fully revealed, thereby portraying the life-cycle of the Ever-normal Granary throughout history, which is characterized by a transition from positive to negative construction and a decline in functionality over time.[15]

Fifthly, as research deepens, the academic community has gradually recognized the complexities and contradictions associated with the Ever-normal Granary in historical changes. For example, while the Ever-normal Granary utilized significant resources, its performance was not always satisfactory; despite institutionalization in its construction, the drawbacks of rule by man remained evident; although there were many

[14] For journal articles, see: Zhong, Yongning. 1990. The Ever-normal Granary and rice exportation in Hunan during the early Qing dynasty. *Seeker (Qiu Suo)*. (1): 107–110; Wu, Tao. 1997. On the storage system in the Suzhou-Songjiang region during the early Qing dynasty. *Agricultural History of China.* (2): 40–49; Hu, Bo. 2002. A tentative study on the changes in the grain storage scale of the Ever-normal Granary in the Loess Plateau Region of Shaanxi during the Qing dynasty. *Journal of Shaanxi Normal University (Philosophy and Social Sciences).* (S1): 157–159; Yao, Jianping. 2005. Internal and external functions: The purchase and sales of grain from the Ever-normal Granary in the Hubei-Hunan regions during the Qing dynasty. *Social Science Journal.* (4): 122–127; Ma, Li, and Fang Xiuqi. 2009. The spatial pattern of grain storage quotas of Ever-normal Granary in Qing dynasty. *Journal of Chinese Historical Geography.* 24(3): 68–74; He, Rong. 2014. The development and management of the Ever-normal Granary in Xinjiang in the Qing dynasty. *Journal of Xinjiang University (Philosophy, Humanities & Social Sciences).* 42(2): 66–69. For monographs, see: Chen, Yao. 2017. *The Modes of Ditiao: The Grain Trade and Local Society in Xiangtan in the Qing Dynasty*. Xiamen: Xiamen University Press; Bai, Liping. 2018. *Warehouse Transformation and Social Change in the Middle Reaches of the Yangtze River in the Late Qing Dynasty*. Beijing: China University of Political Science and Law Press; Chen, Chunsheng. 2020. *Market Mechanisms and Social Change: An Analysis of Rice Prices in Guangdong in the 18th Century* (Revised Edition), Beijing: Beijing Normal University Press; Deng, Yibing. 2019. *Research on Government and Beijing Grain Market in Early Qing Dynasty*. Beijing: Social Sciences Academic Press. For research utilizing granary records, see: Wu, Siwu. 2018. *Institutional Dilemmas of Granary and Its Disaster Relief Practices in the Qing Dynasty*. Beijing: Social Sciences Academic Press.

[15] See: Kang, Peizhu. 1996. The decline of storage systems and famines in the Qing dynasty. *Social Science Front.* (3): 186–191; Li, Fenyang. 2006. *Research on Storage Systems in the Qing Dynasty*. Taibei: Wenhai Press Company; Zhu, Hu. 2014. Food as the Heaven for the people: Policy evolution and structural transformation of disaster preparedness storage in the Qing dynasty. *Journal of Historical Science.* (4): 20–25.

improvements and innovations in Ever-normal Granary system, they were difficult to sustain over the long term; although the principles governing the operation of the Ever-normal Granary were acknowledged, violations of these principles occurred frequently.

It is noteworthy that despite the multifaceted and multi-dimensional portrayal of the Ever-normal Granary in history, the academic community still tends to evaluate it positively. Recently, some overseas studies have even "discovered", through the Ever-normal Granary, the efficient organization and coordination capabilities of ancient Chinese states in response to socio-economic crises, contrary to Western traditions.

In overseas research, Hoshi Ayao, a Japanese scholar, views the Ever-normal Granary and the Community Granary as part of the welfare policies. His book, *A Study of the History of Social Welfare Policies in China: A Monograph on Relief Granaries in the Qing Dynasty*, examines granaries within the context of traditional Chinese charity service and public welfare endeavors. This indicates that ideas and practices similar to welfare economics have a long-standing tradition in China. In his research on the Ever-normal Granary in the Qing dynasty, Hoshi Ayao adopts both macro and micro perspectives. On the one hand, he emphasizes tracing the evolution of granaries and institutional changes; on the other hand, he employs a substantial amount of local historical materials to investigate the functions and operations of local granaries. His work, *A Study of the History of Social Welfare Policies in China: A Monograph on Relief Granaries in the Qing Dynasty*, opens up a new approach to regional granary research through its shift of historical materials and perspectives.[16]

Among European and American scholars, Pierre-Etienne Will and R. Bin. Wong, among others, co-authored the work *Nourish the People: the State Civilian Granary System in China, 1650–1850*. Utilizing numerous archival historical materials, they conduct a detailed and in-depth analysis of the internal operating mechanisms of granaries in the Qing dynasty, and through this also examine the internal workings of the bureaucratic system. They argue that the granary system actively promoted by the mid-Qing government achieved great successes in maintaining economic and social stability and development, and that the administrative efficiency of the government is commendable.[17] Such understanding is also reflected in Pierre-Etienne Will's work *Bureaucracy and Famine in Eighteenth-century China* and R. Bin. Wong's *China Transformed: Historical Change and the Limits of European Experience*. Deviating from the entrenched views that have long prevailed in Western academia, with analysis of granaries they argue that the ancient Chinese states exhibited positive aspects in economic and social management that have generally been overlooked. However, they also point out that the granary system, with the Ever-normal Granary as the representative, also displayed cyclical characteristics of decline following prosperity during its development.[18]

---

[16] Wu, Siwu. 2018. *Institutional Dilemmas of Granary and Its Disaster Relief Practices in the Qing Dynasty*. Beijing: Social Sciences Academic Press. pp. 14–15.

[17] Will, Pierre-Etienne and R. Bin Wong. ed. 1991. *Nourish the People: the State Civilian Granary System in China, 1650–1850*. Ann Arbor: University of Michigan Press.

[18] Will, Pierre-Etienne. 1990. *Bureaucracy and Famine in Eighteenth-century China*. trans. Elborg Forster. Stanford: Stanford University Press; Wong, R. Bin.1997. *China Transformed: Historical Change and the Limits of European Experience*. Ithaca and London: Cornell University Press.

Lilian M. Li, an American scholar, draws a similar conclusion by stating "Storing Grain: Granaries as solution and problem".[19] This summary, as the title of Chap. 6 in her work *Fighting Famine in North China: State, Market, and Environmental Decline, 1600s–1990s,* is quite appropriate.[20] Meanwhile, Helen Dunstan, an Australian scholar, reveals the complex relationship around government intervention and market regulation in the construction of Ever-Normal Granaries during Emperor Qianlong's reign, as well as the various challenges faced by the government in maintaining such a huge storage system.[21] Helen Dunstan's insights resonate with earlier research by the Chinese scholar Gao Wangling.[22] William T. Rowe, an American sinologist, took a different approach. Based on his analysis of the elite consciousness in Chen Hongmou (1696–1771), an influential Chinese official in the eighteenth-century Qing Empire, William T. Rowe analyzes how this outstanding representatives of the bureaucratic class endeavored to resolve conflicts and dilemmas, thereby outlining the practical ideas and paths of making ever-normal granaries and community granaries benefit the people.[23]

The Ever-normal Granary is part of the administrative institution in ancient China. How much insight and practical significance does it hold for contemporary economic society? Can it be adapted and transformed to benefit national welfare? Aside from research in areas such as famine administration (*huangzheng*), agricultural economics, price management, etc., there is relatively little in-depth academic discussion on these issues. The limited number of researches usually lack theoretical depth, making it difficult to establish a cohesive framework. In fact, if we take a broader view and look globally, we can see that Ever-normal Granary system in ancient China was already adopted by Western capitalist societies in the 1930s, where it played a positive role in their national economies. Qian Mu (1895–1990), a prominent Chinese historian known for being an outspoken defender of traditional Chinese culture, in his work *Research Methodology of Chinese History*, reflected on the equalization policy implemented in the Han dynasty (which served as a mechanism for grain regulation, akin to the Ever-normal Granary) and provided a thought-provoking anecdote:

> The equalization policy of the Han Dynasty…has been continuously adapted and applied in Chinese history. Take grain prices as an example: during years of abundance, the government would purchase surplus grain at high prices to prevent farmers from suffering due to low grain prices. When famine struck, the government would sell stocked grain in large

[19] Li, Lillian M. 2007. *Fighting Famine in North China: State, Market, and Environmental Decline, 1600s–1990s*, Stanford: Stanford University Press. p.166.

[20] Li, Lillian M. 2007. *Fighting Famine in North China: State, Market, and Environmental Decline, 1600s–1990s*, Stanford: Stanford University Press.

[21] Dunstan, Helen. 2006. *State or Merchant Political Economy and Political Process in 1740s China*, Massachusetts: The Harvard University Asia Center.

[22] Gao, Wangling. 2005. *Living Tradition: Economic Development and Government Policies in Eighteenth-Century China.* Beijing: Peking University Press.

[23] Rowe, William T. 2001. *Saving the World: Chen Hongmou and Elite Consciousness in Eighteenth-Century China.* Stanford: Stanford University Press.

> quantities at low prices, with the intention of providing relief aid for impoverished farmers… It is said that during the economic panic in the United States under Roosevelt's administration, someone introduced this method of price regulation in Chinese history, attributing it to erroneously Wang Anshi's New Policies. In fact, it was a traditional policy in China. During the Anti-Japanese War, when the U.S. Vice President Henry A. Wallace visited China and just stepped off the plane in Lanzhou, he expressed his great admiration for Wang Anshi to the Chinese government officials who had come to welcome him. However, those officials were dumbfounded and at a loss for words. As in the minds of modern Chinese people, only great figures like George Washington and Abraham Lincoln were known. They believed that everything in China was backward, and under the modern global trend, all historical figures and traditional governance systems were unworthy of being mentioned.[24]

The traditional Ever-normal Granary system, like an old tree with new vitality, had been adopted and further developed abroad, while some Chinese government officials were totally oblivious to it. It is natural for them to believe that "everything in China was backward". However, this was not the case among intellectuals. In 1944, the Chinese agronomist Shen Wenfu introduced in the journal *Economic Forum* (*jingji lunheng*) the agricultural Ever-normal Granary policy promoted by Henry A. Wallace in the United States.[25] In 1945, Shen Wenfu published an article in the journal *Eastern Miscellany*, further elaborating the historical and contemporary significance of the Ever-normal Granary domestically and internationally, and arguing that Chinese people should inherit and further develop this important economic tradition:

> The Ever-normal Granary system has long been adopted and further developed abroad, reaching a level of refinement. However, some Chinese people lament the decline of old Chinese learning, unaware of the need to align their research with economic theories, while others disdain the old institutions and policies, unwilling to inherit and improve such wisdom. Ironically, it was agricultural experts and politicians in the United States who advocated for it, making it a cornerstone of their long-term agricultural legislation and a pillar of their new agricultural adjustment plans. If Li Kui, Geng Shouchang and Sang Hongyang, the forerunners of Ever-normal Granary in ancient China, were aware of it in their lower world, they would surely smile at the far-reaching and ever-successful application of the Ever-normal Granary system. Chinese people, with their intellectual curiosity and abilities still intact, should feel ashamed in front of their predecessors and realize the urgency to catch up with the others.[26]

We may draw inspiration from Shen Wenfu's narration: China's ancient economic traditions embody modern values and should not be abandoned in the modern times. In fact, equating modernity solely with the West and viewing Chinese traditions as backward lacks convincing theoretical foundation. Only by observing China's economic traditions from a broader perspective and over a longer historical time-frame

[24] Qian, Mu. 2001. *Research Methodology of Chinese History*. Beijing: SDX Joint Publishing Co. pp.30–31.

[25] Shen, Wenfu. 1944. On the Ever-normal Granary policy advocated by Wallace in the United States. *Economic Forum*. 2(7–8): 21–26.

[26] Shen, Wenfu. 1945. On the Ever-normal Granary policy throughout history and around the world. *Eastern Miscellany*. 41(6): 23.

can we achieve a deeper understanding and proper assessment of them. This means that the cognition of the Ever-normal Granary should not be confined to a one-dimensional view of the past; instead, it should focus on multiple facets spanning ancient-modern and Chinese-foreign contexts, placing the Ever-normal Granary within a systematic framework across different eras, cultures, and economic forms.

When focusing on cultural exchanges between China and the West in modern times, we find that the opportunity to engage in economic thinking across ancient and contemporary times, as well as between China and the West, first fell upon Chen Huan-chang (1881–1931), a Chinese student who studied in the United States during the period of late Qing dynasty and early Republic of China. While attending Columbia University, Chen Huan-chang completed his doctoral dissertation titled *The Economic Principles of Confucius and His School*, which introduced the ancient Chinese Ever-normal Granary system to the West.[27] As a result, this ancient system gained global recognition and significantly influenced the agricultural reforms vigorously promoted by Henry A. Wallace, the Secretary of Agriculture of the United States in the 1930s. Li Chaomin, a contemporary Chinese scholar, systematically explored how the American agricultural reforms of the 1930s borrowed from and further developed the Chinese Ever-normal Granary, providing new perspectives for the multi-faceted research around this topic. The economic stabilizing function of Ever-normal Granary is not limited to the agricultural sector; Li Chaomin also noted Benjamin Graham's theoretical exploration in the 1930s and 1940s, which extended the concept of agricultural Ever-normal Granary to multiple reserves. Following Shen Wenfu, Li Chaomin broke through the existing research boundaries, which would apparently deepen our understanding of Ever-normal Granary.[28]

---

[27] Chen Huan-chang's doctoral dissertation, titled *The Economic Principles of Confucius and His School*, was published simultaneously in New York and London as 44th and 45th volumes of the series of Columbia University's "Studies in History, Economics and Public Law". In January 1913, Chen Huan-chang published his Chinese translation of the first chapter "Public Expenditures" of "Book IX Public Finance" in the inaugural issue of *The Confucian Association Monthly*. In China, Chen Huan-chang's English work and its Chinese version have been reprinted for several times.

[28] Focusing on Ever-normal Granary, Li Chaomin wrote the following articles: Li, Chaomin. 2000. The influence of the idea of Ever-normal Granary on Henry A. Wallace and the Agricultural Adjustment Act in the New Deal. *Fudan Journal (Social Sciences)*. (3): 42–50; Li, Chaomin. 2000. The Ever-normal Granary: A debate in the 1930s' U.S. *Journal of Shanghai University of Finance and Economics*. (3): 13–20; Li, Chaomin. 2000. A safeguard for the prosperity of modern American agriculture: The Ever-normal Granary and the Agricultural Adjustment Act of 1938. *Journal of Finance and Economics*. (12): 56–62; Li, Chaomin. The Ever-normal Granary: Reflections on the tracing of the source of contemporary economic stability policy to China. *Fudan Journal (Social Sciences)*. (2): 70–76; Li, Chaomin. 2004. The practical significance of agricultural legislation and the Ever-normal Granary program in the United States over the past 70 years. *Issues in Agricultural Economy*. (4): 73–77. Li Chaomin's monographs include the following: Li, Chaomin. 2002. *Ever-normal Granary: A Chinese Idea in the American Systems*. Shanghai: Shanghai Far East Publishers; Li, Chaomin. 2014. *The Mystery of the Rise of the Great Nations: The Chinese Origin of the American Ever-normal Granary System*. Beijing: Central Compilation & Translation Press. In addition, some other domestic scholars also discuss the Ever-normal Granary in their researches on American agricultural policies, such as: Xu, Gengsheng. 2017. *The Agricultural Policies of America*. Beijing: Economy & Management Publishing House. However, due to different focuses,

The "metabolism" of the Ever-normal Granary did not come to an end with Benjamin Graham. In fact, the economic regulation ideas closely related to the Ever-normal Granary underwent a series of significant developments after Graham, with the "Keynesian Revolution" serving as a crucial link between past and future. Li Chaomin has already noticed this, discovering that "Keynes also proposed a stabilization policy for government reserves of food and raw materials in 1938", but "his main ideas were different from those of Benjamin Graham."[29] Searching through Keynes' surviving literature, we may find that as early as the 1920s he introduced the concept of "buffer stocks" in response to the problem of overproduction in capitalism, which bore some similarities with Graham's proposition. In subsequent reflections and research, Keynes gradually refined this concept and elaborated on it with "the theory of short-period prices" in his work *A Treatise on Money* published in 1930. According to Keynes, another book he published in 1936, *The General Theory of Employment, Interest, and Money* (hereinafter referred to as *The General Theory*), was a "natural evolution" of *A Treatise on Money*, yet he acknowledged that this evolution "may sometimes strike the reader as a confusing change of view".[30] Could certain concepts in *The General Theory* embody the "natural evolution" of the buffer stock idea, even though they appear on the surface to be completely "different" theories and propositions? From the perspective of continuity of ideas, such a "natural evolution" possibly do exist, as Keynes elaborated on a detailed buffer stock scheme in the 1940s. He even called it "the internationalization of Vice-President Wallace's 'Ever-normal Granary'",[31] hoping that this scheme, along with another plan he put forward—the "International Clearing Union" for the monetary and financial system (also known as the "Keynes Plan") —would work together to promote post-war world economic stability and the formation of a new order. Although these two plans were ultimately not adopted, Keynesian economics, including the idea of buffer stocks, inspired an important school of thought—Post-Keynesian economics. Post-Keynesian economists continued the Keynesian tradition and proposed the theory of "buffer stock employment" in the 1990s. In fact, this theory had already been implemented on a large scale during the period of "Franklin D. Roosevelt's New Deal" through the "labor relief" policies. However, a glance at Chinese economic history reveals that the so-called "labor relief" was not an invention of the New Deal; its principles were already elaborated in ancient China during the pre-Qin period and later promoted and applied by subsequent generations.

---

these researches focus on American agricultural policies and their evolution across various historical periods, without addressing the Chinese origin of the Ever-normal Granary.

[29] Li, Chaomin. 2002. The Ever-normal Granary: Reflections on the tracing of the source of contemporary economic stability policy to China. *Fudan Journal (Social Sciences).* (2): 75.

[30] Keynes, J. M. 2013. *The General Theory of Employment, Interest and Money*. in *The Collected Writings of John Maynard Keynes,* vol. 7. ed. Moggridge, D. New York: Cambridge University Press. p. xv.

[31] Keynes, J. M. 2013. *Activities 1940–1946: Shaping the Post-War World:Employment and Commodities.* in *The Collected Writings of John Maynard Keynes.* ed. Moggridge, D.vol.27. New York: Cambridge University Press. p. 112.

From this perspective, the repeated "historical transcendence" of the Ever-normal Granary still has many fascinating chapters waiting to be further explored and elaborated upon. So, what are the connections between these chapters? In particular, how did the idea of buffer stocks gradually develop and evolve into modern macroeconomic theory? If delving deeper, we find that there are numerous mysteries that need to be unraveled regarding the relationship between Ever-normal Granary and economic theory. In fact, the story of the Ever-normal Granary unfolds as a "tapestry" interwoven with history and economics. Only through a deep integration of historical-economic, temporal-spatial narratives can we present its rich content more comprehensively.

It is also worth noting that a deeper exploration into the evolutionary thread of economic principles embodied in the Ever-normal Granary reveals other layer of relationship that remains to be clarified between Ever-normal Granary and economic philosophy. We know that any economic thought or policy with far-reaching impacts must rest upon a set of cognitive framework as its ontological foundation. When criticizing Jean-Baptiste Say's "Trinity Formula", Marx stated, "All science would be superfluous if the form of appearance of things directly coincided with their essence".[32] It seems that if we cannot extract a more general worldview, values and methodology for economics from the Ever-normal Granary, and if we don't achieve a holistic understanding based on the three dimensions of philosophical ontology, economic theory, and policy application, it will be difficult for us to have a profound understanding of Ever-normal Granary, the Chinese economic tradition. Consequently, it would be impossible for us to further uncover the more general economic laws hidden within it.

In summary, although abundant achievements have been made in researches on Ever-normal Granary system, there are many questions that need to be answered when viewed from new clues and perspectives, and more systematic and in-depth research efforts need to be undertaken. Firstly, existing researches are often limited to specific historical periods. A comprehensive study of the connotation and historical evolution of Ever-normal Granary remains a rarely explored area, which should have the "continuity" and "change" as the main thread and the relationships between the ancient and modern times and between China and the West as the foothold. Secondly, a deeper integration of economics and history in researches is necessary. For a long time, in-depth exploration of economic principles has been marginalized in the study of Ever-normal Granary. Particularly, analyses that combine modern macroeconomic theories with the buffering regulatory functions of Ever-normal Granary are quite scarce, but the possible connections between them are a worthwhile topic for exploration. Thirdly, it is necessary to find new paths for interpreting the deeper-level "essence" of Ever-normal Granary from the perspectives of its "principles" and "applications". How could the ancient Chinese develop the Ever-normal Granary system? And how did this system evolve into a continuous

[32] Marx, Karl. 1981. *Capital: A Critique of Political Economy*, vol.3. trans. David Fernbach. London: Penguin Books. p. 956.

economic tradition? Existing research has failed to answer this question from the perspective of economic thinking, which would reveal the philosophical ontology underlying the Ever-normal Granary system, and explore the essential connotations and characteristics of China's economic tradition, as well as their possible connections with contemporary Chinese economic theory and practice. Furthermore, from the perspective of making the ancient wisdom serve the present and foreign things serve China, the question of how to apply Ever-normal Granary to contribute to China's economic development nowadays, also requires corresponding answers from perspectives of epistemology and policy.

In summary, by employing interdisciplinary and comparative methods that connect time and space, the study of Ever-normal Granary and its associated Chinese economic traditions as well as their modern values, requires not only the integration of existing cognitive resources but also a fresh start from a higher vantage point. This book attempts to make efforts in this regard, aiming to provide a more comprehensive and in-depth interpretation of relevant issues.

1.3 Research Purpose and Structure

To avoid the shortcomings of a linear analysis lacking systematicity, by drawing from and building upon existing researches, we establish a coordinate system that connects the ancient and the modern, as well as the Chinese and the Western. We embed the Ever-normal Granary within a multifaceted historical and economic context interwoven with ideological, social, and cultural factors. Through the interaction of these factors in historical processes, we aim to conduct a multidimensional interpretation of the Ever-normal Granary, exploring a more holistic research. This approach enables us to clarify the historical and theoretical logic behind the cross-temporal and cross-spatial evolution of Ever-normal Granary, thereby re-evaluating and discovering the multiple values hidden within this Chinese economic tradition. We seek to facilitate mutual discovery and invention among economic thoughts, systems, policies, and practices spanning ancient and modern times, as well as China and the West, achieving a new "handshake", "convergence" and "transcendence". The potential theoretical and practical significance of this endeavor lies in tracing the traditional roots for contemporary Chinese economic development, providing a more comprehensive theoretical support for relevant economic policies through mutual reference to both Eastern and Western perspectives, and contributing to the exploration of constructing a discourse system of economics with Chinese characteristics.

Following this arrangement, the main research methodology and content of this book will be developed from the following aspects.

(1) The Historical Evolution of Ever-normal Granary in Ancient China

By analyzing the theoretical origin of the Ever-normal Granary, the *qing-zhong* theory in *Guanzi*, this study examines how the Ever-normal Granary utilized grain as the "standard" and employed the buffer stock mechanisms such as "*pingdi*" (increased-price purchase) and "*pingtiao*" (reduced-price sales) to regulate the supply and price of grain, thereby stabilizing the economy. The study further analyzes the historical transformation of the Ever-normal Granary from its origins in the pre-Qin period, its formal establishment in the Western Han dynasty, its institutional development in the Tang dynasty, the reforms during the Northern and Southern Song Dynasties, its completion in the Qing dynasty, and its adaptation in modern times, examining its institutional changes, benefits and drawbacks, rise and fall, and the functional effects.

Expanding the definition of Ever-normal Granary in a "broad sense". The "Ever-normal Granary in broad sense" defined in this study includes: the "Ever-normal Granary system" consisting of multiple granary types with the Ever-normal Granary as the core; the "equalization policy" (*pingzhunfa*) that incorporates multiple commodities, materials, and even currencies into buffer regulation; and a special form of "Ever-normal Granary of labor force" represented by the "labor relief" system. The discussion of the Ever-normal Granary in broad sense illustrates the historical practice of ancient Chinese people in adapting the buffer stock mechanism flexibly to specific circumstance and time under the philosophy of "respecting Heaven" (*jing tian*) and "nourishing the people" *(yang min)*. This reveals the originality of macroeconomic regulation thought in ancient China.

(2) The "Ever-normal Granary" in Modern Western Economic Theory and Policy

Examining the U.S. agricultural "Ever-normal Granary" established through agricultural legislation and policy adjustments by Secretary of Agriculture Henry A. Wallace during the Franklin D. Roosevelt's New Deal in the 1930s. Building on this foundation, it further analyzes Benjamin Graham's concept of a "Modern Ever-normal Granary" (or "modern equalization policy" (*pingzhunfa*)) in the context of industrialized societies. The discussion focuses on the theoretical implications of utilizing a buffer stock mechanism to integrate fiscal and monetary policies for stabilizing the macro-economy.

Revisiting Keynes's forgotten idea of buffer stocks. The idea of buffer stocks was first proposed by Keynes in the 1920s and further developed into the theory of short-period prices (also referred to as the "Granary Formula") in his 1930 work *A Treatise on Money*. In the 1940s, Keynes expanded this concept into the scheme of international buffer stocks. By connecting these ideas, this study explores the macroeconomic theory implicit in Keynes's buffer stock ideas and connects it to his 1936 work *The General Theory*, interpreting the "Keynesian Revolution" through the lens of Ever-normal Granary.

Building on Keynes' macroeconomic ideas, post-Keynesian economists proposed the theory of "buffer stock employment" as a means to achieve true full employment (zero unemployment). We will delve into this theory's inheritance and development of Keynesian macroeconomics. By examining the American economic history, it will explore the "labor relief" policy within Franklin D. Roosevelt's New Deal as a typical case of the US government stabilizing the macroeconomy through "buffer stock employment," an "Ever-normal Granary of labor force," during the Great Depression. The pivot point for the implementation of buffer stock employment was "functional finance". By analyzing the theoretical implications of functional finance, the author will further explain how the implementation of buffer stock employment in policy became possible, and the deeper "Kalecki dilemma" that underlies this possibility.

(3) The economic tradition of "Dialectical Equilibrium" and "Maintaining Balance through the Mean" and modern value

Extracting the theoretical connotation of the Ever-normal Granary: In a world full of uncertainties, faced with the unpredictable fluctuations of economic systems and the transitions between stability and crisis, people seek core benchmark that can effectively stabilize the economy based on the economic characteristics of different eras. By establishing a buffer buying and selling mechanism for this benchmark and ensuring it is consistently in a state of "full use" or "full employment", this approach effectively guides the full utilization of production factors and other resources. In doing so, it releases a stabilizing force that converges fluctuations within the economic society, transforming instability into equilibrium and ultimately achieving dynamic stability in the economic society.

Returning to the theoretical source of the Ever-normal Granary, the *qing-zhong* theory in *Guanzi*, and exploring the dialectical thinking behind the theory, this study reveals the economic "Dao" developed in *Guanzi*, of which the essence being "all things are born of the two, Yin and Yang, so that a third comes into being", the principle being "*qing-zhong*-balance", and the application being in the four A-B models (A yet B; A (B) but not A + (B+); neither A, nor B; both A and B). From this, it is further proposed that *Guanzi* achieved a "axial breakthrough of Chinese economic thought", in which the idea of "maintaining balance through the mean"—i.e., coordinating and unifying various aspects of economic affairs through dialectical thinking, thereby achieving dynamic balance—laid the foundation for the epistemology and methodology of Chinese economic tradition. From the perspective of comparative analysis between China and the West, this study uses the theories of John M. Keynes, Karl Marx, and Adam Smith as a reference framework to analyze how the principles of *qing* and *zhong*, equilibrium and "Ever-Normal" are presented in the Western economics. Furthermore, it employs the A-B models to interpret the dialectical view and ever-normal view of contemporary Chinese economics in the context of the reform and opening-up. The study concludes by summarizing the "ever-normal principle" that runs through Chinese history and points out that contemporary socialist China has achieved a historical transcendence of this principle through creative transformation.

Policy Construction. The historical evolution of Ever-normal Granary across different eras and regions, its transcendence through history, and the theoretical insights it offers provide a policy pathway for the modern transformation of China's economic traditions. Based on the practical needs of China's economic strategic transformation, the requirements for economic-social security and sustainable development in the new era, this study proposes incorporating selected elements of population, resources, key products and their production capacity into a buffer regulation mechanism, thereby establishing a Modern Grand Ever-normal Granary.

(4) Spirit of the Mean in Chinese economic tradition

Through a series of in-depth explorations, the study concludes that from the Ever-normal Granary to the ever-normal principle, the Chinese economic tradition of "maintaining balance through the mean" permeates economic ontology, economic thought, and policies and practice, with the embodiment of a simple yet profound spirit of the mean. The spirit of the mean is a significant symbol of Chinese economic wisdom, which continues to thrive in the new era. It enlightens us that economic cognition must be based on an organically systematic view. When facing problems and contradictions, instead of resolving them in an either-or manner, we should embrace things of diverse nature while recognizing their differences, coordinate all parties, adapt flexibly, avoid extremes, and always maintain a sense of vigilance, taking the path of tolerance and moderation. At a higher level, the spirit of the mean requires viewing various opposing yet interdependent objects, such as the ancient and the modern, China and the foreign, heaven and humanity, people and self and objects and self, etc. as a dialectical whole. Only through holistic synthesis and analysis can we derive the mean that harmonizes and integrates all aspects, thereby achieving the ever-normal development of the economic society. The spirit of the mean, enduring and ever-renewing, reflects the essential wisdom of Chinese economic thought. Grounded in this fundamental principle, the exploration of present economic paths and the development of future economic theories will leave us with a broader stage.

To sum up, in the new historical stage of the development of socialism with Chinese characteristics, our research approaches, basic conclusions and practical directions are nothing more than footnotes to the following assertion:

> Cultural confidence is a more fundamental, extensive, and profound kind of confidence. It is a more basic, deeper, and more enduring force for the development of a country and a nation… To strengthen cultural confidence, we must participate extensively in the dialogue among world civilizations with a more confident mindset and a broader horizon, boldly draw upon and absorb the achievements of human civilization, and promote the creative transformation and innovative development of excellent traditional Chinese culture…[33]

[33] Publicity Department of the CPC Central Committee ed. 2018. *Thirty Lectures on Xi Jinping Thought on Socialism with Chinese Characteristics for a New Era*. Beijing: *Xuexi Chuban She* (Learning Press). p.25.

Chapter 2

"Ever-normal Granary": Economic Tradition in China

Grain is the primary undertaking of the king and the great concern of the ruler. It is the path to poss*essing the people and the way to maintaining the state in good order.*

Guanzi: Maintaining the State[1]

In good years, people have surplus grain and the grain is cheap, then the government, taking advantage of this lower price, would buy the grain which drives up the price of grain; in bad years, people are in lack of grain and the grain is expensive, then the government, taking advantage of this high price, would sell the grain which drives down the price of the grain at a fair price. The rulers control the highs and lows of grain prices by buying and selling at the right time to stabilize grain prices for the benefits of the common people. Even monarchs who adopt hegemonic policies would incorporate policies and practices that align with the principles of benevolence in their governance.

Qiu Jun (Ming Dynasty)[2]

Tracing back to its origins, the complete principle of the Ever-normal Granary comes from *Guanzi*'s "light and heavy principles" (*qing zhong* economic policies)[3].

---

[1]Guanzi. 1998. *Political, Economic, and Philosophical Essays from Early China*, vol.2. trans. W. Allyn Rickett. Princeton: Princeton University Press. p. 180.

[2]Qiu, Jun. 2012. *The order for the official acquisition of grain. Supplement to Great Learning*, vol.25. ed. Jing, Liangnian. Shanghai: Shanghai Bookstore Publishing House. p. 229.

[3]The "*qing-zhong* (light and heavy) principles" is articulated in the work Guanzi (Master Guan, named in homage to its author, Guan Zhong, d. 645 B.C., who served as Prime Minister to Duke Huan of Qi.). At over 135,000 characters long, Guanzi is one of the longest early Chinese philosophical texts. It covers broad subject matter, notably expatiating on methods of taking advantage of low (*qing*- literally "light") and high (*zhong*- literally "heavy") prices for price regulation of commodities. As a core text in ancient Chinese economic thought, it is arguably one of the most representative texts of political economy that developed during the Spring and Autumn period. Also explains "Meaning of *Qing Zhong*" with following words, "'*Qing*' means 'light', and by extension 'unimportant', 'inconsequential', or 'cheap'. As a verb, it means to accord little or no value to something. *Zhong* means 'heavy', and by extension 'important', 'serious', or 'expensive'. As a verb, it means to value something. As a compound the two characters together usually mean 'weight', and in economic writings *qing* and *zhong* are often used to refer to the weight of coins.

W. Xian, *Chinese Food Security Strategy*, Research Series on the Chinese Dream and China's Development Path,
https://doi.org/10.1007/978-981-95-7964-8_2

The "light and heavy principles" elaborates the relationship between the value of grain and other things, and establishes the mechanism of food regulation in the form of a general plan - stabilizing economic and social fluctuations through the establishment of grain-based buffer stock. With the purpose of ruling the state by manipulating prices of grain, such a "top-level design" based on "light and heavy principles" theoretically provided the earliest macroeconomic regulation model of the Chinese. The Ever-normal Granary also experienced ups and downs in the history. In a period of economic and social stabilization, Ever-normal Granary would be highly valued by the emperors, thus developing into a key point for national finance, food storage, warehousing, and wasteland management and economic regulation.

Originating in the Pre-Qin period, Ever-normal Granary system was formally created by Geng Shouchang, the Vice Chamberlain, during the reign of Emperor Xuan (74B.C.-48 B.C.) of the Western Han dynasty. It was gradually developed into a more complete system by the royal government of the Tang dynasty (618-907). During the Northern Song dynasty (960-1127), Wang Anshi (1021-1086), the Counsellor-in-chief and a controversial reformer-statesman, promoted the practice of Green Sprouts Act (*qingmiaofa*)[4] to monetize the Ever-normal Granary by way of micro-credit. This unsuccessful new reform provided a historical reference for Zhu

---

Thus, *qing* and *zhong* may be used to refer to the value of money in relation to goods or to the relationship between supply and demand. When supply is greater than demand, it is because things are not valued or *qing*; when the opposite is true, it is because things are valued or *zhong*. As the compound appears in the title of this section, however, *qing zhong* refers to a wide range of policies that were based on the *qing zhong zhifa*, '*qing zhong* method', said to have originated with Guan Zhong. This method involved using money to acquire grain and other critical commodities when they were plentiful and cheap (*qing*),and to sell them when they were in short supply and expensive (*zhong*) in order to control the profits of merchants and gain income for the state. Thus in this section *qing zhong* may refer merely to taking advantage of market conditions to manipulate prices, or it may refer to a broad range of economic policies involving such things as government monopolies, loans to producers, foreign trade and territorial expansion, currency control, and work incentives. See: Guanzi. 1998. *Guanzi: Political, Economic, and Philosophical Essays from Early China*, vol.2. trans. W. Allyn Rickett. Princeton: Princeton University Press. pp. 338-339.

[4] Green Sprouts Act (or Green Sprouts Measures, *qingmiao fa,*), a program of low-interest state loans available to farmers during the lean spring season, was part of the New Policies of Wang Anshi, a reformist intellectual in the Northern Song dynasty. In ancient China, loans were essential to the farmers. To avoid great distress inflicted upon the people caused by the high rate of interest (usually 20-30 percent annually or above), the Green Sprouts Act regulated that during months of insufficient grain supply, usually February and May of any given year, the government would offer loans – in the form of either grain or credit to buy grain – to those in need, with interest to be repaid along with taxes in summer and fall. This loan was called "*Qing Miao* money" or "Green Sprout money", because the loans were disbursed in the spring when the wheat was just sprouting. With the grain purchased and stored by the government during productive seasons and lent out in poor harvest seasons, the program sought to regulate the market price of grain, reduce the usurious exploitation of lenders, lessen the financial burden on the common people, and increase government revenue.

Xi's Community Granary (*zhuzi shecang*) to expand the grass-roots community granaries in the Southern Song dynasty (1127 A.D.-1279 A.D.). The "preparedness granary" (*yubeicang*) is a unique design in the Ming dynasty. Though it took advantages of both Ever-normal Granary and community granary, it put higher requirements for management, therefore it was difficult to last for a long time. In the Qing dynasty, Ever-normal Granary system was more mature and more complete. Chen Hongmou, an important eighteenth-century statesmen-thinker, was a particularly strong proponent for the construction of ever-normal granaries and community granaries. This reveals that the local elites were committed to achieving the organic unity of government, market and society in order to seek stability of economy. "Granaries Subsidized by the State", "Self-funded Granaries", and "Granaries Funded by Local Elites" were the general types of granaries for grain buffer stock. Since the state-run ever-normal granaries undertook the responsibility of stability, security, and welfare in the macro and public perspective, "Granaries Subsidized by the State" played the most important role in the long run. In addition to the government capacity, the unsustainability of subsidies from the governments was another important factor that caused various problems for the development of ever-normal granaries, which would inevitably go through U-shaped cycles.

2.1 Origin of Ever-normal Granary

2.1.1 Long-Standing Tradition of Reserves and the Idea of Economic Regulation

The core area of Chinese civilization is located in the eastern part of the Asia-Europe continent, which is a typical continental monsoon climate area. Rain and high temperature provide good conditions for the development of agriculture. However, the spatial distribution of heat and water is not balanced, and the climate is complex and changeable. The seasonal changes in river runoff lead to frequent drought and flooding disasters, which in turn lead to unstable agricultural production with cyclical fluctuations. In "Biographies of Money-makers" of *Records of the Grand Historian* (*Shi Ji*), there is record of Fan Li's[5] narration on cyclical fluctuations: "Every six years there will be a good harvest, every six years there will be a drought, and every

[5] Fan Li was an ancient Chinese military strategist, politician, and businessman in the Spring and Autumn period. He was an important political and military advisor to Goujian, the king of Yue. He later was known as Tao Zhu Gong, a name he took after achieving a decisive victory for Yue over the state of Wu and retiring to live a secluded life with his wife Xi Shi, one of the most famous beauties in Chinese history.

twelve years there will be one great famine."[6] In "Celestial Patterns"[7] (*tianwen xun*) of *Book of Prince Huainan: Annotated and Commented* (*Huainan Honglie ji jie*), there are following words, "Thuswithin three years, there is a year of famine; within six years, there is a year of epidemic. Twelve years brings a repose."[8] In "*Water and Drought*" (*shuihan*) of *Discourses on Salt and Iron (yantie lun)* there is similar saying: "There is a bad harvest every six years, and a famine every twelve years."[9] Late quantitative studies have shown that the proportion of years below Level 3 is quite large in traditional agricultural societies (Table 2.1).

Food is the paramount necessity of all people. For the ancient people who lived on this land, the irresistible forces of nature meant that abnormal climate and unstable agricultural outputs could have different degrees of impact on the economic society and population survival. This forced the ancestors to adapt to production and life, and the tradition of grain reserves has been developed over time.

In Neolithic archaeology, cellars with large amounts of grain remains have been discovered. For example, archaeologists found 88 rectangular ash pits (1 to 1.5

Table 2.1 Composition of harvest grade from 210 to 1910 B.C.

Agricultural harvest grade	Severe poor-harvest year Level 1	Poor-harvest year Level 2	Partially poor-harvest year Level 3	Normal year Level 4	Relatively good-harvest year Level 5	Excellent harvest year Level 6
Number (years)	180	357	458	725	271	125
Proportion of total years (%)	8.5	16.9	21.6	34.3	12.8	5.9

Source: Fang Xiuqi et al. 2019. *The Impact of Historical Climate Change on China's Society and Economy.* Beijing: China Science Publishing and Media Ltd. p. 80

[6] Sima, Qian. 1993. Biographies of Money-Makers. *Records of the Grand Historian: Han Dynasty*, vol.2. trans. Burton Watson. Hong Kong and New York: Columbia University Press. p. 437. Sima Qian's grand historical work *Records of the Grand Historian* attributes the theory of the fluctuation of the agricultural production and the theory of *pingtiao* (the seasonal purchase, storage and sale of grain at reduced prices) to Ji Ran (also named Jini), Fan Li's teacher. But Cai Mo of the Eastern Han dynasty suggests that Ji Ran was the name of a book written by Fan Li. There are many debates about this issue afterwards. Hu Jichuang reviewed all kinds of literature and proposed: "Even if Ji Ran is not the name of the book, he is the teacher of Fan Li. It is reasonable to attribute his thoughts under Fan Li's name who, as a disciple of Ji Ran, passes them down." See: Hu, Jichuang. 1998. *History of Chinese Economic Thought*, vol.1. Shanghai: Shanghai University of Finance and Economics Press. p. 190. The author hereinafter follows Hu Jichuang's proposal.

[7] The term *tian wen* (celestial patterns) means "astronomy" in modern Chinese, but the classical term has a much broader reach, encompassing also astrology, cosmology, calendrics, mathematical harmonics, and meteorology. See: Liu, An. 2012. *The Essential Huainanzi.* trans. J.S. Major, S. A. Queen, A. S. Meyer and H. D. Roth. New York: Columbia University Press. p. 39.

[8] Major, J. S. 1993. *Heavens and Earth in Early Han Thought: Chapters Three, Four and Five of the Huainanzi.* Albany: State University of New York Press. p. 129.

[9] Wang, Liqi. ed. 1992. Flood and Drought. *Discourses on Salt and Iron: Annotated and Commented*, vol.6. Beijing: Zhonghua Book Company. p. 428.

meters long, 0.5 to 0.8 meters wide, and 1 to 5 meters deep) piled up with a large amount of corn remains at the site of Magnetic Hill in Wu'an, Hebei Province (a representative of the Cishan culture of the Early Neolithic period, 7,200 to 7,300 years old), with a general piling thickness of 0.5 to 0.6 meters (the thinnest is around 0.2 to 0.3 meters, and the thickest up to 2.9 meters). It is estimated that the cellar could store as much as 69,100 kilograms of grain (to avoid errors, the number could be at least 50,000).[10] The amount of grain storage at the site of Magnetic Hill is amazing, which indicates that agricultural production at that time has reached a fairly high level, and planned grain reserves may have become an important part of production and life to avoid possible famine.

In the age of civilization, written records of storage were found in oracle bone inscriptions[11] of Shang dynasty (r. 1600 B.C.-1046 B.C.):

> the king of Shang ordered officials of Wu to inspect the granaries in the south in October (*ling wu sheng cai nan lin, shi yue*)

Chen Mengjia, a Chinese poet and archaeologist, interpreted the word "*lin*" as "a place for grain storage, which is later known as a granary". Therefore the inscriptions means that the king of Shang ordered officials of Wu to inspect the granaries in the south in October.[12] This suggests that there might have been institutionalized, large-scale grain reserve systems during the Shang dynasty. It is worth noting that the latest archaeological work on the culture of Xia dynasty has discovered the earliest known grain storage site for centralized storage of grain at Shizhuang in

---

[10] Tong, Weihua. 1984. Primitive agricultural remains from the site of Magnetic Hill and relevant problems. *Agricultural Archaeology*. (1): 194, 197.

[11] Oracle bone inscription refers to inscriptions carved on turtle shells and animal bones during the Shang and Zhou dynasties. They are also known as "script chiseled out with a knife," "oracles on bones or tortoise shells," or "script from Yin ruins." Such inscriptions include oracles and events recorded on bones or tortoise shells of the. They are the earliest known characters of ancient China dated more than 3,000 years ago. Inscriptions on bones or tortoise shells were first uncovered from among Yin ruins at Xiaotun Village in Anyang in Henan Province, generally believed to have first been discovered in 1899 by Wang Yirong (1845-1900), a late Qing epigrapher. In the Shang and Zhou dynasties, royal families and noblemen would consult heaven about anything ranging from state business to trivial affairs in daily life, such as sacrificial rituals, weather, harvesting, war, hunting, illness, and giving birth. It was the answers they thus elicited that determined what course of action to take. Divination was an important part of a country's governance; the bones and tortoise shells with characters inscribed on them would be stored away as state archives. So far, more than 100,000 bones and tortoise shells have been unearthed, about 4,500 characters have been tallied, and of these, about 1,700 have been understood and interpreted. Characters on bones and tortoise shells have become increasingly systemized, with the six ways of forming Chinese characters (namely, pictographs, self-explanatory characters, associative compounds, pictophonetic characters, mutually explanatory characters, and phonetic loan characters) all reflected in them and a large number of pictophonetic characters (or phonograms) that had merged. Oracles inscribed on bones and tortoise shells are also valuable firsthand material for studying the history of the Shang and Zhou dynasties. It was firstly discovered in Anyang of Henan province in the Qing dynasty. These inscriptions were mainly used for divination and record-keeping.

[12] Chen, Mengjia. 1956. *Review of Yin Ruins Oracle Inscriptions*. Beijing: China Science Publishing and Media Ltd. p. 536.

Huaiyang, Henan Province, dating back from 4,000 to 3,700 years ago.[13] The archaeological research of this site may further reveal the longer history of China's grain reserve system.

In "Offices of Earth on Taxation and Division of land" (*di guan situ*) of *Rites of Zhou* (*Zhou li*)[14], there are various official titles such as "Officers of Gratuities and Public Relief" (*yi ren*), "Quantity Attendants" (*lü shi*), "Granary Officers" (*lin ren*), "Depot Officers" (*cang ren*) and "Seed Workers" (*si jia*) (see Table 2.2), generally reflecting the idea of stabilizing the economy and society through grain reserves in the Pre-Qing period. There are many similar official titles in "In "Offices of Earth on Taxation and Division of land" (*di guan situ*)" of *Rites of Zhou* (*Zhou li*), which indicate that grain reserve was an important issue for the state administration and economic management in the pre-Qin period. In "The Royal Regulations" of *The Book of Rites (Li ji)*, there is regulation on standard of grain reserves, "If in a state there was not accumulated (a surplus) sufficient for nine years, its condition was called one of insufficiency; if there was not enough for six years, one of urgency. If there was not a surplus sufficient for three years, the state could not continue. The husbandry of three years was held to give an overplus of food sufficient for one year; that of nine years, an overplus sufficient for three years. Going through thirty years (in this way), though there might be bad years, drought, and inundations, the people would have no lack or be reduced to (eating merely) vegetables, and then the son of Heaven would every day have full meals and music at them."[15]

Fan Li's theory of *pingtiao*, and Li Kui's theory of *pingdi*[16], can be regarded as the precedent ideas for Ever-normal Granary system. As was stated by Fan Li:

---

[13] Li, Yun. 2020. Five archaeological discoveries make Xia Culture more credible. *Guangming Daily*. Nov. 26. p.1.

[14] Rites of the Zhou (1046 B.C.-256 B.C.), also known as "The Official System of the Zhou Dynasty" or "Classic of the Official System of the Zhou Dynasty", is one of the Confucian classics in China. It is compiled by combining the official system of the Western Zhou dynasty (1046 B.C.-771 B.C.) and the East Zhou dynasty (770 B.C.-256 B.C.), with the Confucian political ideals. Ancient scholars believe that it was compiled by Zhou Gong, the first king of Zhou dynasty, but modern scholars hold that it was completed in the Warring States Period (475 B.C.–221 B.C.). The book is divided into six chapters according to the types of officials, involving important political systems such as the ancient official system, the military system, the farm system, the tax system, and the ritual system. Providing a reference for the construction of state institutions in the following dynasties, it is the first book in China that comprehensively describes the systems and the division of state institutions. The institutional setting in the book is permeated with the Confucian fraternity spirit, which has far-reaching influence in the history of ancient Chinese politics, ideology and culture.

[15] Legge, J. (trans.) 1885. *The Sacred Books of China: The Texts of Confucianism, Part 3–4, The Li Ki*. Oxford: Clarendon Press. p.222.

[16] *pingdi* and *pingtiao* were two ways for grain price adjustment in ancient China. In times of good harvest the local authorities purchased grain (*pingdi*) at favorable prices and stored it in public granaries, as a reserve for times of bad harvest when the grain prices soared. During times of famine when the grain prices soared, the grain reserves were thrown on the market (*pingtiao*) to keep the price at an acceptable level. This kind of economic policy was promoted by Fan Li, a counsellor to the king of Yue during the Spring and Autumn period (770-476 B.C.), and implemented in successive feudal dynasties.

Table 2.2 Officials and documents about grain reserves and suppressing the supply and demand of grain in *Rites of Zhou: the Officer of the Bureau of Land*

Official titles	Responsibilities related to grain reserves, supply and demand
Officers of gratuities and public relief (*yi ren*)	The officials are in charge of the distribution of alms and public relief. They are responsible for managing the state's grain reserves, ready to bestow favors upon the people. The grain stored in the local communities is used to relieve the hungry and destitute; the reserves from the border gates (for taxation upon entry and exit) are used to support the parents and children of those who die in state service; the reserves in the suburbs are for entertaining guests; the reserves in the rural areas are for supplying travelers; and the reserves in the counties are for preparing against famines
Quantity attendants (*lv shi*)	The officials are in charge of storing grain in the fields. They oversee the storage of grain, including the collective grain of farmers (for use in times of famine), the grain penalties of farmers who neglect their fields, and the grain penalties of idle civilians. They utilize contracts as proof, distributing the aforementioned three types of taxes evenly among the people to alleviate their livelihood and production, ensuring benefits for the people and the even enforcement of government policies. The grain is lent out in spring to those in need and collected in autumn
Granary Officers (*lin ren*)	The officials are in charge of managing the grain stored in granaries. They manage the grain supply, preparing it for distribution to the ministers, aiding the populace, or granting gifts, as well as providing food for common officials serving in the government. They calculate the state's expenses based on the annual harvest, determining whether there is sufficient grain, and report to superiors on the principles of grain allocation, establishing different standards for times of abundance or scarcity
Depot Officers (*cang ren*)	The officials are in charge of storing grain. They manage the storage of the grain received, distinguishing between the names and types of various grains for the state's use. If the grain supply is insufficient, they reduce the distribution of the reserves; if there is an excess, they store it for use in times of famine. During significant national events, they supply the grain reserves and other provisions on the roads
Seed Workers (*si jia*)	The officials are in charge of teaching the people about grain cultivation methods. They are responsible for inspecting the crops of the people in the fields, identifying the types of grains, fully understanding their names, and the types of soil they are suited to grow in. They establish cultivation methods and post them at the entrance of the town for people to follow. They monitor the growth of rice in the fields, determining the rules for taxation based on the annual yield, and manage the distribution of grain throughout the realm, responsible for relief efforts in times of scarcity, distributing the collected and stored grain fairly to those in urgent need

Source: Yuan, Ruan, ed. 2009. *Annotations to the Thirteen Classics*. Beijing: Zhonghua Book Company. pp. 1567-1568, 1606, 1614, 1616, 1616-1617

> If grain is sold as low as twenty cash a picul, then the farmers will suffer, but if it goes as high as ninety cash, then those in secondary occupations will suffer. If the merchants and others in secondary occupations suffer, then they will produce no goods, while if the farmers suffer they will cease to clear their fields. If, however, the price does not go over eighty cash nor fall below thirty, then both farmers and those in secondary occupations will benefit.

> If the price of grain is kept level and goods are fairly distributed, then there will be no shortages in the customs barriers and markets. This is the way to govern a country.[17]

Fan Li realized that if the price of grain was allowed to rise or fall freely, the farmers or merchants would suffer from losses. Therefore, he proposed the policy of *pingdi* and *pingtiao*[18] to stabilize grain prices between 30 coins and 80 coins. Then both farmers and merchants could make reasonable profits, thus promoting the joint development of agriculture and commerce. As an early representative of Legalism and the counsellor of Wei during the Warring States period (476-221B.C.), Li Kui had a comprehensive and thorough understanding of the strategy for governing the country. Since agriculture is the foundation of a wealthy and powerful country, he proposed the practice of buying grains in good years. Li Kui analyzed the impact of fluctuating grain prices on production and consumption, "If grain [for storage] was very expensive it would injure the people (other than the farmers); while if it was very cheap it would injure the farmers."[19] He went further to propose that the gov-

[17] Sima, Qian. 1993. *Records of the Grand Historian: Han Dynasty*, vol.2. trans. Burton Watson. Hong Kong and New York: Columbia University Press. p.437.

[18] Unlike *Records of the Grand Historian*, the fourth volume of *The Glory of Yue(yue jue shu)* replaces "selling grain" (*tiao*, 粜) with "buying grain" (*di*, 籴). In the work there are following words, "Jini said: 'When grain costs twenty cash a picul then it harms the farmers, when it costs ninety then it injures tradesmen. If farmers are harmed then grass and trees are not cleared, if tradesmen are injured then goods are not put on the market. Therefore if [the price of] rice does not go higher than eighty nor lower than thirty, farmers and tradesmen both benefit from it.'" See: Milburn, Olivia. 2010. *The Glory of Yue: An Annotated Translation of the Yuejue Shu*. Leiden and Boston: Brill. p.157. The phrase of "farmers and tradesmen both benefit from it" is obviously a statement at the government's stance. For the goal that "the price of rice does not go higher than eighty nor lower than thirty", the government needs both to buy grains in good years and sell stored grains in bad years. Therefore, the "*di*" (buying grain) and"*tiao*" (selling grain) in *Records of the Grand Historian* and *The Glory of Yue* are literally one-sided. Recent research has provided a reasonable explanation for this problem, with Shi Yang arguing that during the periods of the late Warring States period and the Qin and Han dynasties, the Chinese character "糴" (*di*) simultaneously had three meanings: "*di*" (籴, buying grain), "*tiao*" (粜,selling grain), and "grain". The distinguishing between "*di*" (buying grain) from "*tiao*" (selling grain) was occasional phenomena in the late Western Han dynasty. But they became competitive in the middle of the Eastern Han dynasty, and developed into commonly used words in official documents in the late Eastern Han dynasty. See: Shi, Yang. 2023. Historical predecessors of "*di*" and "*tiao*": The usage of "糴" (*di*) in unearthed texts from the Warring States to the Western Jin dynasty. *Journal of Chinese Historical Studies*, (2):68-84. Based on this understanding, the "*tiao*" (selling grain) and "*di*" (buying grain) in *Records of the Grand Historian* and *The Glory of Yue* should therefore be replaced by "糴" (*di*), which simultaneously had three meanings: "*di*" (籴, buying grain), "*tiao*" (粜,selling grain), and "grain". The reason is as follows: firstly, the characters "*tiao*" (selling grain) in *Records of the Grand Historian*and "*di*" (buying grain) in *The Glory of Yue* actually mean "grain"; secondly, when the price of grain goes higher than eighty the government should sell stored grains (*pingtiao*) to keep the price at an acceptable level, and when the price of grain falls lower than thirty, the government should buy grains (*pingdi*) at favorable prices and stored it in public granaries, as a reserve for times of bad harvest. Therefore, the theory of *pingtiao*(平粜) might better be named theory of *pingdi* (平籴), or theory of *pingdi* and *pingtiao* (平籴平粜).

[19] Swann, Nancy Lee. (trans.) 1950. *Food and Money in Ancient China: The Earliest Economic History of China to A.D. 25, Han Shu 24, with Related Texts, Han Shu 91 and Shih-Chi 129.* Princeton: Princeton University Press. p.139.

ernment should see to it that the grain price was balanced into two directions, "If the people were injured the [families] would be separated and scattered [into other places]; and if the farmers were injured, the state would be poor. Consequently whether [the price was] very high or very low, the injury was one and the same. [Therefore], those who were versed in [good] government saw that the people were not injured, and that those who farmed were encouraged the more."[20] As to the detailed policy, Li Kui suggested:

> For these reasons those versed in leveling the priceof grain [through government storage] must carefullywatch yearly [harvests]. There were three [grades] ofgood [crops]: (i) best, (ii) medial, and (iii) good. In abest harvest [the product was] four times [as much as the ordinary harvest]; and after [deducting for food] there would be a surplus of four hundred piculs *shih*. In a medial harvest [the product was] three times [as much], with a surplus of three hundred piculs. In a good harvest [the product was] merely doubled, with a surplus of one hundred piculs. [In a year of] first degree failure of crops there were gathered one hundred piculs; [in that of] a second degree failure seventy piculs; and [in that of] great failure thirty piculs. Therefore, [in a year] of best harvest the government then purchased three parts of it, leaving one part [for use of the people]. [In a year of] medial harvest [the government] then bought two parts, [while in a year of] good harvest it bought one part (that is, one half). This caused the people to have just a sufficiency for all needs; and when the price returned to its ordinary level [purchase] would be stopped. [In a year of] first degree failure [the government] then put on sale [fifty piculs of grain] which had been bought [in a year of good harvest]; [in a year of] second degree failure it then put on sale [two hundred piculs of grain] which had been bought [in a year of medial harvest]; and [in a year of] great failure it then put on sale [three hundred piculs of grain] which had been bought [in a year of best harvest].[21]

To put it simple, Li Kui divided the harvest years into threegrades: (i) best, (ii) medial, and (iii) good, and suggested the purchase of surplus grain accordingly. Correspondingly, the failure years were also divided into three grades: first degree failure, second degree failure and great failure. The government stabilizes the grain price by the following policies: in a year of great failure the government put on sale grains which had been bought in a year of best harvest; in a year of second degree failure it then put on sale grains which had been bought in a year of medial harvest; in a year of first degree failure it then put on sale grains which had been bought in a year of good harvest. There is both purchase and sale of grains in the policies. But from the above material, we can also see that Li Kui attached more importance to the purchase. This is because only in good years is there purchase, and only in failure years is there sale.[22] With these policies, "though there occurred famines from failuresof grain crops and dearth of vegetables, or floods, ordrought, the price of grain was not high and the people did not emigrate, [because of the government

[20] Swann, Nancy Lee. (trans.) 1950. *Food and Money in Ancient China: The Earliest Economic History of China to A.D. 25, Han Shu 24, with Related Texts, Han Shu 91 and Shih-Chi 129.* Princeton: Princeton University Press. pp. 139-140.

[21] Swann, Nancy Lee. (trans.) 1950. *Food and Money in Ancient China: The Earliest Economic History of China to A.D. 25, Han Shu 24, with Related Texts, Han Shu 91 and Shih-Chi 129.* Princeton: Princeton University Press. pp.142-143.

[22] Therefore, it is more reasonable to call Li Kui's policy as "*pingdi*" (buying grains in good years).

policy] of collecting when there was an oversupply in order to supplement when there was a deficiency. When this policy was practiced in Wei, the feudatory thereupon became replete [in resources], and was strong."[23]

Fan Li and Li Kui both emphasized the necessary government intervention in grain circulations, but neither advocated regulation by directive means. However, there are subtle differences between the two. Fan Li's point of observation is the market, and he analyzed grain price fluctuations from both short-term and long-run perspectives. However, Li Kui analyzed grain prices more from the supply side, i.e. the long-term cycle of agricultural production. With the division of various grades of good harvest or failure, Li Kui depicted a complete fluctuating process of a whole year by "carefullywatching yearly harvests". He paid more attention to the long-term solution to the problem, with the intention of leveling grain prices in years with good or bad harvests by means of macro-control.

2.1.2 Systematic Theoretical Exposition and Initial Practice in the Han Dynasty

In addition to Fan Li and Li Kui's narrations, the "light and heavy" (*qing zhong*) chapter in *Guanzi* gives a more systematical explanation of the theory of grain buffer and "*di tiao* policies" (buying and selling grains to stabilize grain prices), which should be given due attention when in examining economic thoughts in the Warring States period.[24] When the work *Guanzi* was written, small-scale peasant economy,

[23] Swann, Nancy Lee. (trans.) 1950. *Food and Money in Ancient China: The Earliest Economic History of China to A.D. 25, Han Shu 24, with Related Texts, Han Shu 91 and Shih-Chi 129.* Princeton: Princeton University Press. pp. 143-144.

[24] There are totally 86 chapters in the original *Guanzi*, but there are only 76 left with content nowadays, andthe other 10 chapters only exist in the catalog. The date for compilation of the work *Guanzi* has long been debated in the academic community. Wang Demin summarizes six different viewpoints, which hold that *Guanzi* was compiled during the Spring and Autumn period, the late Spring and Autumn to the Warring States period, the late Spring and Autumn to the Qin and Han dynasties, the Warring States period, the late Warring States to the Qin and Han dynasties, and the Han dynasty. Scholars today still hold different views on the compilation date, each with a strong argument. Generally it is believed that the main chapters of *Guanzi* might have taken shape by the late Warring States period. As it was circulated through the Han dynasty, multiple versions with varying chapters appeared, until Liu Xiang finished his compilation of the works. The most remarkable feature of *Guanzi* is its rich economic thought. The Chinese scholar Hu Jichuang highly appraises it with following words: "In terms of quantity, there are no less than 100,000 words of *Guanzi*'s discourse on economic issues, which can be regarded as an economic masterpiece that has never appeared in ancient Chinese history. In terms of quality, except for the theory of value and the doctrine of 'economic cycle', it almost touches on all aspects of social and economic activities, and has its unique insights. Even if we expand our perspective to the global scope, in a long period of pre-capitalism, there are few economic treatises as brilliant and abundant as *Guanzi*." Therefore, "*Guanzi*... is a brilliant star in the ancient history of China and even the whole world." See: Hu, Jichuang. 1998. *History of Chinese Economic Thought*, vol.1. Shanghai: Shanghai University of Finance and Economics Press. pp. 366-367, 369. Significant scholarly achievements

commodities, money, markets, and economic fluctuations caused by unsteady agricultural production were typical, common and periodic phenomena. These phenomena, as well as the economic problems brought by their interaction, were already rather complex. For the author of "Light and Heavy" chapter of *Guanzi*, the primary problem is undoubtedly how to convert the concrete "complexity" into abstract "simplicity", so as to have a profound knowledge and grasp of the economy and society. As we know, the "Light and Heavy" chapter reduces economic phenomena and problems into a holistic economic relationship or economic concept that treats "light" and "heavy" in relation to each other. It was developed into a comprehensive theory of light and heavy. Regarding the economic connotations of "light" and "heavy", people generally consider them as the principles of supply and demand of grain as well as its price[25]. There is already a substantial amount of analysis on this topic. For the purpose of discussion, the author briefly illustrates this with Fig. 2.1.

It is noteworthy that from a micro-local perspective, the theoretical abstraction of "light" and "heavy" seems to significantly simplify the understanding of economic phenomena. However, when shifting from the micro to the macro perspective, the analysis of "light" and "heavy" is not "simple" at all, as "all things" generate a vast

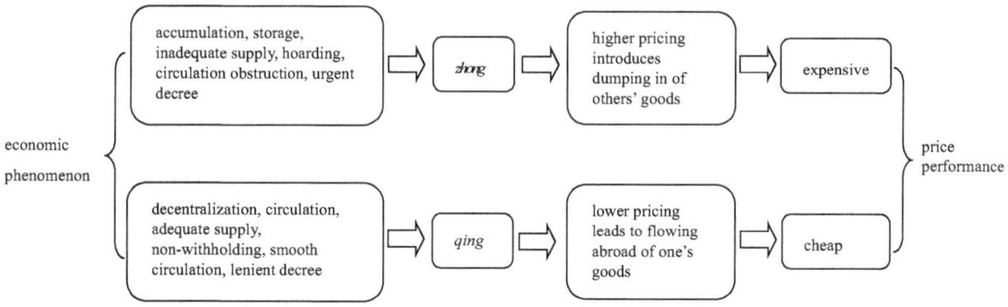

Fig. 2.1 Connotation of "light and heavy"

have been made in the study of Guanzi's economic thought. Notable works, among others, include the following: Liang, Qichao. 1989. Biography of Guanzi. *Thoughts from the Ice-Drinker's Studio*, vol.28. Beijing: Zhonghua Book Company; Huang, Han. 1936. *Guanzi's Economic Thought*. Shanghai: Commercial Press; Ye, Shichang. 1965. On *qing-zhong* Principles in Guanzi, *Economic Research Journal*. (1): 56-61; Wu, Baosan. 1989. *Research on Guanzi's Economic Thought*. Beijing: China Social Sciences Press; Hu, Jichuang. 1998. *History of Chinese Economic Thought*, vol.1. Shanghai: Shanghai University of Finance and Economics Press; Zhao, Jing. 2002. *A Comprehensive History of Chinese Economic Thought*, vol.1. Beijing: Peking University Press; Zhao, Shuzheng. 1989. *Research on Guanzi's Economic Thought*. Shanghai: Shanghai Classics Publishing House; Ren, Jiliang. 2005. *Research on Guanzi's Economic Thought: Historical Analysis of "qing-zhong Principles"*. Beijing: China Social Sciences Press; Ma, Feibai. 1979. *New Interpretation of the qing-zhong Chapters in Guanzi*. Beijing: Zhonghua Book Company. In the Western world, Walter A. Rickett's two-volume translation work, *Guanzi: Political, Economic, and Philosophical Essays from Early China* (Princeton University Press, 1985, 1998), is a representative work of the west that helps understand *Guanzi*.

[25]The area covered by the Guanzi's *qing-zhong* theory is not limited to this; see Section 2 in Chapter 6.

array of fragmented non-additive "light" and "heavy" relationships, holding little value or significance for macro-level governance. Nevertheless, proponents of the "light and heavy principles" have not been entangled in this complexity. Instead, they have focused their attention on the structural aspects of "light and heavy" relationships and have extracted the main contradictions. They find that "grain alone will determine whether things are expensive or cheap".[26] Grain is a special, non-substitutable commodity. Whether it is expensive or cheap not only depend on its own production and demand, but also have the potential to further influence and determine the pricing of other commodities – "when grain is expensive, all other things are cheap; when grain is cheap, all other things are expensive.[27]" In this way, the proponents have grasped the key point of the numerous "light and heavy" relationships, transforming the complex issue of specific "light and heavy" relationships into a general "light and heavy" relationships centered around grain, thereby elevating the "light and heavy" theory to a macro-level perspective.

With focus on grains, the author of *Laozi* also stated, "the five grains and rice are the people's Master of Destiny."[28] "In general the five grains determine the value of all other things."[29] It can be seen that changes in the supply and demand of grain as well as its price have a significant impact on the country's economy and people's livelihood. If grain production is affected by good or bad harvest, there would be different sceneries, "When there is a bumper harvest, no one can sell grain in the market, and dogs and pigs eat the food of people. When there is a bad harvest, grain is sold in the market for ten strings of cash (*jiang*) per *ju*and the roads are filled with starving people."[30] Would grain be sufficient enough to feed livestock in good years, short enough to fill the roads with starving people in bad years? In "The State's Store of Grain" (*guo xu*) of *Guanzi*, the author argues that these extreme situations are the result of leaving the market to develop at its own, "*As the harvest is bad or good, grain will be expensive or cheap. As government demands are relaxed or pressing, commodities become less (qing) or more valued (zhong). Thus it follows that if the prince is not able to control the situation, it will lead to large-scale traders roaming the markets and taking advantage of the people's lack of things to increase their capital a hundredfold.*"[31]

---

[26] Guanzi. 1998. *Political, Economic, and Philosophical Essays from Early China*, vol.2. trans. W. Allyn Rickett. Princeton: Princeton University Press. p. 367.

[27] Guanzi. 1998. *Political, Economic, and Philosophical Essays from Early China*, vol.2. trans. W. Allyn Rickett. Princeton: Princeton University Press. p. 367.

[28] Guanzi. 1998. *Political, Economic, and Philosophical Essays from Early China*, vol.2. trans. W. Allyn Rickett. Princeton: Princeton University Press. p. 377.

[29] Guanzi. 1998. *Political, Economic, and Philosophical Essays from Early China*, vol.2. trans. W. Allyn Rickett. Princeton: Princeton University Press. p. 382.

[30] Guanzi. 1998. *Political, Economic, and Philosophical Essays from Early China*, vol.2. trans. W. Allyn Rickett. Princeton: Princeton University Press. pp. 380-381.

[31] Guanzi. 1998. *Political, Economic, and Philosophical Essays from Early China*, vol.2. trans. W. Allyn Rickett. Princeton: Princeton University Press. p.379.

So how can the upheaval caused by supply shocks be effectively smoothed out when it is difficult to establish a long-term stable relationship between grain production and the market? At the theoretical level, it has been found that although the state has little control over climatic factors in grain production, it does possess an important economic tool — currency. Currency is a "medium of exchange" (*tong shi*) and "means of circulation" (*tong huo*), following the law that "if money is valued (*zhong*), goods will all be cheap (*qing*), but if money is cheap, goods will all be expensive."[32] This suggests that the state can influence the economy by adjusting the relative weight between currency and grain. One of the fundamental principles is to "make use of what is valued to acquire what is not valued and what has been acquired cheaply to ease the price of what has become too expensive" (or "accumulating stores of grain when demand and price are low (*qing*) and distributing them when demand and price are high (*zhong*)"[33]. It means that when the price of a commodity is low, it can be purchased at a slightly higher price, and when the price of a commodity is high, it can be sold at an appropriately lower price. For example, in a year with bumper harvest when there is a surplus of grain, there is the relationship of "cheat grain" and "valued money" in the market, leading to a macro-level price relationship of "cheat grain" and "valued goods". At this point, the state, acting as a demander, promptly injects currency to purchase the surplus grain ("make use of what is valued to acquire what is not valued"). As the relationship between supply and demand of grain in the market changes, the price relationships of "cheat grain" and "valued money", and "cheat grain" and "valued goods" will be adjusted and eventually balanced. In times of famine when the grain harvest is poor, there is a price relationship of "expensive grain" and "cheap money", and the overall situation of relative prices correspondingly shifts to "expensive grain" and "cheap goods". In this situation, the state, acting as a supplier, sells grain at a price lower than the market price ("make use of ...what has been acquired cheaply to ease the price of what has become too expensive"). Then the price relationships of "expensive grain" and "cheap money", and "expensive grain" and "cheap goods" will also undergo a transformation. By integrating both situations, the state regulates the price of grain by tightening or easing currency supply, which in turn affects the value of all other things and ensures overall stability of economic development.

The above analysis establish the foundation for buffer stock mechanism for grain, "those who are good at managing their states distribute their reserves when people do not have enough and intervene in the market when people have surpluses. When the people have a surplus of grain, they value it little *(qing)*. Therefore the prince may acquire grain for storage at a low price (*qing*). When the people are faced with shortages, they value it greatly *(zhong)*. Therefore the prince may

[32] Guanzi. 1998. *Political, Economic, and Philosophical Essays from Early China*, vol.2. trans. W. Allyn Rickett. Princeton: Princeton University Press. p.417.

[33] Guanzi. 1998. *Political, Economic, and Philosophical Essays from Early China*, vol.2. trans. W. Allyn Rickett. Princeton: Princeton University Press. pp. 381-382.

distribute these stores at a high price *(zhong).*"[34] Theoretically, the government purchases grain at the lowest price P_l in a year with bumper harvest [Fig. 2.2 (a) with an infinitely elastic demand curve D_i], and sells grain at the highest price P_h in a famine year [Fig. 2.2 (a) with an infinitely elastic supply curve S_i]. As a result, the supply and demand of grain, as well as its price, are thus controlled within a reasonable range [Fig. 2.2 (a) at any price level between P_h and P_l, assumed to be P_0]. "Therefore the prince controls the alternating superiority of grain and other things by intervening in the market when prices are unstable."[35] The state then would effectively avoid drastic fluctuations in grain prices [Figure 2.2(a)P_1-P_2] caused by supply shocks that leave them to the control of the market, thus preventing the wealthy merchants and large households from taking advantage of the situation for speculation and profiteering. As was stated in the chapter of "The State's Store of Grain" (*guo xu*) in *Guanzi*:

> He sees to it that in every city of ten thousand households there are certain to be stores amounting to ten thousand *zhong* of grain and ten million strings of cash. He also sees to it that in every town of a thousand households there are certain to be stores amounting to a thousand *zhong* of grain and amillion strings of cash. In the spring this is used to support plowing and in the summer to support weeding. Digging forks and plows, tools and imple-

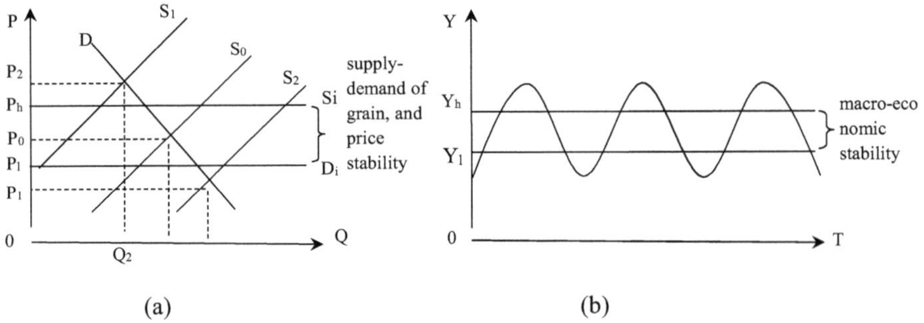

Fig. 2.2 Grain-based buffer stock stabilization mechanisms (Figure-a takes into account the effects of market circulation and nongovernmental reserves on supply; in the absence of these two factors, supply would be an inelastic vertical line, in which case a shift in the supply curve would cause a big change in price. See: Li, Lillian M. 2007. *Fighting Famine in North China: State, Market, and Environmental Decline, 1690s-1990s*. Stanford: Stanford University Press. pp. 203-206.)

[34] Guanzi. 1998. *Political, Economic, and Philosophical Essays from Early China*, vol.2. trans. W. Allyn Rickett. Princeton: Princeton University Press. p. 381. It should be pointed out that the buffer stock policy proposed by Guanzi is consistent with Bai Gui's business strategy of "What others throw away, I take; What others take, I give away." (See: Sima, Qian. 1993. *Records of the Grand Historian: Han Dynasty*, vol.2. trans. Burton Watson. Hong Kong and New York: Columbia University Press. p.438.) But this does not mean that the government has become a businessman. In Guanzi's view, the primary duty of the government is to stabilize the economy and society.

[35] Guanzi. 1998. *Political, Economic, and Philosophical Essays from Early China*, vol.2. trans. W. Allyn Rickett. Princeton: Princeton University Press. p.382.

> ments, seed grains and food rations, all are supplied by the prince. Thus big traders and families engaged in hoarding are unable to force extractions from our people.[36]

With the discovery of the relationship between grain and all other goods, proponents of "light and heavy principles" established a grain-based policy that addressed the main economic conflicts and other relevant issues. The state, by establishing a standard buffer stock mechanism, releases a stabilizing force into the economic society to converge fluctuations. In other words, the grain buffer stock, acting as a "price anchor" and "supply-demand anchor," stabilizes the total supply and demand, keeping the total output within a reasonable range [Figure 2.2 (b) Y_h -Y_l], thus playing the role of an economic stabilizer.

In this way, proponents of the "light and heavy principles" developed the macro-control ideas that regulate the value of grain by currency, and then uses the value of grain to control the value of all other goods. As was pointed out,

> Nowadays, since knife and spade money (*daobi*and *bubi*)[37] is being kept in the government treasury, the counterfeiting of coins and manipulation of prices is completely in the hands of merchants. If money is valued *(zhong)*, goods will all be cheap *(qing)*, but if money is cheap, goods will all be expensive. If grain is expensive, gold will decrease in value; if grain is cheap, gold will increase in value. If the prince is able to maintain a proper balance in the relative values of grain, coinage, and gold, the empire can be rendered stable. Such is the method for preserving the empire.[38]

Guanzi applies the "light and heavy principles" to the analysis of grain buffer stock mechanism, which provides a complete set of theoretical and policy framework for the application and development ever-normal granaries in later generation with far-reaching influence. As an economic policy, the buffer stock of grain was first introduced by Geng Shouchang, a subordinate of the second rank (*da sinong*) in the Ministry of Finance, in the year 57 B.C., the first year of Wufeng period (57–54 B.C.) during the reign of Emperor Xuan in the Western Han dynasty. It is first known as Ever-normal Granary (*chang ping cang*). In "Treatise on Food and Money" (*shi huo zhi*) of *The Book of Han* (*han shu*), there are following words:

---

[36] Guanzi. 1998. *Political, Economic, and Philosophical Essays from Early China*, vol.2. trans. W. Allyn Rickett. Princeton: Princeton University Press. p.382.

[37] Knife Money (*dao bi*) and Spade Money (*bu bi*) were notable types of ancient Chines currency. Knife Money was a unique form of currency in ancient China, which took the shape of iron knives used in trade. Made predominantly of bronze, these coins were issued by various states during the Warring States period. The design of Knife Money not only served as a medium of exchange but also symbolized the power and authority of the issuing state. The coins typically had a sharp edge and a hole at the top, allowing them to be strung together for convenience. Spade Money was a type of currency in ancient China that was modeled after the agricultural spades of the time. These coins were made of bronze and were prevalent during the late Spring and Autumn period and the Warring States period. The design of Spade Money often included inscriptions that indicated the issuing state and the denomination of the coin. Like Knife Money, Spade Money had a hole at the top for easy transport and storage.

[38] Guanzi. 1998. *Political, Economic, and Philosophical Essays from Early China*, vol.2. trans. W. Allyn Rickett. Princeton: Princeton University Press. p.417.

When the emperor Hsüan came to the throne, he employed government authorities (*li*) chosen for the most part for their worth and character. The "hundred clans" (that is, the people) were content on the land; year [after year harvests] were repeatedly abundant and luxuriant. When grain *ku* [fell in price to] five cash a picul *shih* farmers had little profit. At that time [a subordinate of] the second rank in the ministry of agriculture, Keng Shouch'ang (or Geng Shouchang), was favored by the emperor for his skill in calculation, and his ability to devise enterprises for gaining profits. In the *wu-feng* reign period (57-54 B.C.) he memorialized the throne, saying: "In the past each year there was the labor service for transport by water route from east of the Pass (Hsien-ku) four million bushels *hu of* grain for provisions for the capital, which employed sixty thousand men conscripted [*tsu*, for military or labor services]. It is fitting that grain *ku* sufficient to supply the capital should be bought within the provinces of the metropolitan area, [as well as those] of Hung-nung, Ho-tung, Shang-tang, and T'ai-yüan. This would save more than half of the [conscript] man power used in shipments which come by water from east of the Pass."

...

The grand secretary, Hsiao Wang-chih (106-46 B.C.), memorialized the throne, saying: "...At this time [Keng] Shou-ch'ang would like grain *ku* to be bought and transported by water from nearby [territory] within the Pass [Hsien-ku]. Expenses for building granaries and constructing boats [as he suggests] would cost more that two hundred million [cash]. This means an enterprise that will set a great many [people] in motion. [Your minister, however] fears that [because of this measure] there would appear the phenomena of drought, and that the people [thereby] would suffer calamities caused [by visitations from Heaven]. [Keng] Shou-ch'ang is experienced in the matter of devising enterprises and in calculating [to the point of] division of the *shu* but his deep schemes and far-reaching plans are indeed not [good] enough to be trustworthy. It is suitable for the present that [transport be carried on] as [has been done] heretofore." The emperor did not accept the appeal [of Hsiao Wang-chih but followed instead the suggestion of Keng Shou-ch'ang], and the matter of transport by water [of grain from nearby territory] was actually found advantageous.

[Keng] Shou-ch'ang then suggested (54 B.C.) that frontier provinces be ordered to erect granaries so that at times when grain *ku* was cheap it might be bought at an increased price [for storage by government] in order to benefit the farmers; and that at times when grain was expensive [that which had been stored up] might be sold at a decreased price [in order to benefit the people]. [To granaries erected under this government policy of equalization of prices by storage] was given the name of *Ch'ang-p'ing* "ever-level [price]" granaries. The people found them advantageous. So then the emperor issued an imperial edict conferring upon [Keng] Shou-ch'ang [the nineteenth grade of honorary rank], marquis of Kuannei.[39]

During the Western Han dynasty, it was costly to transport grain from various parts of east of the Pass to the capital. During the reign of Emperor Xuan, Geng Shouchang noticed that the grain was abundant and luxuriant for many years and the lower price of grain hurt the farmers, so he suggested the government to purchase a large amount of grains from the central metropolitan area and neighboring areas. On one hand it could reduce the expenditure of transportation by water route; on the other hand, it could increase the income of the farmers. The good results of the policy led Geng Shouchang to try to solve the problem of transporting grain from the interior region to the border areas in the north. Delivering grain to the border areas to meet the needs of national defense was a major economic burden to the state. Since grain

[39] Swann, Nancy Lee. (trans.) 1950. *Food and Money in Ancient China: The Earliest Economic History of China to A.D. 25, Han Shu 24, with Related Texts, Han Shu 91 and Shih-Chi 129.* Princeton: Princeton University Press. pp. 191-196.

prices continued to fall during the reign of Emperor Xuan, it was clearly more cost-saving for the government to purchase grain at lower prices in the border counties for national defense than spending huge sums of money on long-distance grain transportation from the interior region to the border areas. Considering this, Geng Shouchang, inspired the success of the transportation by water route, "suggested that frontier provinces be ordered to erect granaries so that at times when grain *ku* was cheap it might be bought at an increased price for storage by government in order to benefit the farmers; and that at times when grain was expensive that which had been stored up] might be sold at a decreased price [in order to benefit the people. To granaries erected under this government policy of equalization of prices by storage was given the name of Ch'ang-p'ing 'ever-level price' granaries."

It is worth noting that, unlike the previous practice of transporting grain from the east to the capital, the grains for the ever-normal granaries in the border areas were purchased for storage or sold at the suitable time. This not only solved the problem of meeting military needs and saving the cost of grain transportation, but also helped to stabilize the local price of grain and protected the interests of farmers. However, since these ever-normal granaries are not located in the major grain-producing areas, the sustainability for such operation was limited. During the reign of Emperor Yuan of the Han dynasty, natural disasters led to rising grain prices. "(At that time) most of the scholars in substantial government posts stated that...and 'ever level [price] granaries,' [all] should be abolished, and that [the government] ought not to strive with the people for profits. The emperor followed their proposal, and abolished them all (44 B.C.)."[40] In the Eastern Han dynasty (25-220 A.D.), Emperor Ming wanted to restore the ever-normal granaries, which was opposed by some officials. In "Biography of Liu Ban" of *The Book of the Later Han*, there are following words, "The Emperor intended to re-establish the ever-normal granaries, and most officials agreed to it. However Liu Ban rejected, 'Although Ever-normal Granary enjoys the reputation of benefiting the people, it actually is a means to exploit the people. The wealthy and powerful might use it as a means to gain more wealth, while the ordinary people couldn't derive any tangible benefits. Thus, it is not advisable to establish such ever-normal granaries.' Hearing these words, the emperor abandoned the plan."[41]

Inheriting the tradition of the Qin dynasty of attaching importance to the key regions such as capital city and border areas by setting granaries there, the Han dynasty also set granaries. Although the ever-normal granaries set in the Western Han dynasty bore the name "ever-normal", their function was not consistently effective. In fact, the granaries were set primarily for national defense instead of solving the problem of lower grain prices harming farmers or higher grain prices harming the general populace. Although the ever-normal granaries played some role

---

[40] Swann, Nancy Lee. (trans.) 1950. *Food and Money in Ancient China: The Earliest Economic History of China to A.D. 25, Han Shu 24, with Related Texts, Han Shu 91 and Shih-Chi 129.* Princeton: Princeton University Press. p.197.

[41] Fan, Ye.1965. Biography of Liu Ban. *The Book of the Later Han*, vol.39, Beijing: Zhonghua Book Company. p. 1305.

in stabilizing grain prices with the purchase and sale of grains, it is more of the "side effect". However, ever-normal granaries of the Western Han dynasty accumulated a certain amount of grains in the particular periods, which did play a positive role for "ever-normal peace at the border areas". More significantly, the Ever-normal Granary began to be part of the economic policies of the great unified state, which held a pioneering historical position for the economic control and adjustment of later dynasties.[42]

2.2 Government Control and Innovative Regulation

2.2.1 Developing into a Fixed Policy

The basic mechanism for the operation of "Ever-normal Granary" is that the government regulates the price fluctuations of grains in seasons with bumper harvest or poor harvest by purchasing grain at a slightly higher price when it is cheap and selling it at a slightly lower price when it is expensive. At the same time, these activities aim to curb the hoarding and manipulation of grain prices by private merchants and tycoons, thus stabilizing the supply and demand of grains, alleviating the social conflicts, and keeping the grain prices at the "ever-normal" level. Sima Guang[43] summarized the method in Ever-normal Granary as follows:

> In examining the methods of the Ever-normal Granary, it is found that in years of bountiful harvests, the low grain prices harmed the interests of farmers. Therefore, the government purchased grain at a price higher than the market price, leaving those who wished to hoard grain with no opportunity to compel the farmers to sell. In years of poor harvests, when grain prices were too high and harmed the people's interests, the government sold grain at a price lower than the market price, preventing those who hoarded grain from making great

---

[42] Murong, Hao. 2014. Exploring Ever-normal Granary in the Han dynasty. *Inner Mongolia Social Science*. 35(3): 77-79.

[43] Sima Guang (1019-1086 A.D.) was a renowned historian and high-rank official in Northern Song dynasty. With the courtesy name of Junshi, he was a native of Xiaxian county in Shanxi province. He was a successful candidate in the highest imperial examinations. During the reign of the Emperor Yingzong, he first worked as local government officials and then higher-rank officials in the central government. He began to compile the eight-volume history book during the reign of Emperor Yingzong. The book was named Comprehensive Mirror to Aid in Government (*zizhi tongjian*), when he served as a senior official at the imperial academy, or Chinese Hanlin Academy. He was an opponent to the New Policies proposed by reformist Wang Anshi and had launched several debates against Wang and his colleagues. As the reformists won support from Emperor Shenzong, he retreated to Luoyang, devoting 15 years of energy to compiling the Comprehensive Mirror to Aid in Government. During the reign of Emperor Zhezong, he tried to restore the old systems by defeating the reformists under the support of the Dowager Empress Gao. Sima Guang's greatest contribution was the 249-chapter Comprehensive Mirror to Aid in Government, recording history from the Warring States period to Northern Zhou dynasty, aiming to offer historical experiences and lessons to rulers of the country. His poems and literary works were included in the Sima Wengong Collection.

> profits by forcing the people to buy at high prices. With stable prices, both the public and private individuals benefited. This has been a good method of governing the state since the Three Dynasties.[44]

It is the ideal state of practice for ever-normal granaries that "the grain prices are ever-normal and the interest of the people and the state are both protected". However, the actual effect varies considerably in different historical periods. During the Three Kingdoms period, the country was divided and the disasters and wars continued without stop, causing the ever-normal granaries to be abandoned for a long time. From the Western Jin dynasty (266-317 A.D.) to the Northern and Southern Dynasties (420-589 A.D.), the setting of Ever-normal Granary was intermittent, so that its function was not fully developed and it didn't develop into a fixed system. As was recorded in the *Comprehensive Institutions (Tongdian)*:

> During the reign of Emperor Wu (236-290 A.D., the founding emperor of the Western Jin dynasty, reigning from 266 to 290) ...... when the grain was cheap but cotton and silk was expensive, the emperor desired to apply the approach of purchasing grain with cotton and silk at favourable prices (*pingdi*) and have the grain stored in granaries as reserves. However, some officials said that the military funds were still insufficient, thus it was inappropriate to exchange the expensive for the cheap. In 266, the second year of Taishi period, the emperor issued an edict stating, "the ancients people would weigh the national expenses and take profits and disperse the surplus by means of *pingdi*. Such policies have been abandoned for a long time ...... It is time to reintroduce the policy, and those in charge should fairly formulate specific regulations." However, the regulations were not immediately formulated. It was only in the fourth year of Taishi period that ever-normal granaries were set up. In times of good harvest, the state would purchase grain for storage; while in times of bad harvest, the state would sell stored grain for the benefit of the populace.
>
> During the Yuanjia period in the reign of Emperor Wen (407-453 A.D.) of the Southern Song dynasty, the Sanwu region (a region at the lower reaches of the Yangtze River, including the three counties of Wuxian, Wuxing, and Huiji) suffered from severe floods and waterlogging, which led to an increase in the grain prices and starvation among the people. Liu Yikang, Prince of Pengcheng, proposed a plan by stating, "Due to the disaster and famine in the eastern region, people are living in hardship, and the grain prices are increasing. Wealthy merchants hoard large quantities of grain, driving up grain prices every day....... It is necessary to command the households with savings to keep one year's storage, while the rest grains are to be sold compulsively in the market to stabilize the grain prices...". However, the plan which the people were very supportive of, was not actually implemented.
>
> In the middle of Yongming period during the reign ofEmperor Wu of Southern Qi (440-493 A.D.), the grains and textiles were cheap throughout the state. The emperor intended to set up ever-normal granaries for storage of grains and textiles. In the sixth one of Yongming period, an edict was issued to take fifty million coins from the imperial treasury to purchase grains and textiles in the capital...
>
> During the reign of Emperor Xiaowen (467-499 A.D.) of the Northern Wei, Li Biao, the Imperial Secretary submitted a memorial saying, "...... now there is a famine in the area east of the Taihang Mountains, and the capital is also short of supplies. I suggest that two ninths of the regular tax revenues of the sates and prefectures should be allocated. The allocated revenues, together with the surplus of the capital's annual expenses, should be sued to establish official granaries. In years of abundance the surplus grains should be pur-

[44] Sima, Guang.1999. Memorial to the Emperor Zhezong on purchasing grain at the due time for Ever-normal Granaries. in *Memorials Submitted to the Throne in the Song Dynasty.* ed. Zhao, Ruyu.vol.107. Shanghai: Shanghai Ancient Books Publishing House. p. 1156.

> chased and stored in the granaries, while in time of scarcity two tenth of the stored grains should be sold in the market. In this way, people would be encouraged to cultivate land to buy official silk, or save money to buy official grains. In years with good harvest, the granaries would be stored with grains, while in years with famine the stored grains would be sold directly to the populace." ...
>
> During the Heqing period ofEmperor Wucheng (537-569 A.D.) of the Northern Qi, all states and prefectures were ordered to set up Wealthy Granaries (another form of Ever-normal Granary)... When grains were expensive, they were sold at a price lower than the market price; when grains were cheap, the stored goods were sold to purchase the grains at the due price (slightly higher than the market price) for storage.
>
> Emperor Wen (507-556 A.D.) of Later Zhou dynasty set up six official positions, with the Minister of Granaries responsible for managing the grains and measure national spendings accordingly. When there was surplus grain, they would be stored to prepare for disasters and famine; when there was a shortage of grain, excess consumption would be cancelled. When there was a sufficient supply, grain would be lent to the people, which was distributed in the spring and returned in the autumn.[45]

For more than two hundred years, there was not a stable political, economic and social situation for the development of ever-normal granaries due to the frequent changes of regimes, the turbulence of society, the controlling of local magnates and the shrinking of the commodity economy. Among the regimes of the northern ethnic groups, Li Biao put forward a relatively complete policy of Ever-normal Granary during the reign of Emperor Xiaowen of the Northern Wei dynasty, the emperor "read it and approved it, intending to implement all"[46]. After that, in Northern Qi "all states and prefectures were ordered to set up Wealthy Granary".When grains were expensive, they were sold at a price lower than that of the market; when grains were cheap, the stored goods were sold to purchase the grains at the due price (slightly higher than the market price) for storage. The so-called "Wealthy Granaries" actually function as ever-normal granaries.[47] In the Southern Dynasties, although it was suggested to set up ever-normal granaries to "stabilize the grain prices", the plan "was not actually implemented". During the reign of Qi in the Southern dynasty the Ever-normal Granary was rebuilt, and "an edict was issued to take fifty million coins from the imperial treasury to purchase grains and textiles in the capital." According to *the Six Institutions of Tang Dynasty* (*tang liu dian*), ever-normal granaries were established in both Liang State and Chen State of the Southern Dynasties, but "Liang State did not sell the stored grains from the ever-normal granaries, and so did Chen State".[48] Grains were purchased for the ever-normal granaries but were not sold when necessary, thus performing half of its due function. In other words, they probably only serve as reserve for military needs.

---

[45] Du, You. 1988. Food and Money, XII. *Comprehensive Institutions*, vol.12. ed. Wang, Wenjin et al. Beijing: Zhonghua Book Company. pp. 287-289.

[46] Wei, Shou. 1974. Biography of Li Biao. *History of Wei*, vol.62. Beijing: Zhonghua Book Company. p. 1389.

[47] Zhang, Gong. 1986. *A Preliminary Study of Granary System in the Tang Dynasty*. Beijing: Zhonghua Book Company. p. 106.

[48] Li, Linfu et al. 1992.Ever-normal Granary Bureau, Ministry of Agriculture. *Six Institutions of Tang Dynasty*, vol.20. ed. Chen, Zhongfu. Beijing: Zhonghua Book Company. p. 546.

During the Sui dynasty, the country was finally unified into a grand one. Emperor Wen of the Sui dynasty issued an edict in the third year (583) of his reign, "establishing the Liyang Granary in Weizhou (nowadays southwest of Xunxian County, Henan), Heyang Granary in Luozhou (with its administrative center in Luoyang, now in Mengxian County, Henan), Ever-normal Granary in Shanzhou (nowadays Sanmenxia in the west of Henan), and Guangtong Granary in Huazhou (with its administrative center in Huayin, now in Huayin, Shaanxi). Then the grains were stored in the granaries and then transported by water route in a relay manner. In this way the grains from the northwest were sent to the capital."[49] The ever-normal granaries became part of the transportation channel in solving the problem of grain supply. This practice was similar to Geng Shouchang's granary system during the Western Han dynasty that supplied grains to the capital. Emperors of the Sui dynasty emphasized the establishment of large and gigantic granaries to protect the political and economic centers. Although a large amount of grain was stored, it did not widely benefit the common people. As was recorded in *The Political Program of Zhenguan Period* (*zhenguan zhengyao*), Emperor Taizong of Tang dynasty once talked about this with his ministers, considering it a great lesson from the history.[50] With the shift of the short-lived Sui dynasty to the Tang dynasty, the Ever-normal Granary system experienced a period of fast development ever since the Han dynasty.

The setting of official position of Ever-normal Granary Supervisor at the beginning of Tang dynasty (618-690 A.D.), shows the rulers' emphasis on Ever-normal Granary system. On September 22nd of first year (618) of Wude period, Emperor Gaozu of Tang dynasty, the founder and first emperor of the Tang dynasty, issued an edict stating, "it is appropriate to appoint Ever-normal Granary Supervisor for stability of the market prices. When grain prices rise in the market and there is increasing demand for grains, the state should sell the grains in ever-normal granaries at a reduced price in order to stabilize market prices. When there is a good harvest, the state should purchase grains and have them stored in the ever-normal granaries. With such practice, the interests of the state and common populace are both protected, and households have sufficient grains, preventing the great merchants and hoarders of provisions from robbing our people and eliminating social stagnation."[51] Emperor Gaozu explained the operational mechanism and basic functions of the ever-normal granaries with great clarity, indicating that at the founding of the state, rulers had recognized the significance of maintaining stable grain prices and supply-demand balance for the long-term security and stability of the state. However, due to the myriad challenges at the time, the construction of ever-normal granaries was not actually implemented. In the fifth year (622 A.D.) of the Wude period, the

[49] Wei, Zheng. ed. 1973. Food and Money. *The Book of Sui*, vol.24. Beijing: Zhonghua Book Company. p. 683.

[50] Wu. Jing. 2009. Rise and fall of dynasties. *Annotated Political Program of Zhenguan Period*, vol.8. ed. Xie Baocheng. Beijing: Zhonghua Book Company. p.466.

[51] Liu, Xu et al. ed. 1975. Food and money II. *Old History of Tang Dynasty*, vol.49. Beijing: Zhonghua Book Company. p. 2122.

official position of Ever-normal Granary Supervisor was abolished. In the thirteenth year (639) of the Zhenguan period, the imperial court ordered the establishment of ever-normal granaries in the main grain-producing areas of the north, namely the eight states of *Luo, Xiang, You, Xu, Qi, Bing, Qin*, and *Pu*. On one hand, this measure helped prevent grain prices from falling; on the other hand, it was relevant with expanding military reserves in preparation for wars at the border areas. However, from the time until the early Kaiyuan period (713-741 A.D.), records of establishment of ever-normal granaries were not found. This suggests that in the early years of the Tang dynasty, when the economic foundation was not yet solid, it was not a good opportunity for establishment of ever-normal granaries. From the Kaiyuan period to the Tianbao period (742-756 A.D.), the Tang dynasty witnessed economic and social prosperity. Inheriting Emperor Gaozu's idea on construction of ever-normal granaries at the foundation of dynasty, the emperors of later generations attached importance to construction of ever-normal granaries, which were widely constructed with unprecedented levels. After the An-Shi Rebellion[52], the Ever-normal Granary system was restored and revitalized with the support of Liu Yan, the Prime Minister in min-Tang, but it gradually declined thereafter.

According to the research of Zhang Gong, a Chinese scholar, the development of Ever-normal Granary during the reign of Emperor Xuanzong was manifested in the following three aspects. Firstly, the construction of Ever-normal Granary was gradually extended to the whole nation, even to the remote Tien Shan County. The only regions that still did not have Ever-normal Granary during the reign of the Kaiyuan were the Jiangnan Dao (south of the middle and lower reaches of the Yangtze River and north of the South Mountains) and Lingnan Dao (north of the South Mountains). Secondly, during this period, the grain reserves of the Ever-normal Granary were more adequate, fully utilizing its buffer regulating function. The 20% increase in

[52] The An-Shi Rebellion (755-763 A.D.) was an eight-year uprising led by military governors An Lushan and Shi Siming in the last years of Emperor Xuanzong's reign of the Tang dynasty.The rebellion was a turning point of the Tang dynasty from its rise to its decline. It was partly caused by Emperor Xuanzong's lapses late in his life, when he indulged himself in sensual pleasures, pampered his favorite imperial consort Yang Guifei (guifei is the highest rank of imperial consorts aside from empress), and entrusted state affairs to her cousin, Grand Councilor Yang Guozhong. Tang's weakness was exploited by An Lushan, a military governor of three commanderies - Pinglu (today's Chaoyang, Liaoning Province), Fanyang (today's Beijing), and Hedong (southwest of today's Taiyuan, Shanxi Province). He had been contending with the grand councilor for power and was fully aware of the regime's decadence. In the 11th lunar month of 755, An led a revolt in Fanyang against the corrupt grand councilor and soon captured Luoyang and Chang'an. In the first lunar month of 757, An Lushan was murdered by his son An Qingxu. Later, Shi Siming killed An Lushan's son, only to be slain by his own son, Shi Chaoyi. Taking advantage of the infighting, the royalist troops led by Guoziyi and Li Guangbi crushed the rebel armies. In the 10th lunar month of 762, Shi Chaoyi committed suicide in despair, marking tha end of the An-Shi Rebellion. However, remnants of the rebel forces survived and eventually split north China into semi-independent regions as the Tang dynasty declined. The Tang government was much weakened, however, and the second half of the Tang dynasty and the subsequent Five Dynastiesperiod were troubled by chronic warlordism. See: "An-Shi Rebellion", Encyclopedia of China, https://www.zgbk.com/ecph/words?SiteID=1&ID=390056.

price for purchasing grain and the 20% decrease in price for selling grain may have been the general range for regulating grain prices at the ever-normal granaries during the reign of Emperor Xuanzong. In order to enhance the granary's ability to regulate the supply and demand, Emperor Xuanzong also use reserves from imperial granaries and charity granaries to regulate grain price in key areas. Thirdly, in terms of management, during the Kaiyuan period a management system was established in which the funds for granary storage were directly allocated by the central government, and rights of management went to local *dao* (province) and *zhou* (prefecture, county). In practice, the money and grain were dominated by Dao Inspector appointed by the imperial court, and the individual states followed the instructions on purchasing and selling grains.[53] From the Western Han dynasty to the Sui dynasty, Ever-normal Granary finally went into its heydays in the Tang dynasty, with widespread establishment of the reserve system, a more complete institutional framework, and the capacity to function as an economic regulator. Judging from these three aspects, we may say Ever-normal Granary had stepped into a new stage of development in the prosperous Tang dynasty.

After the An-Shi Rebellion, the imperial court rebuilt ever-normal granaries. In January of the second year (764) of the reign of Emperor Daizong of the Tang dynasty, "Di Wuqi suggested, 'Ever-normal granaries should be established in all prefectures. When the grain prices are low, grains would be purchased with prices slightly higher than those of the market; when the grain prices are high, the stored grains would be sold with prices slightly lower those of the market.'"[54] The war in the middle of Tang dynasty made national strength decline significantly. The capital for ever-normal granaries was originally funded by the state, then it had to be funded by the local government. However, the recovery of ever-normal granaries was still relatively good, otherwise Liu Yan would find it difficult to implement his economic policy. "Liu Yan made use of the ever-normal granaries, which involved purchasing surplus grain from the people at higher prices during years of abundance, selling it back at lower prices during time of famine. Approximately three million *hu* of grain were stored in each prefecture with this policy."[55] In possession of a certain amount of reserves, Liu Yan didn't passively buy or sell grain; instead, he made timely and accurate decisions, allowing the ever-normal granaries to play a more proactive role in regulation supply and demand. "Every ten days and at the end of each month, the local officials were required to report on the conditions of rain, snow, abundance, and shortage in their respective prefectures and counties (*zhou* and *xian*) to the Transportation Commissioner. In times of good harvest, grain was purchased at higher prices, and in times of shortage, it was sold at lower prices....When the scheduled time arrived, Liu Yan did not wait for applications from the prefectures

[53] Zhang, Gong. 1986. *A Preliminary Exploration of Granary System in the Tang Dynasty*. Beijing: Zhonghua Book Company. pp. 108-112.

[54] Liu, Xu et al. ed. 1975. Food and money II. *Old History of Tang Dynasty*, vol.49. Beijing: Zhonghua Book Company. p. 2124.

[55] Ouyang, Xiu and Song Qi. 1975. Biography of Liu Yan. *New History of Tang Dynasty*, vol.149. Beijing: Zhonghua Book Company. p. 4798.

and counties (*zhou* and *xian*) but directly submitted a proposal to the emperor for implementation, meeting the urgent needs of the people without ever missing the right moment. He did not wait until the people were exhausted, displaced, or had died of hunger before providing relief."[56] Thanks to the government's ability to obtain information and make decisions quickly, as well as a high degree of administrative efficiency, Ever-normal Granary could "meeting the urgent needs of the people without ever missing the right moment". Liu Yan set a good example in this regard.

In addition to buying or selling grain and providing relief, the Ever-normal Granary in the Tang dynasty might have been used for lending as early as the Kaiyuan period (713-741 A.D.). Contract documents unearthed in Turpan from the third year (765A.D.) of Guangde period reflect situations where multiple households guaranteed loans of grain from Ever-normal Granary.[57] A larger scale of relief loans by ever-normal granaries likely started in the later period of the Tang dynasty. In February of the sixth year (807 A.D.) of Emperor Xianzong's reign, when there was a grain shortage in the capital region, the imperial court lent the reserves of the ever-normal granaries and charity granaries to the people to alleviate their plight. "It was decreed that 240,000 *shi* of grain from the ever-normal granaries and charity granaries should be lent to the people. In areas where there was a shortage of grain seeds, local officials were also instructed to borrow the grains from the ever-normal granaries and charity granaries."[58]

In the Tang dynasty the Ever-normal Granary already revealed many problems and contradictions in its operation.[59] A system always has its pros and cons. Undoubtedly, Ever-normal Granary that was matured and standardized in the Tang dynasty has become the meeting point of various policies. It is not only a basic public product provided by the government to the society but also an important tool for economic regulation. From then on, Ever-normal Granary became a key term in the management of economy and society in ancient China.

2.2.2 *New Ever-Normal Granary Policy*

In the third year (992) of the reign of Emperor Taizong in the Northern Song dynasty, the Ever-normal Granary was first established in the capital area, "At that time, the capital region was experiencing a bumper harvest and grain prices were extremely

[56] Sima, Guang. 1956. *Comprehensive Mirror to Aid in Government*, vol.226. Beijing: Zhonghua Book Company. pp. 7285-7286.

[57] Zhang, Gong. 1986. *A Preliminary Exploration of Granary System in the Tang Dynasty*. Beijing: Zhonghua Book Company. pp. 119-121.

[58] Liu, Xu et al. ed. 1975. Food and money II. *Old History of Tang Dynasty*, vol.49. Beijing: Zhonghua Book Company. p. 2126.

[59] Zhang, Gong. 1986. *A Preliminary Exploration of Granary System in the Tang Dynasty*. Beijing: Zhonghua Book Company. pp. 117-123.

low". Taking advantage of this opportunity, the officials "dispatched envoys to set up markets at the four gates of the capital, where they purchased grain at prices higher than the market prices. Relevant departments were ordered to empty the nearby granaries so as to store the purchased grains. These granaries, managed by officials, were called ever-normal granaries. When there was a famine, the stored grain would be sold at reduced prices to the poor. This system was later made permanent."[60] In the third year (1006) of Emperor Zhenzong's reign, the imperial court began to implement the Ever-normal Granary policy throughout the country:

> Initially, someone proposed that natural disasters such as floods and droughts can only be avoided with readiness, so ancient ever-normal granaries should be resumed. It was requested to calculate the number of households in east and west of the capital, Hedong, Shaanxi, Jianghuai, and Liangzhe[61]. Depending on the number of households, a portion of the tax money should be set aside, ranging from 1,000 to 20,000 strings of coins. The transfer ambassadors should be ordered to choose honest and capable officials to manage it in each city, and the agricultural department should be entrusted specifically with the general leadership. The three departments of finance should not use the money without authorization. The operation method was to buy grain from farmers at a higher price than the market during the summer and autumn each year. If there was a disaster and grains were expensive, the stored grains should be sold at a lower price. Ten years later when there was a certain surplus of the money, the capital should be returned to the three financial departments. The emperor issued an imperial edict for the three finance departments to implement. They agreed to do as proposed, but not to set up additional ever-normal granaries in the border areas. Thus, the officials of Ministry of Agriculture built office, prepared register documents and set up ever-normal granaries.[62]

This promotion of the Ever-normal Granary involved a wide range of areas and established a framework for the system, laying the foundation for the development of the Ever-normal Granary system during the Northern and Southern Song dynasties. In 1018 and 1020, Emperor Zhenzong further established reserve standards for each prefecture and expanded the construction regions,[63] gradually developing a large-scale Ever-normal Granary system. By 1021, the ever-normal granaries had "purchased over 183,000 *hu* of grains and sold over 243,000 *hu* of grains."[64] Emperor

---

[60] Li, Tao.2004. *Supplement to Historical Mirror to Aid in Government*, vol.33. Beijing: Zhonghua Book Company. p. 737.

[61] Liangzhe, or Liangzhe Circuit (997–1160s), was one of the major circuits during the Song dynasty (960–1279). Its administrative area corresponds roughly to modern Zhejiang, Shanghai, and southern Jiangsu (the portion east of Changzhou, between Lake Tai and the Yangtze River). The fertile Yangtze River Delta lay within Liangzhe Circuit, as did Lake Tai. Liangzhe was the wealthiest circuit in Song. The capital of Liangzhe Circuit was Hang Prefecture (renamed Lin'an Prefecture in 1129, when it became the Song capital). The name Liangzhe ("Two Zhe's") originally referred to the two Tang dynasty (618–907) circuits Zhejiang East Circuit and Zhejiang West Circuit.

[62] Li, Tao. 2004. *Supplement to Historical Mirror to Aid in Government*, vol.62. Beijing: Zhonghua Book Company. p. 1385.

[63] Xu, Song. ed. 2014. Food and money, LIII (6-7). *Draft for the Collected Statutes of Song Dynasty*. Shanghai: Shanghai Ancient Books Publishing House. pp. 7198-7199.

[64] Toqto'aet al. 1985. Food and money I (4). *History of Song Dynasty*, vol.176. Beijing: Zhonghua Book Company. p. 4276.

Renzong and Emperor Yingzong continued to promote the construction of the Ever-normal Granary. In the third year (1066) of Emperor Yingzong's reign, "501,048 *shi* of grains were stored in the ever-normal granaries, and 471,157 *shi* of grains were sold."[65] This was a great expansion in the scale compared to the that in 1021.

In the second year (1069) during the Xi'ning period in the reign of Emperor Shenzong (reigned 1067-1085), Wang Anshi[66] implemented comprehensive reforms to solve the prominent economic and social problems of the Northern Song dynasty. Green Sprouts Act, an important part of the New Policies, pushed the Ever-normal Granary system to a higher level. In the year 1069, the Department of Regulations (*tiaoli si*) made the following explanation of the Green Sprouts Act:

> The rough calculation shows that the grain stored in the ever-normal granaries and public welfare granaries (*guanghui cang*) across various regions can reach over 15 million *shi*. The way of purchasing and selling the grains at due time has not been appropriate, so the benefits have not been maximized. Now, it is intended to sell the stored grain at a price slightly lower than the market price when grain prices are high, and to buy at a price slightly higher than the market price when grain prices are low. Grain taxes and money under the control of the Transport Commission can also be used flexibly for exchange. In addition, with the current money, following the precedent of the Green Sprouts Loan in Shaanxi, those willing to borrow in advance can be lent withmoney. Repayment is made with grain when taxes are paid, half when the summer tax is paid, and half when the autumn tax is paid. If the price of grain is high when repaying with grain, those who wish to pay with money are allowed to do so according to their wishes. In case of natural disasters and poor harvests, repayment

[65] Toqto'aet al. 1985. Food and money I (4). *History of Song Dynasty*, vol.176. Beijing: Zhonghua Book Company. p. 4279.

[66] Wang Anshi (1021-1086) was a reformer, thinker and litterateur of the Song dynasty (960-1279). Wang was born in Linchuan, Jiangxi (today's Fuzhou, Jiangxi Province) and was known as Mr. Linchuan. His courtesy name was Jiefu, literary name Banshan. He came fourth in the imperial exam in 1042, and worked in local governments for many years. Wang thought that the ultimate cause of social poverty was annexation of land. Therefore, in 1058, Wang submitted to Emperor Renzong a ten-thousand-character memorandum in which he proposed to comprehensively reform the policies that had been implemented since the founding of the Song dynasty. In 1069, he was appointed participant in determining governmental matters. The following year, he became grand councilor, and began to put his reform policies into practice. Wang clearly stated that finance was the top priority for a grand councilor, and explained the close relationship between state affairs and finance. He believed that only on the basis of production development could the state financial problems be effectively dealt with. In his reform program, Wang set production development as the urgent and utmost priority. While emphasizing the leading role played by state power, Wang opposed its excessive intervention in social production and economic life. He insisted that there should not be too many monopolies and taxations. Under the guidance of Wang's thoughts, reformers stipulated a series of new policies. Reform was widely carried out, covering agriculture, handicraft and businesses in both rural and urban areas. However, his reform infringed on the benefits of landlords and bureaucrats, and thus received a hostile reception from conservative scholars, empress dowagers, the royal members, and many others, leading to Wang's first removal from his position in 1074.The following year, he was reinstated but failed to gain sufficient support to continue the reform. In 1076, Wang resigned. He returned to Jiangning Prefecture (today's Nanjing), and spent the rest of his life there. In 1086, Emperor Zhezong took office. The conservatives resumed their power, and abolished all of the new reform policies. This led to Wang suffering from depression and finally his death of illness. See: "Wang Anshi", Encyclopedia of China, https://www.zgbk.com/ecph/words?SiteID=1&ID=390233&Type=bkztb&SubID=681

> can be postponed until the next tax collection. Not only is it sufficient to prepare for times of famine and disaster, but also, once the people have borrowed, they will not worry about food during the farming season. Therefore, officials can be chosen to encourage and persuade them to develop water and soil, and then agricultural practices in all directions will naturally improve. People's poverty often occurs during the time of harvest gap between the new and old crops, and the rich and powerful take advantage of this urgency to lend at high interest rates and demand double interest, causing borrowers to suffer. The stored grain in the ever-normal granaries and public welfare granaries has been accumulated, and it is only sold when there is a poor harvest and the grain prices are high, benefiting only those who are idle in the city. Now, within a region, the supply and demand are connected, and grain is sold when prices are high and bought when prices are low, which increases savings and stabilizes prices, allowing farmers to engage in agricultural labor according to the agricultural season, and the rich and powerful cannot take advantage of people's difficulties. All of the above are for the benefit of the people, and the state does not gain any income from it. This is also in line with the intention of the ancient emperors to distribute benefits to the people as an aid to agriculture. By regulating grain prices and supply and demand it helps to prevent the rich and powerful from taking advantage of the situation.[67]

The Green Sprouts Act still retained the buffer mechanism of purchase and sale of grains, so the Department of Regulations (*tiaoli si*) explained that "the old policy is still retained in the new reform", and "the old policy was not perfect enough in terms of extensive grain storage, suppression of the wealthy and powerful from hoarding, and relief for the poor and weak … Therefore, it is necessary to draw on the credit and loan system in *Rites of Zhou* and revise a new policy".[68] The "credit and loan" in *Rites of Zhou* provided a theoretical basis for the Green Sprouts Act.[69] Apparently, the New Policies focused on providing low-interest loans to the people with the grain reserve of public welfare granaries and ever-normal granaries (the Green Sprouts Act was also known as the New Ever-normal Granary Act): loans were delivered once or twice a yearwith an annual interest rate of 20%, either in the form of money or grain at the wish of the borrower, which was paid back along with the summer and fall taxes. This policy is based on two important considerations: Firstly, for the people, official loans can help the weak and the poor. "For private loans, the interest rate is at least 50%~70%, but sometimes it is even double of the capital."[70] In comparison, the 20% interest of official loans is really low. "In the past, the poor would borrow from the wealthy at high interest rates, but now the poor would borrow from the government. The government offers loans with low

[67] Xu, Song. ed. 2014. Food and money IV (16). *Draft for the Collected Statutes of Song Dynasty*. Shanghai: Shanghai Ancient Books Publishing House. p. 6041.

[68] Xu, Song. ed. 2014. Food and money IV (25). *Draft for the Collected Statutes of Song Dynasty*. Shanghai: Shanghai Ancient Books Publishing House. p.6051.

[69] For an in-depth discussion of this issue, see: Yu, Jinghui and Lei Bo. 2016. The Green Shoots Lending policy in Xining Period of Northern Song dynasty and the debate on the meaning of the classics. *Historical Research*. (2): 20-39.

[70] Yang, Shi. 1986. *Collection of Yang Shi*, vol.12. in *Complete Library in the Four Branches of Literature (Wenyuange Edition)*, *Ji* section, vol.1125. Taibei: Commercial Press of Taiwan. p. 227.

interest rates, and the people are helped out of their difficulties."[71] Such "policy-supported" loans must be very effective in preventing hoarding activities. In addition, public welfare granaries and ever-normal granaries have limited grain reserves. If the reserves are fully utilized to for loans, more people would be benefited. Secondly, as far as the official institutions are concerned, their active lending could improve the operational benefit. With the previous policy, the circulation of money and grains in granaries were obstructed, in that "in many regions the grains were purchased at high prices, and in some cases they had not been sold for several decades, failing to contribute to relief efforts."[72] Coupled with the difficulty of maintaining adequate reserves in the granaries, it was difficult to sustain the operation of ever-normal granaries and public welfare granaries, "resulting in the need for relief lending from other prefecture-level granaries"[73]. In the new reform, the ever-normal granaries and public welfare granaries are proactive in lending loans, charging an interest rate of twenty percent. Such an arrangement not only covers administrative costs and normal losses but also generates profit, creating a circulation of funds that allows the policy to be implemented for long-term. Wang Anshi provided a clear explanation for this, "When it comes to the interest on loans, a rate of twenty percent is inferior to ten percent, and ten percent is inferior to lending without interest. Lending without interest is still not as good as giving it away. So, why do we charge twenty percent interest instead of giving it away? It is to ensure that this work can continue in the future. If it cannot continue, then this matter is merely a favor to the people, not a policy. Governance is not just about giving benefits without incurring costs. Therefore, it is necessary to lend loans to them with interest. Moreover, we must also pay the salaries of the officials for this work, plus the costs of transportation, and the losses from floods, droughts, rats and birds. Hence, it is essential to implement and expand the Green Sprouts Act. Only then can we provide assistance when they are lack of food and clothes in years of famine. Could this possibly be done without the twenty percent interest?[74]

As an important innovation to the policy of ever-normal granaries, the Green Sprouts Act "was not ill-intentioned in its legislative purpose"[75]. From personnel management, operation procedures, loan targets and loan amounts to supervision processes and credit guarantees, each aspect had detailed arrangements, and the

[71] Wang, Anshi. 2017. *Collected Works of Wang Anshi*, vol.41. in *Complete Works of Wang Anshi*, ed. Wang, shuizhao.vol.6. Shanghai: Fudan University Press. p. 794.

[72] Xu, Song. ed. 2014. Food and money IV (25). *Draft for the Collected Statutes of Song Dynasty*. Shanghai: Shanghai Ancient Books Publishing House. p. 6051.

[73] Prefecture-level granary, or county-level granary, is part of the national granary, whose reserves are derived from taxes collected in accordance with legal procedures. Its main function is to maintain the administrative functioning of the government.

[74] Wang, Anshi. 2017. *Collected Works of Wang Anshi*, vol.73. in *Complete Works of Wang Anshi*, ed. Wang, shuizhao. vol.7. Shanghai: Fudan University Press. pp. 1306-1307.

[75] Zhu, Xi. 2002. *Collected Works of Zhu Xi*, vol.79. in *Complete Book of Zhu Xi*. ed. Zhu Jieren et al. vol.24. Shanghai: Shanghai Ancient Books Publishing House; Hefei: Anhui Education Publishing House. p. 3777.

legislative provisions could be described as very comprehensive and thorough. However, upon deeper investigation, we may find the hidden flaws and defects in the design of Green Sprouts Act,[76] among which the crucial one was the important policy orientation of the new reform - monetary operations. In the research of Yu Jinghui and Lei Bo, this issue was revealed from two aspects. Firstly, as was stated in the memorial of Han Qi (1008–1075), one of the most influential statesmen in the Northern Song and an opponent to Wang Anshi's New Policies, from the perspective of the government, although the Green Sprouts Act stipulated that repayment with money or grain was voluntary, grain was not suitable for long-term storage and would easily cause losses. The cost for grain reserves was also high. In addition, in years of bumper harvest, grain prices would necessarily be low, making grain repayment unfavorable for the government. Moreover, returned grain would occupy the capitals, affecting monetary circulation and subsequent lending. Therefore, Han Qi believed that the government would induce farmers to sell grain to repay with money. Then, from the perspective of the borrowers, would farmers prefer to repay with money or grain? According to the provisions of the Green Sprouts Act and corresponding regulations, during the loan process, the determination of the benchmark price for grain should be based on the intermediate price of grain over a period of time. However, since official capital could not be lost, it was likely in practice that the lower price within ten years would be used as the conversion standard. As such, whether farmers chose to repay a grain loan with money or grain, the actual interest rate would be higher than twenty percent. This meant that the greater the gap between the benchmark price for converting grain to money and the current market price of train, the more apparent the tendency of people to pay loans with money.[77]

In fact, even if you repay a loan with money, the actual interest rate is bound to be higher than the nominal twenty percent. We know that small-scale peasant economy is subsistence-type economy, and that small-scale peasants are both the vulnerable group in the market and the group who desire for market stability. Under the old system, Ever-normal Granary also lent to the farmers, but the borrowings and repayments were both in the form of grain, which avoided market risks. However, with the Green Sprouts Act, farmers were more likely to borrow money, so they had to engage in market transactions to obtain necessary production and living materials. When there was a rush to trade, the market was clearly dominated by sellers (a seller's market). And with the "money supply" increasing sharply in the short term, the purchasing power of money would significantly decline, placing farmers in a disadvantageous position. During the harvest season, farmers would once again flock to the market to exchange grain for the money needed to repay the loan. Then the market would be dominated by buyers (a buyer's market) due to the large supply of grain, causing the value of the grains held by the farmers to decline again. It is

[76] Li, Jinshui. 2007. *Researches on Wang Anshi's Economic Reform*. Fuzhou: Fujian People's Publishing House. pp. 96-109.

[77] Yu, Jinghui and Lei Bo. 2016. The Green Shoots Lending policy in Xining Period of Northern Song dynasty and the debate on the meaning of the classics. *Historical Research*. (2): 20-39.

worth noting that compared to the short-term increase in money caused by "borrowing Green Sprouts Loans - exchanging money for goods", the long-term shortage of money caused by "exchanging goods for money - repaying Green Sprouts Loans" brought greater losses to farmers. "Now, the Green Sprouts Act… demands that people should pay money for loans. This is why all goods are cheap, and only money is the most expensive."[78] This caused the "money shortage" that had already appeared in the early Northern Song dynasty to be an even more serious problem during the Xi'ning years. It is not difficult to see that the two trading links in the implementing of Green Sprouts Act borrowing and repayment, i.e., exchanging money for goods and exchanging goods for money, greatly increased the transaction costs dominated by the market, invisibly adding to the losses. In addition to the interest stipulated for the loans, the actual interest rate borne by farmers was no longer twenty percent, but much higher than that.

Reflecting on the ever-normalgranary system, we can further recognize its protective function: ever-normal granaries "exogenously" created a market that could protect the interests of farmers through the mechanisms of purchase and sale of grain or lending and repaying grain. The government, acting as a "market maker", aimed to separate farmers from the unstable market during special periods, reducing the uncertainty and creating another stable trading environment for farmers as buffer. However, the operating model of the Green Sprouts Loan precisely violated this principle - the monetary loan that could not directly bring goods pushed farmers back into the volatile market, making it difficult for ever-normal granaries to effectively keep the stability of the market. Therefore, although some scholars argue that the monetary orientation of the Green Sprouts Act aligns with the trend of commodity economic development in the later period of traditional Chinese society, a more in-depth understanding of the Green Sprouts Loan can be achieved by analyzing the specific transaction process.

The issues arising from the implementation of the Green Sprouts Act led Emperor Shenzong to reflect. In September of the seventh year (1074) of the Xi'ning period, the emperor questioned: "For the grains in ever-normal granaries, if half are used as loans for interest and half are for sales at reduced prices, and the two rely on each other with a balance but without favoring one over the other, then the people will surely be benefited. Now, the officials are eager to implement the New Policies. They desire to lend loans, while the old rules for ever-normal granaries are not supervised by anyone. Generally, the policies of past dynasties that are feasible should be strictly adhered to. Now, without considering the benefits or harms of the past policies, everything is changed. Is this reasonable?"[79] After the Green Sprouts Act was enacted, the old Ever-normal Granary system of distributing grain at

[78] Su, Zhe. 1990. Reflections on current affairs on my return from Qi Zhou. *Collections of Su Zhe*, vol.35. ed. Chen, Hongtian and Gao Xiufang. Beijing: Zhonghua Book Company. p. 619.

[79] Li, Tao. 2004. *Supplement to Historical Mirror to Aid in Government*, vol.256. Beijing: Zhonghua Book Company. p. 6256.

reduced prices and providing relief loans was still in effect.[80] However, because the officials focused more on implementing the New Policies, the old Ever-normal Granary system did not receive enough attention. The practice of "loans for interest" and "sales at reduced prices" did not achieve the expected balance, resulting in more severe situations when disasters struck and the use of provincial granaries was required.[81] Nevertheless, according to the hydraulic work law *(nongtian shuili fa)*[82], the practice of "labor relief"[83] promoted by implementing monetary loans of the new policy further expanded the old Ever-normal Granary system and achieved multiple benefits.

Amidst the struggle between the old and new parties, the retention or abolition of the Green Sprouts Act became a focal point. The content of the new policy was also adjusted during the time, but the dominant idea of collecting and lending money for interest remained unchanged. In the first year (1086) of the Yuanyou period, the Green Sprouts Act was abolished, and later it was reinstated and then abolished again. In the second year (1128) of the Jianyan period of the Southern Song dynasty, the ultimate fate of the Green Sprouts Act was announced, "the Green Sprouts Act shall never be implemented again[84]". The monetary operation in the Green Sprouts Act was an attempt to address the issue of sustainable development for the old Ever-normal Granary system. Although Wang Anshi, in the face of the financial difficulties of the Northern Song dynasty, provided a "classical" theoretical basis from the *Rites of Zhou* for the reform, this new policy was easily influenced by pursuit of interests. There were irreconcilable contradictions between supporting the needy, stabilizing the economy, and enriching the treasury, as well as between the moral, public, and profitable aspects.

[80] For example, in the third year of Xi'ning Years (1070) "an edict stated: 'The Sovereign has heard that the states of Chang'an and Tonghua suffered a particularly severe drought in the fall, so stragglers already wandered to the western regions of the capital city in search of food. The Sovereign hereby orders the transport commissioners in Shaanxi and western capital to investigate the situation and provide relief as soon as possible by selling grain in ever-normal granaries at lower prices to help them tide over their difficulties.'" (Li, Tao. 2004. *Supplement to Historical Mirror to Aid in Government*, vol.214. Beijing: Zhonghua Book Company. p. 5202.) In in the fifth year of Xi'ning Years (1072), "the Emperor issued an edict to the transport commissioner of Shaanxi: 'Because the valleys of Huazhou have collapsed, and there are houses and farmland in the regions ...... if they are short of grain seeds and plowing oxen, you'd lend them the money and grain in the ever-normal granaries, with exemption from interest and loose requirement for the repayment date." See: Li, Tao. 2004. *Supplement to Historical Mirror to Aid in Government*, vol.239. Beijing: Zhonghua Book Company. p. 5807.

[81] Wei, Tian'an. 2007. Some issues concerning the Ever-normal Granary system. in *The Song History Research Forum*. ed. Jiang, Xidong et al. vol.8. Hebei University Press. p. 58.

[82] "Hydraulic works law" (*nongtian shuili fa*) was a method to ameliorate local organization of building dykes and dams for irrigating fields. It was part of the Reform Policy of Wang Anshi (1021-1086) in the Northern Song dynasty.

[83] It means to relieve people in disaster areas by providing them employment instead of outright grant. This is to be further discussed in Chapter 2,

[84] Li, Xinchuan. 2000. The revenue II. *Miscellaneous Records of Historical Documents from Jianyan Period*, Section 1, vol.15. Beijing: Zhonghua Book Company. p. 252.

Wang Anshi's monetary reform of the ever-normal granaries might have been ahead of its time. Chen Huanzhang, in his work *The Economic Principles of Confucius and His School*, commented that Wang Anshi was "born at the wrong time". However, from another perspective, the new Ever-normal Granary policy was a failed attempt in its time but not so to future generations. It provides a "modern history" reference for Zhu Xi's grassroots ever-normal granaries—"She Granaries"—more than a hundred years later.

Wang Anshi's monetization reform of the Ever-normal Granary is foreward-looking. Chen Huan-Chang, in *The Economic Principles of Confucius and His School*, said that Wang Anshi "lived either too late or too early".[85] But in another way, unsuccessful Ever-normal Granary law is an attempt beneficial to future generations. It provides "modern history" for Zhu Xi's grass-roots Ever-normal Granary, i.e., community granary.[86]

2.2.3 Zhu Xi's Community Granary

The term "community granary"[87] first appeared in the Sui dynasty (581-618 A.D.), but actually it meant "charity granary". Community granary can be traced back to the charity tenancy *(yizu)* in state of Northern Qi (550-577 A.D.),[88] and the system of community granary originated from the Sui dynasty. In the fifth year (585) of Kaihuang period, Zhangsun Ping, the minister of the Ministry of Works, thought that there must be a fixed pattern for helping the people and governing the state. "During the Sui dynasty, Zhangsun Ping observed that many prefectures and counties (*zhou* and *xian*) throughout the country were suffering from floods and droughts, and the people were unable to support themselves. He submitted a memorial to the imperial court, requesting an imperial decree for the people and soldiers of each

85 Chen, Huan-chang. 1911. *The Economic Principles of Confucius and His School.* New York: Columbia University Press.p. 596.

86 See Chapter 3 for Henry A. Wallace's Ever-normal Granary policy in the U.S.

87 Community granaries were themselves originally created as a response to official abuses after the rejection of Wang Anshi's "green sprout loans"; rather than have the state mismanage a program, officials relied on the people themselves to create a nongovernment alternative. The community granary, championed by no less a figure than the famous philosopher Zhu Xi (1130-1200), was formed outside the geographical centers of government and meant to be managed by local people instead of officials. Funded in principle by private contributions, these granaries provided a means for the educated and wealthy to nourish the people without direct state control. See: Wong, R. Bin. 1991. Chinese traditions of grain storage. in *Nourish the People: The State Civilian Granary System in China, 1650-1850.* ed. Will, Pierre-Etienne and R. Bin Wong. Ann Arbor: The University of Michigan Press. p.7.

88 Wei, Zheng. ed. 1973. Food and money. *The Book of Sui*, vol.24. Beijing: Zhonghua Book Company. pp. 667-678.

prefecture to donate money and grain to their Community Association[89] to establish charity granaries (*yi cang*). In the harvest season, they were encouraged to donate an appropriate amount of grain, such as millet and wheat, according to their individual harvests. These grains were then stored in the local charity granaries, with the responsibility of managing the granaries entrusted to the community officials. They were to inspect and verify the annual receipts and stored amounts against the ledgers to prevent damage. If there was a poor harvest, and families in the Community Association faced famine, the grains from the charity granaries were used to provide relief and support."[90]

From the perspectives of the source of grain, the location of the granaries, management and basic functions, the charity granary initially was grain reserves for civil mutual assistance. They were also called "community granary" because they were set up and managed at local communities. In the fifteenth (595) and sixteenth (596) years of Kaihuang period, the charity granaries were handed over to the prefectures and counties (*zhou* and *xian*), and the irregular "donation" which was not fixed, was replaced by grain collection based on the amount of assets, with upper, middle and lower grades.[91] Following the Sui dynasty's system, in the second year (628) of Zhenguan period, "Han Zhongliang, the Minister of Revenue (*hubu shangshu*), submitted a proposal: 'All land cultivated by commoners should contribute two liters of grain per *mu*. As for the types of grain, such as millet, wheat, glutinous rice and common rice, they should be determined based on local production. These grains should be stored at the prefectures or counties (*zhou* or *xian*) to prepare for disaster years.' This proposal was accepted. From then on, prefectures and counties (*zhou* and *xian*) throughout the empire began to establish charity gra-

[89] Community Association (*lishe*) was an ancient Chinese social and administrative unit that played a crucial role in local governance and community life. Originating from the Western Zhou dynasty and becoming more formalized during the Qin and Han dynasties, Community Association functioned as a small-scale, rural community organization. It was typically composed of approximately 25 to 100 families, depending on the geographical and demographic circumstances of the time. Community Association served multiple purposes. Primarily, it was a unit for local administration, where officials appointed by the central government would oversee the collection of taxes, recruitment of labor, and maintenance of public order. Additionally, Community Association was a hub for social and communal activities. It organized collective labor for public projects like irrigation systems, road repairs, and disaster relief efforts. It also played a role in local education, moral guidance, and the enforcement of social norms, reflecting the Confucian values of harmony, respect for elders, and communal welfare. One of the significant contributions of the Community Association was the establishment and management of the charity granaries (*yicang*), which were community-based grain reserves. These granaries were used to provide relief during times of famine or natural disasters, demonstrating Community Association s role in local self-sufficiency and mutual aid. TheCommunity Association system, with its emphasis on local autonomy and communal solidarity, was an integral part of China's traditional rural society and administration for centuries, lasting until the late imperial period when it was gradually replaced by other forms of local governance.

[90] Wei, Zheng. ed. 1973. Food and money. *The Book of Sui*, vol.24. Beijing: Zhonghua Book Company. p. 684.

[91] Wei, Zheng. ed. 1973. Food and money. *The Book of Sui*, vol.24. Beijing: Zhonghua Book Company. p. 685.

naries. Whenever famine struck, the granaries were opened for relief distribution."[92] Although the charity granaries experienced three rises and falls in the Tang dynasty, they eventually reached a certain scale and played an important role in regulating and stabilizing the economy and society.[93]

The community granary system was first found in the Southern Song dynasty. In the twentieth year (1150) of Shaoxing period, Wei Yanzhi set up a charity granary in Changtanpu Town, Jianyang County of Jianning Prefecture. In *History of Song Dynasty* there are following words, "the charity granaries in townships started with Wei Yanzhi"[94]. Zhu Xi provided detailed accounts of this,[95] but the formation and popularization of community granary system was largely attributed to Zhu Xi himself. In the fifth year (1169) of Qiandao years, Zhu Xi established a community granary in Kaiyao Town, Chong'an County (now Wuyishan City) of Jianning Prefecture, due to the famine there caused by a flood in the previous year. At that time, Zhu Xi was residing in the countryside there. Entrusted by the county magistrate Zhuge Tingsui, he and the local gentleman Liu Ruyu borrowed 600 *shi* of grains from the Ever-normal Granary for the relief efforts. In the winter of the same year, the people of Kaiyao Town returned all the grains. With this as the basis, Zhu Xi and Liu Ruyu planned for the to build granaries for the local communities, stipulating an annual loan and an interest rate of twenty percent upon return. Initially, the grains of the community granaries were stored in the homes of the people. In the seventh year (1171) of the Qiandao years, Zhu Xi received a subsidy of 60,000 coins from the magistrate of the prefecture, and several months later the Wufu Community Granary[96] of Chong'an County was formally established.[97] In the eighth year (1181) of the Chunxi years of the Southern Song dynasty, there was a famine in the eastern part of Zhejiang. Zhu Xi, as the Supervisor of Public Business Concerning Trade in Tea (*tiju changping chayan gongshi*) in eastern Zhejiang, was responsible for disas-

---

[92] Liu, Xu et al. ed. 1975. Food and money II. *Old History of Tang Dynasty*, vol.49. Beijing: Zhonghua Book Company. p. 2123.

[93] See: Pan, Xiaowei. 1984. On Charity Granary in Tang dynasty. *Agricultural History of China*. (4): 18-23; Pan, Xiaowei. 1998. Further studies on Charity Granary in Tang dynasty. *Agricultural History of China*. (3): 32-38.

[94] Toqto'a et al. 1985. Biography of Wei Yanzhi. *History of Song Dynasty*, vol. 459. Beijing: Zhonghua Book Company. p. 13469.

[95] Zhu, Xi. 2002. *Collected Works of Zhu Xi*, vol.79. in *Complete Book of Zhu Xi*. ed. Zhu Jieren et al.vol.24. Shanghai: Shanghai Ancient Books Publishing House; Hefei: Anhui Education Publishing House. p. 3777-3779.

[96] Zhu Xi's community granary was originally named "Wufu Community Granary". It was first erected successfully in 1171 in Wufu Town, Chongan County, Fujian Province, the hometown of Zhu Xi, thus known as the "Wufu community granary" in history. The granary, composing of three storerooms, was initiated and named by Zhu Xi as a privately operated community granary. To commemorate the benevolent governance of the sage Zhu Xi, the locals changed the name of the "Wufu Community Granary" to "ZhuXi's Community Granary".

[97] Zhu, Xi. 2002. *Collected Works of Zhu Xi*, vol.77. in *Complete Book of Zhu Xi*. ed. Zhu Jieren et al.vol.24. Shanghai: Shanghai Ancient Books Publishing House; Hefei: Anhui Education Publishing House. pp. 3720-3721.

ter relief. He took the opportunity to report the successful experience of the community granary in detail, and wrote the article "Management of Community Granary". With the approval of the imperial court, the community granary was transformed into a granary system for nationwide promotion.[98]

The operation of Zhu Xi's community granary involved obtaining the necessary grain either by borrowing from the governmental Ever-normal Granary or through voluntary donations from households. In normal years, households borrowing grain from the community granary with an interest rate of twenty percent; in years with poor harvest, the interest rate was reduced by half; and in times of severe famine, the interest was waived entirely. The community granary accumulated the interest from the grain loans over the years. Once it reached a self-sustainable scale, the grain borrowed from the Ever-normal Granary as initial capital was repaid, and the left grain was used to continue the circulation. In practice, after fourteen years of operation, the community granary of the Kaiyao Town had accumulated a total of 3,700 *shi* of grain. After repaying 600 *shi* of grain to the Jianning Prefecture, the remaining 3,100 *shi* of grain continued to be lent out. However, from then on, no longer was the twenty-percent interest collected; instead, for every *shi* of grain repaid by the farmers, an additionional three liters were charged in the name of losses.[99]

At the beginning of the operation of the community granary, a twenty-percent interest was charged, which inevitably reminded people of the Green Sprouts Act, hence the oppositional opinions, "The Ministry of Revenue (*hubu*) considered it feasible, but at the time some people argued that charging two *dou* of interest per *shi* of grain was similar to the practice of the Green Sprouts Act, so they launched attacks".[100] Zhu Xi, living in the Southern Song dynasty which was a century away from Wang Anshi's New Reform in Xi'ning years. As an observer of the "modern history", he had an in-depth critique and reflection on the Green Sprouts Act:

> In general, the reasons why the common people criticize this are merely based on the Wang Anshi's Green Sprouts Act. From my observation of the discussions of the previous men and the verification of present practice, the Green Sprouts Act was not ill-intentioned in its legislative purpose. However, it provided funds instead of grain, it was managed at the county level rather than the township level, the responsibilities were bestowed to officials and instead of local gentlemen and scholars, and it was implemented with the intention of disaster relief rather than with a compassionate and loyal heart for the public welfare. Therefore, Wang Anshi's act could be implemented in one county but not in the whole country.[101]

---

[98] Zhu, Xi. 2002. *Collected Works of Zhu Xi*, vol.99. in *Complete Book of Zhu Xi*. ed. Zhu Jieren et al.vol.25. Shanghai: Shanghai Ancient Books Publishing House; Hefei: Anhui Education Publishing House. p. 4596-4603.

[99] Zhu, Xi. 2002. *Collected Works of Zhu Xi*, vol.13 andvol.77. in *Complete Book of Zhu Xi*. ed. Zhu Jieren et al. vol.20 andvol.24. Shanghai: Shanghai Ancient Books Publishing House; Hefei: Anhui Education Publishing House. p. 649. pp. 3720-3721.

[100] Shi, Su. 1986. Community granary. *Annals of Huiji*. vol.13. in *Complete Library in the Four Branches of Literature (Wenyuange Edition)*, *Ji* section, vol.486. Taibei: Commercial Press of Taiwan. p. 275.

[101] Zhu, Xi. 2002. *Collected Works of Zhu Xi*, vol.79. in *Complete Book of Zhu Xi*. ed. Zhu Jieren et al. vol.24. Shanghai: Shanghai Ancient Books Publishing House; Hefei: Anhui Education Publishing House. p. 3777.

"The verification of present practice" actually refers to the practice of community granary. When comparing Green Sprouts Loan and the community granary, we may find that later has certain advantages. Firstly, although the community granary, learning the lessons from the Green Sprouts Act, operated through loans at the very beginning, it provided grain instead of money. Thus there was no market transaction process, reducing transaction costs and isolating market risks. The twenty-percent interest for grain loans was the actual interest without any additional burden, which can truly play a role in suppressing rural usury and stabilizing grain prices. Secondly, the community granary was set up in the countryside, making it convenient for borrowing and returning, thus meeting the actual needs of farmers. It is worth noting that although one important reason for the implementation of the Green Sprouts Loan was that the old system couldn't benefit the majority of farmers, as "the grains of Ever-normal Granary and public welfare granary... mainly benefit the idle people in cities". However, it did not improve much in actual operation of Green Sprouts Act, in that "since the implementation of the Green Sprouts Act, farmers are busy traveling to and from counties for loans or repayments."[102] Unlike the top-down system design of Ever-normal Granary and Green Sprouts Loan, the community granary operated in a bottom-up way. It was situated at the grassroots level, and could receive assistance from the prefecture or county (*zhou* or *xian*), thus it had an advantage in management layout. Finally, the community granary was a mutual-assistance organization established cooperatively by the government and the people, but primarily managed by the people. It was initiated and managed by benevolent and prestigious scholars and local gentry in the community. Although the establishment, support, and supervision of the community granary were associated with the government in various ways, the local community could independently make regulations and operations according to the specific time and space, thus avoiding the harassment of officials. Moreover, the mutual supervision among people of the community ensured that the management and operations were more aligned with the interests of the local households.

Zhu Xi's design and practice provided a model for the promotion of community granary. However, the community granaries in various places were adjusted and varied in the course of later development. Liu Zai, a literati of the Southern Song dynasty, summarized with following words, "The community granary was originally established by the government, by individual households, or by the populace, each with its own distinct circumstances. It was run in a town, or in a county. Some sell grain without lending, while others lend grain without sale. In our county, grain is lent in the village and sold in the market, each with its own unique approach."[103]

[102] Bi, Zhongyou. 2016. On Green Shoots Law. *Xitai Collection*, vol.5. in *Xitai Collection (with Three Other Works)*, ed. Shanyou Academy of History and Culture. Shanghai: Shanghai Ancient Books Publishing House. p. 63.

[103] Liu, Zai. 1986. Community granary of Hu's family in Nankang. *Collections of Liu Zai*, vol.22. in *Complete Library in the Four Branches of Literature (Wenyuange Edition)*, *Ji* section, vol.1170. Taibei: Commercial Press of Taiwan. p. 587.

These words address two key aspects for operation of community granary: the raising of capital for the granary, and the mode for grain collection and distribution.

In his article "Community Granaries in the Southern Song Dynasty", Liang Gengyao listed the 65 community granaries distributed in various regions during the Southern Song dynasty.[104] Based on this sample, Wang Wenshu calculated the fund-raising patterns and proportions of capital for these granaries: 34 were funded by the government (52.3% of the total); 15 were privately funded (23.1% of the total); 8 were financed by the populace (12.3% of the total); 4 were jointly funded by the government and the populace (6.2% of the total); and the funding sources for 4 were unclear (6.2%). The sum of government funding and joint government-public funding totaled 58.5%. This data confirms Liu Zai's statement that "the community granary was originally established by the government, by individual households, or by the populace", and it also indicates that a high proportion of community granaries were built with official involvement. As for the source of official funding, when promoting community granaries, the imperial court required local officials to use the grain from charity granaries as capital, which was the additional tax from regular taxes. However, local officials, afraid of criticism for increasing taxes, essentially followed Zhu Xi's approach, using the grain from ever-normal granaries or local finances to replenish the capital for commodity granary.[105]

The above discusses an advantage of the Wufu Community Granary, namely providing physical grains rather than monetary loans like the Green Sprouts Loan would better meet the actual needs of farmers. However, credit loans inherently bore risks, and even with regulations for joint guarantee and compensation, defaults would still occur. If the grain could not be repaid, the community granary would face difficulties in maintaining its circulation. Therefore, shortly after the promotion of community granaries, managers of the community granariesimitated the practices of other public serves and purchased land as loan capital, relying on land rent for interest-free loans to reduce the burden on farmers. In this way they tried to solve the problems of "collectinggrains but not daring to distribute"or"distributing grain but being unable to recollect". Sustainable operation is a core issue to the small-scale community granaries. In addition to buying land for rent, community granaries also developed operations like "*pingdi*" (buying grains with prices higher than the market ones in good years) and "*pingtiao*" (selling grains with prices lower than the market ones in bad years), which Liu Zai described with the words "others

[104] Liang, Gengyao. 2005. Community Granary of Southern Song dynasty. in *Economic Pulse*. ed. Chen, Guodong et al. Beijing: Encyclopedia of China Publishing House. pp. 149-153.

[105] Chen, Zhiping. 2016. Zhu Xi's Design of Community Granary and its evolution. *Researches in Chinese Economic History*. (6): 18-31. The charity granary reserves in the Northern and Southern Song dynasties were mainly derived from additional taxes rather than regular taxes, which were usually stored in a warehouse together with the provincial and county tax grains. However, these reserves suffered from the disadvantage of being misappropriated (See: Li, Huarui. 2012. The development and changes of the disaster relief storage system in the Song dynasty. in *Jinan Historical Science*. vol.7. ed. Ma, Mingda. Guilin: Guangxi Normal University Press. pp. 512-514.) This is also one of the main reasons for the development of community granaries in the Southern Song dynasty in "increment".

lend grain without sale". *Pingtiao* involves direct grain-money exchange: only when distribution (e.g. sale of grain) is done can the collection (e.g. purchase of grain) be carried out. So compared with credit lending, the practice of *pingdi* and *pingtiao* (purchase and sale of grain) carries less risks. In addition, compared with the ever-normal granaries set up at the prefectures and counties (*zhou* and *xian*), community granaries had more advantages in implementing *pingdi* and *pingtiao* operations. Dong Ying believed that one important reason why ever-normal granaries at the prefectures and counties (*zhou* and *xian*) could not benefit rural areas was the cost of transportation and dissipation, leading to the fact that "villages are hesitant to request from the county". However, "during famine years, people worry about the lack of rice instead of money."[106] Extending ever-normal granaries from the prefectures or counties (*zhou* or *xian*) to the countryside was costly, which was precisely where community granaries had an advantage. Located in rural areas, community granaries could offer help to farmers directly with no additional transportation costs, saving unnecessary expenses; for the practice of *pingtiao* (sale of grain), farmers had significant demand of exchanging grain for money. Thus it was beneficial for both the farmers and the granaries. For the practice of *pingdi* (purchase of grain), extending ever-normal granaries from the prefectures or counties (*zhou* or *xian*) to the countryside in a vertical-management line was inefficient and time-consuming. "Although they want to buy grain in time, the process involvesthe county reporting to the prefecture, the prefecture reporting to the Judicial Commission (*tidian xingyu si*), and the Judicial Commission reporting to the Ministry of Agriculture (*sinong si*), during which there is long-time wait for instructions. By the time the request is approved, it's already months later. Losing the opportunity, the grain price has already doubled."[107] In contrast, community granaries could operate *pingdi* (purchase of grain) independently by storing local grains flexibly without missing the time, hence more efficient use of the funds. It seems that the *pingtiao*-style community granaries that appeared in many places in the Southern Song dynasty were a rational choice in practical exploration, and they seemed to be model for later community granaries.[108]

From the above analysis, we can draw the following conclusion: in the Southern Song dynasty the community granaries gradually aligned with the ever-normal granaries in their development process. Firstly, nearly sixty percent of the community granaries (based on Liang Gengyao's sample analysis and Wang Wenshu's statistics) were established with the support of local ever-normal granaries or financial assistance, and the initiation and operation of even more community granaries were inseparable from government support and supervision. Therefore the community

---

[106] Liang, Gengyao. 2005. Community Granary of Southern Song dynasty. in *Economic Pulse*. ed. Chen, Guodong et al. Beijing: Encyclopedia of China Publishing House. pp. 156-157.

[107] Sima, Guang.1999. Memorial to the Emperor Zhezong on purchasing grain at the due time for Ever-normal Granaries. In *Memorials Submitted to the Throne in the Song Dynasty.* ed. Zhao, Ruyu.vol.107. Shanghai: Shanghai Ancient Books Publishing House. p.1156.

[108] Liang, Gengyao. 2005. Community Granary of Southern Song dynasty. in *Economic Pulse*. ed. Chen, Guodong et al. Beijing: Encyclopedia of China Publishing House. pp. 157-158.

granaries can be seen as "non-state-run branch offices" of the ever-normal granaries at the grassroots level. Secondly, the ever-normal granaries primarily focused on purchase and sale of grain, as well as providing relief loans and relief aids. After a period of development, the community granaries "might sell grain without lending, while others lend grain without sale', or both depending on the different relief recipients.[109] In this way the community granaries performed similar functions as the ever-normal granaries. Based on these two points, the community granaries, as the "fulcrum" of the ever-normal granaries, effectively filled the gap in rural areas as "grassroots ever-normal granaries" or "small and micro ever-normal granaries". In this regard, Yuan Xie illustrated as follows:

> Since ancient times, there have never been laws that can be implemented alone. The benefits of the Ever-normal Granary system are not comprehensive and widespread. Through careful consideration and thorough discussion, people try to seek complementary methods to implement them together, thereby broadening the scope of benefits. The community granaries are surely complements to the ever-normal granaries! When there is a surplus of grain, they are collected; when there is a shortage of grain, the reserves are distributed. In this regard there is no difference between ever-normal granaries and community granaries. However, while the ever-normal granaries accumulate grain in prefectures and counties (*zhou* and *xian*), community granaries are distributed throughout the countryside. The officials are spared the labor of long-distance transportation, and the people enjoy the convenience of purchasing grain nearby, which is enough to extend the intention of the ever-normal granaries in poverty relief. This is what is meant by complementing the system.[110]

The emergence of community granaries in the Southern Song dynasty was an adaptive adjustment to the granary system in the face of economic, social and cultural changes, such as the absence of a system for land allocation and administration, population increase, diversification of grassroots governance entities and the rise of Neo-Confucianism. It was an important practice of transforming the ever-normal granaries towards a "flat" structure by learning from the pros and cons of the old ever-normal system and the Green Sprouts Act. It reduced transaction costs and better addressed the issue of unbalanced information. However, even after the imperial court promoted it nationwide, the local people was not so enthusiastic. It was only after the vigorous promotion by the disciples and fellow Neo-Confucianists of Zhu Xi that the development of community granaries gradually gained support from local governments and the populace, leading to significant improvements.[111] Nevertheless, the status of community granaries in the Southern Song dynasty should not be overestimated. As Chen Zhiping pointed out, its establishment did not reach a state of widespread administrative proliferation, which "may be closer to the

[109] Liang, Gengyao. 2005. Community Granary of Southern Song dynasty. in *Economic Pulse*. ed. Chen, Guodong et al. Beijing: Encyclopedia of China Publishing House. p. 158.

[110] Yuan, Xie. 1986. Community granaries of Hongdu Prefecture. *Collected Works of Yuan Xie,* vol.10. in *Complete Library in the Four Branches of Literature (Wenyuange Edition)*, *Ji* section, vol.1157. Taibei: Commercial Press of Taiwan. p. 122.

[111] Liang, Gengyao. 2005. Community Granary of Southern Song dynasty. in *Economic Pulse*. ed. Chen, Guodong et al. Beijing: Encyclopedia of China Publishing House. p. 148, p.154.

basic fact of the community granaries in the Southern Song Dynasty".[112] In particular, with the emergence of issues such as insider control and excessive intervention by local governments, the functions of community granaries were continuously diminishing. Zhen Dexiu, a disciple of Zhu Xi's disciple, once remarked, "In my youth, I indeed witnessed its benefits. But over the years, the system has deteriorated, and I cannot help but sigh over it."[113] Even so, one thing remains certain: Zhu Xi's community granaries, by help of scholar-officials and local elites, embedded an economic stabilizer within grassroots organizations, and compensated for the defects of the ever-normal granaries under the bureaucratic hierarchical management system. It would be appropriate if we therefore regard Zhu Xi as a pioneer in the "flattening" and "distributive" transformation of the ever-normal granaries, exploring the establishment of a "social economic organization" that coordinates official and public efforts and fosters trust and mutual assistance in communities. Zhu Xi's community granaries created a new tradition that was further developed in later generations.

After discussing the community granaries, we must also address a much-debated question: How should we view the relationship between community granaries and charity granaries? Are they the same or similar, or are they completely different? Setting aside the differences in their names, the origins of both community and charity granaries can be traced back to Zhangsun Ping of the Sui dynasty. According to the design of storing grain among the people ("donate money and grain to their Community Associationto establish charity granaries) and being managed by the people themselves ("with the responsibility of managing the granaries entrusted to the community officials. They were to inspect and verify…"), there is no difference between charity granaries and Zhu Xi's community granaries. The difference lies in the original purpose: charity granaries were primarily set up for relief, while community granaries focused on loans. In the Tang dynasty, charity granaries also took on the function of loans,[114] occasionally engaging in grain sales.[115] In the Song dynasty, grain sales and purchases became more frequent.[116] With the previous

[112] Chen, Zhiping. 2016. Zhu Xi's Design of Community Granary and its evolution. *Researches in Chinese Economic History*. (6): 25.

[113] Zhen, Dexiu. 1937. Memorial to set up community granaries in twelve counties. *Collected Works of Zhen Dexiu*, vol.10. Changsha: Commercial Press. p. 176.

[114] Pan, Xiaowei. 1984. On Charity Granary in Tang dynasty. *Agricultural History of China*. (4): 21-23.

[115] In September in the eighth year of Taihe period, the emperor issued an edict: "Huai River, Zhexi and other regions have suffered from years of floods and waterlogging... It is hereby ordered that the local officials should sell the rice stored in the official granaries at half price to the poor and weak. If there is no storage, they should sell the rice from the charity granaries." See: Wang, Qinruo et al. 2006. Benefiting the people II. *Prime Tortoise of the Record Bureau*, vol.106. Nanjing: Phoenix Publishing House. p. 1159.

[116] Li, Huarui. 2012. The development and changes of the disaster relief storage system in the Song dynasty. in *Jinan Historical Science*.vol.7. ed. Ma, Mingda. Guilin: Guangxi Normal University Press. p.518.

analysis of community granaries, it can be seen that the functions of charity and community granaries have gradually converged in the process of development.

An important change occurred in Zhangsun Ping's design of charity granaries in the fifteenth year (595) of the Kaihuang period in the Sui dynasty, where the charity granaries were transferred from the communities to the prefectures and counties (*zhou* and *xian*). As the source of the granary grain became the three-tiered taxes from the upper, middle, and lower households, the operation of the charity granaries necessarily was taken over by the government. In Tang and Song dynasties, the reserves of charity granaries were continuously incorporated into the financial system, effectively making the charity granaries a specialized fiscal institution in name. This setup was prone to misappropriation and confusion with other granary systems, which was clearly different from the relative independence and grassroots nature of ZhuXi's community granaries. However, these situations were not static and invariable. In the Qing dynasty greater emphasis was attached to the construction of community granaries than previous dynasties, and community granaries reached the peak in Emperor Qianlong's reign (1736-1796). Nevertheless, after the widespread establishment of community granaries, the influence of the government gradually increased, leading to a situation where "people considered them to be public granaries rather than community granaries"[117]. In such circumstances, the establishment of charity granaries was actually aimed at achieving greater independence. In this sense, the widespread charity granaries established by Fang Guancheng in Zhili[118] was very similar to Zhu Xi's community granaries.[119]

The community granaries and charity granaries are seemingly alike yet different, or seemingly different yet alike, leading to the sayings that "the two types of granaries are same" and "the two types of granaries are different"[120] from ancient times to the present. If one gets bogged down in the numerous details, whether the community granaries and charity granaries are different or the same becomes a complex and confusing issue. However, if one observed it from a broader perspective, it is easier to see their similarities in that the establishment of both types of granaries aims to stabilize fluctuations and maintain the stable development of the economy and society. When we examine historical records, a phenomenon that requires attention is that there are records indicating the joint use of community granaries and charity granaries in the Tang dynasty, which was also frequently seen during the Song dynasty. Moreover, the co-reference to ever-normal granaries, community granaries and charity granaries was even more common in the Qing dynasty. This indicates that behind the different names, there is a main line connecting them: "collecting when there is surplus, and distributing when there is shortage". The timely

---

[117] Fang, Guancheng. 2017. *Maps of the Charity Granaries in the Capital Area*. ed. Cui, Guangshe et al. Baoding: Hebei University Press. p. 34.

[118] *Zhili*, literally meaning "directly ruled (by the Imperial Court)", was the name of Hebei before 1928.

[119] See Section 2, Chapter 2, for a discussion of the charity granaries in Fang Guancheng's work.

[120] See: Wu, Siwu. 2018. Differentiation of the concepts of charity granary and community granary. *Collected Essays on Qing History*. (2): 287-300.

collection and distribution help to achieve constant stability between supply and demand. Therefore, although community granaries and charity granaries can be distinguished in a narrow sense, they should be viewed as a whole in a broader sense. They are both important supplements to the Ever-normal Granary system. Together with ever-normal granaries, they form a grand "Ever-normal Granary system".[121]

2.2.4 Preparedness Granaries of Ming Dynasty

The preparedness granary (*yubei cang*) is "the system of Ever-normal Granary in previous dynasties"[122], and also a unique granary system of the Ming dynasty. "In the early years in Emperor Hongwu's reign[123], the emperor called for the establishment of four preparedness granaries in each county, with the officials responsible for purchasing and storing grain for relief purposes."[124] There are differing opinions in the academic world about when the preparedness granaries were initially established in the Ming dynasty: the most common view is that it was firstly established in "the first year in Emperor Hongwu's reign" (1368); others say it was established in "the third year in Emperor Hongwu's reign" (1370); still others, after comparative study and textual research, say it was established in "the twenty-first year in Emperor Hongwu's reign" (1388)[125]. According to local chronicle records, the establishment of preparedness granaries was not frequently seen in the early period in Emperor Hongwu's reign, but there was a significant change after the twenty-first year in Emperor Hongwu's reign.[126] It is likely that Emperor Hongwu had a plan to establish preparedness granaries nationwide as early as the first year of his reign, but the implementation of the plan should have been postponed until the twenty-first year. At the beginning of the dynasty, there were many things waiting to be done. It

[121] See Section 2 of Chapter 2 for further discussion of the Ever-normal Granary system.

[122] Long, Wenbin. 1998. Preparedness Granary. Food and money, IV. *Economic and Political Structures of Ming Dynasty*, vol.56. Beijing: Zhonghua Book Company. p. 1073.

[123] Emperor Hongwu, or Emperor Taizu, with the name Zhu Yuanzhang (1328-1398), was the Chinese emperor (reigned 1368–1398) who founded the Ming Dynasty that ruled China for nearly 300 years. During his reign, Emperor Hongwu instituted military, administrative, and educational reforms that centred power in the emperor.

[124] Shen, Shixing et al. 1995. Granary II. *Code of Great Ming Dynasty*, vol.22. in *Supplement to Complete Library in the Four Branches of Literature*. ed. Committee for Compilation of Supplement to Complete Library in the Four Branches of Literature. *Shi* section, vol.789. Shanghai: Shanghai Ancient Books Publishing House. p. 383

[125] Chen, Xu. 2010. A new study on the creation of the preparedness granary in the Ming dynasty. *Agricultural Archaeology*. (1): 236-247.

[126] Wu, Tao. 1996. A preliminary study of the granary system in the Suzhou-Songjiang Region during the Ming dynasty. *Agricultural History of China*. (3): 53-61; Chen, Xu. 2010. A new study on the creation of the preparedness granary in the Ming dynasty. *Agricultural Archaeology*. (1): 236-247; Li, Jing.2015. A preliminary study of the relief granary during the Ming dynasty: a case study of the Southern Zhili Region. *Journal of Chinese Architecture History*. (1): 330-363.

was normal that there were more plans than action at the beginning of a new dynasty, and the implementation of the plans had to be delayed until years later. It is also true for the establishment of the ever-normal granaries in the Tang and Song dynasties.

Compared to the ever-normal granaries of previous dynasties, the preparedness granaries established during the Hongwu period of the Ming dynasty had the following two distinct features.

Firstly, they relied on the elderly system, with the selection of "local elderly and honest people to participate inthe management"[127]. To strengthen grassroots governance, in imitation of the Three Elderly (*san lao*[128]) system of Han dynasty, the Ming government selected elderly individuals from wealthy and influential families who were respected for their morality, competence, and generosity to the people, to participate in local government management. They were known as "district elders", "elders", "respectable elders", "venerable elders" or "official elders", with a status similar to that of public servants. Depending on local needs, positions such as post elders, market elders, shop elders, granary elders, water conservancy elders, floating bridge elders, kiln factory elders, etc., were established.[129] Among these, the granary elders were responsible for the management of the preparedness granaries. "Emperor Taizu ordered various prefectures and counties (*zhou* and *xian*) to establish granaries, with the elders responsible for their management by collecting and storing grain during bumper years and distributing stored grain during lean years."[130] The government coordinated planning, organized construction and raised funds for grain purchases, with the assistance of the "elderly administrators overseeing the granaries" who were familiar with the local communities.[131] Correspondingly, the government appointed supervisory officials to inspect the preparedness granaries to prevent the emergence of various issues.[132]

[127] Shen, Shixing et al. 1995. Granary II. *Code of Great Ming Dynasty*, vol.22. in *Supplement to Complete Library in the Four Branches of Literature*. ed. Committee for Compilation of Supplement to Complete Library in the Four Branches of Literature. *Shi* section, vol.789. Shanghai: Shanghai Ancient Books Publishing House. p.383.

[128] *san lao*, lit., the 3 stages of old age, presumably the 50s, 60s, and 70s; hence someone in one of these age groups: Elder, one of the 3 appointees from among the resident population in the quasiofficial sub-district (*hsien*) administration of a Township (*hsiang*); normally a man of good character more than 50 years old, responsible for providing moral leadership and discipline. From among the Township Elders, one was commonly designated District Elder (*hsien san-lao*); and at least in Later Han there were some Commandery (*chün*) Elders, presumably chosen from among the District Elders. See: Hucker, Charles O. 1988. *A Dictionary of Official Titles in Imperial China*. Taipei: Southern Materials Center, Inc. p.399

[129] Wang, Xingya. 1993. The pros and cons of implementing the elderly administration system in the Ming dynasty. *Journal of Zhengzhou University (Philosophy and Social Sciences Edition)*. (2): 22-23.

[130] Yang, Shiqi et al. 1962. *Veritable Records of Emperor Taizong in Ming Dynasty*. ed. Institute of History and Philosophy. *Academia Sinica*. p.1068.

[131] Hu, Huojin, and Zhang Hanyu. 2012. Elderly administrators overseeing the granaries for famine relief in the townships of the Ming dynasty. *Chinese Social Sciences Today*. January 18. p. A05.

[132] In the fourth year of the Zhengtong Years, Grand Scholar Yang Shiqi submitted a memorial to the emperor stating the shortcomings of the preparedness granary with following words, "the

Secondly, in terms of layout, unlike the ever-normal granaries in the previous dynasties, the preparedness granaries were established "at four different places in each county", with a decentralized distribution in the east, west, south, and north. "Within a county, four sub-granaries should be established in places where the inhabitants congregated."[133] Taking Changshu County as an example, in the 23rd year (1390) in Emperor Hongwu's reign, four sub-branches of preparedness granaries were established: "The Eastern Granary was set up in Kaiyuan Town, the Western Granary in Guizheng Town, both with the 26 districts. The Southern Granary was set up in Jishan Town with 44 districts, and the Northern Granary in Chongsu Town with 9 districts."[134] Expanding to the Southern Zhili region (a bigger district) in which Changshu was located, scholars have documented the establishment of preparedness granaries in 29 counties. The specific distribution of the various preparedness granaries can be observed as follows (see Table 2.3). Among them, there are 22 counties with four granaries, and 1 county with five granaries, accounting for 79% of all the counties. Based on this, it can be inferred that the local governments relatively adhered to the imperial court's planning quite effectively at the beginning.

Table 2.3 Layout of preparedness granaries in South Zhili

Distribution of granaries in urban and rural areas	Distribution of granaries in the rural areas			Distribution of granaries in both urban and rural areas		Distribution of granaries in urban areas
Total granaries in one county	2	4	5	3 (rural area) 1 (urban area	2 (rural area) 2 (urban area)	1
Number of counties	1	18	1	2	2	5

Source of data: Li, Jing. 2015. An exploration of Relief Granaries in Ming dynasty: Taking the South Zhili as an example. *Journal of Chinese Architectural History*. (1): 331-332

supervisory officials have failed to fulfill their duties." He suggested that "officials in charge of supervision and inspection should focus on examining and reviewing. Those who are found to have committed fraud, neglected their duties, or shown dereliction will be reported and punished." This shows that in the design of the preparedness granaries, officials responsible for supervising and disciplining were tasked with the responsibility of supervision. In the sixth year of the Zhengtong Years, Yu Qian, another high-ranking official, further proposed that these officials strengthen their supervision through a system of post-departure audits, stating, "When officials in counties and prefectures have completed their terms and are ready for transfer, if the grain in preparedness granary is not sufficient, they should not be allowed to leave their posts. Furthermore, officials responsible for supervising and disciplining should be instructed to conduct regular inspections." See: Long, Wenbin. 1998. Preparedness Granary. Food and money, IV. *Economic and Political Structures of Ming Dynasty*, vol.56. Beijing: Zhonghua Book Company. p. 1074.

133 Xu, Xueju. 1996. Granary. *Collection of Canons of the Ming Dynasty*, vol.101. Beijing: Bibliography and Document Publishing House. pp. 1315-1316.

134 Gao, Shi, and Yang Zhenzao. 1991. Government offices. *Records of Changshu County*, vol.3. Nanjing: Jiangsu Ancient Books Publishing House. p. 48.

The preparedness granary, with the elderly system (selection of local elderly and honest people to participate in the management) and specific layout (distribution of one granary at four or more locations), is quite different from the granaries in previous dynasties. It manifests the care and thought of the rulers. The distribution of one granary at multiple locations avoids the drawback of the ever-normal granaries, which, established at the center of prefectures and counties (*zhou* and *xian*), were difficult to reach rural areas to benefit more people. However, this approach significantly increases the operational costs of the preparedness granaries and the intervention of officials in rural affairs. The solution lies in fully utilizing grassroots forces by means of inviting the elderly to manage the granaries in the way similar to management of Zhu Xi's community granaries, thus avoiding the intervention of local officials. In addition, there was government supervision to the management, thus forming a cooperative relationship between the officials and local people. The establishment of the preparedness granaries was promoted in a top-down pattern by national finance and administrative power, and then managed in a down-top pattern with the help of social resources, and further supervised in a top-down pattern for its development, thus creating a new model that might be called "Ever-normal Granary + community granary". However, this design places high demands on all parties involved and on the various operational aspects, especially the morality of the elderly in charge of the granaries. The development of the preparedness granaries in later periods showed that once there were issues with the management by the people, and if supervision was not timely and effective, the features of the preparedness granaries became a burden for the imperial court and a source of various problems. To address these issues, the government made several rectifications but in vain. Finally, the originally decentralized management shifted towards centralized management, and the cooperative management between officials and local people moved towards direct management by the government. As a result, the preparedness granaries seemed to revert back to the ever-normal granaries of the previous dynasties.[135]

Initially, the preparedness granaries mainly offered famine relief loans, and later implemented grain sales and provided relief aid,[136] thus taking on multiple functions for economic regulation and disaster relief. In the early Ming dynasty, the system of preparedness granaries was comprehensive and the management was strict, so they generally operated well. In the mid-Ming dynasty, they developed in a zig-zag with ups and downs. In the late Ming dynasty, due to financial difficulties, the functions

[135] "In the mid-Yongle period, edicts were issued for the establishment of more granaries in the prefectures and counties throughout the country. Those preparedness granaries located in the rural areas were relocated within the city walls." "In March of the third year of Emperor Hongzhi's reign... Initially, each preparedness granary had its own management officials, but by this time, they were abolished, and the county and prefecture officials, as well as those in charge of preparedness granaries, were instructed to oversee these matters." See: Long, Wenbin. 1998. Preparedness Granary. Food and money, IV. *Economic and Political Structures of Ming Dynasty*, vol.56. Beijing: Zhonghua Book Company. pp. 1073, 1075-1076.

[136] Chen, Guanlong. 1991. On the storage system for famine relief in the Ming dynasty. *Seeker (Qiu Suo)*. (5): 118.

of the preparedness granaries gradually weakened and finally they declined.[137] "During the Longqing period (1567-1572), larger counties at most had a grain storage of 6,000 *shi*, while smaller counties had only 1,000 *shi*.... During the Wanli period (1573-1620), the upper-grade counties at most had a grain storage of 3,000 *shi*, whereas some smaller counties had only 100 *shi*."[138] In the late Ming dynasty during the Chongzhen period, Chen Longzheng, a scholarly-official sighed, "There were no longer any preparedness granaries throughout the empire."[139]

2.3 Balance in Ever-Normal Granary Regulation

2.3.1 Government, Market and Society in the Ever-normal Granary System

Since the Northern Song dynasty, with economic and social development and more convenient land and water transportation, commerce and markets entered a new stage of development, shifting from fragmented distribution to integrated distribution. By the Qing dynasty, grain markets of various regions had been closely linked, breaking through the market limitations that "one does not buy rice from a thousand *li*[140] away".[141] When more and more merchants and regional merchant guilds entered the grain trading market and became an important force in the grain circulation system, the market price, supply and demand and competition mechanism would play a more significant role. In pursuit of profits, when there was a bumper harvest causing grain prices to be low in a certain place, grain merchants from various places would compete to purchase grain at favorable prices (*pingdi*) and stored it in granaries, as a reserve for times of bad harvest. Conversely, when a region suffered from poor harvest or a shortage of grain causing prices to be high, grain merchants from various places would compete to sell the stored grain (*pingtiao*), thus the volume of grain on the markets would increase and its market price remain on an acceptable level. Fan Zhongyan (989-1052), a prominent statesman and literary figure of the Northern Song dynasty, had already utilized this market mechanism to cope with grain supply shocks:

---

[137] Zhou, Zhiyuan. 2014. Re-exploration of preparedness granary in the Ming dynasty. in *Studies on the Institutional Systems of the Ming Dynasty*. ed. Wu, Yanhong. Hangzhou: Zhejiang University Press. pp. 262-279; Wang, Weiping and Wang Hongxu. 2017. Evolution and characteristics of the Preparedness Granary policy in the Ming dynasty. *Academics*. (8): 198-208.

[138] Long, Wenbin. 1998. Preparedness Granary. Food and money, IV. *Economic and Political Structures of Ming Dynasty*, vol.56. Beijing: Zhonghua Book Company. p. 1077.

[139] Chen, Longzheng. 2010. *The Strategies of Famine Relief*, vol.5. ed. Xia, Mingfang. in *Collections of Chinese Books on Famine Administration*. ed. Li, Wenhai, et al. Tianjin: Tianjin Ancient Books Publishing House. p. 469.

[140] *li*, a Chinese unit of length (= 1/2 kilometre).

[141] The sentence "one does not buy rice from a thousand *li* away" comes from: Sima, Qian. 1982. *Records of the Grand Historian*, vol.129. Beijing: Zhonghua Book Company. p. 3271.

> When Fan Zhongyan governed in Hangzhou, there was severe famine in the regions of Liangzhe (resent-day Zhejiang Province and the southeastern part of Jiangsu Province). Grain prices were skyrocketing, with one *dou* of grain costing one hundred and twenty coins. Fan Zhongyan then increased the price to one hundred and eighty coins per *dou*, leaving the public bewildered. Despite this, Fan ordered his men to post notices along the river, detailing the famine in Hangzhou and the rise in grain prices. Upon hearing this, merchants raced day and night to transport grain, fearing that they might be left behind and others would go ahead. As the grain came in large quantities, Fan Zhongyan lowered the price back to the original, namely one hundred and twenty coins per *dou*.[142]

Fan Chunren (1027-1101), the second son of Fan Zhongyan and a famous statesman, followed his father's approach. "When he was the magistrate of Xiangyi County, he anticipated a famine in the following year due to a severe drought. Therefore, he registered as many passenger ships as possible in his territory, and persuaded their owners to transport grain by promising to sell grain for them. As a result, a large supply of guest grain arrived the following spring. This ensured that the people of Xiangyi County could rely on this supply to avoid famine."[143] To maximize the impact of effective policies, targeted institutional arrangements need to be planned. Su Shi (1037-1101), one of China's greatest poets and essayists, and an accomplished calligrapher and a public official, advocated for the reduction or exemption of grain transaction taxes to encourage market circulation, thereby leveraging market forces to stabilize prices between bumper and poor harvests, "The state should lift the grain tax that hinders the circulation of grain. Stimulated by profits, merchants would compete to purchase grain in areas with abundant harvests, causing low grain prices to rise. At the same time, merchants would also rush to sell grain in disaster-stricken areas, thus high grain prices would also fall....In this way, the years of bumper harvests and those of scarcity would complement each other, benefiting both farmers and people in other industries. Even in the event of floods or droughts, there would be no severe famines."[144]

However, this does not mean that the government can extricate from the market. As a matter of fact, the more the market develops, the more necessary government regulation becomes. Ye Shi, a statesman and literary figure of the Southern Song dynasty, noticed the following phenomenon: "Of the output of the land cultivated by farmers, rice occupies the most proportion, but there is no stored rice in the houses of the farmers. I have carefully observed the reasons for this. Rivers and lakes are interconnected, and the land transportation is also convenient. A boat can go wherever as one wishes without any obstructions. For their livelihood, farmers, apart from planting rice for their own consumption for the year, sell the remaining rice in the local market... Even in a year with small bumper harvests, there is no surplus

---

[142] Wu, Zeng. 1985. Start of things. *Nenggaizhai Studio's Random Records, vol.*2. Beijing: Zhonghua Book Company. p.83.

[143] Dong, Wei. 2018. Miscellaneous records for famines relief. *A Book on Relieving Famine and Reviving the People*, vol.3. Beijing: China Bookstore. p. 183.

[144] Su, Shi.1986. A petition for exemption from the taxation on grain transportation. *The Collected Works of Su Shi*, vol.35. ed. Kong, Fanli. Beijing: Zhonghua Book Company. pp. 990-991.

rice in storage. This is caused by the situation."[145] Convenient transportation promoted the circulation of goods. Convenient transportation facilitates the circulation of goods. In pursuit of immediate benefits, the farmers sell all their surplus grain, making it difficult to sustain themselves even in years of minor shortages. It seems, therefore, that a buffer reserve of grain remains indispensable. However, the reality is always complex. Sima Guang found that if the officials didn't know the actual market price of grain, the buffer operation would easily be exploited by speculators. "Some officials are unable to accurately grasp the actual market price per *hu* and per *dou*, and instead rely on hearsay, causing damage to the national interest as those who speculate in grain. When grain is freshly harvested and farmers are in urgent need of money, they deliberately lower the grade and price of the train, preventing the state from collecting grain and causing it to flow into the hands of speculators with slightly higher price. After the procurement season, households that have accumulated grain have already had their granaries filled to the brim, and only then do they start to raise the price and grade, selling grain into the national granaries. As a result, farmers sell their grain at low prices, while the state often buys at high prices, with the substantial profits going to those 'middlemen.'"[146]

The market mechanism must be utilized, and speculative behavior must be curbed, which placed higher demands on the government's mastery of market conditions, timely action and market regulation. With the development of a commodity economy, the regulation with ever-normal granaries must take into consideration the complex relationship between the government and the market under specific circumstances and cannot deal with the problems in a simple way. Dong Wei, a scholar and statesman of Southern Song dynasty, gave an example to illustrate that if mandatory measures were taken to regulate the price of grain, it would be difficult to achieve the desired effect. "In recent years, those in charge of government affairs do not understand the intent of legislation. They assume that the common people have no money and therefore believe it necessary to enforce strict measures to control grain prices. They don't know that if the government lowers grain prices, merchants will be discouraged from bringing their grains. If grain prices surge in other places while they are low here, who would be willing to transport grains here? With the lack of large-scale transportation, there will be a shortage of grain within the region. The well-to-do families, those with savings, will be even more hesitant to sell. The hungry, even with money in hand, will have unending anxiety all day with no place to buy grain".[147] In his work "*A Book on Relieving Famine and Reviving the People*" (*jiuhuang huomin shu)*, Dong Wei advocated for a dual approach to regulation with ever-normal granaries that involved both government management and market adjustment, and he even

[145]Ye, Shi. 2010. A petition to Emperor Ningzong. *The Collected Works of Ye Shi*, vol.1. ed. Liu Gongchun et al. Beijing: Zhonghua Book Company. pp. 2-3.

[146]Sima, Guang.1999. Memorial to the Emperor Zhezong on purchasing grain at the due time for Ever-normal Granaries. In *Memorials Submitted to the Throne in the Song Dynasty.* ed. Zhao, Ruyu.vol.107. Shanghai: Shanghai Ancient Books Publishing House. p.1156.

[147]Dong, Wei. 2018. On not suppressing prices. *A Book on Relieving Famine and Reviving the People*, vol.2. Beijing: China Bookstore. pp. 109-110.

emphasizes the role of the latter at times. He believed that the best strategy was that the government should follow market principles and adapt to circumstances, working in a cooperative way. His ideas adapted to the new changes in economic and social development and resonated with the mercantilism in modern China.

In the Qing Dynasty, the national commodity market was basically formed, and the voice of valuing the market regulation was constantly heard. "There are two ways of stabilizing grain prices: when grain prices are low, the government purchases grain at increased prices so as not to harm the farmers; when grain prices are high, the government sells stored grain at decreased prices so as not to harm the populace and to prevent grain prices from being too high. This is the way the government purchases and sells grain from the benefits of people. Stimulated by profits, merchants would compete to purchase grain in areas with abundant harvests, causing low grain prices to rise. At the same time, merchants would also rush to sell grain in disaster-stricken areas, thus high grain prices would also fall. This is the way merchants buy and sell grain from for the benefits of people."[148] Further, "The government's purchase and sale of grain is limited, whereas the people's transactions are boundless"[149], "If trade does not flourish, the people cannot be saved; if prices are not suppressed, merchants will surely come. This is the unchanging truth."[150] Some even think that "where there is money, there will be grain trade", and "where there is trade, there will be granaries".[151] In terms of policy orientation, the imperial court also had self-reflection. A typical example was the grain policy in the early years of Emperor Qianlong's reign (1736-1796). In order to implement benevolent governance, Emperor Qianlong continued the policies of Emperor Kangxi (reigned 1654-1722) and Emperor Yongzheng (reigned 1722-1735) who attached emphasis on granary construction. He focused on a substantial expansion of the ever-normal granaries, requiring each province to set new reserve quantities and procurement plans to meet the needs. However, with years of development, grain reserves were intentionally increased, and years of poor harvests led to market supply shortages, which resulted in sustained rises in grain prices. This not only failed to achieve the initial policy objectives but had the opposite effect. A major debate ensued throughout the empire about whether to reduce reserves and whether to make greater use of market resources.[152] Emperor Qianlong himself also had the reflection:

---

[148] Zhang, Tingyu et al. 2000. Grain purchase, V. *Comprehensive Textual Research of Historical Documents of Qing Dynasty*, vol.36. Hangzhou: Zhejiang Ancient Books Publishing House. p.5193.

[149] Lu, Zengyu. Twenty policies for coping with emergencies. *Imperially Authorized Compendium of Disaster Relief*, vol.3. ed. Zhao, Li and Xu Na. in *Collections of Chinese Books on Famine Administration*. ed. Li, Wenhai, et al. Tianjin: Tianjin Ancient Books Publishing House. p. 1821.

[150] Lu, Zengyu. Twenty policies for coping with emergencies. *Imperially Authorized Compendium of Disaster Relief*, vol.3. ed. Zhao, Li and Xu Na. in *Collections of Chinese Books on Famine Administration*. ed. Li, Wenhai, et al. Tianjin: Tianjin Ancient Books Publishing House. p. 1826.

[151] Yuan, Mei. 1993. Reply to Governor-general of Jiangnan Province and Jiangxi Province on matters of revitalization and reform. *Collected Works of Yuanmei (xiao cangshanfang wenji)*, vol.15. in *Complete Works of Yuan Mei*, vol.2. ed. Wang, Yingzhi. Nanjing: Jiangsu Ancient Books Publishing House. p. 289.

[152] Gao, Wangling. 2005. *Living Tradition: Economic Development and Government Policies in Eighteenth-Century China*. Beijing: Peking University Press, p.114-123 ; Dunstan, Helen and

> After observing the situation in various places, I find that the price of rice has not decreased, instead it has increasingly increased. This is not only the case in provinces with poor harvests. Even in places where there is bumper harvest and places known for rice production, the prices have doubled compared to before. Do you think this is caused by the increasing population? Then how could the population have increased so much in just a decade? You might think it's caused by poor harvests. Then during the reigns of Emperor Kangxi (reigned 1654-1722) and Emperor Yongzheng (reigned 1722-1735) there were also years of poor harvest, why didn't this happen? Upon careful consideration, I think the real reason is that all provinces are competing to buy grain toadd to the storage of their granaries, which has led to the rise in rice prices.[153]

Competing for grain storage rather than purchasing grain at favorable prices (*pingdi*) as a reserve for times of bad harvest, led to excessive government involvement in the market, resulting in an artificial shortage of supply and leaving negative impact on grain policy and the market.[154] In the thirteenth year (1748) of Emperor Qianlong's reign (1736-1796), storage capacity of ever-normal granaries was cut to the quota of the Emperor Kangxi and Emperor Yongzheng's reign, and "the quantity of grain stored in ever-normal granaries of various province should be set exactly the same as the previous quotas in Emperor Kangxi and Emperor Yongzheng's reign."[155] However, as can be seen from the following Table 2.4, the actual storage of the ever-normal granaries in the provinces remained at a high level in the late period of Emperor Qianlong's reign.

In fact, the imperial court maintained a considerable vigilance towards the market. After all, merchants were profit-driven, and their monopolistic speculative behaviors exposed the negative side of the market. "Every year during the autumn with harvest of wheat, wealthy merchants in local areas would take their substantial capital to major towns and thoroughfares on land and water to buy new wheat, and then sell it to households that make wine yeast. They would set up open storehouses to collect and store as much wheat as possible, fearing that it might not be large enough. Ordinary farmers, ignorant of the whole situation, would sell their wheat at the current price in order to seek profits, without considering saving for the whole year. These unscrupulous merchants, however, are only concerned with

---

Wang Jiang. 2007. 1748 Re-examined: Raison D'état and policy change towards the Ever-Normal Granaries. *The Qing History Journal*. (2): 1-11.

[153] Qing, Gui and Dong Gao et al. 1985. *Factual Record of Qing Dynasty: Records of Emperor Gaozong*, vol.189. Beijing: Zhonghua Book Company. p. 429.

[154] As early as the Northern Song dynasty, Su Shi observed a similar situation: when a region experienced poor harvest in grain, if military and administrative departments competed to purchase grain for their respective duties, it would inevitably lead to rising grain prices and increased procurement costs. Although the government held grain in storage which was purchased at high prices, it would suffer another round of losses when the grain supply was scarce in the following year and the stored grain needed to be sold at reduced prices to stabilize the market prices. See: Shi, Tao. 2010. *A Study of Natural Disasters and Governmental Management Systems in the Northern Song Dynasty*. Beijing: Social Sciences Academic Press. p. 120.

[155] Zhang, Tingyu et al. 2000. Grain purchase, V. *Comprehensive Textual Research of Historical Documents of Qing Dynasty*, vol.36. Hangzhou: Zhejiang Ancient Books Publishing House. p.5194.

Table 2.4 The amount of grain stored in the ever-normal granaries of various province in the Qing Dynasty (unit: *shi*)

Provinces	13th year (1748) of Qianlong	54th year (1789) of Qianlong	Amount of change	Rate of change	Provinces	13th year (1748) of Qianlong	54th year (1789) of Qianlong	Amount of change	Rate of change
shengjing	1200000	520000	−680000	−0.56	Jiangxi	1370713	1405832	+35199	0.026
zhili	2154524	2198520	+43996	−0.02	Hubei	520935	2091628	+1570693	3.02
Shandong	2959386	2945000	−5386	−0.002	Hunan	702133	1522682	+820549	1.17
He'nan	2310999	2866499	+555500	0.24	Fujian	2566449	2984620	+418171	0.16
Shanxi	1315837	2110031	+794194	0.60	Guangdong	2953661	2850038	−103623	−0.035
Shaanxi	2733010	3558504	+825494	0.30	Guangxi	1294829	1294829	0	0
Gansu	3280000	6892250	+3612250	1.10	Sichuan	1029800	3118004	+2098204	2.03
Jiangsu	1528000	1538000	+10000	0.006	Yunnan	701500	835246	+133746	0.19
Anhui	1884000	1894000	+10000	0.005	Guizhou	507010	2258496	+1751486	3.45
Zhejiang	2800000	2926561	+126561	0.045	total	33812786	45810740	+11997954	0.35

Source: Liu, Cuirong. 2005. Review of the stability function of the Qing dynasty warehousing system. in *Economic Pulse*. ed. Chen, Guodong et al. Beijing: Encyclopedia of China Publishing House. p. 319-320 monopolizing the market, without considering the difficulties people face in obtaining food. They are indeed the great pests of the common people."[156]

In the early years of Emperor Qianlong's reign, there were even speculative behaviors where merchants profited from the grain trade without real capitals, relying solely on the pawn broking industry: "Recently, it has been heard that there is practice of buying and pawning grain in the pawnshops.... Unscrupulous merchants and cunning dealers take the short-term loans from pawnshops to buy grain at a low price... They buy and immediately pawn out, turning it over and over. It is estimated that with a small amount of silver, they could buy grains worth four to five times of the original capital (with the help of pawnshops). In the next spring or late summer and early autumn, when the previous season's crops are almost eaten up and the new ones are not yet ripe, the price of grain is bound to be high... They redeem and sell the grain in batches. Therefore, the common people's harvested grain of the year, is sold at first to merchants at a low price, and bought back in the end by themselves at a high price."[157] "We know, for example, that the latter (Suzhou) indulged in such practices as *qihang*, the concerted launching of false and alarming rumors about weather conditions in order to drive up prices. Such practices were certainly very common, even on a smaller scale, and the guilds in which merchants associated provided an ideal framework for all kinds of manipulative maneuvers."[158]

It should be noted that, from the "light and heavy principles" in *Guanzi* to the later Ever-normal Granary, prudent theoretical and policy thinkers would not take an either- or attitude to the two forces, i.e. market and government, but take both into consideration. As Sima Guang illustrated as follows,

> In each prefecture and county (*zhou* and *xian*), whenever there is a year of bumper harvest and the price of grain per *dou* falls to the lower grade, the government should purchase grain at the right time at a price higher than the market price. In years of famine when the price of grain rises to the upper grade, the government should sell grain at the right time at a price lower than the corresponding market price. If the current market price is within the medium range, the government should neither buy nor sell the grain."[159]

The government did not need to intervene in the market "if the current market price is within the medium range", and it would take regulative actions "at the right time" if it exceeds the reasonable range. "At the right time" indicates that the government did not aim to suppress or excluded the market, but to bring the price of grain back

[156]Qing, Gui and Dong Gao et al. 1985. *Factual Record of Qing Dynasty: Records of Emperor Gaozong*, vol.65. Beijing: Zhonghua Book Company. p.50.

[157]Tang, Pin. Petition to ban pawning grain in the pawnshops.*Collection of Memorial to the Throne of Qing Dynasty*, vol.45. in *Supplement to Complete Library in the Four Branches of Literature.* ed. Committee for Compilation of Supplement to Complete Library in the Four Branches of Literature. *Shi* section, vol.473. Shanghai: Shanghai Ancient Books Publishing House. p.388.

[158]Will, Pierre-Etienne. 1990. *Bureaucracy and Famine in Eighteenth-Century China.* trans. Elborg Forster. Stanford: Stanford University Press. p. 212.

[159]Sima, Guang.1999. Memorial to the Emperor Zhezong on purchasing grain at the due time for Ever-normal Granaries. In *Memorials Submitted to the Throne in the Song Dynasty.* ed. Zhao, Ruyu.vol.107. Shanghai: Shanghai Ancient Books Publishing House. p.1156..

within a reasonable range. "Generally, the price cannot be reduced too much, nor can it be increased too much, ensuring that neither should go beyond its original value."[160] The market mechanism should both be utilized and regulated. The key is to grasp the "degree" of government intervention. This "degree" includes not only the scale of the Ever-normal Granary reserve, but also the time, price and quantity of grain buying and selling. So, how should "the right time" of government intervention be grasped? Here how to better understand the "unity of opposites" relationship between the government and the market, and how to use intervention means to guide the market to participate in the regulation, has become a high-level operational art. In Emperor Yongzheng's reign (1722-1735) of the Qing dynasty, E Mida, the Viceroy of Liangguang[161] (Guangdong and Guangxi), once proposed the following suggestions on the strategy of selling grain:

> In sale of grain from ever-normal granaries, the grain price should not be immediately reduced. The common people are very careful about every little bit, and if the official price for the grain sale differs significantly from the market price, then the speculators will definitely hoard grain in the hope of a price increase. The common people who rely on purchase of grain to cook will all be waiting for aid from the government. The state's grain storage is limited, and the merchants will take advantage of the situation. This is the planning for *pingtiao* (seasonal purchase and storage, and sale of grain for price stability), but the prices are still not stable at all! It has always been the case that when goods pile up, prices fall. Since the common people can buy grain from the government, they are not entirely dependent on the grain from the merchants' shops. When the shopkeepers see that the price reduction of government's grain is limited, they will also lower their prices slightly in the hope of promoting circulation. Please reduce the price by one-tenth of the market price, then decrease it successively, and stop after a certain period of time. In this way, the shopkeepers will have little opportunity to manipulate the market, and the state's grain supply will not be in danger of shortage.[162]

"In sale of grain from ever-normal granaries, the grain price should not be immediately reduced." Instead the reduction of price should be conducted step by step according to the market price. The government should "reduce the price by one-tenth of the market price, then decrease it successively". If the price of grain drops sharply, merchants would make no profit, and thus the supply of grain would inevitably decrease significantly. When the government granaries were empty, the merchants would dominate the market and sell grain at high prices, leading the market to develop in the direction opposite to government regulation. However, "when the shopkeepers see that the price reduction of government's grain is limited, they will also lower their prices slightly in the hope of promoting circulation." Therefore, only

---

[160] He, Chunzhi. 2010. *pingtiao*, VI. *A Compendium on Famine Relief.* ed. Chen, Zhe and Luo Xinglian. in *Collections of Chinese Books on Famine Administration*, vol.1. ed. Li, Wenhai, et al. Tianjin: Tianjin Ancient Books Publishing House. p. 133.

[161] Viceroy of Liangguang, or Governor-General of Guangdong and Guangxi (*liangguang*) was the highest-ranking official in charge of Guangdong and Guangxi during the Ming and Qing dynasties, responsible for civil and military affairs as well as military provisions. He was one of the nine regional ministers appointed to govern the provinces.

[162] Zhao, Erxun. 1977. Food and money, II. *Draft of Qing Dynasty*, vol.121. Beijing: Zhonghua Book Company. p 3557.

when the government could effectively guide the market could the Ever-normal Granary system better exert its effect for price stability, thus "the shopkeepers will have little opportunity to manipulate the market, and the state's grain supply will not be in danger of shortage". It is really the effect of "moving a thousand*jin*[163] with four ounces", or achieving huge results with minimal effort. In the view of E Mida, the government should make good use of the power of the market in the process of grain price regulation, making flexible adjustments instead of being restricted by rigid rules.

In summary, if the government rejected the market and relied solely on the ever-normal granaries and overemphasized the role of the government, the result might very well be that "Ever-normal Granary is not ever-normal at all". However, if the government could effectively make use of the market and mobilize market resources, it could achieve the effect that both the government and the market would be beneficial to each other instead of causing harms, hence the effect of "one plus one being bigger than two". Of course, in the case of severe disasters, disorder and loss of control would still occur. Especially, with the development of the grain circulation market in the Qing dynasty, market connections (links) between various regions gradually became closer, and the impact of imbalances between supply and demand extended far beyond the actual disaster-affected areas. If the disaster-affected areas were grain-producing regions, then the grain prices in areas that normally relied on these regions for grain supply would rise, so did the grain prices in the surrounding areas. In particular, "the parallel trend — the enlarged role of merchants in food distribution — increased the risk of runaway prices.... But if ... local merchants were unable to cope with the situation or simply unwilling to forgo unexpected opportunities for profit, prices might easily run out of control."[164]

At to the balance of the delicate relationship between the government and the market, Chen Hongmou (1696-1771), a scholarly official who served in many places in the reign of Emperor Yongzheng (reigned 1722-1735) and Emperor Qianlong, had rich practical experience. Research by William T. Rowe shows that Chen Hongmou was an official who valued both local particularities and market laws, making important contributions to the management of ever-normal granaries. Chen Hongmou regarded the Ever-normal Granary as a basic means to "storing wealth among the people" (*cang fu yumin*)[165], maintain local self-sufficiency, and

[163] *jin*, a unit of weight (=1/2 kilogram).

[164] Will, Pierre-Etienne. 1990. *Bureaucracy and Famine in Eighteenth-Century China*. trans. Elborg Forster. Stanford: Stanford University Press. p.179.

[165] The concept of "storing wealth among the people" (*cang fu yumin*), or "keeping wealth with the people", has long been a part of Chinese political economy. Prior to the Qin dynasty, the Confucian, Mohist, Daoist, and Legalist scholars as well as military strategists all expounded on this subject. A ruler is expected to be frugal and will not compete with the people for benefits, nor plunder their riches. Policies that are generous towards the people should be adopted, so as to permit and encourage them to become rich through justified means. The underlying assumption here is that a wealthy populace and a wealthy state are one and the same. A wealthy populace is the foundation of a state's wealth as well as the fundamental guarantee for the state to win popular support. A state's wealth is more than just about its riches, but about people's support as well. This is an extension of the concept of "putting the people first", and in the present day, keeping wealth with the people has

ensure social stability. He adapted to local conditions and with the times, allowing the government to play an active role while making the best use of market. He introduced an unprecedented centralized management of the Ever-normal Granary at the provincial level without reverting to a model of economic intervention based on mandatory commands, thereby enabling the people to overcome difficulties and maintain sustainable productivity. For example, Chen Hongmou centralized the allocation of local storage funds, which improved the efficiency of fund usage; in purchase of grain, he emphasized the significance of calculating generously the grain price based on the actual market conditions; to prevent speculation and manipulation of the market, he chose to sign purchase contracts with farmers at negotiated prices based on the area of cultivation; in sale of grain, he advocated increasing market supply as a temporary measure to lower prices through market mechanisms; to achieve better effects with the policy, he required local officials to be well-acquainted with the history of local prices so as to understand the long-term trends and cyclical changes each year.[166]

On one hand, Chen Hongmou actively explored and improved the Ever-normal Granary system, and on the other he tirelessly promoted the construction of community granaries (*shecang*). He believed that community granaries and ever-normal granaries were complementary to each other, and community granaries could benefit the farmers who were not reached by ever-normal granaries. In the view of William T. Rowe, perhaps no one else was more enthusiastic about the community granary than Chen Hongmou in the early years of Emperor Qianlong's reign. Chen Hongmou established a series of policies for community granaries in provinces he served, to ensure effective social management and support for the rural economy. According to his plan, community granaries should be closely integrated with local social organizations. "Depending on terrain, *shecang* should be situated no more than twenty *li* from each cultivator—that is, within one day's round-trip travel. Depending on the local population density, they should be capitalized at between four hundred and one thousand *shi* of grain. When holdings surpassed this amount, it was time to think about further subdivision and branch establishment."[167] Chen Hongmou believed that community granaries, different from ever-normal granaries, were important economic resources owned and operated by the community. Although the establishment of community granaries required government support, and the form of management for community granaries approximated the distinctive "popular management with official oversight" (*guandu minban*) formula, the granaries belonged to the farming residents of the community instead of the government. "Community granary grain was 'local public property' (*difang gongwu*), or 'public property of that particular place' (*gaishe gongwu*), or 'collective property of

become a defining feature of modern civilization. See: https://www.chinesethought.cn/EN/shuyu_show.aspx?shuyu_id=4052.

[166] Rowe, William T. 2001. *Saving the World: Chen Hongmou and Elite Consciousness in Eighteenth-Century China*. Stanford: Stanford University Press. pp. 252-273.

[167] Rowe, William T. 2001. *Saving the World: Chen Hongmou and Elite Consciousness in Eighteenth-Century China*. Stanford: Stanford University Press. p.277.

neighboring villagers' (*fujin cunmin zhi wu*)." [168] Therefore they should not be subject to any government intervention except during special periods. Chen Hongmou emphasized that the community granary was also an instrument of local moral-cultural regeneration (*jiaohua*) by inspiring people to practice charity, mutual aid, self-discipline, and frugal consumption, thus playing an important role in changing customs and habits.[169] It is easy to see that in Chen Hongmou's planning, community granaries were intended to benefit both economic stability and social governance, and had become an effective means of comprehensive rural governance.

Chen Hongmou, a capable official, learned from the Neo-Confucianism of Song and Ming dynasties. In his life he emphasized both the promotion of moral consciousness and the spirit of actively transforming the world. As a social elite in the reign of Emperor Yongzheng (reigned 1722-1735) and Emperor Qianlong, Chen Hongmou provides us with a sample of utilizing the traditional storage system to realize the Confucian ideal society, from which we can observe the reflection of the traditional culture in the economic field: in the context of valuing agriculture, Chen Hongmou endeavored to find an "equilibrium solution" for stability and development through the storage system, so as to realize the goal of harmonious integration of righteousness and profits (*yili heyi*) and "storing wealth among the people" (*cang fu yumin*). He integrated government regulation with market adjustment together, making the Ever-normal Granary an important means for local economic stability and development. In the practice of promoting community granaries, he used government support and supervision to mobilize and organize grassroots social forces, filling the gaps that the Ever-normal Granary could not reach. Chen Hongmou utilized and integrated resources from various aspects, and constructed a top-down system of the Ever-normal Granary that integrated government, market and society as a trinity. He had unconsciously or consciously found a simple equilibrium solution:

ever-normal economy = government resources + market resources + social resources

In his view, the government must play a pivotal role in coordinating the relationship of all parties in this balance. Only when the government could set reasonable boundaries, fully respect and utilize the market, and carefully protect people's private ownership from infringement, would government, market, and social resources form a collective force. Chen Hongmou also emphasized that when the economy and society were hit by a big shock, the active intervention of the government would remain the last line of defense. Throughout the history of the development of the Ever-normal Granary, reformers have constantly explored ways to improve this relationship in conjunction with specific circumstances. Whether they were successful or not, they have all provided important references to later generations. And if we view Chen Hongmou of the Qing dynasty as a "summarizer" in theory and practice, we have already clearly obtained a complete answer from him.

[168] Rowe, William T. 2001. *Saving the World: Chen Hongmou and Elite Consciousness in Eighteenth-Century China*. Stanford: Stanford University Press. p. 280.

[169] Rowe, William T. 2001. *Saving the World: Chen Hongmou and Elite Consciousness in Eighteenth-Century China*. Stanford: Stanford University Press. pp. 278-279.

2.3.2 Purchase and Sale of Grain and Financial Support for Granaries

The state-led Ever-normal Granary, as a "last resort" in critical moments, were necessary. The "leisurely" approach of E Mida mentioned in previous text would obviously be ineffective in the case of severe supply shocks. Rulers in the history were acutely aware of this. In the fifth year of Yongzheng's reign (1722-1735), the emperor issued a decreed, "The grain in the Ever-normal Granary is crucial for the lives of the people, and is the most important aspect for the local governance."[170] During the reigns of emperors Kangxi, Yongzheng, and Qianlong, the government, relying on its growing economic strength, developed and strengthened the Ever-normal Granary system. The system was so complete and well-developed that it could be considered as a master that synthesized all achievements of previous generations. It played a positive role in stabilizing the economy and society.

During the reigns of emperors Kangxi, Yongzheng, and Qianlong, the rulers attached great importance to the grain reserves of Ever-normal Granary, and made detailed regulations on the reserves of prefectures and counties (*zhou* and *xian*) and even various smaller regions. In the forty-third year (1704) of the Emperor Kangxi's reign, the ever-normal granaries in various provinces had developed to a certain scale, then the specific quotas of reserves were specified: large prefectures and counties (*zhou* and *xian*) were required to store 10,000 *shi* of grain, medium prefectures and counties 8,000 *shi*, and small prefectures and counties 6,000 *shi*. Due to regional differences, the reserve quotas were different according to the specific situation.[171] In the reign of Emperor Kangxi, the Ever-normal Granary had already experienced deficits. In the reign of Emperor Yongzheng (reigned 1722-1735), strict regulations were implemented, and central government officials were dispatched to various regions to supervise the granaries to ensure that they maintained sufficient reserves.[172] In the reign of Emperor Qianlong, the total reserves of the national ever-normal granaries continued to grow. However, due to the large amount of government purchases, grain prices rose continuously. Therefore, in the 13th year (1748) of Emperor Qianlong's reign, the government adjusted the provincial reserves quotas as the old system. Although the reserves of the national ever-normal granaries decreased to some degree in the middle of Emperor Qianlong's reign, they soon rose and remained at a high level.

In the Qing dynasty, the Ever-normal Granary was planned and implemented uniformly by the central government, with the governors and generals responsible

---

[170] Xi, Yufu and Shen Shixu. 1974. Granary XIII: Reserves. *Classified Anthologies of Imperial Regulations*, vol.153. Taibei: Wenhai Press Company. p. 2084.

[171] Zhang, Tingyu et al. 2000. Grain purchase III. *Comprehensive Textual Research of Historical Documents of Qing Dynasty*, vol.34. Hangzhou: Zhejiang Ancient Books Publishing House. p.5173.

[172] Zhang, Tingyu et al. 2000. Grain purchase IV. *Comprehensive Textual Research of Historical Documents of Qing Dynasty*, vol.35. Hangzhou: Zhejiang Ancient Books Publishing House. p. 5181.

for the overall implementation in provinces, the directors and commissioners supervising specific implementation, and the officials of prefectures, counties and cities handling the specific operations. The operation and management of the Ever-normal Granary went through a process of continuous development during the Qing dynasty. In order to solve the problem of ineffective implementation by local governments, supervision of the grain sales system was implemented during the reign of Emperor Kangxi. For example, officials from the *Ducha Yuan* (Ministry of Supervision, the central government's censorate institution) were dispatched to supervise the implementation of the policy of grain sale in local ever-normal granaries.[173] In the reign of Emperor Yongzheng and Emperor Qianlong, the central government more frequently sent officials to various regions to supervise and inspect the storage system in order to rectify the accumulated problems. With regard to the proportion between grain storage and sale, the policy of seventy percent for storage and thirty percent for sale was initially implemented in the reign of Emperor Kangxi. However, the inflexible implementation of this policy hindered the full performance of the Ever-normal Granary. Starting from Emperor Yongzheng's reign, the government began to make flexible adjustments based on local conditions. By the 7th year (1742) of Emperor Qianlong's reign, it was decreed that "when a province encounters a situation where local rice is scarce and prices are high, more sales of grain from the ever-normal granaries should be made to provide for people's food, and no one should rigidly adhere to past practices."[174] For another example, the standard for price reduction in the sale of grain from Ever-normal Granary was a highly delicate issue. The initial regulation stated that when grain prices were high, the reduction shouldn't exceed one *qian* (one tenth of tael) per *shi* of grain. However, the decree in the 7th year (1742) of Emperor Qianlong's reign stated that in years with high grain prices, a reduction of only one *qian* per *shi* was clearly insufficient. Therefore, provinces were required to propose standards for price reductions based on their specific local conditions.[175] In the late period of Emperor Qianlong's reign, after years of practical exploration and summarization, a set of standard regulations was gradually formed. (See Table 2.5) During the reigns of emperors Kangxi, Yongzheng, and Qianlong, the ever-normal granaries in the Qing dynasty gradually formally established a complete system encompassing fund raising and management, granary construction, types of stored grains, grain preservation, loss handling, storage and sale proportions, reserve replenishment and circulation, grain purchase and sale prices, as well as statistical record-keeping, assessment management, and

---

[173] Zhang, Tingyu et al. 2000. Grain purchase IV. *Comprehensive Textual Research of Historical Documents of Qing Dynasty*, vol.35. Hangzhou: Zhejiang Ancient Books Publishing House. pp. 5174-5175.

[174] Zhang, Tingyu et al. 2000. Grain purchase V. *Comprehensive Textual Research of Historical Documents of Qing Dynasty*, vol.36. Hangzhou: Zhejiang Ancient Books Publishing House. p. 5192.

[175] Zhang, Tingyu et al. 2000. Grain purchase V. *Comprehensive Textual Research of Historical Documents of Qing Dynasty*, vol.36. Hangzhou: Zhejiang Ancient Books Publishing House. pp. 5191-5192.

Table 2.5 Established rates for reduced-price sales of government grain

Market price (tael/*shi*)	Reduction (tael)	Market price (tael/*shi*)	Reduction (tael)
<0.9	No sales	1.2–1.3	0.20
0.9–1.0	0.05	1.3–1.4	0.25
1.0–1.1	0.10	1.5–1.7	To be discussed by with Board (maximum 0.30)
1.1–1.2	0.15		

Source: Will, Pierre-Etienne. 1990. *Bureaucracy and Famine in Eighteenth-Century China*. trans. Elborg Forster. Stanford: Stanford University Press. p.185.

supervision and punishment. Of course, as time passed and bureaucratic corruption set in, the problems with these systems also gradually came to light.

The main functions of the Ever-normal Granary in the Qing dynasty were to buy and sell grains to stabilize grain prices, provide loans, and offer relief. In the third year (1725) of Emperor Yongzheng's reign, three-level standard for releasing grain were set according to the annual harvest, "selling grains at stable prices for years with minor shortages, lending grains for years with moderate shortages, and providing relief for years with major shortages"[176]. Under normal situation, the ever-normal granaries would be engaged in buying and selling or lending operations[177] every year to periodically update their reserves, and in years of bumper harvest they would increase their replenishment efforts to maintain sufficient reserves. As is shown in Fig. 2.3, the layout of the ever-normal granaries across the country were specially arranged, with targeted differences in reserve quantities in different regions. In the southeastern coastal and mountainous areas, which were far from the main grain-producing regions and difficult to access, the per capita occupancy of grain reserves in ever-normal granaries was higher than that in other southern provinces. This, to some extent, confirms the conclusion of previous studies: "the observations of Chuan and Kraus for the 1720's and 1730's show that at Canton and Fuzhou (in Guangdong and Fujian, respectively) prices responded 'much more violently' to unfavorable harvests than in surplus-producing regions like Jiangxi and Hunan."[178]

[176] Zhang, Tingyu et al. 2000. Grain purchase IV. *Comprehensive Textual Research of Historical Documents of Qing Dynasty*, vol.35. Hangzhou: Zhejiang Ancient Books Publishing House. p. 5178.

[177] Lending was generally intended to address the issue of food rations and seeds during the lean season while enabling the reserve to be renewed cyclically. In normal years, loans carried a 10% interest rate, but in years of poor harvest only the principal was collected without interest. According to local chronicles of Shanxi and Shaanxi, the Ever-normal Granary followed the principle of "storing 70% of the grain and selling 30%" when grain prices were high, and "storing 70% and lending out 30%" (with an additional 10% interest) when prices were stable. In years with harvests below seven-tenths of the normal, loans were provided "interest-free". See: Ni, Yuping. 2013. *Finance and Society during the Jiaqing and Daoguang Reigns of the Qing Dynasty*. Beijing: The Commercial Press. pp. 41-42.

[178] Will, Pierre-Etienne. 1990. *Bureaucracy and Famine in Eighteenth-Century China*. trans. Elborg Forster. Stanford: Stanford University Press. p. 179.

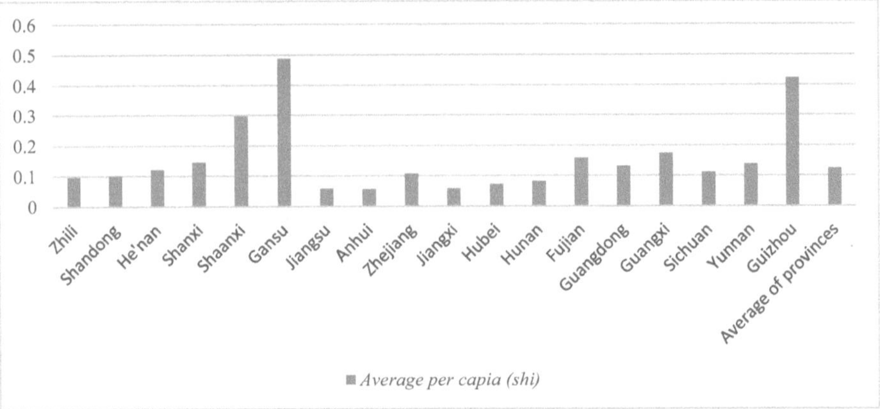

Fig. 2.3 Average amount of grains per Ever-normal Granary in provinces during the Qing dynasty at the time of maximum national storage (1789 quota). Source of data: Liu, Cuirong. 2005. Review of the stability function of the Qing dynasty warehousing system. in *Economic Pulse*. ed. Chen, Guodong et al. Beijing: Encyclopedia of China Publishing House. p. 340

In provinces with frequent natural disasters such as Zhili, Shandong and Henan, which were also of great significance for safeguarding the capital, the construction of ever-normal granaries necessarily received attention of the imperial court. In provinces along the Yangtze River, where the inland river network were rich and market circulation were well developed, the per capita occupancy of grain reserves in ever-normal granaries could be correspondingly reduced.[179] As for the northwest and southwest regions, raising the standard of the Ever-normal Granary was of greater significance, both in terms of agricultural development conditions, geographic remoteness (far from the main grain trade routes) and the importance of national defense.[180] It can be seen that within the limit of the state's power, the imperial court played an active role, adapting to local conditions to establish a nationwide Ever-normal Granary system, allowing it to function as a stabilizer.

Pierre-Etienne Will's research shows that during the great drought in Zhili from 1743 to 1744, enough grain from ever-normal granaries were transported to the disaster-stricken area to sustain the lives of more than two million people for eight full months. The efficient operation of the regulation system, including the Ever-normal Granary, played an important role, and it was not just an isolated case of the 18th century. Pierre-Etienne Will emphasized,

[179] Li, Fenyang. 2006. *Research on Storage Systems in the Qing Dynasty*. Taibei: Wenhai Press Company. pp. 181, 187.

[180] For a discussion of the geographic distribution characteristics of the storage capacity of the Ever-normal Granary, see: Ma, Li and Fang Xiuqi. 2009. The spatial patterns of grain storage quota in the Ever-normal Granary in Qing dynasty. *Journal of Chinese Historical Geography*. (3): 68-74.

> The skepticism I spoke of would suggest that relief operations existed mainly on paper, ...But the very fact that this system had been elaborated over a long period of time, was nourished by a venerable tradition, and had reached an advanced stage of inventiveness and complexity—the very well-attested fact, finally, of its durability—argues that it could and did work relatively well.[181]

However, the development of the Ever-normal Granary in the Qing dynasty also followed a cyclic process. "The *changpingcang* seem to have had a succession of ups and downs (not to mention considerable regional variations); typically, each period marked by an effort on the part of the central government to update the granaries' operations and place them under tighter control was followed by a gradual deterioration at the local level until the next tightening of control."[182] The will of the state and the governance capabilities of the government were important factors that affected the development of the Ever-normal Granary. Initiated as a way for good governance, the Ever-normal Granary system gradually evolved into an issue of many problems, which was reflected in its periodical development.

It is noteworthy that in his recent research, Wu Siwu focused on a problem that cannot be ignored in the rise and fall of ever-normal granaries in the Qing dynasty, namely the difficulties in the operation of this system. From the perspective of institutional design, with financial appropriations and donations, the ever-normal granaries mainly took advantage of the grain price fluctuations (the gap between buying and selling prices) to generate profits and maintain the normal operation of the granaries, which is known as the model of "granaries supported by granaries". However, in practical implementation, on one hand due to the huge costs and risks associated with storage losses, management expenses, and purchasing to replenish stocks, the profit margin of the ever-normal granaries was very limited. On the other hand, the actual operation of the granaries often resulted in expenses exceeding income, mainly due to excessive price reductions in grain sales and higher purchase prices (without considering losses and management costs).[183] When the ever-normal granaries was in the process of growing from nothing to something, or from smaller ones to larger ones, these issues could be resolved through continuous increases in financial input. However, when financial investment and the storage capacity of the granaries reached a certain scale and needed to be maintained at that scale, the "deficit" between buying and selling became an inevitable big problem. The ideal state should be that the ever-normal granaries could offset losses according to actual conditions, which would ensure their normal operation and relieve officials of any additional financial pressure. However, the choices made in various regions were

---

[181] Will, Pierre-Etienne. 1990. *Bureaucracy and Famine in Eighteenth-Century China*. trans. Elborg Forster. Stanford: Stanford University Press. p. 272.

[182] Will, Pierre-Etienne. 1990. *Bureaucracy and Famine in Eighteenth-Century China*. trans. Elborg Forster. Stanford: Stanford University Press. p. 187.

[183] Wu, Siwu. 2018. *Institutional Dilemmas of Granary and Its Disaster Relief Practices in the Qing Dynasty*. Beijing: Social Sciences Academic Press. pp. 33-109. Also see: Will, Pierre-Etienne and R. Bin Wong. ed. 1991. *Nourish the People: the State Civilian Granary System in China, 1650-1850*. Ann Arbor: University of Michigan Press. pp. 141-193.

either to accumulate losses in order to maintain the reserves, or to temporarily suspend purchases to avoid visible losses, leading to a continuous decline in reserves. All these reflect the long-term operational dilemmas faced by the ever-normal granaries in the context of limited fiscal budgets.

Certainly, this was a cyclical and cumulative evolutionary process, with new explorations born out of various problems in the nineteenth century. Wu Siwu believes that this marked the modern transformation from the mode of "granaries supported by granaries" to the mode of "granaries supported externally". The catalyst for this transformation was the Taiping Rebellion[184], which severely disrupted the grain storage system, primarily ever-normal granaries and charity granaries, in Jiangnan (south of the middle and lower reaches of the Yangtze River). Amidst the reconstruction of Jiangnan led by local gentry, Grain-storage Granaries (*jigu cang*) was introduced, soon followed by the emergence of a number of well-managed and developed new-style Grain-storage Granaries (*jigu cang*). Among them, the Changzhou-Yuanhe-Wuxian Abundant Store Charity Granary (*Chang-Yuan-Wun fengbei yicang*) was a typical case. As a local granary in Suzhou, the Changzhou-Yuanhe-Wuxian Abundant Store Charity Granary was the first one in modern China to decouple the processes of grain storage, relief, and profit-making. It achieved a shift from the model of "granaries supported by granaries" to the mode of "granaries supported externally". Under the management model led by the gentry with official participation and cooperation, the Changzhou-Yuanhe-Wuxian Abundant Store Charity Granary operated like a "dual-track" enterprise: on one hand it achieved self-sufficiency through its own profits, and on the other hand it effectively fulfilled its social assistance function. In particular, in terms of self-sustaining profits, the Changzhou-Yuanhe-Wuxian Abundant Store Charity Granary achieved sustainable development through diversified operations such as land leasing, pawnshop interest collection, real estate and securities investments.[185]

The dilemmas and solutions of the storage system in the Qing dynasty can be traced back to the Northern and Southern Song dynasties. In an effort to enhance the self-sustaining capabilities of the ever-normal granaries, Green Sprouts Act was implemented in the in Northern Song dynasty as the first large-scale practice of "granaries supported by granaries". In the Southern Song dynasty, community granaries had already adopted a business model of using land property as capital and

[184] The Taiping Rebellion, also known as the Taiping Civil War or the Taiping Revolution, was a large-scale and protracted uprising that occurred in China from 1850 to 1864. It was led by Hong Xiuquan, who claimed to be the brother of Jesus Christ. It started due to social and economic discontent and spread rapidly, establishing the Taiping Heavenly Kingdom. Despite initially gaining significant control, internal divisions and external pressures led to its downfall. The rebellion had a profound impact on China, weakening the Qing dynasty and contributing to future political instability.

[185] Wu, Siwu. 2018. *Institutional Dilemmas of Granary and Its Disaster Relief Practices in the Qing Dynasty*. Beijing: Social Sciences Academic Press. The charity granary that emerged in Guangdong at the end of the Qing dynasty also had a distinct nature of investment and business management. See: Chen, Chunsheng. 1994. On the rise of charity granary in Guangdong at the end of Qing dynasty. *Journal of Chinese Social and Economic History*. (1):50-66.

utilizing land rentals for interest-free credit, which was an early form of "granaries supported externally". This approach expanded operational scope to achieve sustainable development of granaries and could be seen as a precursor to the Changzhou-Yuanhe-Wuxian Abundant Store Charity Granary. The emergence of new-style granaries represented by the Changzhou-Yuanhe-Wuxian Abundant Store Charity Granary in the late Qing dynasty provided a successful example of operating grain buffer reserves under conditions of a more developed commodity economy. However, it should be realized that the Changzhou-Yuanhe-Wuxian Abundant Store Charity Granary was a local granary, and the success of granaries supported externally largely depended on a more developed regional economy and certain social conditions. If the dual-track system of the Changzhou-Yuanhe-Wuxian Abundant Store Charity Granary was transplanted to regions with lower levels of economic development and inferior water and land transportation conditions compared to Jiangnan (south of the middle and lower reaches of the Yangtze River), it might not be as effective.

On the whole, the grain buffer reserves that undertook the functions of economic and social stability could operate with three business models. In addition to "granaries supported by granaries" and "granaries supported externally", "granaries supported by finance" cannot be ignored. From both theoretical and practical perspectives, each of these three models had its applicability, depending on the type of storage. In particular, the systematic state-run ever-normal granaries, ranging from central government to local governments, bear important responsibilities such as stabilizing the economy, regulating distribution, and providing social assistance. Therefore, "granaries supported by finance" should be the dominant model, with profit-making as a supplementary means. Utilizing "granaries supported by granaries" and "granaries supported externally" to achieve sustained profits can easily lead to competition with the market and small-scale agricultures for benefits, making it difficult for these models to become the main maintenance mode for large-scale state-run storage.

Back to the Northern Song, regulations on planning the Ever-normal Granary in Emperor Gaozong's reign, as was mentioned earlier, stipulated that "a portion of the tax money should be set aside" as the capital for the Ever-normal Granary. "Ten years later when there was a certain surplus of the money, the capital should be returned to the three financial departments." In practical operation, besides selling at a price lower than the market price, the Ever-normal Granary sometimes needed to sell at even lower prices or even provide non-reimbursable aids.[186] In this way, it

[186] For example, in the third year (1051) of Huangyou period, "Chen Shengzhi, the governor of Huainan and Liangze, and other officials made a petition stating, 'Some prefectures and garrisons have suffered from natural disasters, and we ask for the sale of grain from the Ever-Normal Granaries for relief.' The emperor issued an imperial edict saying, 'When each Ever-normal Granary initially purchased grain, it was during abundant harvests when prices were low. If the grain is now sold at the original purchase price, there will be considerable expenses involved in setting up markets, dispatching officials for purchase, storage, as well as paying for packaging and wastage. Therefore, the Justice Departments of Huainan, Liangzhe, East and West Jiangnan, North and South Jinghu should be ordered to conduct an investigation and, based on the original purchase

is already the best state for the Ever-normal Granary to maintain a balance between income and expenditure. If the Ever-normal Granary is expected to have an "a certain surplus of the money" and to return the capital to the central treasury, it is obviously difficult to realize. In addition, the funds of the Ever-normal Granary were often misappropriated, so these granaries would find it difficult to maintain the continuous operation without financial support. In the fourth year (1069) of Jiayu period during the reign of Emperor Renzhong, the imperial edict stated, "Throughout the realm, the ever-normal granaries often have their stored grain reallocated for other uses, with the leftover grain insufficient to meet the demands in famine years. An order is issued for the Imperial Treasury and the three financial commissions to jointly disburse one million strings of cash, which would then be distributed to the various regions to assist in the purchase and storage of grain."[187] To the time of Emperor Zhezong' reign, although the central government had put at least three batches of large amounts of funds into the Ever-normal Granary,[188] this approach of directly allocating funds from the central government to replenish the capital of the Ever-normal Granary was not a regular or institutionalized arrangement. "Due to the lack of capital, even during years with bumper harvest, the prefectures and

price, increase the price by ten to fifteen cash coins per *dou* (a unit of dry measure for grain which equals 1 decalitre) to meet the needs of the sale.' Chen Shengzhi further remarked, 'If additional money is added, it is contrary to the purpose of showing concern for the people.' Consequently, the emperor issued another imperial edict decreeing that the grain should be sold at the original purchase price." See: Xu, Song. ed. 2014. Food and money, LIII (7, 8). *Draft for the Collected Statutes of Song Dynasty*. Shanghai: Shanghai Ancient Books Publishing House. pp. 7199-7200. In the second year (1079) of Yuanfeng period, "the emperor issued an imperial edict stating, 'It is reported that the price of grain in Qizhou, Yanzhou, and Yunzhou is extremely high, reaching almost 200 cash coins per *dou*. The people are struggling to find food, and there are many displaced people wandering around. The Department of Agriculture (*shi nong si*) should instruct the prefectures and counties to sell the grain stored in the Ever-Normal Granaries, especially those originally purchased at a price of less than 10 cash coins per *dou*. The same policy applies to Binzhou, Dizhou, and Cangzhou.'" See: Xu, Song ed. 2014. Food and money, LVII (8). *Draft for the Collected Statutes of Song Dynasty*. Shanghai: Shanghai Ancient Books Publishing House. p. 7334. In the first year (1086) of the Yuanyou period, "An imperial edict was issued instructing the supervisors of ever-normal granaries in the Eastern and Western Huainan to assess the severity of the famine and to provide relief using the grain from the charity granaries and ever-normal granaries according to regulations, and to report to the court upon completion." Additionally, "another imperial edict was issued stating: 'The circuits and their respective judicial supervision departments should investigate and understand the disaster situations in the counties and prefectures, regardless of the tax reduction ratio due to the disaster or whether there are complaints from the people, and should promptly provide relief using the grain from the charity granaries and ever-normal granaries to prevent people from becoming displaced.'" See: Xu, Song. ed. 2014. Food and money LVII (9). *Draft for the Collected Statutes of Song Dynasty*. Shanghai: Shanghai Ancient Books Publishing House. p.7335.

[187] Xu, Song. ed. 2014. Food and money LIII (8). *Draft for the Collected Statutes of Song Dynasty*. Shanghai: Shanghai Ancient Books Publishing House. p.7200.

[188] Shi, Tao. 2010. *A Study of Natural Disasters and Governmental Management Systems in the Northern Song Dynasty*. Beijing: Social Sciences Academic Press. p.111.

counties (*zhou* and *xian*) had no money to purchase grain for storage."[189] Wang Anshi's reform with Green Sprouts Act reform can be said to have been forced out of this dilemma to some extent. However, the failure of the reform further indicates that when financial support is weakening, the mode of "granaries supported by granaries" is prone to various problems, which seriously weakens the basic function of the Ever-normal Granary. The preparedness granary in the Ming dynasty also faced the same problem of financial support. A typical example is that in order to replenish the preparedness granaries, the government had grains for atonement stored in granaries. "In the eighth year of Hung-chih (1505) a law was enacted to allow criminals to redeem their crimes by paying fines in grain which would be then stored for relief purposes. Officials who had been convicted of corruption and bribery were allowed to do likewise. A decree issued during the Cheng-te period (1506-1521) stated that a prisoner upon whom the court had imposed a fine could pay to the government's granary an amount of grain equivalent to 80 percent of the imposed fine. Military officials who had committed crimes were allowed to do likewise."[190] The laws in the Ming dynasty were extremely strict. In the mid and late period, the funds collected from criminals' redemption payments were used as capital for the granaries, which provides the financial weakness of the government at the time.[191]

The rulers of the Qing dynasty attached more importance to the construction of ever-normal granaries compared to previous dynasties. However, when the imperial court attributed various problems with the ever-normal granaries primarily to the lack of competent personnel, it did not fully recognize another underlying reason: as analyzed earlier, when the cycle of grain purchase and sale (*ditiao*) could not be sustained due to a lack of continuous financial support, the operational problems and risks at the practical level were difficult to resolve. Li Fenyang pointed out that demanding high moral standards from local administrators was not the complete solution. Ever-normal granaries in the Qing dynasty were bestowed with important responsibilities, and the system was strict with multiple layers of prevention and control. However, local governments, operating with limited personnel and budgets, found it challenging to handle complex and difficult tasks.[192] By the end of the 18th century, the imperial court found it increasingly difficult to require local prefectures and counties (*zhou* and *xian*) to maintain full reserves in the ever-normal granaries. At the same time, local governments increasingly relied on direct appropriations from the imperial court or "tribute held back" to deal with disasters and injuries[193].

---

[189] Sima, Guang.1999. Memorial to the Emperor Zhezong on purchasing grain at the due time for Ever-normal Granaries. In *Memorials Submitted to the Throne in the Song Dynasty.* ed. Zhao, Ruyu.vol.107. Shanghai: Shanghai Ancient Books Publishing House. p.1156.

[190] Li, Dun. J. 1967. *The Essence of Chinese Civilization.* Princeton: Van Nostrand. p.126.

[191] Gu, Ying. 1993. A preliminary exploration of the problem of grain accumulation in the preparedness granaries in the Ming dynasty. *Collected Papers of Historical Studies.* (1): 22-23.

[192] Li, Fenyang. 2006. *Research on Storage Systems in the Qing Dynasty.* Taibei: Wenhai Press Company. pp. 232-233.

[193] Will, Pierre-Etienne. 1990. *Bureaucracy and Famine in Eighteenth-Century China.* trans. Elborg Forster. Stanford: Stanford University Press. p. 287, p. 293, p. 296.

As the national situation deteriorated, the ever-normal granaries found it difficult to secure continuous financial support from both central and local governments, leading to a clear degradation of their functions. In the twenty-second year (1817) of the Jiaqing period, the ever-normal granaries were described as something "longly neglected with accumulated problems"[194].

In summary, if grain storage is taken as the main evaluation criterion, the development of state-run ever-normal granaries in the Qing dynasty may exhibit an "inverted U-shaped" pattern. Liu Cuirong utilized local chronicles to depict the changing trends of grain storage in ever-normal granaries in five counties of Zhili, ten counties of Shanxi, five counties of Hubei, five counties of Hunan, and five counties of Guangdong from the periods of Emperor Kangxi and Emperor Yongzheng to the periods of Emperor Tongzhi and Emperor Guangxu.[195] It can be observed that they generally developed in the inverted U-shaped pattern. Liu Cuirong's statistics should have a certain degree of representativeness: if grain storage of various regions are summed up, the ever-normal granaries of the whole country should also follow this trend at the macro level, which can be confirmed by Li Fenyang's research.[196]

Of course, the above analysis does not imply a negation of the policy. The long history of the ever-normal granaries in Chinese history demonstrates the state's efforts to take on the responsibilities of welfare assistance and macroeconomic stability, employing feasible regulatory measures to maintain the steady development of the economy and society. Su Shi once said, ""However, during my two-year tenure in Hangzhou, I personally managed the relief efforts for famines. I knew that simply by selling the relief grain, without implementing any other measures, the price of rice could be kept stable, ultimately preventing the people from starving and becoming refugees."[197] Su Shi's affirmation of the effective function of the ever-normal granaries based on his personal experience should not be considered hollow words. Moreover, the numerous books on famine relief that emerged during the Qing dynasty, which offered advice on how to better manage and utilize the ever-normal granaries, deserve serious consideration. As long as one understands the history with empathy rather than harsh criticism, the ever-normal granaries constructed during the mid-Qing dynasty and their role in stabilizing the economy and society can be said to be unparalleled worldwide. Lillian M. Li, through a quantita-

---

[194] Liu, Jinzao. 2000. Grain purchase, V. *Sequel to Comprehensive Textual Research of Historical Documents of Qing Dynasty*, vol.60. Hangzhou: Zhejiang Ancient Books Publishing House. p. 8164.

[195] Liu, Cuirong. 2005. Review of the stability function of the Qing dynasty warehousing system. in *Economic Pulse*. ed. Chen, Guodong et al.Beijing: Encyclopedia of China Publishing House. pp.321-325.

[196] Li, Fenyang. 2006. *Research on Storage Systems in the Qing Dynasty*. Taibei: Wenhai Press Company. p. 183.

[197] Su, Shi. 1986. Petition for an edict to allocate grain from the annual tributes and granaries for sale in Zhexi prefectures ensuring continuous distribution. *The Collected Works of Su Shi*, vol.33. ed. Kong, Fanli. Beijing: Zhonghua Book Company. p. 932.

tive analysis of grain prices in North China, believes that "*quantitative analysis confirms the strong role that the state played in promoting economic stability during the high Qing. It did so by ... maintaining price stability through measures such as price equalization, grain storage, and famine relief.*"[198] *She also made a comparison of price rises of 20 to 70 percent over normal in Emperor Qianlong's reign and the prices rises in Europe by stating, "Crop failures, or harvest shortfalls of 40–60percent, were certainly serious, and price rises of 20 to 70 percent over normal could have grave social consequences. Yet by comparison with the worst European famines where prices doubled, tripled, or quadrupled, they were moderate.*"[199] In the typical agriculture-centric society of ancient China, it is hard to imagine the repercussions if the state had not taken action in terms of grain reserves. Although Kung-Chuan Hsiao analyzed the various defects of the storage system (including the ever-normal granaries) in the Qing dynasty in his work "Rural China: Imperial Control in the Nineteenth Century", he still cautiously concluded,

> We are not arguing that the grain reserve system was not a useful institution.... An unsatisfactory method of famine control was better than no method at all, ... But the reserve system, like any other imperial institution, did not operate in a historical vacuum. Its performance was conditioned by circumstances-physical, economic, and political. For this reason it could not produce all the results of which it was theoretically capable when other major factors in the historical situation tended to undermine the imperial structure as a whole, or when other elements in the imperial system did not work satisfactorily.[200]

Throughout the history, there are repeated discussions surrounding the Ever-normal Granary. While there are many debates over their advantages and disadvantages, there are few arguments about whether or not they should be abolished. The Ever-normal Granary emerged from the fragile simple reproduction of small-scale peasant economy at the micro level, and the macro-demand of a unified country seeking long-term stability and security. In the "non-vacuum" reality, the apparent and potential problems did not hinder the construction and development of the Ever-normal Granary in various dynasties. Rather than fading out of the historical stage, they evolved into a significant feature of China's economic accumulation of various dynasties, sharing the destiny of these dynasties.

The connotation of the Ever-normal Granary is rich. Broadening our horizons and conducting a thorough analysis, we can see that the Ever-normal Granary is not just one or two types of "grain granaries", but rather a coordinated system of various "granaries". This integration reveals that the ancient Chinese were flexible and versatile, incorporating a variety of resources and factors into a broad buffer reserve system.

---

[198] Li, Lillian M. 2007. *Fighting Famine in North China: State, Market, and Environmental Decline, 1600s-1990s*. Stanford: Stanford University Press. p.220.

[199] Li, Lillian M. 2007. *Fighting Famine in North China: State, Market, and Environmental Decline, 1600s-1990s*. Stanford: Stanford University Press. p.247.

[200] Hsiao, Kung-chuan. 1960. *Rural China: Imperial Control in the Nineteenth Century*. Seattle: University of Washington Press. pp. 182-183.

Chapter 3

"Ever-normal Granary in Broad Sense": Policy Expansion and Governance for Nourishing the People

> Then, ifthereis a year of severe droughts or floods and the people lose their primarysource of income, he builds palaces and pavilions, thereby providingemployment for those households so poor that they have neither a dogin front nor a pig behind. Thus, his building of palaces and pavilions isnot to gratify his pleasure, but to maintain equilibrium in the economicpolicies of the state.
>
> —*Guanzi:The Art of Fiscal Management* (*cheng ma shu*)[1]

> In ancient times, those who were adept at governing their countries and cherished their people would certainly establish stable and simple laws, ensuring that those above cherished resources to nurture those below, while those below exerted their utmost efforts to support those above. In this way, those above would be prosperous without causing those below to suffer poverty.
>
> —*Old History of Tang: Treatise on Food and Money (shi huo zhi)*[2]

In this chapter, the concept of the Ever-normal Granary is expanded into a broad-scope buffer reserve system, which includes the following three: (1) the Ever-normal Granary itself, and various types of granaries that supplement and assist it, which collectively form the "Ever-normal Granary system"; (2) the "equalization policy" (*pingzhunfa*)[3] that incorporates a variety of commodities and even currency into the

[1] Guanzi. 1998. *Guanzi: Political, Economic, and Philosophical Essays from Early China*, vol. 2. trans. W. Allyn Rickett. Princeton: Princeton University Press. p.365.

[2] Ouyang, Xiu and Song Qi. 1975. Food and money, I. *New History of Tang Dynasty*.vol. 51. Beijing: Zhonghua Book Company. p. 1341.

[3] "Equalization policy" (*pingzhunfa*), also called "balanced standard" or "price stabilization", a policy of state buying and selling to balance supply and demand, particularly for the price of grain, was advocated by Sang Hongyang, a statesman, during the Han period (206 B.C -220 A.D.), and remained a substantial aspect of economics policy through the aged. In 110 B.C. Emperor Wu (141-87 B.C.) decided to introduce the price adjustment policy, organized by an institution called Bureau of Standards (*pingzhun*). The Bureau controlled the prices of all "tribute products" delivered from the provinces to the capital, as well as various objects manufactured for the court and the capital. The procedure was the same as with the ever-normal granaries (*changing cang*) which followed a system of buying commodities when and where the price was low. They were kept in

W. Xian, *Chinese Food Security Strategy*, Research Series on the Chinese Dream and China's Development Path,
https://doi.org/10.1007/978-981-95-7964-8_3

buffer regulation; (3) a special "Ever-normal Granary of labor force" – the "labor relief" system. These aspects are collectively referred to as the "Ever-normal Granary in broad sense" in this chapter for the following reasons: the classic work *Guanzi* firstly narrated the theoretical implications and policy value of the grain buffer reserve; compared to the "equalization policy" (*pingzhunfa*) and the "labor relief" system, the Ever-normal Granary was implemented most extensively and had the greatest impact in Chinese history; the term "ever-normal" more intuitively expresses the goal of seeking macro stability for economic policies. From using granaries to buffer grain reserves to using public projects to buffer labor reserves, from tangible granaries to intangible granaries, ancient Chinese continuously explored flexible applications of basic economic principles. Among these, the "Ever-normal Granary of labor force", or the labor relief system, was an important institutional invention. In the Song dynasty governments began to consciously implement the labor relief policy, which illustrates that under the conditions of population increase and the absence of a system for land allocation and administration, the state was actively exploring the possibilities of adaptive transformation of economic regulation policies. The reason why China was able to foster macroeconomic stability policies and develop the Ever-normal Granary tradition over a long history can be attributed to at least the following three conditions: the instability of agricultural production caused by unpredictable climate changes; the widespread and fragile small-scale peasant economy; the unified national governance structure, and the economic ethics and macro welfare demands rooted in the traditions of "people-orientation" (*minben*) and "benevolent governance" (*renzheng*).

3.1 Stabilizing Grain Prices Ensures Stability of Other Commodities

Among the various types of agricultural economies, small-scale peasant economy has the lowest degree of self-sufficiency. The traditional Chinese small-scale peasant economy, with farming and weaving as the mainstay, relies on market exchange for salt, iron, and other production and living materials, as well as for the currency needed to pay taxes and for some miscellaneous needs. The small-scale peasant

storehouses and granaries, and brought in higher quantities on the market in times of inflation, in order to lower the market prices. This method would on one hand stabilize prices of staple goods, and on the other hand curb speculative purchase and selling. It must be notified that the government did only set upper limits for prices, but did not request a minimum price for the commodities in question. The price adjustment policy directly influenced the creation of ever-normal granaries in 54 B.C. by Geng Shouchang. Sang Hongyang (152–80 B.C.) was a prominent official of the Former Han dynasty, who served Emperor Wu of Han and his successor Emperor Zhao. He is most famed for his economic policies during the reign of Emperor Wu, the best known of which include the state monopolies over iron and salt - systems which would be imitated by other dynasties throughout history. He installed the office of price control in the capital to prevent merchants from buying cheap and selling expensive.

economy is an important creator of the market while also being highly dependent on it. However, due to the fragmentation of production and the vulnerability of survival, peasants were often the weaker party in the market. A stable market is therefore crucial for them.

If the productive sectors of China's traditional society are divided into agricultural and non-agricultural sectors, there is no doubt that the exchange between food, the main product of small-scale peasant economy, and non-agricultural products, become the largest node for the commodity exchange in the entire traditional market, and also a key link for the successful realization of reproduction in the entire agricultural society. In Western classical political economics, François Quesnay (1694-1774) of the French Physiocratic School clearly expressed the importance of agriculture to reproduction through a schema of arithmetic and zigzag connecting lines – the "Tableau Économique" (*Economic Table*). Although agriculture and the circulation of its products were placed at the core in the "Tableau Économique", and Quesnay believed that "a kingdom ought, above all things, to be well flocked with husbandmen",[4]no reasonable place was given to the "uncertainty" of agricultural production. Grain, when it becomes a commodity for exchange, often has a greater elasticity in supply than in demand, making it difficult for prices to converge. (In mathematics, convergence requires that the absolute value meets the condition: (Qd2-Qd1) / (Pd2-Pd1) > (Qs2-Qs1) / (Ps2-Ps1)). The market risks for the grain and their artificial amplification (e.g. commercial manipulation and speculation) are often closely linked to the conditions of production – climate fluctuations, the largest uncertainty factor. Therefore, grain prices are decided by various unstable factors. However, grain is the most important production and living material in traditional agricultural societies. The production, exchange, distribution, and consumption of grain occupy a dominant position in the economic system, making the balance of supply and demand and price stability extremely important for the entire system. Based on this judgment, the "Sunspot Theory"

Food, if becomes an exchange commodity, its supply elasticity will often be greater than that of demand, and the price is not easy to converge. (Convergence mathematically requires absolute values to satisfy conditions: (Qd2-Qd1)/(Pd2-Pd1) > (Qs2-Qs1)/(Ps2-Ps1)). This market risk and its artificial amplification (commercial manipulation and speculation) are often closely linked to the greatest uncertainty of production conditions—climate fluctuations, so food prices are influenced by multiple volatility factors. However, food is the most important means of production and subsistence in traditional agricultural society. With its production, exchange, distribution and consumption of grain dominant in the economic system, the supply-demand relationship and price stability of food are extremely important for the whole system. Judging from this, the "sunspot theory" proposed by William Stanley Jevons and his son H. Stanley Jevons – that cyclical behavior of sunspots causes

[4] Mirabeau, Victor de Riquetti, marquis de. 1968. *François Quesnay: The Economic Table, an Attempt towards Ascertaining and Exhibiting the Source, Progress, and Employment of Riches with Explanations*. New York: Bergman Publishers. p. 91.

changes in climate and agricultural output and therefore general economic activity, hence cyclical economic fluctuations[5] – is really reasonable.

Therefore, whether it is a year of bumper harvest with ample supply leading to a significant drop in grain prices, or a year of poor harvest with supply shortages causing a significant rise in grain prices, both scenarios will bring varying degrees of risk to market exchange. This not only hinders the reproduction of the small-scale peasant economy, but can also further spreads and affects other industries and even the macro economy. In this light, the grain buffer purchasing and selling mechanism performs a special leverage function. The Chinese classic work *Guanzi* had a profound understanding of this point and was the first to systematically explain it with the "light and heavy principles". Chen Longzheng, a Chinese scholar in the Ming dynasty, inherited this important theory and elaborated on it in the context of the Ever-normal Granary (*changping cang*):

> The Ever-normal Granary doesn't simply stabilize grain prices; when grain prices are stable, the prices of various foodstuffs and commodities also do not become excessively high... Therefore, the Ever-normal Granary also stabilizes the prices of all other goods... Only when the prices of grains are stable, do the prices of other goods naturally keep stable as well.[6]

In terms of policy, Dong Wei of the Southern Song dynasty inherited Li Kui's theory that the Ever-normal Granary should be implemented in all years from "year of best harvest" to "year of great failure", making buffering grain trade a regulating tool even in "every year":

> With the Ever-normal Granary, the government purchased grain every year, and also sold grain every year. In a year of best harvest the government then purchased three parts of the harvest, leaving one part for use of the people. In a year of medial harvest the government then bought two parts, while in a year of good harvest it bought one part (that is, one half). This is the way the government purchased grain every year. In a year of first degree failure the government then put on sale grain which had been bought in a year of good harvest; in a year of second degree failure it then put on sale grain which had been bought in a year of medial harvest; and in a year of great failure it then put on sale grain which had been bought in a year of best harvest. This is the way the government sold grain every year.[7]

Recent studies have quantitatively analyzed the corresponding relationship between climate change and socio-economic changes in Chinese history, pointing out that agricultural abundance or scarcity is an important background and foundation that leads climate change into the depth, affecting the prosperity or decline of the economy and society. However, the researchers specifically noted that such impact is

---

[5] Jevons, W. S. 1981. Papers on Political Economy.in *Papers and Correspondence of William Stanley Jevons,* vol. 7.ed. R. D. Collison Black. London: Macmillan.

[6] Chen, Longzheng. 2010. *The Strategies of Famine Relief,* vol. 4. ed. Xia, Mingfang. in *Collections of Chinese Books on Famine Administration,* vol. 1. ed. Li, Wenhai, et al. Tianjin: Tianjin Ancient Books Publishing House. p. 459.

[7] Swann, Nancy Lee. (trans.) 1950. *Food and Money in Ancient China: The Earliest Economic History of China to A.D. 25, Han Shu 24, with Related Texts, Han Shu 91 and Shih-Chi 129.* Princeton: Princeton University Press. pp. 142-143.

often based on the premise of failure of various regulations. If a state has strong regulatory capabilities, even if the climate has an adverse effect on agriculture, the economy and society may still develop in a favorable way (as Dong Wei's words mentioned above, "with the Ever-normal Granary, the government purchased grain every year, and also sold grain every year". This is the essence of the governments' regulatory capabilities). During the reigns of emperors Kangxi and Qianlong, though the weather was generally colder than usual, better practiced this essence, it was a flourishing age in the history, which proves the above saying.[8] During the reigns of emperors Kangxi, Yongzheng, and Qianlong, the Ever-normal Granary, based on the achievements of previous dynasties, continued to develop and mature. It not only confirmed the aforementioned research results, but also further proved that the buffer purchasing and selling mechanism can play the role of firewall in preventing or reducing the malignant transmission effects brought about by climate changes. Throughout history, whenever state capacity allowed, establishing a grain buffer adjustment mechanism and releasing stabilizing forces that reduce fluctuations and maintain balance in the economic system became an inevitable policy choice. The efforts of successive dynasties in this regard confirmed the insight in the book *Guanzi*: "If the prince is able to maintain a proper balance in the relative values of grain, coinage, and gold, the empire can be rendered stable. Such is the method for preserving the empire.[9]"

It should also be noted that, since grain occupied a considerable share in the ancient Chinese state taxation, grain can be regarded as a special type of "currency" that could be widely accepted. Liang Qichao (1873–1929), the famous scholar, philosopher and reformist, stated in his work "Biography of Guanzi" (*Guanzi zhuan*) that grain "contains two natures: one being the nature of a common consumer product, the other the nature of currency." Therefore, when grain serves as a special currency or asset, "its price often influences the prices of other items."[10] This means that the purchasing and selling mechanism of the Ever-normal Granary could perform the function of stabilizing interest rates: the Ever-normal Granary acts like a central bank during seasonal fluctuations or years of abundance or scarcity, by buying and selling grain (expanding or contracting the currency supply) to regulate the "grain currency" supply in the economic system, thereby stabilizing the interest rate and restraining usurious lending. Liang Qichao's understanding goes further than that of Chen Longzheng. The Ever-normal Granary actually plays the dual roles for"fiscal policy" and "monetary policy".

The fundamental purpose for establishment of Ever-normal Granary is to stabilize the economy and society and ensure the smooth progress of reproduction. Compared to years of bumper harvest, years of poor harvest had much greater

---

[8] Fang, Xiuqi et al. 2019. *The Impact of Historical Climate Change on China's Society and Economy.* Beijing: China Science Publishing and Media Ltd. p.206, p. 208.

[9] Guanzi. 1998. *Political, Economic, and Philosophical Essays from Early China*, vol. 2. trans. W. Allyn Rickett. Princeton: Princeton University Press. p.417.

[10] Liang, Qichao. 1989. Biography of Guanzi. *Thoughts from the Ice-Drinker's Studio*, vol. 28. Beijing: Zhonghua Book Company. pp. 59-60.

impact on agricultural reproduction and social stability. Under the conditions of traditional agricultural societies, material scarcity, especially food shortages, was a common problem in the society. In addition to *pingdi* (increased-price purchase) and *pingtiao* (reduced-price sales), and relief loans, relief aid gradually became a main task of the Ever-normal Granary operations. Therefore, although initially established only for *pingdi* (increased-price purchase) and *pingtiao* (reduced-price sales), by the Tang dynasty, the Ever-normal Granary had already incorporated all these three functions: purchasing and selling of grain, relief loans, and relief aid. Jia An (1022-1065), a statesman of the Northern Song dynasty, stated,

> The establishment of the Ever-normal Granary was primarily aimed at stabilizing grain prices to prevent the common people from suffering due to excessively high or low prices. Occasionally, in time of poor harvests and famines, opening the granaries for relief aid not only went against the original purposeinbuilding the granaries, but also resulted in expenses drawn from the official finance. Currently, the national finance is in difficulty and savings not abundant. There is indeed Ever-normal Granary in the state. However, in recent years, even slight floods or droughts would lead to people leaving their homes, starving to death, or even resorting to rebellion and becoming thieves, which clearly indicates that Ever-normal Granary is really incapable to cope with disasters.[11]

Jia An pointed out the overwhelming burden of the Ever-normal Granary. But in face with the plight of the displaced and the starving, the granary could not but participate in relief efforts. As such, it was impossible for the Ever-normal Granary to rely solely on the theoretical cycle of *pingdi* (increased-price purchase) and *pingtiao* (reduced-price sales) for its long-term maintenance. The actual sources of grain for the Ever-normal Granary were not limited to what was purchased through *pingdi* (increased-price purchase), but also included donations from the public, the government's regular purchases, and allocations from the grain transport system. This placed high demands on the government, as only continuous financial support to ensure sufficient capital and ample storage could buffer the impact of supply shocks as much as possible during years of minor to major shortages, allowing the economy and society to navigate through difficult times more smoothly. However, this was precisely a problem that had plagued rulers throughout the dynasties.

During the Northern Song dynasty, Wang Anshi introduced the Green Sprouts Act to address this issue, hoping to maintain the Ever-normal Granary's normal operation through interest-bearing loan. The loan function of the Ever-normal Granary had appeared at least by the Tang dynasty. However, the policy of borrowing grain and repaying with grain was more in line with the characteristics of the small-scale peasant economy and could meet the needs of peasants better than the policy of borrowing money and repaying with money in the Green Sprouts Act. More importantly, the practice of earning profits through agricultural loans to support the granaries (granaries supported by granaries) deviated from the original goal of the Ever-normal Granary of supporting the people with granaries. Consequently, the Green Sprouts Act was inevitably doomed to failure.

[11] Li, Tao.2004. *Supplement to Historical Mirror to Aid in Government*, vol. 175. Beijing: Zhonghua Book Company. p. 4243.

Over the course of history, the Ever-normal Granary system originated in the pre-Qin period, reached its initial stage during the Han dynasty, and saw further development with establishment of rules and regulations during the Tang dynasty. During the period, the Ever-normal Granary not only gradually developed into a systematic institution but also expanded significantly in scale. The Ever-normal Granary "became a fixed system in the Song dynasty"[12], with the "Ever-normal Granary applied throughout the state"[13]. Although the reform of the Ever-normal Granary system with Green Sprouts Act ended in failure, it provided important lessons for future generations. Zhu Xi of the Southern Song dynasty developed the community granary system based on the review of the Green Sprouts Act, which filled the gap at the grassroots level and benefited more farmers. Learning from the experiences of previous dynasties, the Ming dynasty integrated the methods of Ever-normal Granary and community granary to develop its unique preparedness granary. Carried through to the Qing dynasty, the Ever-normal Granary system reached maturity and completeness, with its capability to intervene and regulate the economy reaching unprecedented levels in the mid-Qing dynasty. According to statistical analysis by Liu Cuirong, in the 54th year (1789) of Emperor Qianlong's reign, the total storage of ever-normal granaries was sufficient for grain needs of the population in the entire state for 16.5 days. If the ever-normal granaries and community granaries were put together, their maximum stockpile could meet the needs of the national population for about half a month to 20 days. Although this does not meet the standards of a modern country, the achievement is still significant for a traditional society, which should not be neglected.[14]

3.2 Developing from Grain Storage to Labor Storage

Qiu Jun (1421-1495), a scholar, politician and economist in the Ming dynasty, expanded the design of the Ever-normal Granary system since the Western Han dynasty. Hu Jichuang summarized Qiu's contributions into five main points: first, the expansion of the category of grains for purchase and sale; second, the flexibility of the ever-normal granaries to adjust and allocate grains among different regions; third, allowing the common people to exchange goods, in addition to money, for

[12] Jiang, Pu. 1986. Rites of Zhou. *Explanations to the Classics and Histories for Imperial Review*, vol. 25. in *Complete Library in the Four Branches of Literature (Wenyuange Edition)*, *Zi* section, vol. 723. Taibei: Commercial Press of Taiwan. p. 620.

[13] Dong Wei stated, "The Ever-normal Granary was mainly implemented in the northern regions, and it still failed to reach the lower reaches of the Yangtze River in the Tang dynasty. In the present Song dynasty, it is implemented throughout the state, surpassing those in Han and Tang dynasties." See: Dong, Wei. 2018. *A Book on Relieving Famine and Reviving the People*, vol. 1. Beijing: China Bookstore. p. 32.

[14] Liu, Cuirong. 2005. Review of the stability function of the Qing dynasty warehousing system. in *Economic Pulse*. ed. Chen, Guodong et al. Beijing: Encyclopedia of China Publishing House. pp. 340-341.

grains from the ever-normal granaries; fourth, the Ever-normal Granary institutions should also engage in the trade of various commodities; fifth, adopting different management approaches according to local conditions.[15] In fact, the Ever-normal Granary system had already performed various functions during the Song dynasty – it was not only used for its original purpose of grain storage but also extended to new welfare activities such as constructing water conservancy projects, building fortresses, suppressing thieves, assisting child-rearing, and caring for beggars.[16] Although the economic system in traditional agricultural society was much less complex than that in modern society, economic regulation was still a systematic project, and the Ever-normal Granary alone could not bear the entire responsibility of economic stability. Therefore, the widespread application of this mechanism, whether to supplement and strengthen the functions of the Ever-normal Granary or to expand into new areas of ever-normal regulation, led to the development of a policy system that could be called the "Ever-normal Granary in broad sense" in the historical exploration and practice.

3.2.1 Ever-Normal Granary in Broad Sense: Ever-normal Granary System

In traditional Chinese agricultural society, there was a vast granary system. As the granary system matured during the Tang and Song dynasties, its main components were functionally divided into following categories: the "official granary system"(*zhengcang xitong*) that supported national administration, like funding official salaries, through central and local reserves; the "military granary system" (*juncang xitong*) that supported national defense and military preparedness, which was strategically distributed across various regions; the "turnover granary system" (*zhouzhuancang xitong*) that was established at key transportation hubs and strategic locations, responsible for grain distribution among different types of granaries across various regions, including the "canal granaries" established along the water transport routes; and the "Ever-normal Granary system" that was aimed at stabilizing grain supply and demand, controlling grain prices, and ensuring economic and social stability within the state.

When examining the Ever-normal Granary within the larger granary system, we should pay attention to two key points. Firstly, the subsystems within the larger system were not mutually exclusive or isolated. Instead granaries in different subsystems could join the Ever-normal Granary system when necessary to fulfill its function of stabilizing grain prices. During the Tang dynasty, for instance, the

[15] Hu, Jichuang. 1998. *History of Chinese Economic Thought*, vol. 2. Shanghai: Shanghai University of Finance and Economics Press. p.365.

[16] Kong, Xiangjun. 2009. Research on Ever-normal Granary in the Two Song Dynasties. *Journal of Nanjing Agricultural University (Social Sciences)*. 9(4):102-108.

"official granary system", including the central "imperial granary" (*taicang*), and the "military granary system" participated in "*hedi*" (grain requisition)[17]; the "official granary system", "military granary system", and "turnover granary system" were involved in *pingtiao* (reduced-price sales); and the "official granary system" along with the "turnover granary system" participated in relief loans.[18] The transformation of different specialized granary systems into ever-normal granaries, or the coordination and mutual assistance among ever-normal granaries in different regions, was a common phenomenon even after the Tang dynasty.[19]

The second point, which is more important and requires detailed discussion, concerns the emergence of a variety of granary types within subsystems of the Ever-normal Granary system, which primarily played the role of stabilization and regulation. During the Northern Song dynasty, there were increasing types of granaries that performed the functions of adjustment and stability. In addition to the ever-normal granaries, the main national granaries included the public benefit granaries (*huimin cang*), public welfare granaries (*guanghui cang*), and charity granaries (*yicang*). Initially, the ever-normal granaries were primarily responsible for reduced-price sales (*pingtiao*), supplemented by the public welfare granaries (*guanghui cang*) (hence, the two were also referred to collectively as the "ever-normal public welfare granaries"). The charity granaries (*yicang*) were in charge of relief loans and relief aid, while the public benefit granaries (*huimin cang*) were responsible for poverty relief. In subsequent developments, most granary types assumed additional functions.[20] In the Southern Song dynasty, national granaries included the ever-normal granaries, public welfare granaries (*guanghui cang*), public benefit granaries (*huimin cang*), abundant storage granaries (*fengchu cang*), and charity granaries (*yicang*). Their functions often overlapped, with the public welfare granaries (*guanghui cang*), public benefit granaries (*huimin cang*), abundant storage granaries (*fengchu cang*), and charity granaries (*yicang*) all incorporating the ever-normal function by "buying high and selling low".[21]As was analyzed in the previous chapter,

[17] *hedi*, similar to *pingdi*, was a method of grain procurement in ancient China, where the government would purchase or exchange grain from farmers using negotiated prices or other goods. It was also an important economic policy for dynasties to increase grain purchases and replenish reserves beyond the collection of land taxes. This policy played a positive role in vitalizing grain circulation and adjusting surpluses and shortages under the conditions of a natural economy. For more information, please see: Geng, Hu. 2002. Further exploration of the relationship between *hedi* and *pingdi*. *Journal of Chinese Social and Economic History*. (2): 48-56.

[18] Zhang, Gong. 1986. *A Preliminary Study of Granary System in the Tang Dynasty*. Beijing: Zhonghua Book Company. pp. 148-150.

[19] Of course, there are also cases where ever-normal granaries support other granary systems, and a typical example is that Ever-normal Granary allocate military supplies to support military granary.

[20] Zhang, Wen. 2001. *Study of Social Relief in the Song Dynasty*. Chongqing: Southwest Normal University Press, pp. 57-58.

[21] Li, Huarui. 2012. The development and changes of the disaster relief storage system in the Song dynasty. in *Jinan Historical Science*. vol. 7. ed. Ma, Mingda. Guilin: Guangxi Normal University Press. p. 518, pp. 521-522.

community granaries (*shecang*) played the role of ever-normal granaries at the grassroots level in practical applications. Besides community granaries, in the Southern Song dynasty there were a variety of locally operated granaries that performed the functions of economic regulation and relief. According to Zhang Wen's summary, there were over twenty types of such granaries, including Purchase and Storage Granary (*dina cang*, Changzhou), Extensive Relief Granary (*guangji cang*, Jiankangfu), Prosperous Origin Granary (*fengben cang*, Fuyang County), Aid Sale Granary (*zhentiao cang*, Jianyang County), Comprehensive Relief Granary (*jianji cang*, Xinzhou), Regional Relief Granary (*zhouji cang*, Yuanzhou), Circular and Comprehensive Relief Granary (*xunhuan tongji cang*, Kuizhou), Relief Sale Granary (*jitiao cang*, Taizhou), Fair Purchase Granary (*pingdi cang*, Jiankangfu), Regional Storage Granary (*zhouchu cang*, Yuanzhou), Resolution and Stabilization Granary (*pingzhi cang*, Jiankangfu), Advanced Preparation Granary (*xianbei cang*, Guiyangjun), Equal Benefit Granary (*junhui cang*, Yongzhou), Continuous Benefit Granary (*xuhui cang*, Yongzhou), Thorough Relief Granary (*tongji cang*, Huangyi County), Fair Sale Granary (*pingtiao cang*, Puyang County), Equal Relief Granary (*junji cang*, Tingzhou), Balance and Equality Granary/Actual Preparation Granary (*duanping cang/shi bei cang*, Huizhou), Equal Sale Granary (*juntiao cang*, Yanping), Frugal Love Granary (*jie'ai cang*, Guiyangjun), Universal Benefit Granary (*tonghui cang*, Guiyangjun), Stablizing Relief Granary (*pingji cang*, Xiangxiang County).[22] With this as the basis, Li Huarui added some other types of granaries, such as Stump Granary (*zhuangji cang*), Assistance Relief Granary (*zhuji cang*), and Fair Price Granary (*pingjia cang*).[23] It is reasonable to imagine that there were even more similar granaries in the history of the Southern Song dynasty. They almost uniformly performed the functions of the ever-normal granaries, either due to limited reserves and declining functions of the ever-normal granaries, or because the ever-normal granaries could not reach the vast rural areas, or to avoid the various defects of the ever-normal granaries. They cooperatively created a system that merged with the ever-normal granaries in both organization and function.[24]

From the perspective of hierarchical distribution, various national granaries, including the ever-normal granaries, were set up from top to bottom, but they extended at most to the county level; local granaries, including the community granary (*shecang*), were established from bottom to top, at the levels of both counties and townships.[25] This indicates that the grain buffer reserves, with efforts from both

---

[22] Zhang, Wen. 2001. *Study of Social Relief in the Song Dynasty.* Chongqing: Southwest Normal University Press, pp. 73-76.

[23] Li, Huarui. 2012. The development and changes of the disaster relief storage system in the Song dynasty. in *Jinan Historical Science*.vol. 7. ed. Ma, Mingda. Guilin: Guangxi Normal University Press. p.520.

[24] Li, Huarui. 2012. The development and changes of the disaster relief storage system in the Song dynasty. in *Jinan Historical Science*.vol. 7. ed. Ma, Mingda. Guilin: Guangxi Normal University Press. pp. 522-523.

[25] Zhang, Wen. 2001. *Study of Social Relief in the Song Dynasty.* Chongqing: Southwest Normal University Press, p. 81.

central and local governments, achieved full coverage from top cities to grassroots villages and communities at least in terms of institutional arrangements. Li Huarui quoted the words of a scholar in Qing dynasty that "Ever-normal Granary was firstly initiated by Geng Shouchang, and became a fixed system in the Song dynasty", and pointed out that if this view merely mean the widespread establishment of ever-normal granaries, it is not entirely accurate. However, if the viewrefers to the widespread promotion of the "ever-normal" function of granaries, then it is indeed correct say that Ever-normal Granary "became a fixed system in the Song dynasty". [26]

The preparedness granary (*yubei cang*) was a distinctive type of "Ever-normal Granary" in the Ming dynasty. In the mid-to-late Ming dynasty, facing the challenges of various defects of preparedness granary, empty granaries, and diminishing functions, advices to re-establish ever-normal granaries, community granaries (*shecang*), and charity granaries (*yicang*) were frequently proposed. "In the eighth year (1529) of Emperor Jiajing's reign, due to consecutive years of famine, there were numerous proposals and suggestions for establishment of charity granary (*yicang*) and community granary (*shecang*)."[27] However, due to the state's financial limits, ever-normal granaries, community granaries (*shecang*), and charity granaries (*yicang*) were restored to varying degrees based on actual conditions, to fill the gaps brought by the insufficiency of preparedness granary. Consequently, in the mid-to-late Ming dynasty, there was the phenomenon that four types of granaries coexisted with each other. Among them, the preparedness granary (*yubei cang*) and Ever-normal Granary were operated by the government, while the community granaries (*shecang*) and charity granaries (*yicang*) were constructed and operated by the local people under government initiative. Additionally, in the Jiangnan region (south of the middle and lower reaches of the Yangtze River), the aiding-peasants granary (*jinong cang*), which had distinct regional characteristics, emerged. The aiding-peasants granary (*jinong cang*) was created by Zhou Chen, the governor of Jiangnan, during the Xuande period, to regulate and stabilize the regional economy. Later, in its development and evolution, it gradually merged with the preparedness granary (*yubei cang*), therefore it could be renamed as the preparedness granary or given the alternative name of preparedness aiding-peasants granary (*yubei jinong cang*).[28]

The rulers of the Qing dynasty, while strengthening the construction of the state-run ever-normal granaries, attached more emphasis on granaries at the grassroots level. According to the layout of the granaries during the Kangxi period, ever-normal granaries were established in prefectures or counties (*zhou* or *xian*), with "community granaries (*shecang*) established in rural areas, and public welfare

[26] Li, Huarui. 2012. The development and changes of the disaster relief storage system in the Song dynasty. in *Jinan Historical Science*.vol. 7. ed. Ma, Mingda. Guilin: Guangxi Normal University Press. p.523.

[27] Shen, Defu. 1959. Ministry of Revenue. in *Anecdotes and Unofficial Stories during Emperor Wanli's Reign*, vol. 12. Beijing: Zhonghua Book Company. p.318.

[28] Cui, Yun. 2004. On the storage system for famine relief in the Ming dynasty. *The Northern Forum*. (5): 81-83.

granaries (*yicang*) established in urban areas"[29]. Due to the fact that a vast majority of the population resided in rural areas, "nothing is more convenient for the people than the community granary"[30]. The construction of community granaries received attention earlier than that of charity granaries. During the reigns of Kangxi and Yongzheng, community granaries were cautiously and gradually established, adapting to local conditions. They were piloted in specific areas before being widely promoted, laying the solid foundation for their extensive implementation during the Qianlong period.[31] By the middle of Qianlong period, community granaries were universally established in the state, developing a considerable scale of reserves (see Table 3.1), and effectively filling the geographical gaps of the ever-normal granaries.

The community granary (*shecang*) was mainly initiated and subsidized by the state. Donations from local residents, self-management by the local people, and moderate and reasonable supervision by the state were the guarantees for the healthy operation of community granary. However, if they are included in the government's registration and assessment system, all management decisions had to be submitted for approval, hence the increase of intervention from the state. In this situation, the significance of charity granary (*yicang*) was apparent. In the 13th year of Qianlong period, Fang Guancheng, the Governor General of Zhili province, stated, "Previously, the community grain (*shegu*, the grain stored in community granaries) was managed by the local people. Since it was included in the official accounts for reporting and verification, the common people regarded it as belonging to the public granaries of the state, rather than to their own community granaries. Consequently, whether it was used in emergencies or for regular purposes, reporting to the government department was required...Now, the charity granaries (*yicang*) is establishment with the intention of supplementing the inadequacies of the ever-normal granaries and community granaries."[32] The typical form of charity granary (*yicang*) in the Qing dynasty was the charity granary of salt (*yan yicang*) established with the donation of salt merchants in Huainan and Huaibei during the Yongzheng period.[33] In the early period of Qianlong's reign, charity granary was systematically built in Zhili province under the guidance of Fang Guancheng. In the 18th year (1753) of Qianlong's reign, "the total amount of grain in the charity granaries reached 285,300

[29] Zhang, Tingyu et al. 2000. Grain purchase, III. *Comprehensive Textual Research of Historical Documents of Qing Dynasty*, vol. 34. Hangzhou: Zhejiang Ancient Books Publishing House. p. 5169. This arrangement is only an overall situation, and the geographical distribution of the two warehouses in some regions did not have such strict differentiation.

[30] Zhang, Tingyu et al. 2000. Grain purchase, IV. *Comprehensive Textual Research of Historical Documents of Qing Dynasty*, vol. 35. Hangzhou: Zhejiang Ancient Books Publishing House. p.5177.

[31] Bai, Liping. 2013. Emperor Kangxi and the construction of Community Granary: a case study of Zhili. *Social Sciences of Beijing*. (5): 42-46; Chang, Jianhua. 2018. A study of civilian-run granary in the period of Kangxi and Yongzheng. *Collected Papers of History Studies*. (1): 14-28.

[32] Fang, Guancheng. 2017. *Maps of the Charity Granaries in the Capital Area*. Baoding: Hebei University Press. pp. 34-35.

[33] Zhang, Yan. 1993. Charity granary of salt in the Qing dynasty. *Salt Industry History Research*. (3): 50-58.

Table 3.1 Reported provincial grain reserves in ever-normal granaries and community granaries in the 31st year (1766) of Emperor Qianlong's Reign

Province	Ever-normal Granary reserves (*shi*)	Community granary reserves (*shi*)	Community granary/ ever-normal Granary (%)	Province	Ever-normal Granary reserves (*shi*)	Community granary reserves (*shi*)	Community granary/ ever-normal Granary (%)
Zhili	1975275	396524	20%	Shandong	2563305	186048	7%
Fengtian	241618	93614	39%	Shanxi	2303263	579643	25%
Jiangsu	1271857	323751	25%	Shaanxi	2656610	620870	23%
Anhui	1235708	505285	43%	Gansu	1831711	31677	2%
Jiangxi	1341921	731768	55%	Sichuan	1856437	900518	49%
Zhejiang	407363	260481	70%	Guangdong	2901576	422471	15%
Fujian	2289718	492657	22%	Guangxi	1380121	258276	19%
Hubei	763579	654003	85%	Yunnan	844355	569896	67%
Hunan	1438349	532537	37%	Guizhou	881848	30912	4%
Henan	2391600	643110	27%	total	30576214	8234041	27%

Notes: Data of Zhili, Fengtian, Jiangxi, Zhejiang, Hubei, Hunan, Shanxi, Sichuan, Guangxi, and Guizhou are those of the 31st year (1766) of the Qianlong period; data of Jiangsu, Fujian, Henan, Shandong, Shaanxi, Guangdong, and Yunnan are those of the 30th year (1765) of the Qianlong period; data of Anhui is that of the 29th year (1764) of the Qianlong period; data of Gansu is that of the 28th year (1763) of the Qianlong period

Data source: Zhang, Tingyu et al. 2000. Grain purchase, VI. *Comprehensive Textual Research of Historical Documents of Qing Dynasty*, vol. 37. Hangzhou: Zhejiang Ancient Books Publishing House. pp. 5205-5206 *shi*" and "in the 39,687 villages of the state there were 1005 charity granaries."[34] During the reigns of Emperor Jiaqing (reigned 1796-1820) and Emperor Daoguang (reigned 1820-1850), with the decline of Ever-normal Granary and community granary, charity granary gained prominence and achieved significant development. In particular under the active promotion of Tao Shu, a surge in constructing the abundant store charity granary (*fengbei yicang*) emerged in the Jiangnan region (south of the middle and lower reaches of the Yangtze River) during the Daoguang period. In the late Qing dynasty, the scale of charity granary in regions like Jiangnan was much larger than in previous generations.[35] The word "charity" (*yi*) in the term "charity granary" (*yicang*) reflects the spirit of "public righteousness", which involves a communal love and preparation to offer help in times of need. Rich merchants and wealthy households were most active sponsors, and local gentry were mainly responsible for management of charity granaries, with relatively less intervention from the local government compared to the community granaries. During the Qing dynasty, community granary was mainly engaged in making seasonal loans, as well as providing relief aid and selling stored grains at reduced prices in bad years (*pingtiao*); community granaries were "close to the people", while charity granaries "accumulated grain to complement ever-normal granaries and community granaries"[36], creating a unified system that was "integrated near and far"[37]. In the Qing dynasty, the three types of granaries - Ever-normal Granary, community granary, and charity granary - complemented each other in space, time and function, thus forming an integrated whole.

In summary, Ever-normal Granary, which has undergone several generations of development and changes, should not be viewed in isolation. The logic of this evolving practice is roughly as follows: when the preferentially established Ever-normal Granary was limited in function or affected by various defects that hindered its effectiveness, various parties would seek solutions to the problem by increasing the types of granaries. Consequently, they were gradually layered and improved upon, leading to an Ever-normal Granary system that was interdependent, with government, market, and social resources complementing and interacting with each other. Within this system, the state was an important but not the sole constructor; the governance model involving various parties formed a layered structure of granaries as follows,

Stage 1: Ever-normal Granary1
Stage 2: Ever-normal Granary1+(Auxiliary) granary 2
Stage 3: [Ever-normal Granary1+(Auxiliary) granary 2]+(Auxiliary) granary 3

---

[34] Fang, Guancheng. 2017. A petition on establishment of charity granary. *Maps of the Charity Granaries in the Capital Area*. ed. Cui, Guangshe et al. Baoding: Hebei University Press. pp. 6-7.

[35] Wu, Siwu. 2018. *Institutional Dilemmas of Granary and Its Disaster Relief Practices in the Qing Dynasty*. Beijing: Social Sciences Academic Press. pp. 110-220.

[36] Liu, Jinzao. 2000. Grain purchase, V. *Sequel to Comprehensive Textual Research of Historical Documents of Qing Dynasty*, vol. 60. Hangzhou: Zhejiang Ancient Books Publishing House. p.8163.

[37] Zhang, Tingyu et al. 2000. Grain purchase, I. *Comprehensive Textual Research of Historical Documents of Qing Dynasty*, vol. 32. Hangzhou: Zhejiang Ancient Books Publishing House. p.5143.

Stage 4: {[Ever-normal Granary1 +(Auxiliary) granary 2]+(Auxiliary) granary3}+ (Auxiliary) granary 4

This process seems to provide a good explanation for why, although some people in the past or at present have regarded community granaries and charity granaries as the same or similar storage systems, it is more common to distinguish between them.[38] However, we must also recognize that although each type of granary differs in terms of the source of funds, management mode and location, and each type might lay particular stress on donations, *pingdi* (increased-price purchase), *pingtiao* (reduced-price sales), relief loans, or relief aid in economic regulation, overall each type of granary attempts to fully mobilize the forces of all parties to participate in the stabilizing mechanism for grain purchase and sale. In fact, donations, relief loans, and relief aid were all aimed at stabilizing the supply and demand and grain prices, and could be seen as extensions of *pingdi* (increased-price purchase) and *pingtiao* (reduced-price sales), all of which can be included in the mechanism of grain purchase and sale in broad sense —"collecting when there is surplus, and distributing when there is shortage". Therefore, the every-normal granaries and other granary types with economic regulation functions should not be artificially separated; each granary system was designed to maintain the sustainable economic and social development. It is a more comprehensive and objective understanding to view various granaries as part of an Ever-normal Granary system with broad coverage, instead of being overly concerned with the specific type of reserve or granary. As was stated by Lu Zengyu, a literati and statesman in the Qing dynasty, "Thus, when every village has reserves and everywhere has granaries, the people will be prosperous, and there will be no urgent worries about floods or droughts."[39]

If the pattern of overlapping and complementary distribution of various grain reserves could be maintained for a long time, the traditional agricultural society in China could weave a "regularly balanced network of granaries" with an appropriate density. This network would optimize allocation and strengthen regulation in both time and space. In the early years of Emperor Qianlong's reign in the Qing dynasty, Yan Sisheng (1682-1752), a literati and statesman, while promoting community granaries (*shecang*), intended to establish a network system where community granaries and *Baojia* system (an traditional administrative system organized on basis of households for mutual surveillance in ancient China) complemented each other. He believed that "community granaries and *Baojia* system have interrelated principles and a tendency to overlap. Between them, one serves as the longitude line and the other latitude line, thus the two would develop at a considerable scale." However, Yan Sisheng also considered that such an ideal plan "was very difficult to achieve all at once, but seemingly easy to try out in a simplified manner". Therefore, he

[38] Wu, Siwu. 2018. Differentiation of the concepts of charity granary and community granary. *Collected Essays on Qing History*. (2): 290.

[39] Lu, Zengyu. Six strategies after thedisaster. *Imperially Authorized Compendium of Disaster Relief*, vol. 4. ed. Zhao, Li and Xu Na. in *Collections of Chinese Books on Famine Administration*, vol. 3. ed. Li, Wenhai, et al. Tianjin: Tianjin Ancient Books Publishing House. p. 1859.

suggested building the network with one granary for every fourfortified villages (*bao*) as a node. "The granary of the four *bao* (fortified villages) would be managed in turn by the heads of *Baojia* system, with joint and mutual inspections. Then the accounts would be settled annually, making it particularly easy for heads of the villagesto fulfill their duties, and the accumulated issues would also be completely resolved."[40]

In Fang Guancheng's "Map of Charity Granaries in Capital Region" (*jifu yicang tu*) during Emperor Qianlong's reign, the "regularly balanced network of granaries" was presented more directly. According to Fang Guancheng's design, the various prefectures, counties, and military guards (*wei*) in Zhili province were divided into standardized administrative and topographical grids, with each unit covering five *li*[41]. Based on this, the charity granaries were planned according to the size of the regions and the number of villages, with one granary established every "ten *li*", "fifteen *li*", "twenty *li*", "twenty-five *li*", or "thirty *li*". Eventually, 1,005 charity granaries were established among the 39,687 villages in the Zhili province, storing over 285,300 *shi* of grain. Fang Guancheng managed the granaries by the map, and checked the grain reserves by the granary, fully implementing grid management in the grain reserve system.[42] Of course, this is only an ideal state that can be achieved in specific and special regions. Establishing a larger and more complex network of granary system nationwide requires adapting to local conditions and meeting various requirements such as manpower, funds, and materials, and it will encounter various difficulties and challenges to maintain such a state for the long time. Then it is necessary to find more approaches to further enrich and optimize the content and structure of the buffer grain reserves.

3.2.2 Ever-Normal Granary in Broad Sense: Equalization Policy

The term "*pingzhun*" (equalization) originally referred to the uniform dyeing of fabrics without any difference. As was documented in the "Weaving and Dyeing Bureau" in*General Historical Documents (wenxian tongkao*), "The position of *Pingzhun* Commander was established in the Qin dynasty". Ma Duanlin quoted Wei Zhao's annotation in *Discrimination and Explanation of Names* (*bian shi ming*), "The *Pingzhun* Commander is in charge of dyeing, which has a method of evenness and fairness, hence it is standardized and regulated."The Han dynasty inherited the

[40]Yan, Sisheng. 2004. On the interconnection between Community Granaries and Bao-Jia System. in *The Complete Works of Wei Yuan, vol.* 15. ed. Editing Committee of *The Complete Works of Wei Yuan*. in *Collected Essays on Statecraft of Qing Dynasty*, vol. 40. ed. He, Changling and Wei Yuan. Changsha: Yuelu Publishing House. pp. 286-287.

[41] *li*, a Chinese unit of length (= 1/2 kilometre).

[42] Fang, Guancheng. 2017. *Maps of the Charity Granaries in the Capital Area*. ed. Cui, Guangshe et al. Baoding: Hebei University Press.

system of Qin dynasty and expanded the concept of "*pingzhun*" to economic regulation, "including controlling prices and managing the dyeing".[43] During the reign of Emperor Wu of Han dynasty, Sang Hongyang implemented the "equalization policy" (*pingzhunfa*), which was an economic policy that went in glove with the "balanced-delivery law" (*junshu fa*)[44] by which the government controlled the purchase, transport and selling of selected products. "Discourses on Salt and Iron: Chapter on Fundamental Discussions" (*yantielun: benyi*) discusses both as follows:

> In former times the peers residing in the provinces sent in their respective products as tribute, but there was much confusion and trouble in transporting them and the goods were often of such poor quality that they were not worth the cost of transportation. For this reason transportation offices have been set up in each district to handle delivery and shipping and to facilitate the presentation of tribute from outlying areas. Therefore the system is called "equitable marketing (*junshu*)." Warehouses have been opened in the capital for the storing of goods, buying when prices are low and selling when they are high. Thereby the government suffers no loss and the merchants cannot speculate for profit. Therefore this is called the"balanced level" [stabilization] (*pingzhun*). [45]

The balanced-delivery law (*junshufa*) stipulates that the central government establishes transportation offices in various districts. The tribute that each district should submit is generally converted into local specialty products that are abundant and inexpensive locally, according to local market prices, and handed over to the transportation officials. These officials are responsible for transporting the goods to other areas with higher prices for sale. This approach not only reduces the difficulties of transporting tribute to the capital from various districts and laboring burdens of the people, but also prevents damage and spoilage of the tribute during transportation.

---

[43] Ma, Duanlin. Official positions, XI. *Comprehensive Textual Research of Historical Documents*. Beijing: Zhonghua Book Company. p.1682.

[44] The balanced-delivery law (*junshufa*) was a method to curb the prices of commodities delivered to the imperial household during the Northern Song period (960-1126) and to have a better control over the spending of tax revenue on the local level of administration. It was part of the reform politics of Wang Anshi (1021-1086). The law was introduced in 1069 and had been inspired by similar methods once proposed by Sang Hongyang (152-80 B.C.) during the Former Han period (206 B.C.-8 C.E.) and Liu Yan (716-780) during the Tang period (618-907). Commodities needed by the court and government institutions were to be purchased by the financial institutions in the six circuits of southeast China and the transport commissioners (*fayunshi*) responsible for tribute tea, salt, alum and liquors. For this purpose the central government treasury provided 500 strings of copper cash and ordered to prepare annually an amount of 3 million *shi* of rice. These amounts were flexible and geared to the financial situation of the central treasury. The commissioners bought articles at low prices wherever and whenever possible and stored them in government warehouses or transported them to places where prices were higher (*xi gui jiu jian, yong jin yi yuan*).In this way, government expenditure was not only lowered, but the supply of items needed was secured. Critics argued that Wang Anshi was carrying out a price war with merchants. Marxist historians, however, see in this measure an implementation of state monopoly capitalism (mainly because the state was able to sell the stored goods at higher prices, and thus profited from this business). Yet others interpret it a measure to levy the tax burden imposed on the population. See: "*junshufa*, balanced-delivery law", http://www.chinaknowledge.de/History/Terms/junshufa.html

[45] De Bary, William Theodore and Irene Bloom. eds. 1999. *Sources of Chinese Tradition (2nd ed.)*, vol. 1. New York: Columbia University Press. p.361.

At the same time, it also increases the state's fiscal revenue. After the implementation of the balanced-delivery law (*junshufa*), a portion of the goods purchased in various districts still needs to be transported to the capital for sale. Therefore, the central government could use the commodities at its disposal to regulate the supply and demand, as well as the prices of commodities.

In the first year (110 B.C.) of the Yuanfeng period, Sang Hongyang implemented the "equalization policy" (*pingzhunfa*) to regulate the flow of goods and stabilize the market in the capital. This not only prevented wealthy merchants from hoarding goods and manipulating the economy but also generated revenue. "All the institutions under the Ministry of Finance (*dasinong*) monopolized the goods of the state, selling when prices were high and buying when they were low. In this way, wealthy merchants and traders were unable to make large profits, and would revert to farming instead. As a result, there would be no phenomenon of sudden price fluctuations for all commodities."[46] In the Western Han dynasty (202-8 B.C.), the "equalization policy" (*pingzhunfa*) was an economic stability system that incorporated a variety of commodities into a buffer grain mechanism with purchase and sale. It can also be referred to as a "mixed Ever-normal Granary" or "diversified buffer reserve". During the Xin dynasty (9-23 A.D.) with Wangmang[47] as the emperor, the "*wujun*" reform[48] was implemented, which stipulated the regulated goods and their target prices. The price-controlling policy (*pingzhun*) was implemented in six major commercial cities across the country (Chang'an, Luoyang, Handan, Linzi, Yuan, and Chengdu), expanding the geographical scope of Sang Hongyang's "equalization policy" (*pingzhunfa*).[49] Due to various constraints, it is difficult to implement buffer regulation for important commodities in a vast area. Therefore, the equalization method was mainly applied in cities with convenient transportation and easy access to information, especially in urban commercial areas. For example, during the Tang

[46] Sima, Qian. 1982. Treatise on Price Stabilization. *Records of the Grand Historian*. Beijing: Zhonghua Book Company. p.1441.

[47] Wang Mang (45 B.C.- 23 A.D.) was the founder and the only emperor of the short-lived Chinese Xin dynasty. He was originally an official and consort kin of the Han dynasty and later seized the throne in 9 A.D. The Han dynasty was restored after his overthrow, and his rule marked the separation between the Western Han dynasty (before Xin) and Eastern Han dynasty (after Xin). During his reign, he abolished slavery and initiated a land redistribution program.

[48] A reform project of Wang Mang was the state monopoly on the production and merchandise on salt, iron, ferments, coins and ores and other "products of mountains and swamps" (*wujun liuguan*, "the five [markets, apart from *Chang'an*] to be [balanced] justly and the six [goods] to be controlled"). Instead of vending the monopoly of the production and sales of salt and iron to private entrepreneurs that, as tax farmers, took over the collection of levies on these products, the state should better directly control the merchandise of such products. The markets of Chang'an (today's *Xi'an, Shaanxi*), Luoyang (*Henan*), Handan (*Hebei*), Linzi (*Shandong)*, Wan (today's *Nanyang, Henan*), and Chengdu (*Sichuan*) were to be tightly controlled by the government so that merchants would not be able to establish monopolies and extort customers or farmers by exorbitant prices or usurious credits. The resistance of the merchant associations and of many local officials also led to the abortion of this reform.

[49] Ban, Gu. 1962. Treatise on Food and Money, II. *Book of Han*.vol. 24. Beijing: Zhonghua Book Company. pp. 1180-1181.

dynasty, Court of Imperial Treasury (*taifusi*) set up four "Equalization Bureau" (*pingzhunshu*) in the four commercial markets of Chang'an and Luoyang (i.e. Eastern Market and Western Market of Chang'an, Northern and Southern Market of Luoyang.)[50]

Until the middle Tang dynasty, "Liu Yan (715-780) applied the equalization policy (*pingzhunfa*) to transport the products of mountains and seas, excluding merchants' trade and controlling the prices of all goods. He often managed the surplus resources of the state to assist with military expenses.... In the mid-Tang Dynasty, when the state fell into decline and then revived, Liu Yan made meritorious contributions."[51] The information revealed by "controlling the prices of all goods" should be that Liu Yan greatly expanded the types of goods and the regions regulated by the equalization policy (*pingzhunfa*). For this purpose, Liu Yan established an informational network. "He recruited fast walkers at high prices from the various provinces and inspection institutes to the capital, setting up post stations at regular intervals." As a result, "the fluctuations in commodity prices throughout the empire, even in the most remote areas, could be known within four to five days. Therefore, the government was able to control the prices of grains and other commodities. The imperial court reaped substantial profits, while the people across the state were free from worries about excessively high or low prices."[52]

The history recorded the "ever-normal salt policy" (*changing yan*) implemented by Liu Yan was a special policy within the equalization policy (*pingzhunfa*). Liu Yan reformed the government's monopoly on salt, transforming it from a system of production and sales by the government to one of production by the government and sales by the merchants. This not only reduced the government's burden and the cost of salt but also improved the efficiency of transportation and sales.[53] In regions closer to salt production sites and where salt merchants were more active, the price of salt was regulated through competition among merchants. However, in regions far from the salt production areas, there was a phenomenon of "salt becoming expensive due to the absence of merchants". In response to this situation, Liu Yan implemented the "ever-normal salt policy" (*changing yan*), in which the government established salt reserves in these areas. If the price of salt rose too high, the salt selling agencies would "sell salt at reduced prices" to stabilize the market. "In regions like *Jiangnan* (south of the middle and lower reaches of the Yangtze River) and *Lingnan*[54], which are far from salt production areas, there were ever-normal salt

[50] Liu, Xu et al. ed. 1975. Treatise on official positions, III. *Old History of Tang Dynasty*, vol. 44. Beijing: Zhonghua Book Company. p. 1889.

[51] Ouyang, Xiu and Song Qi. 1975. Biography of Liu Yan. *New History of Tang Dynasty*, vol. 149. Beijing: Zhonghua Book Company. p.4806.

[52] Liu, Xu et al. ed. 1975. Biography of Liu Yan. *Old History of Tang Dynasty*, vol. 123. Beijing: Zhonghua Book Company. p. 3515.

[53] Ouyang, Xiu and Song Qi. 1975. Treatise on Food and Money, IV. *New History of Tang Dynasty*, vol. 54. Beijing: Zhonghua Book Company. p. 1378.

[54] *Lingnan*, lit. "South of the [Nanling] Mountains", is a geographic area referring to the lands in the south of the Nanling Mountains. The region covers the modern Chinese subdivisions of

reserves. Whenever merchants didn't come, the government would sell the salt to the people at reduced prices. Thus the government earned substantial profits, and the people didn't think the salt was expensive."[55]

In the reform promoted by Wang Anshi in the Northern Song dynasty, the market exchange law[56] could find its theoretical prototype in the chapter "Treasury" (*quanfu*) in *Rites of Zhou* (*zhouli*)[57], but fundamentally it was also an equalization (*pingzhun*) mechanism. This can be seen from the remarks of Wei Jizong, who first proposed the market exchange law (*shiyifa*), "It is advisable to set up a market exchange bureau (*shiyisi*) to stabilize the supply and demand....The bureau should keep watch on the high and low prices of market commodities. When prices are too low, it would slightly increase the purchase price to avoid harming merchants; when prices are too high, it would slightly reduce the selling price to avoid harming the people.[58] After the promulgation of the market exchange law, the imperial court set up the market exchange bureau (*shiyisi*) in Kaifang and 21 market exchange offices (*shiyiwu*) in other cities. The government purchased goods that were stranded in the market (to prevent large merchants from taking advantage of the opportunity to suppress prices and exploit), and then distributed them through methods such as extending credit and providing loans to merchants to stabilize the market and limit commercial monopolies. As was stted by Emperor Shenzong (reigned 1067-1085), "The royal court implements the market exchange law (*shiyifa*) to stabilize the prices of all commodities."[59] However, during the implementation of the policy, the government acquired goods at suppressed prices and then took advantage of the opportunity of extending credit and providing loans to merchants so as to charge

Guangdong, Guangxi, Hainan, Hong Kong & Macau and Northern Vietnam.

[55] Ouyang, Xiu and Song Qi. 1975. Treatise on Food and Money, IV. *New History of Tang Dynasty*, vol. 54. Beijing: Zhonghua Book Company. p. 1378.

[56] The market exchange law (*shiyifa*), also called the guild avoidance law (*mianshangfa*), targeted large trading companies and monopolies. A metropolitan market exchange bureau was set up in Kaifeng and 21 market exchange offices in other cities. They were headed by supervisors and office managers who dealt with merchants, merchant guilds, and brokerage houses. These institutions fixed prices for not only resident merchants but also itinerant traders. Surplus commodities were purchased by the government and stored for later sale at a lower price, disrupting price manipulation by merchant monopolies. Merchant guilds that cooperated with the market exchange bureau were allowed to sell goods to the government and buy commodities from government storehouses using money or credit at an interest rate of 10 percent for six months or 20 percent for a year. Small or mid-sized companies and groups of five merchants could provide guarantee with their assets for credit. After 1085, the market exchange bureau and offices became profit making institutions, and bought cheap goods and sold at higher prices. The system stayed in place until the end of the Northern Song dynasty in 1127.

[57] Yu, Jinghui. 2014. "Rites of Zhou dynasty: Treasurer of Taxes" and market exchange law in Xining years: An in-depth reading of the article and Wang Anshi's practical philosophy. *Journal of Capital Normal University*. 4: 23-33.

[58] Li, Tao.2004. *Supplement to Historical Mirror to Aid in Government*, vol. 231. Beijing: Zhonghua Book Company. p. 5622.

[59] Xu, Song. ed. 2014. Food and money XXXVII (31). *Draft for the Collected Statutes of Song Dynasty*. Shanghai: Shanghai Ancient Books Publishing House. p. 6822.

interest for profits. Thus the market exchange bureau (*shiyisi*) and market exchange office (*shiyiwu*) transformed into profit-making organizations, violating the principle of "buying high and selling low" to stabilize the market prices. As a result, the market exchange law (*shiyifa*) was abolished ten years later after its implementation. Of course, the original intention of the market exchange law (*shiyifa*) was to address the serious issue of private merchant monopolies in the cities in Song dynasty,[60] which is undeniable.

Generally speaking, the equalization policy (*pingzhunfa*) uses buffer grain purchase and sale mechanisms to regulate the relationship between "currency" and "commodities". It is noteworthy that in the Song dynasty, a type of equalization policy emerged that adjusted "currency" with "currency" in the monetary field, which is known as "equilibrium maintenance" (*chengti*)[61] in the currency realm. Qiu Jun (1421-1495), a scholar, politician and economist of the Ming dynasty, once summarized the main ideas on "equilibrium maintenance" (*chengti*) of Dai Zhi, a poet, scholar, and statesman of the Southern Song dynasty with following words, "The theory of *chengti* is similar to the so-called 'equalization' (*pingzhun*). With 'equalization' (*pingzhun*) the fluctuation of commodity prices are regulated with currency, while with *chengti* the circulation of paper money is adjusted with metal coins."[62] In the history, the concept of "equilibrium maintenance" (*chengti*) was predominantly discussed during the Southern Song dynasty, involving discussions of various monetary policies.[63] One important aspect, as Qiu Jun described, was the regulation of paper money circulation with metallic currency ("the circulation of paper money is adjusted with metal coins"). "Equilibrium maintenance" (*chengti*), as a whole, is a two-way regulation of the withdrawal and reissue of paper money. As was stated by Yang Guanqing, a poet and official of the Southern Song dynasty, "equilibrium maintenance" (*chengti*) had a similar working mechanism as purchase and sale of ever-normal granaries, "When the value of paper money is low, the

[60]There was a serious problem of private monopoly in the market of Song dynasty. See: Jiang, Xidong. 1996. Merchants' market monopoly and government's anti-monopoly measures in the Song dynasty. *Researches in Chinese Economic History*. (2): 32-41.

[61]The term "equilibrium maintenance" (*chengti*) refers to a policy implemented in the Southern Song dynasty to maintain or restore the purchasing power of paper money. This policy involved the government routinely repurchasing excess paper money from the market. Song officials recognized the importance of maintaining a balance between the supply and demand for means of exchange, which was crucial for people to continue accepting paper money as a valid medium of exchange. The main methods of "equilibrium maintenance" (*chengti*) included the following: redeeming depreciated paper money with metal coins, limiting the total amount of paper money issued, and stipulating a period for regular replacement. During the Southern Song dynasty, some people also referred to maintaining the normal circulation of copper coins as "equilibrium maintenance".

[62]Qiu, Jun. 2012. Copper and paper money, II. *Supplement to Great Learning*, vol. 27. ed. Jing, Liangnian. Shanghai: Shanghai Bookstore Publishing House. p. 241.

[63]Ye, Tan. 1990. A survey of theories on paper money in Song dynasty. *Researches in Chinese Economic History*. 4: 133-145; Zou, Jinwen and Huang Ailan. 2010. Monetary policies in ancient China: An exposition on adjusting paper money's value. *Journal of Central China Normal University*. (5): 56-61.

government uses metallic currency to purchase it, preventing it from being low for too long. When the value of paper money is high, the government distributes it to achieve the goal of 'equilibrium maintenance' (*chengti*), maintaining a stable market without the problem of some being too expensive and others too cheap."[64] However, during the Southern Song dynasty, there was an excessive issue of paper money, and "equilibrium maintenance" (*chengti*) was mainly adopted to withdraw paper money from circulation. Therefore, using metal coins to redeem paper money to stabilize its circulation and value was an important operation of "equilibrium maintenance" (*chengti*). However, this required a sufficient supply of metal coins as a reserve. Faced with the rampant issue of paper money, metallic currency was obviously "insufficient for the capital of granaries". In this situation, the imperial court of the Southern Song dynasty adopted "securities" with uneven and unstable value (such as tax-exemption certificates for Buddhist monks and nuns,[65] official decree, and certificates of monopolistic business) and commodities to "secretly assist the operation of *chengti*"[66]. This was similar to the use of bad coins or adulterated grain in increased-price purchase (*pingdi*) and reduced-price sales (*pingtiao*) in the ever-normal granaries. This would greatly reduce the "equalization" (*pingzhun*) effect of the ever-normal granaries. However, applying the concept of "equalization" (*pingzhun*) to monetary policy, both theoretically and practically, enriched the policy for regulating supply and demand in the history. It is worth noting that "equilibrium maintenance" (*chengti*) is quite similar to the open market operations of central

---

[64]Yang, Guanqing. 1986. Attaching importance of paper money, *keting leigao*. vol. 9. in *Complete Library in the Four Branches of Literature (Wenyuange Edition)*, *Ji* section, vol. 1165. Taibei: Commercial Press of Taiwan. p.500.

[65]Tax-exemption certificates for the Buddhist clergy (*dudie*) were used during the Tang (618-907) and Song (960-1279) periods. Monks and nuns, but also any owner of such a type of certificate was spared payment of the land tax or labour for the community (*yaoyi*). The Buddhist clergy was registered in special household registers (*senghu*) which were not used by the Ministry of Revenue (*hubu*). Tax exemption certificates were issued by the Ministry of Sacrifices (*cibu*), and were therefore also known by the name *cibudie*. State officials were allowed to purchase such certificates, thus profiting from the privilege of the clergy. The government deliberately allowed the trade with exemption certificates to profit from the revenue, which was particularly earmarked for military expenditure. In some cases, the government even allowed the extraordinary issuance of such certificates. During the Tianbao reign-period (742-755), for instance, the Counsellor-in-chief Yang Guozhong (700-756) dispatched Censor Cui Zhong to Taiyuan, where he sold tax extemption certificates and yielded more than 10,000 cash. In 1067, the transport commission (*zhuanyunsi*) of Shaanxi sold one thousand tax exemption certificates. The revenue was used for disaster relief. The Southern Song (1127-1279), in dire need for higher revenue to finance their military campaigns against the Jurchens, largely expanded the business of *dudie* certificates. The Ming dynasty (1368-1644) reorganized the system and demanded that purchasers travel to the capital and undergo a professional examination in religious matters. In this way, only educated monks and nuns would have the chance to obtain certificates. These were issued by two new institutions, namely the Central Buddhist Registry (*senglusi*) and the *Central Daoist Registry* (daolusi). The sales of clergy certificates was stopped in 1645, but was revived in 1736 on a small scale.

[66]Ye, Tan. 1990. A survey of theories on paper money in Song dynasty. *Researches in Chinese Economic History*. (4): 144-145.

banks,[67] and therefore it can be considered as one of the pioneers of modern financial systems.

3.2.3 Ever-Normal Granary in Broad Sense: Labor Relief

As was discussed in previous text, stabilizing grain supply and prices through the Ever-normal Granary system inherently implies keeping farmers on the land to sustain agricultural reproduction as much as possible. This is a most fundamental economic goal for a state striving to keep its people committed to their "primary occupation" and "content with farming". Extraordinary fluctuations in grain supply and prices can disrupt farmers' engagement in stable reproduction, leading them to scatter around in search of food and become unmanageable "vagrants". Economic disruptions in local areas would then spread to broader regions, triggering systemic crises such as banditry and uprisings and posing significant threats to national governance. Du You, a historian, financier and official in the Tang dynasty, succinctly sighed, "When people wander around, the nation is in peril!"[68] During the Southern Song dynasty, Dong Wei statedthat in the absence of government measures to limit land consolidation, the common people would be compelled to leave their homes and roam about in the face of floods and droughts: "With the collapse of the traditional land system and the widespread practice of land consolidation, there has been a significant increase in the number of poor and lower-class households, while middle-class families are unable even to fend for themselves. In the event of natural disasters such as floods or droughts, these families find themselves in dire straits with no means of support. They have no choice but to leave their homes and starve to death."[69] Dong Bing accepted the ancient saying that "preventing trivial matters is easy, but rescuing from a crisis is difficult."[70] He emphasized that once the displaced population reached a certain scale, it would be extremely difficult to control. He said, "Displaced people are like flowing water; it is easier to manage the source, but difficult to contain the flow."[71] Therefore, it is apparent that behind the release of grain from the ever-normal granaries during years of agricultural production fluctuations, especially during famine years, there is a deeper policy orientation: the

[67] Zou, Jinwen and Huang Ailan. 2010. Monetary policies in ancient China: An exposition on adjusting paper money's value. *Journal of Central China Normal University.* (5): 60.

[68] Du, You. 1988. Food and money, XII. *Comprehensive Institutions*, vol. 12. ed. Wang, Wenjin et al. Beijing: Zhonghua Book Company. p 296.

[69] Dong, Wei. 2018. *A Book on Relieving Famine and Reviving the People*, vol. 1. Beijing: China Bookstore. p. 52.

[70] Fan, Ye.1965. Biography of Huan Rong and Ding Hong. *The Book of the Later Han*, vol. 37. Beijing: Zhonghua Book Company. p. 1267.

[71] Dong, Wei. 2018. Caring for the displaced people. *A Book on Relieving Famine and Reviving the People*, vol. 2. Beijing: China Bookstore. p. 134.

government is striving to stabilize the labor force that is "directionless" and prone to abandon their homes and villages due to "unemployment".

"Act before events occur; Decision can prevent disorder."[72] These words encapsulates the proactive wisdom of traditional Chinese thinking on governance. Hence, we can consider "labor relief"[73] as a more profound "ever-normal" stability mechanism[74]. As is shown in Fig. 3.1 below, similar to the grain purchase and sale system, the impoverished people who have lost their livelihood or have no means to earn a living were recruited and gathered through public projects - special types of "ever-normal granaries, such as water conservancy facilities, municipal construction, transportation, and afforestation. This will create a relatively stable economic and social environment during famine years. When the economy recovers, the labor force is then released from this "granary" to return to farming or other productive activities. In the short term, labor relief can mitigate economic fluctuations caused by disasters; in the long run, the construction of public works (such as irrigation systems) helps prevent disasters and achieve long-term stability. Labor relief has the advantages of achieving multiple benefits with half the effort and addressing both symptoms and root causes. This is best described by Yang Jingren, a scholar and

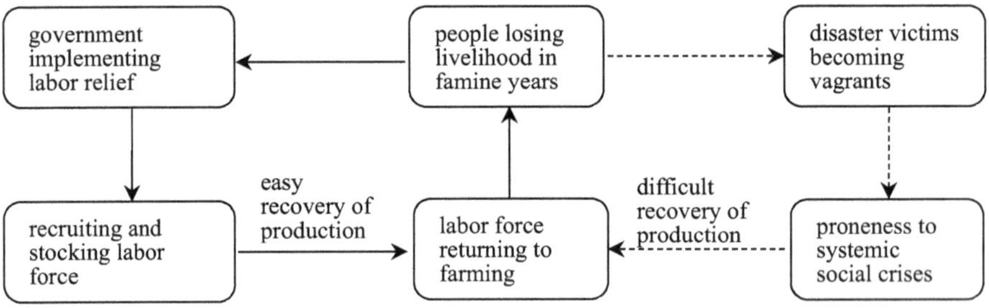

Fig. 3.1 Labor relief: ever-normal granary of labor force

[72] Laozi. 2001. *Dao De Jing: The Book of the Way*. trans. Moss Roberts. Berkeley, Los Angeles and London: University of California Press. p.158.

[73] "Labor relief", also known as "work relief", is a type of social assistance program where the government provides employment to individuals who are unemployed or underemployed, particularly during times of economic hardship such as recessions or disasters. Instead of giving direct financial aid or charity, the program offers jobs that are typically related to public works projects. These jobs help the unemployed to earn a wage, maintain their dignity, and contribute to the community while also stimulating the economy. Labor relief programs can include a variety of projects such as building infrastructure, maintaining public spaces, or engaging in other productive activities that benefit the public good. The goal is to provide immediate assistance to those in need while also creating long-term benefits for society.

[74] Guo Moruo and Yang Lien-sheng were among the earliest Chinese scholars who paid attention to labor relief. See: Guo, Moruo. 1954. A study of the chapter "on Extravagance in Spending". *Historical Research*. (3): 27-62; Yang, Lien-sheng. 1961. *Studies in Chinese Institutional History*. Cambridge: Harvard University Press. pp. 65-74.

official in the Qing dynasty, in his work "Compilations for Relief and Aid" (*chou ji bian*), "Dredging rivers and building dikes provide immediate benefits to alleviate the current famine, while the labor expended on these projects helps prevent future floods and droughts."[75]

"Among the famine relief policies, none are more crucial than initiating public works projects to gather the impoverished."[76] Labor relief, in essence, constructs a unique reserve with public works as the "granary" and "people" as the buffer objects, hence the Ever-normal Granary of labor force. It highlights a more proactive and efficient approach to economic assistance. Even tasks that "seem less urgent", such as "repairing temples and monasteries", can achieve the effect that "those who spend money do not incur wasteful expenses, and those who are employed do not have the shame of idleness."[77]

Compared to the Ever-normal Granary that is engaged in the storage and sale of important commodities, the Ever-normal Granary of labor force has a distinct characteristic: in the former, the commodities are stored in a static state, which incurs high maintenance costs and is subject to a certain percentage of loss and depreciation; however, the latter allows the "living" labor force in the "granary" to "increase in value". Studies show that during the Qing dynasty, labor relief projects enhanced the self-reliance ability and self-rescue consciousness of disaster victims. Many of the impoverished people collected lacked skills or craftsmanship, but the large-scale public works provided them with the opportunity to master skills and crafts that they previously had no chance to learn. This, in turn, improved their future labor and survival capabilities.[78]

"The key to governing a state lies in winning the support of its people."[79]Human beings are the most important element of production. As the Chinese classic *The Great Learning* (*daxue*) states, "With the support of the people, one can possess land; with land, one can accumulate wealth; and with wealth, one has enough for use." Zhu Xi made annotation as follows, "'With the support of the people' means gaining their support; 'with land' means ruling the state; by 'ruling the state' the king has no worry about wealth."[80] With people's support and land, there is state and wealth. The policy of "labor relief" prioritizes gathering and securing people, which

---

[75]Yang, Jingren. 2010. On construction. *Compilations for Relief and Aid*, vol. 13. ed. Hao, Bingjian. in *Collections of Chinese Books on Famine Administration, vol.* 5. ed. Li, Wenhai, et al. Tianjin: Tianjin Ancient Books Publishing House. p. 3197.

[76]Qing, Gui and Dong Gao et al. 1985. *Factual Record of Qing Dynasty: Records of Emperor Gaozong*, vol. 50. Beijing: Zhonghua Book Company. p. 850.

[77]Yang, Jingren. 2010. On construction. *Compilations for Relief and Aid*, vol. 13. ed. Hao, Bingjian. in *Collections of Chinese Books on Famine Administration, vol.* 5. ed. Li, Wenhai, et al. Tianjin: Tianjin Ancient Books Publishing House. p. 3197.

[78]Zhou, Qiong. 2011. Research on relief systems in the Qianlong period *Providing Jobs Instead of Reliefs. Journal of Tsinghua University (Philosophy and Social Sciences).* (4): 75-77.

[79]Ye, Shi. 2010. Civilian affairs. *The Collected Works of Ye Shi*, vol. 2. in *The Collected Works of Ye Shi*. ed. Liu Gongchun et al. Beijing: Zhonghua Book Company. p. 653.

[80]Zhu, Xi. 2016. *Collected Commentaries on the Four Books*. Beijing: Zhonghua Book Company. p.11.

aligns with the people-centric philosophy. The concept of "labor relief" first appeared in the Chinese classic work *The Spring and Autumn Annals of Master Yan* (*yanzi chunqiu*)[81] and was further elaborated in *Guanzi*.[82] During the Xin dynasty ruled by Wangmang, a large-scale discussion on managing Yellow River floods involved the labor relief policy, but it was not actually implemented. The earliest historical record of labor relief occurred during the Zhenguan period (785-805) of the Tang dynasty, when Zheng Yi, a subordinate of Pei Zhou, the military governor (*jiedushi*) of Jingnan, suggested labor relief for famine relief, which was accepted and implemented.[83] A large-scale labor relief practices was observed starting from the Northern Song dynasty. According to Shen Kuo's work *Brush Talks from Dream Brook* (*mengxi bitan*), "in the second year[84] of Huangyou period of the reign of Renzong, a serious famine prevailed in Wuzhong.... At that time, Fan Zhongyan was governing the west part of Liangzhe region..He took different measures to cope with famine such as distributing food to the poor and advising rich people to donate food to the needed....He also gathered the abbots of the Buddhist temples and told them, 'In the year of famine, construction workers can be hired at very low expenditure. You should take this opportunity to build more temples.' Therefore many new temples were under construction. He also rebuilt food warehouses and officials' residences, hiring over one thousand people every day. The chief prosecutor reported to the emperor that Fan Zhongyan, chief administrator in Hangzhou, neglected administrative affairs and went in for amusement excessively. He also accused Fan of launching a lot of construction projects draining the wealth of local people. Fan wrote a report to the emperor, listing reasons of holding banquets and starting construction projects. He said that he intended to make use of extra wealth to provide relief to the poor. Every day there were at least tens of thousand people

---

[81] "In the time of Lord Jing there was a famine. Master Yan asked permission to give grain to the people but his lordship refused. Instead Master Yan constructed the Luqin Tower. Master Yan ordered the officials in charge to double the salaries of the workmen and to make the whole thing as large as possible, while setting an extremely generous deadline with no suggestion that they needed to press on with the construction. Three years later the tower was finished and the people had recovered; thus the ruler was delighted with his new travelling palace and the people had enough to eat." See: Milburn, Olivia. (trans.) 2016.*The Spring and Autumn Annals of Master Yan*. Leiden and Boston: Brill. p.313.

[82] Guanzi once stated, "rather than giving them food, it is better to avoid taking them away from production." See: Guanzi. 1998. *Political, Economic, and Philosophical Essays from Early China*, vol. 2. trans. W. Allyn Rickett. Princeton: Princeton University Press. p. 327. Guanzi also commented, "Then, if there is a year of severe droughts or floods and the people lose their primary source of income, he builds palaces and pavilions, thereby providing employment for those households so poor that they have neither a dog in front nor a pig behind. Thus, his building of palaces and pavilions is not to gratify his pleasure, but to maintain equilibrium in the economic policies of the state." See: Guanzi. 1998. *Political, Economic, and Philosophical Essays from Early China*, vol. 2. trans. W. Allyn Rickett. Princeton: Princeton University Press. p. 365.The "labor relief" policy is further discussed in 5.2 and 6.3.

[83] Zhang, Zhaoyu. 2016. Study on labor relief in the Ming dynasty. *Historical Research in Anhui*. (6): 22.

[84] The year was 1050.

who engaged in commerce, catering industry, construction industry and tourism. To the needed in the famine year, these measures were the best they could hope for. As a result, in the year of famine people in Hangzhou were spared and not a single person in the region led a wandering life in poverty. All these were due to the favor Fan bestowed upon his people."[85]

With Shen Kuo's promotion, the practice of labor relief developed into an institutionalized governmental action in the Northern Song dynasty.[86] Especially when it was integrated with an essential component of Wang Anshi's reforms - the hydraulic work law[87], labor relief reached its peak since its implementation, with various related projects being carried out across the state (see Table 3.2). It is noteworthy that these projects were primarily funded by allocated money and grain from the state granaries, highlighting the stabilization function of labor relief and enriching the regulatory means of the ever-normal granaries. In June of the sixth year (1073) of the Xining period, the imperial court officially issued an edict to implement the labor relief policy. It stated, "From now on, in years of disaster and famine, in addition to the relief aid required by law, those in need of further assistance should be anticipated. The numbers of laborers needed for agricultural and hydraulic projects should be calculated in advance, and funds for hiring laborers should be allocated from the state granaries. In case of disasters and famine, those who do not comply with the previous and subsequent imperial commands for relief aid should be reported to the court by the Ministry of Agriculture."[88] To better implement labor relief, the imperial court required disaster-stricken areas to conduct statistic surveys on potential public works projects, weighing their pros and cons and making the planning in advance. In March of the seventh year (1074) of the Xining period, another edict ordered, "In disaster-affected areas, local officials should inspect and calculate the feasibility of projects such as agricultural and hydraulic works, dike construction, river and road maintenance, and tree planting, for which laborers would be needed. They should report back with detailed assessments of the benefits and drawbacks."[89]

The labor relief policy of the Ming dynasty served as a bridge between the previous and the later dynasties. It is noteworthy that this policy was not popular in the early Ming dynasty, but became widespread after the middle period. The

[85] Shen, Kuo. 2008. *Brush Talks from Dream Brook, vol.* 1. trans. Wang Hong and Zhao Jing. Chengdu: Sichuan People's Publishing House. p. 359.

[86] Yang, Guo and Zhao Zhile. 2014. The countermeasures against famine by different scholar-officals in Song dynasty. *Wuhan University Journal (Philosophy & Social Science).* (2):49.

[87] The hydraulic works law (*nongtian shuili fa*) was meant to improve local organization of irrigation works. It was part of the reform policy of Wang Anshi (1021-1086) during the Northern Song dynasty. Instead of using corvée labor, each circuit was supposed to appoint officials to loan money to the people using the local treasury, so that they could hire laborers.

[88] Li, Tao.2004. *Supplement to Historical Mirror to Aid in Government*, vol. 245. Beijing: Zhonghua Book Company. p. 5966.

[89] Li, Tao.2004. *Supplement to Historical Mirror to Aid in Government*, vol. 251. Beijing: Zhonghua Book Company. p. 6111.

Table 3.2 Examples of labor relief during years of Wang Anshi's reform (1069-1085)

Project categories	Historical facts	Bibliography
Irrigation and water conservancy	On the Renzi day in the February of the fifth year (1072) during the Xining period, the imperial court granted the Zhejiang Circuit Transport Commissioner 100,000 *shi* of grain from the ever-normal granaries for relief aid to the western Zhejiang regions affected by floods, and continued to recruit the impoverished to undertake water conservancy projects	*Extended Continuation to Zizhi Tongjian*, vol.230. p. 5586
Irrigation and water conservancy	In the fifth year (1072) of the Xining period, faced with a famine, the emperor issued an edict instructing the Ministry of Agriculture (responsible for grain storage, granary management, and supplying grain for the salaries of officials in the capital) to release 100,000 *shi* of grain from the ever-normal granaries. This grain was allocated to Nanjing, Suzhou, Bozhou, and Sizhou, where local officials were tasked with recruiting the hungry to dredge rivers	*Extended Continuation to Zizhi Tongjian*, vol.238. p. 5796
Construction of border forts and stockades	On the Renyin day of the lunar December of the fifth year(1072)of the Xining period, the emperor issued an edict to the Zhaoyan Regulatory Commissioner stating, "For the border cities and forts affected by disasters and famine, you'd quickly assess and provide relief aid. Moreover, you may consider recruiting Han and ethnic minority people who lack food to repair nearby cities and forts and undertake other labor tasks before they become hungry and exhausted. If you use funds and grain from the ever-normal granaries, the expenditure should not exceed 20,000 strings of cash and 20,000 *shi* of grain"	*Extended Continuation to Zizhi Tongjian*, vol.241. p. 5887
Irrigation and water conservancy	On the Wushen day of the lunar September in the sixth year (1073) of the Xining period, the Huainan East Transport Commissioner reported, "The people of Zhenzhou and Yangzhou are moving to Sizhou in search of fertile land for cultivation, and they are in need of relief aid." Additionally, the Liangzhe Circuit Procuratorate reported, "Runzhou is experiencing a drought; we request the opening of the provincial granaries for relief aid, or the distribution of a certain number of Buddhist Clergy's Certificates, Purple Robes for Buddhist Clergy, and Buddhist Title Decrees (all three are tax-exemption certificates for the Buddhist clergy, so they may be sold at the time for money), to encourage people to contribute grain, in preparation for relief aid." An imperial edict was issued to allocate thirty thousand *shi* of grain from the Ever-normal Granary Agency to each area, and to recruit the hungry to work on irrigation and water conservancy projects in exchange for food and lodging	*Extended Continuation to Zizhi Tongjian*, vol.247. p. 6011

(continued)

Table 3.2 (continued)

Project categories	Historical facts	Bibliography
Irrigation and water conservancy for farmland	On the Guiwei day of the lunar November in the sixth year (1073) of the Xining period, the imperial court granted the Huainan West Transport Commissioner thirty thousand *shi* of grain from ever-normal granaries, to recruit the hungry to engage in water conservancy projects	*Extended Continuation to Zizhi Tongjian*, vol.248. p. 6059.
Construction of city walls and fortifications	On the first day of the lunar May in the seventh year (1074) of the Xining period, an imperial edict was issued to recruit the hungry people from Hebei to repair the city of Yingzhou	*Extended Continuation to Zizhi Tongjian*, vol.253. p. 6187
Construction of city walls and fortifications	On the Wuchen day of the lunar August in the seventh year (1074) of the Xining period, an imperial edict was issued to recruit displaced people suffering from food shortages in Zhending Prefecture, Xingzhou, Mingzhou, Cizhou, Xiangzhou, and Zhaozhou to repair city walls and moats. The task in Zhending Prefecture was entrusted to the local official Sun Gu, while the rest was overseen by the Transport Commissioner Li Ji. They were also instructed to report every half month on the progress of the construction and the amount of money and grain that had been disbursed	*Extended Continuation to Zizhi Tongjian*, vol.255. p. 6231
Irrigation and water conservancy; Construction of city walls and fortifications	On the Jichou day of the lunar August in the seventh year (1074) of the Xining period, the Hebei West Transport Commissioner requested that in disaster-stricken areas, those who were lack of food or displaced be recruited for labor. In addition to the grain already provided by the imperial court, those who engaged in farming, water conservancy, and the repair of city walls and moats would be supplied with funds and grain from the Ever-normal Granary Agency. The court approved this request	*Extended Continuation to Zizhi Tongjian*, vol.255. p. 6242
Locust extermination	On the Guici day of the lunar October in the seventh year (1074) of the Xining period, an imperial edict granted twenty thousand *shi* of grain from ever-normal granaries to the Huainan region, which were further distributed to the Ever-normal Granary Agency pf Huainan West Commission, to exchange for the locust eggs dug up by the hungry people	*Extended Continuation to Zizhi Tongjian*, vol.257. p. 6282

(continued)

Table 3.2 (continued)

Project categories	Historical facts	Bibliography
Construction of border forts and stockades	On the Jia Yin day of the lunar January in the eighth year (1075) of the Xining period, Zhao Qi, the Fuyan Regulatory Commissioner reported that since the beginning of spring, many of the lower-class households still lacked food. Currently, there were more than four hundred thousand laborers' worth of work to be done on the construction of forts, stockades, city walls, and moats that had not yet commenced. He wished to draw two hundred thousand strings of cash and twenty thousand *shi* of grain from the ever-normal granaries to recruit the poor to fill these labor positions. The imperial court approved this request	*Extended Continuation to Zizhi Tongjian*, vol.259. p. 6320
Irrigation and water conservancy, construction of city walls and fortifications	On the Gengxu day of the lunar March in the eighth year (1075) of the Xining period, the imperial court granted fifty thousand *shi* of grain from ever-normal granaries to the Jingdong region. This was done in accordance with the previous imperial directive: "It has been reported that the states of Xuzhou, Shanzhou, Yizhou, and Huaiyangjun in the Jingdong region have suffered from disasters for several consecutive years. Although there is a bumper harvest this summer, the people are still in hunger. We may grant ten thousand *shi* of grain, and instruct the supervisory commissioners to recruit the people in a timely manner to construct water conservancy facilities and to complete the dredging of city moats, so that the common people will not lack food." Hence, the court took such measures	*Extended Continuation to Zizhi Tongjian*, vol.261. pp. 6361-6362

government was the leading force in the labor relief of the Ming dynasty, with wealthy individuals also participating. However, although the imperial court gradually attached importance to this policy, its nature of being "temporary" was evident, and the corresponding system was not ultimately established.[90] The "initial suppression followed by promotion" of the labor relief policy was likely related to the "initial prosperity followed by decline" of the preparedness granaries, and financial constraints were probably the main reason why the labor relief policy never developed into a systematic institution.

In the Qing dynasty, the labor relief policy had already been implemented during Emperor Kangxi's reign. The institutionalization of this policy during Emperor Qianlong's reign indicated that this special type of "Ever-normal Granary of labor force" had reached its maturity. In order to prepare for unforeseen circumstances, the imperial court inherited the beneficial experiences from the Song dynasty, requiring local governments to plan engineering projects in advance, categorize them by levels, register them in ledgers, and establish contingency plans. This

[90] Zhang, Zhaoyu. 2016. Study on labor relief in the Ming dynasty. *Historical Research in Anhui.* (6): 22-24.

ensured that this special Ever-normal Granary was always in a state of readiness to meet any emergency needs:

> The annual harvest is uncertain, with alternating years of abundance and scarcity. However, the projects that require maintenance must be planned in advance to ensure they can be initiated at any time. Among the various projects within a province, none is more significant than the city walls. It is essential to identify which localities are most critical and which should be addressed first. Governors and lieutenant-governors of each province should conduct detailed investigations, prioritize tasks based on urgency, make preliminary estimates, and compile registers to be submitted to the ministry. In times of uneven distribution of water and drought, if labor relief is to be implemented, it can be quickly executed by referring to these records, preventing delays and significantly benefiting the people's livelihood.[91]

The work "Trifles on Famine Administration" (*huangzheng suoyan*), completed during the Qianlong period, provides a description of the "current regulations" that involves the government's labor relief planning. As was stated in this work, "for projects valued at more than one thousand taels, the government should await years of uneven water and drought to initiate repairs with state funds, in the form of labor relief."[92] Such planning, linking project budgets to labor relief, was clearly well thought out. "Preference was given to water projects because of their crucial role in the protection against natural disaster: the building or repair of dikes, the dredging of waterways and canals, and the construction or restoration of irrigation reservoirs. Such projects had the additional advantage of mobilizing vast numbers of unskilled workers, without requiring much in the way of costly materials. At times, however, more 'specialized' projects, not directly related to the agricultural infrastructure, were also started: city walls, administrative buildings, and so forth."[93] Labor relief in the Qing dynasty, unlike that in the Ming dynasty, was not a temporary response to disasters. The state had developed a more mature long-term mechanism to calmly address unexpected calamities. Throughout the implementation of labor relief, the government had specific regulations on costs, targets of construction, project requirements, and selection of management personnel, etc. As a result, labor relief was implemented in much wider regions in the Qing dynasty. Almost all localities with prefectural, state, and county administrative centers adopted labor relief measures to varying degrees after disasters.[94]

From grain storage to labor storage, the above discussion suggests that to effectively stabilize market and economic fluctuations, the "commodities" for the purchase and sale in the Ever-normal Granary system were not limited to grain alone. Other commodities, monetary resources, and even labor could become objects of

---

[91] Qing, Gui and Dong Gao et al. 1985. *Factual Record of Qing Dynasty: Records of Emperor Gaozong*, vol. 46. Beijing: Zhonghua Book Company. p. 795.

[92] Wan, Weihan. 2010. Labor relief. Miscellaneous Remarks on Famine Relief Policies. ed. Li, Wenhai. in *Collections of Chinese Books on Famine Administration*. ed. Li, Wenhai, et al. Tianjin: Tianjin Ancient Books Publishing House. p. 1906.

[93] Will, Pierre-Etienne. 1990. *Bureaucracy and Famine in Eighteenth-Century China*. trans. Elborg Forster. Stanford: Stanford University Press. p. 259.

[94] Zhou, Qiong. 2011. Research on relief systems in the Qianlong period *Providing Jobs Instead of Reliefs. Journal of Tsinghua University (Philosophy and Social Sciences)*. 4: 66-79.

buffer reserves for purchase and sale. During the Northern Song dynasty, such an expansion had already emerged. In "Biography of Liu Huan" in *History of Song* (*song shi*), we can even find records on what could be called the "ever-normal cattle":

> During the Zhiping years, an earthquake struck Hebei, leaving the common people short of food and leading them to sell their plowing oxen at low prices just to scrape by from day to day. At that time, Liu Huan was the prefect of Chaozhou. He spent all the public funds from the treasury to purchase the oxen. The following year, when the people had no oxen for plowing, the price of oxen immediately increased tenfold. Liu Huan then sold the oxen he had bought in the previous year back to the farmers at the original price, thereby ensuring that the farmers of Chaozhou would not lose their livelihood.[95]

Such practice was not an isolated case. During the Mingdao period of Emperor Renzong's reign, Wu Zunlu ingeniously combined buffer buying and selling with "labor relief", achieving the effect of benefiting both the government and the people:

> Toward the end of the Mingdao period of Emperor Renzong's reign, the state was plagued by locusts and drought. Wu Zunlu, the magistrate of Tongzhou, took action before famine struck the common people. He raised money from wealthy households, collecting a total of ten thousand strings of coins. Then, he sent military officers across the Yangtze River to Suzhou and Xiuzhou to buy rice, which was transported back to supply the people of Tongzhou, thus preventing a rise in prices. He also instructed the people to gather firewood and straw, which the government would purchase at a set price. The people then used the money from selling firewood and straw to buy rice. By winter, when heavy snow fell and the weather turned cold, Wu Zunlu sold the firewood and straw back to the people at the original price. This approach did not deplete the government's funds and benefited the people greatly.[96]

In years of disasters and hardships, it is common for people to sell their important production and living resources at low prices due to the pressure of survival. Based on this, Wei Xi, an essayist in the Qing dynasty, suggested applying the mechanism of buying and selling grain to the tools and utensils needed for farmers' production and living, in order to ensure the smooth continuation of people's livelihoods and agricultural reproduction.[97] This idea is consistent with the suggestion made by Qiu Jun of the Ming dynasty, that ever-normal granaries should also engage in the buying and selling of various commodities. It seems that if important production and living resources, and even labor force, can be strategically included in the buying and selling mechanism, then the Ever-normal Granary in Chinese history can be categorized in "narrow" and "broad" senses—the Ever-normal Granary in narrow sense only has grain as the object of buying and selling, while Ever-normal Granary in broad sense (see Table 3.3) is an expanded and diversified buffer reserve. From

---

[95] Toqto'a et al. 1985. Biography of Liu Huan. *History of Song Dynasty*, vol. 324. Beijing: Zhonghua Book Company. p. 10494.

[96] Wang, Pizhi. 1981. Ability and insight. in *Fleeting Gossip by the River Sheng*. ed. Lü Youren. Beijing: Zhonghua Book Company. p.41.

[97] Wei, Xi. 2010. Solution to problems. *The Strategies of Famine Relief*. in *Collections of Chinese Books on Famine Administration, vol.* 2. ed. Li, Wenhai, et al. Tianjin: Tianjin Ancient Books Publishing House. p. 933.

Table 3.3 Ever-normal granaryin broad sense: policies and objects of buying and selling

Names of policy	Ever-normal Granary (system)	"equalization policy" (*pingzhunfa*)	"equilibrium maintenance" (*chengti*)	Labor relief	"ever-normal tools and utensils"
Objects of Buying and Selling	Grains	Important commodities	Currency	Labor force	People's daily production and living resources

the buffer reserve of grain to the buffer reserve of human resources, from tangible granaries to intangible granaries, ancient Chinese people continuously explored the flexible application of basic economic principles according to time, trends, and circumstances. Among them, the "Ever-normal Granary of labor force" is an important institutional innovation. The Song dynasty government began to implement the policy of labor relief consciously, which indicates that under the conditions of population increase and the absence of a system for land allocation and administration, the difficulty of stabilizing the economy also increased, and the regulatory policies were actively explored for possibility of adaptive transformation.[98]

Sang Hongyang's establishment of the governmental institutions in the capital to implement the equalization policy (*pingzhunfa*), preceded Geng Shouchang's construction of the ever-normal granaries in the border regions. However, it was the work *Guanzi* that first systematically elaborated on the theoretical implications and policy values of Ever-normal Granary. The tradition of valuing agriculture and grain further highlighted the role of Ever-normal Granary in Chinese history, making its impact more profound and lasting. Therefore, we use the term "Ever-normal Granary in broad sense" to refer to the expansion of these policy implications. It should be mentioned that the term "ever-normal" more directly points out the policy's orientation towards stability and its macro characteristics as follows: stabilizing the market and economic fluctuations, and combating monopolies and consolidations, so as to adjust wealth distribution; protecting labor force, and restoring and

[98]Yang Jingren remarked: "The Analects of Confucius records that Confucius advised Emperor Jing of Qi State: 'In years of famine, laboring should be suspended.' Though later generations adopted the policy of 'labor relief' (providing relief in exchange for work), which appears contradictory to Confucius' words, it preserves the essence of the ancients' compassionate governance. Why is it so? Under the ancient 'nine squares' system of land ownership in China (one large square divided into 9 small ones like the Chinese character 井, with the 8 outer ones being allocated to serfs who had to cultivate the central one for the serf owner), each person cultivated about 100 *mu* of land, yielding a surplus after three years' cultivation. With specialized granaries for emergencies and famine relief measures, mutual support was ensured, making it appropriate to suspend laboring and allow the people to recuperate. In later times, with the abolition of the 'nine squares' system and the increase of population, even extensive relief efforts during famines often proved insufficient. Hence, reviving public works projects enabled the destitute to earn wages through labor, preventing the self-reliant from starvation while repairing neglected infrastructure. This dual benefit truly captures the spirit of ancient compassion without being constrained by its specific methods." See: Yang, Jingren. 2010. On construction. *Compilations for Relief and Aid*, vol. 13. ed. Hao, Bingjian. in *Collections of Chinese Books on Famine Administration, vol.* 5. ed. Li, Wenhai, et al. Tianjin: Tianjin Ancient Books Publishing House. p. 3196.

developing productivity, so as to ensure the smooth development of social reproduction; maintaining social governance, and preventing social unrest caused by economic fluctuations. Of course, this does not mean that a richer policy menu will necessarily yield more significant positive effects. If major relationships such as those between the government (*guan*) and the market (*shang*), and between the government (*guan*) and society (*min*) are not handled well, the result of Ever-normal Granary policies might be the opposite of stability. For example, the government of the Northern Song dynasty, exceeding its duties in the market exchange law (*shiyifa*), disrupted the basic balance and ultimately ended in failure, much like the Wang Anshi's implementing of Green Sprouts Act.

3.3 Revering Heaven, Nourishing the People, and Macro Welfare

Zhang Gong believes that from a comparative perspective between China and the west, the Ever-normal Granary is an economic policy with distinct Chinese characteristics. Under the typical landlord governance of European feudal society, such as the Frankish Kingdom, the territory of the feudal lords determined their scope of rule, and the king was merely a largerlandlord among them. Besides the tithe collected by the church, the Frankish Kingdom did not have a unified tax system, thus there was no need for a granary system like that in China.[99] R. Bin Wong further points out that even in the process of "centralization drives of early modern state formation", "European governments never created even modest networks of granaries to cushion bad harvest years and the machination of the market."[100] A wide examination of world history shows that even when countries with different cultural backgrounds and from various regions have had grain storage systems, they often faced issues such as weak functionality, difficulty in sustainability, mere supply for military purpose, and neglect of the grassroots needs (with facilities only established in large cities). These systems cannot be compared with the vast Ever-normal Granary system represented by that in the Qing dynasty.[101]

In ancient China, along with the deepening understanding of the functions of the state, there was a distinctive characteristic in state governance: the primacy of maintaining and improving the welfare of the people. From the perspective of the economic base, since the establishment of the system of prefectures and counties, traditional Chinese agrarian society gradually developed a vertical management structure from the center to the localities. The state had a unified monetary and

[99] Zhang, Gong. 1986. *A Preliminary Study of Granary System in the Tang Dynasty*. Beijing: Zhonghua Book Company. p. 4.

[100] Wong, R. Bin. 1997. *China Transformed: Historical Change and the Limits of European Experience*. Ithaca and London: Cornell University Press. pp. 98-99.

[101] Will, Pierre-Etienne and R. Bin Wong. ed. 1991. *Nourish the People: the State Civilian Granary System in China, 1650-1850*. Ann Arbor: University of Michigan Press. pp. 507-525.

taxation system, which was linked to each small-scale peasant economy. The core system of this structure was the bureaucratic hierarchy and the corresponding administrative organizations at various levels. With them, the scattered small-scale peasant economy was effectively organized and integrated, forming a unified national economic system that spanned a vast territory and had a large population resource. It is no exaggeration to say that this system not only had the substance of an overall "macro-economy" but also the intrinsic need for "macro-control". In reality, once the economy experienced significant fluctuations, such as the unpredictable floods and droughts causing a substantial reduction in grain production, the vulnerable small-scale peasant economy would be pushed to the brink of bankruptcy and a desperate situation for survival. If the rulers were not virtuous in their governance or managed poorly, the most important economic foundation of their rule and the source of taxation would be shaken and undermined, leading to the replacement of the dynasty by a new one.

From the perspective of the superstructure, the concept of the Mandate of Heaven[102] left by the Western Zhou dynasty for later generations provided an important theoretical basis for the implementation of active and effective social governance by the state. Represented by the Duke of Zhou (*zhou gong*), the people of Zhou dynasty learned from the fall of the Shang dynasty and no longer viewed the Mandate of Heaven as an eternal grant as the people of Shang did. Instead, they developed the ideas that the Mandate of Heaven is impermanent, that it favors virtue, and that the will of Heaven resides with the people. People should no longer blindly worship or make sacrifices to Heaven in exchange for good fortune. On the contrary, Heaven was endowed with ethical character, where manifesting virtue and ensuring the well-being of the people, along with reverence and diligence, became the definitive connotations of the "Mandate of Heaven". Since Heaven is rational, it is also observable through human actions, which means that the ruler of the people must be accountable for his actions and the authority of his mandate.[103] This further stipulated that the authority and legitimacy of the ruler depend on the demand of the people as the "Mandate of Heaven":

> After "Heaven" entrusts the "Mandate" to a new dynasty, it does not stand by idly; on the contrary, "Heaven" watches over the movements of the "people" at all times. If the dynasty that has received the "Mandate" works hard and establishes an order of "rites" that satisfies the "people", this proves that it "reveres virtue", and thus it can continue to hold the

[102] The Mandate of Heaven (*tianmin*, lit. "Heaven's command") is a Chinese political ideology that was used in Ancient China and Imperial China to legitimize the rule of the king or emperor of China. According to this doctrine, Heaven (*tian*) bestows its mandate on a virtuous ruler. This ruler, the Son of Heaven, was the supreme universal monarch, who ruled *tianxia* ("all under heaven", the world). If a ruler was overthrown, this was interpreted as an indication that the ruler was unworthy and had lost the mandate. It was also a common belief that natural disasters such as famine and flood were divine retributions bearing signs of Heaven's displeasure with the ruler, so there would often be revolts following major disasters as the people saw these calamities as signs that the Mandate of Heaven had been withdrawn.

[103] Chen, Lai. 2017. *Ancient Religion and Ethics: The Roots of Confucianis*m (Revised Edition). Beijing: Peking University Press. pp. 222-223, p. 230.

> "Mandate of Heaven". Conversely, if it fails to do so, it will lose the "Mandate of Heaven", as what is meant in the saying "Only when one does not revere virtue, will one's mandate soon be lost." ("The Announcement of the Duke of Shao" (*Shaogao*), *Book of History*)[104]

The concept of "Mandate of Heaven" generally puts "people" first. As was stated in the chapter "The Great Speech" (*tai shi*) of Book of History (*shang shu*), "What the people desire,/ Heaven is sure to grant."[105] "Heaven sees as my people see,/ Heaven hears as my people hear."[106] Therefore, the primary task for a dynasty, bestowed by "Heaven" for long-term stability, is to establish a solid material foundation to ensure the people can live and work in peace and stability. "Heaven" continuously watches over the welfare of "people" and their attitude towards the dynasty, determining the duration and shift of the "Mandate of Heaven". As was stated in "King Wen" (wen wang) of "The Book of Songs" (*shi jing*), "Heaven-bestowed supreme power is not eternal."[107] Zheng Xuan's commentary explains, "by the phrase "not eternal", if it is good, it is kept; if it is evil, it is abandoned."[108] The "Mandate of Heaven" which is "not eternal", demands that rulers and bureaucratic organizations should continuously make efforts to respect virtue and protect the people, matching virtue with "Mandate of Heaven", thus illustrating the legitimacy of their rule through benevolent policies that nourish the people (*yang min*). When the ruler governs a state improperly or commits grave errors and fails to protect the people, Heaven will issue a warning to the ruler through a feedback mechanism of "bringing calamity", such as natural disasters like floods and droughts, leading to severe famine and social unrest. If the state does not handle these issues properly and fails to self-correct (from the emperor blaming himself to taking concrete actions), the "Mandate of Heaven" will turn into revolution, and the bestowal of the mandate will shift to the withdrawal of the mandate, making the replacement of dynasties inevitable.

Viewed from the perspective of modern times, the concept of Mandate of Heaven encapsulates an extremely important "principal-agent" relationship. The ultimate

---

[104] Yu, Yingshi. 2014. *On Heaven and Man: An Exploration of the Origins of Ancient Chinese Thought.* Beijing: Zhonghua Book Company. p.96.

[105] Zuo, Qiuming. 2016. *Zuo Tradition/Zuozhuan: Commentary on the "Spring and Autumn Annals"*. trans. Stephen Durrant, Wai-yee Li, and David Schaberg. Seattle and London: University of Washington Press. p.1275.

[106] Mencius. 2009. *Mencius*. trans. Irene Bloom. New York: Columbia University Press. p.104.

[107] This term first appears in *The Book of Songs*. It means that there is no one who can forever remain a recipient of the bestowed supreme power by the Ruler of Heaven. The ancients believed that the heavenly order determined to whom the supreme royal power belonged. However, the choice of the recipient of such a conferment was not forever. Replacement of the Shang dynasty by the Zhou dynasty was brought about by the change of the recipient of Heaven's bestowal of the mandate to rule. However, the change of the recipients of the mandate followed a fixed principle: such bestowal could fall only on a ruler who was virtuous. Once he had lost virtue, the mandate to rule would be withdrawn from him. Therefore, the concept of the change of the recipient of Heaven's mandate served as a warning to the ruler, who must constantly cultivate his virtue in order to keep his rule. See: https://www.chinesethought.cn/EN/shuyu_show.aspx?shuyu_id=4142

[108] Ruan, Yuan. ed. 2009. *Annotations to the Thirteen Classics*. Beijing: Zhonghua Book Company. p. 1086.

principal, in simple terms, is the divine heaven that represents the will of the people, while the rulers and the bureaucratic hierarchy are the agents of various levels who bear the mission and responsibility. The principal-agent model characterized by the Mandate of Heaven, combined with the economic foundation of small-scale peasant farming, gave rise to the deep-rooted traditions of prioritizing agriculture, people-centric values, and macro welfare thoughts in traditional Chinese society. It also accordingly led to the development of economic management policies - to ensure the well-being of the people and to prevent or stop the turmoil from escalating into the loss of the empire, the ruling class must effectively allocate resources and actively intervene in the economy. "He who knows why heaven is heaven will achieve great imperial endeavors; he who does not know why heaven is heaven will not achieve great imperial endeavors. A ruler should regard the people as heaven, and the people regard food as heaven."[109] These words by Li Yiji during the Chu-Han Contention (between Liu Bang and Xiangyu for sovereignty) encapsulate the key to state governance. Rulers must realize that the government needs to provide small-scale farmers with favorable conditions for living and development, and implement effective economic management and control so as to prevent economic fluctuations from destroying the fragile small-scale farming and thus incurring the punishment of the Mandate of Heaven. The establishment of theEver-normal Granary is a product of such thought and action. Although the real impact of the Ever-normal Granary system may vary with the strength of the state and the efficiency of governance in different historical periods, its overall evolutionary trend shows that the state has been continuously striving to develop an effective and comprehensive Ever-normal Granary system to ensure the basic material welfare of the people.[110]

It is worth discussing the traditional concept of "the people regard food as heaven". If we consider "food", which is equated with "heaven" in importance, as the people's most basic demand for survival and development, and thereupon regard this demand as a fundamental right, then the Mandate of Heaven to "protect the people" is to entrust the rulers with the authority to protect this right. In this light, from the perspective of Amartya Sen's view of "entitlement" in his work *Poverty and Famines: An Essay on Entitlement and Deprivation*, there seems to be certain connection between the Ever-normal Granary and the "food entitlement".

Amartya Sen realized that different social classes have significantly different control and commanding powers over general goods, especially food, which is reflected in the society as entitlement relationships. Therefore, the struggle of the general labor class and the lower class to survive in the face of a famine often stems largely from the loss of their food entitlements. "...different groups typically do

---

[109] Sima, Qian. 1982. Biography of Li Sheng and Lu Jia. *Records of the Grand Historian, vol.* 97. Beijing: Zhonghua Book Company. p. 2694.

[110] Microscopically, for scholars, responding to the state, participating in public affairs and promoting the welfare of the people is an effective way to realize Confucian ideals and improve their morals. Such bottom-up grassroots Ever-normal Granary as Zhuzi civil storehouse is a typical manifestation of this practice.

have very different commanding powers over food, and an over-all shortage brings out the contrasting powers in stark clarity."[111] In fact, the actual need for food, rather than marketable demand with purchasing power, is the abundant fact during a famine. "The government's thinking on the nature of the food problem seems to have been persistently influenced by attempts to estimate the size of the 'real shortage' based on 'requirements' and 'availability'; it was a search in a dark room for a black cat which wasn't there."[112] As a result, Amartya Sen emphasizes, "there is also need for a mechanism for directly tackling the problem of vulnerability through public institutions guaranteeing food entitlement. ... What is needed is not ensuring food availability, but guaranteeing food entitlement."[113] One important implementation program is that "no matter how a famine is *caused,* methods of *breaking* it call for a large supply of food in the public distribution system. This applies not only to organizing rationing and control, but also to undertaking work programmes and other methods of increasing purchasing power for those hit by shifts in exchange entitlements in a general inflationary situation."[114]

From Amartya Sen's perspective, the granaries established by the Chinese government in ancient times were essentially part of the welfare systems designed to safeguard the food and exchange entitlements of small farmers. Let us return to *Guanzi*. The chapter "The State's Store of Grain" (*guo xu*) of the book is an important text on the significance of establishing a buffer reserve of grain. It states as follows, "a country of ten thousand chariots will have traders who have accumulated ten thousand catties of gold while a country of a thousand chariots will have traders who have accumulated a thousand." However, "it follows that if the prince is not able to control the situation, it will lead to large-scale traders roaming the markets and taking advantage of the people's lack of things to increase their capital a hundredfold."[115] The text clearly recognizes the significant differences in control over food among different social classes. "If the prince is not able to control the situation", the market will provide conditions for these differences to be magnified: "When there is a bumper harvest, no one can sell grain in the market, and dogs and pigs eat the food of people. When there is a bad harvest, grain is sold in the market for ten strings of cash (*jiang*) per *ju* and the roads are filled with starving people." [116] In response to such problems, the author hopes that "the prince is able to control

[111] Sen, Amartya. 1981.*Poverty and Famine: An Essay on Entitlement and Deprivation.* Oxford: Clarendon Press. p.43.

[112] Sen, Amartya. 1981.*Poverty and Famine: An Essay on Entitlement and Deprivation.* Oxford: Clarendon Press. p. 80.

[113] Sen, Amartya. 1981.*Poverty and Famine: An Essay on Entitlement and Deprivation.* Oxford: Clarendon Press. p. 129.

[114] Sen· Amartya. 1981.*Poverty and Famine: An Essay on Entitlement and Deprivation.* Oxford: Clarendon Press. p. 79.

[115] Guanzi. 1998. *Guanzi: Political, Economic, and Philosophical Essays from Early China*, vol. 2. trans. W. Allyn Rickett. Princeton: Princeton University Press. p. 379.

[116] Guanzi. 1998. *Guanzi: Political, Economic, and Philosophical Essays from Early China*, vol. 2. trans. W. Allyn Rickett. Princeton: Princeton University Press. pp. 380-381.

the situation", explicitly stating the attitude while proposing the reserve policy, "big traders and families engaged in hoarding are unable to force exactions from our people."[117] From Amartya Sen's perspective, is this not a declaration against cunning seizures and a proposal for protecting people's food and exchange entitlements? Though Amartya Sen does not discuss the granaries in Chinese history in his book *Poverty and Famines*, he thinks that "no matter how a famine is *caused*, methods of *breaking* it call for a large supply of food in the public distribution system."[118] Although Amartya Sen focuses on contemporary economic and social issues, he should also recognize the value of the ancient Chinese system.

If the above explanation seems too vague, we may further illustrate it with reference to studies on "registration" (*chao zha*) from the mid-Northern Song dynasty to the Southern Song dynasty. During this period, the government, to better implement relief efforts with grain reserves, widely conducted"registration" to investigate and verify the population, providing a detailed basis for relief aid, relief loans, and food distribution to ensure that no one was left out.[119] Therefore, "despite the numerous defects of the registration process, which may cause discrepancies between registration data and actual data, it is undoubtedly certain that the population statistics of the relief registration in the Song dynasty included the entire population, including men, women, the elderly, and children."[120] Based on this, it can be seen from historical documents that Amartya Sen's proposal that "there is also need for a mechanism…through public institutions guaranteeing food entitlement" was already implemented as early as the Song dynasty in China. The mechanism was quite complete at the time, which included not only the Ever-normal Granary system, but also specific measures such as "registration" (*chao zha*) to ensure the implementation of food entitlements.

When the government of a traditional agricultural society bore the responsibility for the livelihood of its people, the Ever-normal Granary system that evolved in the history indeed possessed a sense of "modernity". Apart from welfare economics, such policies undoubtedly had a strong flavor of macroeconomics - the state coordinated various forces to establish an effective intervention system and a corresponding institutional structure. By buffering the purchasing and selling of grain, it aimed to "level out" economic fluctuations caused by climate change and natural disasters (if we disregard other factors). Although the reasons for such fluctuations differ from those in the modern economic system, the basic policy orientation of taking timely action and counter-cyclical regulation is essentially the same as that of modern macroeconomics.

---

[117] Guanzi. 1998. *Guanzi: Political, Economic, and Philosophical Essays from Early China*, vol. 2. trans. W. Allyn Rickett. Princeton: Princeton University Press. pp. 382.

[118] Sen, Amartya. 1981. *Poverty and Famine: An Essay on Entitlement and Deprivation*. Oxford: Clarendon Press. p. 79.

[119] Li, Huarui. 2012. The registration system and statistical survey of households needing disaster relief in the Song dynasty. *Historical Research*. (6): 30-42.

[120] Li, Huarui. 2012. The registration system and statistical survey of households needing disaster relief in the Song dynasty. *Historical Research*. (6): 42.

When the government in a traditional agricultural society had a significant responsibility for people's livelihoods, the system of Ever-normal Granary that developed in history had essentially possessed modernity. In addition to welfare economics, such policies also bore a strong resemblance to macroeconomics. The state was coordinating various forces to establish an effective intervention system and a corresponding institutional structure. The aim of this system was to smooth out economic fluctuations caused by climate change and natural disasters (excluding other factors) through buffering grain trading. Although the reasons for such fluctuations differ from those in a modern economic system, the basic policy orientation of acting opportunistically and counter-cyclically is fundamentally the same as in modern macroeconomics.

In the 17th and 18th centuries, policies of economic intervention like mercantilism were implemented in Western European countries, primarily to break feudal separation, promote domestic economic integration, and expand international trade. After the establishment of the capitalist system in Europe and America, the laissez-faire market economy model gradually took dominance. In the 1920s and 1930s, Western societies experienced an unprecedented economic crisis, leading to the idea of counter-cyclical state intervention in macroeconomic theories, represented by the "Keynesian Revolution".

Western macroeconomics was born in a period of great changes. Keynes was not the only one at the time who made the proposal for the state to actively intervene in economic life and influence the material welfare of the people. In fact, behind the "Keynesian Revolution" was successive groups of people and the historical development of a new trend of thought. Interestingly, the macro-intervention ideas advocated by these groups had close connection with the ancient Chinese Ever-normal Granary system. History presents a picture of a successful "handshake" between China's economic traditions and Western economic theories and policies in the 1920s and 1930s, with far-reaching impact for the latter.

Chapter 4
Transformation of Ever-Normal Granary in Modern Times: From Chen Huan-Chang to Benjamin Graham

> It isprobably true quite generally that inthehistory of human thinking the most fruitful developments frequently take place at those points where two different lines ofthought meet. These lines may have their roots in quite differentparts of human culture, in different times or different cultural environments or different religious traditions.
>
> —Werner Heisenberg[1]

> From the standpoint of the national interest, the consuming interest, and the agricultural interest, the increased stability of supply and price that would come with the Ever-normal Granary is essential.
>
> —Henry. A. Wallace[2]

Due to the great economic depression in the Western world during the 1920s and 30s, and the ensuing spread of governmental macro-level interventions, the ancient Chinese price-stabilizing mechanism of Ever-normal Granary found new life in the new era. The exposure of Ever-normal Granary to the West is largely due to a significant work, *The Economic Principles of Confucius and His School* written by the Chinese scholar Chen Huan-Chang, which introduced the ancient Chinese economic traditions to the west. The discussion of the Ever-normal Granary inspired Henry A. Wallace, the U.S. Secretary of Agriculture (1933-1940) during the Franklin D. Roosevelt administration. Wallace advocated effective governmental intervention to buffer price volatility and end the damage to the U.S. economy caused by laissez-faire policies in agriculture. Wallace promoted the enactment of two "Agricultural Adjustment Acts" (AAA) and implementation of relevant reforms in the 1930s, achieving a historical transformation of ancient Chinese Ever-normal Granary system. The Ever-normal Granary reform in agriculture in the 1930s, i.e.

[1] Heisenberg, Werner. 1958. *Physics and Philosophy: The Revolution in Modern Science.* New York: Harper & Brothers Publishers. p.187.

[2] Wallace, Henry. A. Statement before the House Agricultural Committee, May 27, 1937. *qtd.* in: Graham, B. 1937. *Storage and Stability: A Modern Ever-normal Granary*. New York and London: McGraw-Hill Book Company. p. 179.

W. Xian, *Chinese Food Security Strategy*, Research Series on the Chinese Dream and China's Development Path,
https://doi.org/10.1007/978-981-95-7964-8_4

supporting the ever-normal development of agriculture with both the government and the market, symbolized the maturing of the American agricultural economy. Inspired by the success of Henry A. Wallace, Benjamin Graham, an influential American investor known as the "Father of Value Investing", proposed the "Modern Ever-normal Granary", a buffer stock scheme based on a "basket" of widely-used commodities including industrial and agricultural products, hence the creation of the Commodity Reserve Currency system which coexists with the gold standard system. The Modern Ever-normal Granary proposed by Graham, is actually the application, in an industrialized society, of the "equalization policy" (*pingzhunfa*) (or Multiple Buffer Stock) of Ever-normal Granary in broad sense, a policy implemented in ancient agricultural China. Graham extended its application to the modern world, and the "Modern Ever-normal Granary" was later updated to the "World Ever-normal Granary". The ancient Chinese Ever-normal Granary found its resurrection and new development in the U.S. with its creative transformation in the new era.

4.1 "East to West": Chen Huan-Chang and Henry A. Wallace

4.1.1 Chen Huan-Chang and The Economic Principles of Confucius and His School

Chen Huan-Chang occupies a special place in the history of Chinese economic thought. In the context of "Eastward Spread of Western Learning"[3] in modern China, he published *The Economic Principles of Confucius and His School* in English which spread Chinese wisdom to the west in a "counter-current" way. The book not only won full affirmation with its academic value in the Western intellectual communities, but also soon influenced the agricultural economic policies in U.S. with its "modernity", contributing to the modern transformation of ancient Chinese Ever-normal Granary system.

Chen Huan-Chang (or ChenHuanzhang, 1881-1933) was a great thinker and social activist during the late Qing dynasty (1644-1911) and early Republic of China (1912-1949). At the age of fifteen, he was enrolled to the academy Wanmu Caotang (*Thatched Hall among Ten Thousand Trees*) in Guangzhou and was tutored

[3] "Eastward Spread of Western Learning" (*xixue dongjian*), historically refers to the process by which Western learning, science, technology, and cultural ideas were introduced and gradually adopted in Eastern countries, particularly in China. Originating in the late 19th century and continuing through the early 20th century, "Eastward Spread of Western Learning" was a response to the rapid industrialization and military advancements of Western nations, which had become apparent to the Chinese during a series of defeats and unequal treaties following the Opium Wars. In essence, it was a transformative period that marked the beginning of China's modernization and its engagement with the global community.

by Kang Youwei (1858-1927), a prominent political thinker and reformer of the late Qing dynasty. He achieved scholarly honor as *Jinshi* Degree[4] in 1904, and was sent to study in the U.S. in 1907. He became a student in the Economics Department of Columbia University, where he obtained his doctoral degree in 1911, and returned to China in the following year. Back in China, he launched the State Religion Movement (*guojiao yundong*), and, in imitation of Christian activities, founded the National Confucian Association[5] in Shanghai for which he was the director (Kang Youwei was the chairman). In 1913 he became the editor-in-chief of the journal *The Confucian Association Monthly*, and was later appointed legal adviser to President Yuan Shikai[6]. He, together with Yan Fu, Liang Qichao and other elites made efforts to induce the Parliament to adopt Confucianism as the state religion of China. As was pointed out by some scholars, it was perhaps because of his political "errors" of involvement in the State Religion Movement, a movement considered by some New Culture Movement activists to be closely related with Yuan Shikai's restoration of the hereditary monarchy in China in 1915, that Chen and his proposals were lost in history.[7]But now it is considered that his greatest "error" might be his failure to have his doctoral dissertation, *The Economic Principles of Confucius and His School,* translated into Chinese before it was too late. As was stated by Chen Huan-Chang in the first issue of *The Confucian Association Monthly* which was published in 1913, "Many people in my country have urged me to translate the book into Chinese. Though I have planned to do so, I fail to because I am really tired out."[8]Who would have expected that his work wouldn't be translated and published in China until almost one hundred years later? In comparison, Yan Fu[9] was celebrated for his

[4] *Jinshi* was the highest and final degree in the imperial examination in imperial China. The examination was usually taken in the palace of the imperial capital. Recipients are also called Imperial Scholars.

[5] The Confucian Association (*kongjiao hui*) was a non-governmental organization which aimed at promoting Confucian as the nation's major religion in order to enhance the cohesion of the Chinese nation. It followed Confucius's teachings to provide students with relevant knowledge. The teachings were based on a moral code for human relations, which emphasized the importance of tradition and rites.

[6] Yuan Shikai (1859–1916) was a Chinese political and military figure who played a significant role during the late Qing dynasty and the early Republic of China. Born in Henan Province, he rose to prominence by training the first modernized army in Tianjin and later suppressed the Yihetuan Movement. In 1911, he forced the abdication of the last Qing emperor and became the provisional president of the Republic of China. However, in 1915, he declared himself emperor, sparking widespread opposition. Facing nationwide condemnation, he abdicated shortly after and died in Beijing in 1916.

[7] Han, Hua. 1999. Chen Huan-zhang's interpretation of Confucius' "Economical Principles" in the modern era. *Social Science Research.* (1): 88.

[8] Chen, Huan-Chang. 1913. *The Economic Principles of Confucius and His School* and Its Application in China. *The Confucian Association Monthly*. 1(1): 1.

[9] Yan Fu (1854-1921) was a prominent Chinese enlightenment thinker and translator. He was most known for his translation principle of "faithfulness" (*xin*信), "expressiveness" (*da*达) and "elegance" (*ya*雅), and translation of eight major works including T. H. Huxley's *Evolution and Ethics*,

translation of eight major works, and Liang Qichao[10] was renowned as a prolific writer. It is no wonder such a book published overseas, together with its author, was neglected and even totally forgotten by the Chinese for quite a long time. However, as intellectual elites of the time, they shared similar knowledge structure and educational background: "the educational background of this generation must be unique in the Chinese history — receiving both traditional and modern education, acquiring both old and new knowledge, and incorporating Western thoughts together, etc. ...While receiving traditional knowledge, they studied foreign languages and pursued Western learning in a comparatively systematic way. In the rise of studying abroad in modern China, which started around 1900, they were pioneers who had the opportunities to see foreign countries firsthand, and many had the opportunities to receive higher education in the Western universities. Because of such historical conditions and opportunities, they were unique intellectuals in Chinese history who had relatively balanced knowledge of the old and the new, and the east and the west."[11]Accordingly, the book *The Economic Principles of Confucius and His School* written by Chen Huan-chang, the holder of two doctoral degrees (*jinshi* degree in imperial examination of China and Ph.D. degree from Columbia University), could be considered as a great intellectual achievement at the meeting of Chinese and Western civilizations at the time.

The book *The Economic Principles of Confucius and His School* gives a detailed account of economic thinking of Confucius and his school, and their ideas on consumption, production and public property, etc. As was stated by Chen Huan-chang in the "Author's Preface", although "my arrangement of the material follows that which has become conventional among western writers", "this is the first attempt to present The Economic Principles of Confucius and His School in a systematic form in any language", "it is a survey of the Chinese thought and Chinese institutions which developed independently of the Occident", and "I have been very careful not to read into the writings of the ancient Chinese ideas drawn from modern western economists." The book of course cannot be free from the influence of Western economics. However, Chen Huan-chang's statements were generally based on the words or the spirit of the original Confucian classics. The Western economic theories mostly served as tools for interpreting the Confucian economic principles, hence the interactive interpretation between the east and the west. To Chen Huan-chang, "the Confucian writings may be compared to a great mountain containing

Adam Smith's *The Wealth of Nations*, and Herbert Spencer's *The Study of Sociology,* etc. that introduced key ideas of Western thoughts to China.

[10] Liang Qichao (1873-1929) was a Chinese politician, social and political activist, journalist, and intellectual. His thought had a significant influence on the political reformation of modern China. He inspired Chinese scholars and activists with his writings and reform movements. His translations of Western and Japanese books into Chinese further introduced new theories and ideas and inspired young activists.

[11] Chen, Wanxiong. 1997. *Origin and Development of May Fourth New Culture Movement.* Shanghai: SDX Joint Publishing Company. p. 183.

rich mineral resources", and he is "in the position of a miner, extracting a particular ore and contributing it to the world's production"[12]

The Economic Principles of Confucius and His School, after its publication, attracted the attention of Western scholars with its unique value and appeal.[13] Our focus here is the subtle connection between Ever-normal Granary in this book and the adjustment of agricultural economic policies in the U.S. in the 1930s and 40s, namely the modern transformation of Ever-normal Granary, promoted by Henry A. Wallace, the U.S. Secretary of Agriculture since 1933.Tsuen-HsuinTsien, a most renown scholar of Chinese bibliography and paleography, stated as follows, "The most interesting and significant case transmitted entirely through academic channels is the American adoption of the so-called 'Ever-normal Granary,' … This Chinese economic theory… was first discussed in a doctoral dissertation by ChenHuanzhang of Columbia University in 1911. This piece of research chanced to fall into the hands of Henry Wallace, who had held great admiration for this Chinese institution since 1918, when he was editor of a weekly paper. This alien idea was finally realized in America in 1933, when Mr. Wallace became Secretary of Agriculture…. The first Agricultural Adjustment Act of 1933, which was an integral part of the New Deal Policy, embodied the general principle of this Chinese institution of the "Ever-normal Granary."[14]As a Chinese-American scholar, Tsuen-Hsuin Tsiendid't deliberately attribute the reforms of U.S. agricultural policies to the classical Chinese economic policies. Prof. Derk Bodde from University of Pennsylvania once wrote to Henry A. Wallace for confirmation of the issue, who replied as follows:

> I first learned about the Ever-normal Granary by reading a doctor's degree thesis written by Chen Huan-chang, a Chinese scholar at Columbia University. The title of his thesis was "The Economic Principles of Confucius and His School." As a result I wrote several editorials for *Wallaces' Farmer* during the decade of the twenties entitled "The Ever-normal Granary."[15]

In his diary, which reflected his own thoughts, Henry A. Wallace wrote as follows:

> Madame Chiang told me how deeply interested she was in agriculture, that she had been told by the President that part of our agricultural program was based on Chinese philosophy. I then told her the story of how I had gotten the phrase "Ever-normal Granary" out of a

[12] Chen, Huan-chang. 1911. *The Economic Principles of Confucius and His School.* New York: Columbia University Press. pp. xi-xii.

[13] Han, Hua. 2015. Chen Huan-Chang and *The Economic Principles of Confucius and His School.* in: Chen Huan-Chang. *The Economic Principles of Confucius and His School.* trans. Han Hua. Beijing: The Commercial Press. pp. 603-605.

[14] Tsien, Tsuen-Hsuin. 1959. Asian Studies in America: a historical survey. in *Asian Studies and State Universities.* ed. Teng, Ssu-yu. Bloomington: Indiana University. pp. 108-121. Also: Han, Hua. 2015. Chen Huan-Chang and *The Economic Principles of Confucius and His School.* in: Chen, Huan-Chang. *The Economic Principles of Confucius and His School.* trans. Han Hua. Beijing: The Commercial Press. pp. 604-605.

[15] Bodde, D. 1946. Henry A. Wallace and the Ever Normal Granary. *The Far Eastern Quarterly.* 5(4): 412.

> book, Economic Principles of Confucius. … She said she was very eager to have me come to China to study Chinese agriculture.[16]

In the diary, Wallace narrated in detail his conversation with Song Meiling, the wife of Chiang Kai-shek and a famous political figure in China, on February 25, 1943 (Song was raising money in the United States at the time). From his narration, we learn that both Franklin D. Roosevelt and Henry A. Wallace admitted frankly that the American agricultural policies were inspired by traditional Chinese thoughts, the "Americanization" process of which started from Chen Huan-Chang. In Chapter XXX "Government Control of Grain" of his work, Chen Huan-Chang analyzed in detail the Ever-normal Granary system with its merits and demerits,[17]which might be most valuable for Henry A. Wallace to learn from.

4.1.2 The Demand for Ever-normal Granary in America

Why was the Americanized Ever-normal Granary proposed? To answer the question, it is necessary to learn about the background of agricultural development in the U.S. at the time. The period from 1910 to 1914 was known as the Golden Age of American agriculture, characterized by high and stable prices for agricultural products. During World War I (1914–1918), the significant increase in international demand for foodstuffs propelled an unprecedented boom in American agriculture. Although the continuous occurrence of farm bankruptcies in 1915 led to a decline in agricultural product prices, they recovered and grew in 1916. From 1916 to the middle of 1920, the level of agricultural product prices more than doubled. Correspondingly, the price of farmland across the nation rose by 70 percent between 1913 and 1920.[18] During this period, the degree of agricultural mechanization also continued to increase. Taking tractors as an example, in 1915 there were 25,000 farm tractors in the U.S., while in 1919 the number grew up to 158,000.[19] However, at the start of the 1920s, American agriculture was among the first to feel the chill of the Great Depression. Due to the changes in consumption demand, a slowdown in population growth, and competition in the international market, the agricultural sector found itself with a surplus of supply over demand. In the summer of 1920, agricultural product prices began to plummet. Within a year, the price of wheat fell drastically from $2 per bushel to $1 per bushel, and the overall level of agricultural

[16] Blum, J.M., ed. 1973. *The Price of Vision: The Diary of Henry A. Wallace 1942-1946*. Boston: Houghton Mifflin Company. p. 196.

[17] Chen, Huan-chang. 1911. *The Economic Principles of Confucius and His School*. New York: Columbia University Press. pp.568-585.

[18] Cochrane, Willard. W. 1993. *The Development of American Agriculture: A Historical Analysis (Second Edition)*, Minneapolis: University of Minnesota Press. p.100.

[19] Schlebeker, John T. 1975. *Whereby We Thrive: A History of American Farming, 1607-1972*. Iowa: The Iowa University Press. p. 202.

product prices nearly halved.[20] "With the decline in prices, the bankruptcy rate jumped from 6.4 percent of all farms in 1920 to an average for 1924-1926 of 17.7 percent, after which it drifted downwards to 8.7 in 1929."[21]

By the end of the 19th century, agriculture was no longer the leading sector of the national economy in the United States. The arrival of the industrial era made agricultural issues more complex. Confronted with the disproportionately low prices of agricultural products compared to industrial goods and the continuously rising costs of agricultural inputs caused by socialized production, the agricultural sector fell into a dilemma of dual price-cost squeeze, becoming a sacrifice for industrial development. On the other hand, the U.S. government lacked proactive and targeted agricultural policies throughout the 1920s. *The McNary-Haugen Bills*, which were actively promoted by farm groups to raise agricultural prices, were denied twice by President John C. Coolidge in 1927 and 1928, who believed that agricultural policies would distort the market development. The *Agriculture Marketing Act of 1929*passed by the Congress in 1929 was of little help for agricultural plights during the period of Great Depression between 1929 and 1933.[22]The capitalist agricultural production still relied primarily on self-regulation of the markets, therefore the conflict between socialized mass production and decentralized market and farming decisions was not properly solved by the government with unified policies. "Farmers were unable to adjust their production to market demands as quickly as manufacturers. Indeed, when prices fell they tended to work harder to produce more in order to maintain total income, and this only added to the oversupply."[23]

Henry A. Wallace had an in-depth understanding of the long-term accumulated contradictions of American agriculture. Growing up in a family with generations of farmers in the Corn Belt, Wallace was greatly influenced by the devotion of his grandfather and father to American agriculture. With his knowledge of Ever-normal Granary in ancient China, Wallace tried to find a solution for agricultural overproduction, and for the series of economic and social problems caused thereby.[24] Wallace's own writings reveal that this is a gradually-deepening process. His article entitled "Storage of Food", which was published in the newspaper *Wallaces' Farmer* (for which he was the editor-in-cheif) in December, 1918, pointed out the significant role the government should play in regulating the supply and demand of agricultural products:

---

[20]Cochrane, Willard. W. 1993. *The Development of American Agriculture: A Historical Analysis (Second Edition)*, Minneapolis: University of Minnesota Press. p.100.

[21] Scheiber, H. N., et al. 1976. *American Economic History*. New York, Hagerstown, San Francisco, London: Harper & Row. p. 345.

[22]Xu, Gengsheng. 2007. *American Agricultural Policies*. Beijing: Economy and Management Publishing House. p. 98.

[23] Scheiber, H. N., et al. 1976. *American Economic History*. New York, Hagerstown, San Francisco, London: Harper & Row. p. 345.

[24]Li, Chaomin. 2002. *Ever-normal Granary: A Chinese Idea in the American Systems*. Shanghai: Shanghai Far East Publishers.

> The dealers in eggs, butter and other surplus food products are rendering a distinct service both to the producers and the consumers, when they buy these products when they are plentiful and store them up to be used during the time when they are scarce. No doubt it is quite true that some of these men make more of a profit than they ought to make, but certainly their operations tend to equalize the price of food and to make it cheaper than it would otherwise be during that season of the year when the supply is smallest.
>
> If any government shall ever do anything really worthwhile with our food problem it will be by perfecting the plan tried by the Chinese three thousand years ago; that is, by building warehouses and storing food in years of abundance, and holding it until the years of scarcity.[25]

In October, 1926, Wallace published his article "The Ever-normal Granary" in *Wallaces's Farmer*, in which he stated that "Ever-normal Granary shows more administrative ability than can be found in the vast majority of other American agriculture relief plans." He also pointed out that the policy should be adjusted according to the American agricultural situation. Though a certain degree of government intervention is inevitable for agricultural production, Wallace believed that Americans were not ready for such a change. He then emphasized as follows:

> It must be remembered that the government is continually meddling with agriculture and that it is in large measure responsible for the present surplus of agricultural products…. In times like the present, the government should either stop boosting agricultural production or should go ahead and work out an agricultural program designed to safeguard the future welfare of the nation.[26]

To highlight the importance of Ever-normal Granary in American agricultural policies, Wallace published another article with the same title "The Ever-normal Granary" in *Wallaces' Farmer* in January 1927. In the article, "a Californian" suggested the application of "Ever-normal Granary to cotton" as follows: Let the federal government each year decide what has been the average price of cotton during the preceding five years. If the current price is 10% below or above the said average price, let the government purchase and store the cotton or sell the stored supply. The government should carry the interest and warehouse charges as a legitimate contribution to the public welfare. What is noteworthy here are comments by Wallace on the Ever-normal Granary proposed by the anonymous "Californian":

> There is merit in this idea. It would stabilize prices, and the chief criticism we can see is that it accepts the 1922-1926 scale of prices as normal and desirable for farm products. Someday the "ever normal granary" idea will be made to fit modern conditions.[27]

---

[25] Wallace, H.A. 1918. Storage of food. *Wallaces' Farmer.* 43 (49): 1772. December 6. *qtd.* in: Bodde, D. 1946. Henry A. Wallace and the Ever-normal Granary. *The Far Eastern Quarterly*. 5(4): 415-416.

[26] Wallace, H.A. 1926. The Ever Normal Granary. *Wallaces' Farmer*. 51 (41), October 8. p. 1314. *qtd.* in: Bodde, D. 1946. Henry A. Wallace and the Ever-normal Granary. *The Far Eastern Quarterly*. 5(4): 416.

[27] Wallace, H.A. 1927. The Ever Normal Granary. *Wallaces' Farmer*. 52(3). January 21. p. 85. *qtd.* in: Bodde, D. 1946. Henry A. Wallace and the Ever-normal Granary. *The Far Eastern Quarterly*. 5(4): 416-417.

In Wallace's view, the markets of 1922-1926 no longer reflected the real prices for agricultural products due to the depression in American agriculture, which in turn led him to believe that such price distortion sooner or later should be changed by Ever-normal Granary system. Wallace's predictions revealed his determination to change the status quo of American agriculture: when he became the Secretary of Agriculture during the Great Depression, Wallace started his ambitious reform with Ever-normal Granary.

4.2 Ever-normal Granary of Henry A. Wallace and Benjamin Graham

Different from a laissez-faire set of agricultural regulations, the American Ever-normal Granary constructed by Henry A. Wallace aims at stabilizing agricultural development through price and income support policies. However, Graham's "Modern Ever-normal Granary" involved incorporating bulk commodities into a buffer reserve mechanism, which is more similar to the "equalization policy" (*ping-zhunfa*) in ancient China. Its novelty lies in its attempt to create a more stable monetary system with a composite of commodity reserves (instead of a single gold reserve).

4.2.1 Symbol of Maturing Agricultural Economy: American Ever-normal Granary in 1930s

The Agricultural Adjustment Act of 1933 (AAA of 1933), the first American farm bill, took effect on May 12th, 1933 with the promotion of Henry A. Wallace. It was an emergency legislation enacted at the early stage of Franklin D. Roosevelt's New Deal to deal with the farm crisis. The act primarily aimed at tackling the issue of declining agricultural product prices and credit problems resulting from overproduction. As was stated in the beginning of the bill:

> That the present acute economic emergency being in part the consequence of a severe and increasing disparity between the prices of agricultural and other commodities, which disparity has largely destroyed the purchasing power of farmers for industrial products, has broken down the orderly exchange of commodities, and has seriously impaired the agricultural assets supporting the national credit structure, it is hereby declared that these conditions…have affected a national public interest, …."[28]

Under the provisions of the AAA of 1933, farm owners entered into agreements with the government to limit the production of basic commodities in the form of

---

[28] *Agricultural Adjustment Act of 1933*. https://nationalaglawcenter.org/farmbills/, accessed on Nov., 12, 2022.

acreage allotment. Any farm owner who entered into an agreement could receive government subsidies. The AAA aimed to re-establish a new price level for agricultural commodities on the basis of balanced production and consumption, and restore the parity[29] between agricultural and industrial commodities and farm purchasing power to the level of the prosperous 1909-1914 period, a period chosen as the base because it was a time when farm family incomes were equal to or at parity with income of non-farm families.

As a supplement to the AAA of 1933, the Department of Agriculture of the United States launched a program for surplus products disposal. The Federal Surplus Relief Corporation, later renamed the Federal Surplus Commodities Corporation, was established by the government on October 4, 1933. This company, in collaboration with the Department of Agriculture and the Federal Emergency Relief Administration, purchased surplus agricultural commodities and distributed them to poverty-stricken families. With such purchase and distribution activities, the surplus agricultural commodities were not allowed to flood freely into the market to lower the prices. The Commodity Credit Corporation (CCC) was established by the government on October 17 of the same year to issue *price-support loans*, now commonly referred to as non-recourse loans (the commodity itself was security on the loan), for farmers participating in the controlled production program to obtain cash using crops as collateral. The aim of the non-recourse loan was to allow the farmers to make their own decisions on marketing behavior after harvest. To be more specific, the Commodity Credit Corporation set the loan rates and provided a certain amount of funds to the farmers based on the parity price of the commodities. After harvest, if the market prices were comparatively low, the farmers could have their crops as collateral against the loan to the Commodity Credit Corporation and obtain a short-term loan, holding their products off the market until prices improved. If the market prices were above the loan rate plus interest, the farmers could choose to sell their crops to repay the loan. If the market prices remained low, the farmers could give their products to the Commodity Credit Corporation without repaying the loans, and the latter had no right to demand the farmers to repay the loans. The loan is therefore called a non-recourse loan.[30] Non-recourse loans guarantee the farmers' basic profit calculated at the parity price. With the support of policies guaranteeing the minimum price and income, the farmers were placed in a consistently protected

---

[29] Parity means to "re-establish prices to farmers at a level that will give agricultural commodities a purchasing power, with respect to articles that farmers buy, equivalent to the purchasing power of agricultural commodities in the base period" (1909-1914). However, the parity formula neglected the impact of higher productivity on prices. Therefore, the Agricultural Act of 1949 regulated that a new parity formula was to be phased in from the beginning of the year1950. See: Xu, Gengsheng. 2007. *American Agricultural Policies*. Beijing: Economy and Management Publishing House. p. 100. It is worth noting that Wallace's parity pricing policy didn't necessarily mean "full" parity for the farmers, for its effect was decided by the funds allocated to the Secretary of Agriculture by the American Congress. See: Scheiber, H. N. et al. 1976. *American Economic History*. New York, Hagerstown, San Francisco, London: Harper & Row. p. 300.

[30] Xu, Gengsheng. 2007. *American Agricultural Policies*. Beijing: Economy and Management Publishing House. p. 100.

and advantageous position. This is much similar to the *pingdi* of the Ever-normal Granary system in ancient China. The key lies in the combination of government intervention (parity price support) with market regulation (granting farmers the right to make decisions based on market prices), thereby maintaining the flexibility of the policy. At the same time, the agricultural products mortgaged by farmers to the Commodity Credit Corporation established a national buffer stock, which could be utilized to stabilize market fluctuations.

It is worth noting that Chen Huan-Chang described the Green Sprouts Act in his book *The Economic Principles of Confucius and His School* as follows:

> This law was introduced in 1620 of Confucius Calendar (1069 A.D.). If people wished to get money in advance, they were allowed to borrow it from the government; and when they paid taxes, they should return grain for the money they had borrowed. If they wanted to borrow grain instead of money, or if they wanted to return money instead of grain because at the time of return the price of grain was high, they were allowed to do so.[31]

The Green Sprouts Act is akin to a recourse loan, but its institutional design empowers farmers with the discretion to choose whether to borrow money or grain, and whether to repay money or grain according to their real interests.[32] It is on this basis that some scholars argue that Wallace's non-recourse loans were inspired by the Green Sprouts Act.[33]Bodde originally had a similar view. However, Wallace, in his letter to Bodde, clarified that he didn't know Wang Anshi when he advocated agricultural legislation.[34] Although both the Ever-normal Granary and the Green Sprouts Act were mentioned in *The Economic Principles of Confucius and His School*, they were placed in different sections of the book: the Ever-normal Granary was discussed in Chapter 30 "Government Control of Grain" and the Green Sprouts Actin Chapter 31 "Government Loans and Public Relief". From the perspective of the titles alone, it is reasonable to assume that Wallace would have been most drawn to the chapter "Government Control of Grain", thus reasonably neglecting the chapter "Government Loans and Public Relief".

With the implementation of the AAA of 1933 and relevant policies, the economic situation for farmers was much better than before. In comparison with that of the Golden Age (1910-1914, indexed as 100), the index of farm prices declined to 65 in 1932, rose to 70 in 1933, then to 81 in 1934, and to 108 in 1935.[35]Correspondingly, "the average cash farm income in 1933-35 exceeded the average cash farm income in 1932", and "farm income in 1935 was more than 50 percent higher than farm

[31] Chen, Huan-chang. 1911. *The Economic Principles of Confucius and His School*. New York: Columbia University Press. p.590.

[32] The Green Sprouts Act showed an obvious tendency towards monetization in practice, as is discussed in chapter 1.2.

[33] Li, Chaomin. On the influence of Wang Anshi's economic thoughts on the Ever-normal Granary of the New Deal in the United States. *Journal of Southwest Normal University*. 2002 (6): 96-100.

[34] Bodde, D. 1946. Henry A. Wallace and the Ever-normal Granary. *The Far Eastern Quarterly.* 5 (4):411-412.

[35] Novak, J. L et al. 2022.*Agricultural Policy in the United States: Evolution and Economics* (Second Edition). London and New York: Routledge. p.55.

income during 1932"[36]. However, the new policies also attracted criticism after their implementation: "No part of the New Deal program inspired more widespread criticism than that pertaining to agriculture. The whole idea of curtailing the production of foodstuffs while millions were on the point of starvation seemed to humanitarians little short of insanity."[37] Meanwhile, the policy of imposing a special tax on processors of farm products to support agricultural subsidies aroused fierce opposition. In the United States v. Butler, 297 U.S.1 (1936), the U.S. Supreme Court held that the processing taxes were not collected for the general welfare of the public, therefore they should be repealed. The court also held that regulation of agriculture was a state responsibility, rather than a federal one. "Congress and the Supreme Court had voided all the old contracts between farmers and the secretary of agriculture."[38]

After the experimental AAA of 1933 was ruled unconstitutional, another act, the *Soil Conservation and Domestic Allotment Act*, was hurriedly approved by the Department of Agriculture on February 29, 1936. The act introduced the concept of "income parity"[39], integrating the efficient use and conservation of agricultural resources with support of farmers' income. The act divided agricultural products into two categories: soil-depleting crops and soil-conserving crops. The former included surplus agricultural crops such as grains, cotton and tobacco, while the latter included crops such as legumes and grasses. Under the law, the farmers would be subsidies for their voluntary transition of acreage from soil-depleting crops into soil-conserving crops. The *Soil Conservation and Domestic Allotment Act* may be understood as Ever-normal Granary with a special function: it didn't reserve the grains but the soil. Wallace called it "storing the grain in the soil" instead of "storing it in the bin".[40]The Ever-normal Granary of soil addresses the issue of surplus production while conserving land resources and providing income support to farmers, thus achieving multiple benefits.

However, the *Soil Conservation and Domestic Allotment Act* was still an incomplete law. Due to the severe drought in 1934 and 1936, the previously accumulated grain conservations were consumed, and there was even shortage of agricultural products. But in 1937, the good weather brought a new surplus. The unpredictable shift in abundance and shortage demanded a more complete "all-weather" program.

---

[36] Rasmussen, W.D. et al.1976. A short history of Agricultural Adjustment, 1933- 75. *National Economic Analysis Division, Economic Service, U.S. Department of Agriculture, Agriculture Information Bulletin.* 391: 4.

[37] Scheiber, H. N., et al. 1976. *American Economic History*. New York, Hagerstown, San Francisco, London: Harper & Row. p. 371.

[38] Schlebeker, John T. 1975. *Whereby We Thrive: A History of American Farming, 1607-1972*. Ames: The Iowa State University Press. p. 241.

[39] Income parity means "the maintenance of a continuous and stable supply of agricultural commodities adequate to meet consumer demand at prices fair to both producers and consumers". in "Soil Conservation and Domestic Allotment Act (1936)", https://nationalaglawcenter.org/wp-content/uploads/assets/farmbills/soilconserv1936.pdf.

[40] Davis, J.S. 1938. The Economics of the Ever-normal Granary, *Journal of Farm Economics*. 20(1): 10.

"On February 8, 1937, a group of farm leaders from all over the country met in Washington to discuss the situation. They listened to Mr. Wallace's appeal for an Ever-normal Granary, and then, the following day, unanimously passed a resolution demanding the adoption of such legislation."[41] The resulting AAA of 1938 was signed by President Franklin D. Roosevelt on February 16, 1938. As was stated by Bodde,

> Since 1938 the term Ever-normal Granary has appeared frequently in publications of the U.S. Department of Agriculture. It is commonly used in a general rather than a specific sense, to cover a whole group of broadly related activities, rather than a particular piece of legislation. Some of these activities antedate the AAA of 1938, but they were coordinated by that Act into a comprehensive and unified program. To quote the Department of Agriculture itself:
>
> The Ever-normal Granary program, in a broad sense, includes the various activities concerned with the supply of agricultural products. It is designed to provide abundance from year to year and in the future with reserves in the store-houses and reserves in the soil. It is concerned with efficiency of production, adjustment of production, conservation, balancing the flow of market supplies, and insuring crop yields.[42]

The laws and policies around the AAA of 1938 covered various aspects of agricultural production and consumption, highlighting the multiple functions of Ever-normal Granary in America. We will summarize the key points and make a brief explanation of this scheme. Firstly, the government provides income support to farmers participating in acreage allotments. Accordingly, the Soil Conservation program was further implemented to establish the first level of land reserve, by decreasing the production of soil-depleting crops in favor of increased production of soil-conserving crops. In addition, special payments were made to farmers in ten states participating in the land retirement plan. Secondly, balancing the flow of agricultural product supplies: when the oversupply of agricultural products leads to prices falling below a certain percentage of the parity price, farmers participating in the marketing quota (which may not be used unless approved by at least two thirds of the farmers voting in referendum on the question) may obtain non-recourse loans, to ensure price support for major agricultural products based on the historical parity price. At the same time, the loan institutions (Agricultural Credit Corporation) establish a national reserve system by mortgaging agricultural products, forming a second level of physical agricultural product reserves on the basis of land reserves. Thirdly, the insurance program for crops was implemented. The U.S. Department of Agriculture, through the Federal Crop Insurance Corporation, protected farmers from losses caused by agricultural disasters. Fourthly, The Department of Agriculture participated in and provided funds for research and promotion of new crop varieties,

[41] Bodde, D. 1946. Henry A. Wallace and the Ever-normal Granary. *The Far Eastern Quarterly*. 5 (4): 420.

[42] Achieving a balanced agriculture, p.23. *qtd.* in: Bodde, D. 1946. Henry A. Wallace and the Ever-normal Granary. *The Far Eastern Quarterly*. 5(4): 420.

new farming methods and new chemical fertilizers, etc. to increase agricultural productivity.[43]

In the AAA of 1938, achieving parity between prices and incomes was an important goal, which was similar to the "*pingdi*" in the Ever-normal Granary system in ancient China. In addition to supporting prices and incomes, building up food and soil reserves was a strategy similar to "*pingtiao*" to prepare for lean years. The surplus food disposal plan of the American Department of Agriculture, "which began with the distribution of surplus pork in 1933" and "was supplemented by a nationwide school lunch program, a low-cost milk program, and a food stamp program"[44] after 1938, were also similar to assistance and relief aid of the Ever-normal Granary. Henry A. Wallace not only inherited the fundamental principles of the ancient Chinese Ever-normal Granary system but also creatively developed specific measures in accordance with national conditions of the U.S.. Wallace focused on addressing the issue of agricultural surplus under the conditions of capitalist large-scale farming and a highly market-oriented environment. He combined policy guarantees with market regulation through fiscal and financial means and democratic mechanisms. Additionally, he significantly expanded the boundaries of the agricultural Ever-normal Granary system to the fields of the protection of agricultural resources, nutrition security, insurance plans, and the promotion of agricultural productivity. Wallace, through a comprehensive plan, constructed the agricultural Ever-normal Granary which achieved a successful historical transcendence in the industrial era. The U.S. Department of Agriculture ever since developed from "growing stage" to "maturity stage", starting to protect agriculture with the help of "two hands", i.e. the market and government.

During the 1920s and the 1930s, the U.S. government, deeply mired in a crisis, could no longer take the laissez-faire pathway for its agricultural development. The ancient Chinese economic ideas and policies, through Chen Huan-chang's publishing in the English world, inspired Wallace who firmly believed that the active role of the government would be the key to solving American agricultural problems and safeguarding the farmers' interests. If Franklin D. Roosevelt's New Deal is regarded as a pioneering activity of systematic government intervention in economy in the Western world at the industrial age, the Ever-normal Granary must be its pioneer in the agricultural field.[45]In this sense, Henry A. Wallace was an agricultural economist

[43] Bodde, D.1946. Henry A. Wallace and the Ever-normal Granary. *The Far Eastern Quarterly*. 5(4): 420-421.

[44] Rasmussen, W. D. et al.1976. A short history of Agricultural Adjustment, 1933- 75. *National Economic Analysis Division, Economic Service, U.S. Department of Agriculture, Agriculture Information Bulletin*. 391: 8.

[45] It should be noted that there was an overlooked driving force behind the New Deal, the institutionalist movement in American economics which, founded by Thorstein B Veblen (1857-1929), sprang up in the 1920s and 1930s. The movement embraced the need for more government interventions. With the theoretical explanations and participation in the decisions and implementation of New Deal policies, the institutionalists had a great impact on the New Deal. For example, Ezekiel, an institutionalist and an economist in the Department of Agriculture, was a leading economist by the side of Roosevelt at the beginning of the New Deal and an important author of AAA

with far-reaching influences in American economics.[46] In particular, what should not be overlooked is that the agricultural legislation in the 1930s not only changed the path of American agriculture, but also played an important role in the anti-fascist war. During the Second World War, American agricultural reserves were shipped to the Allies, which strongly supported the anti-fascist war. Even the laissez-faire groups who criticized Wallace's agricultural policies reluctantly admitted: "The war, of course, saved the situation by creating a big demand for farm products – whereupon the size of the stored-up surpluses became a proof of Wallace's foresight!"[47] The so-called "ever-normal" is a state opposite to that of "non-normal". How could people be optimistic to the free market economy so much so that they turn a blind eye to natural or man-made disasters?

Agriculture has positive externalities, and agricultural products belong to public goods or quasi-public goods. The vast industrial chain associated with agriculture provides considerable employment positions. Even though the agricultural support policies of the U.S. government may result in efficiency losses, these losses are still smaller than the harm caused to the economy and society by spontaneous disorder. As was stated in the book *Agricultural Policy in the United States: Evolution and Economics*, "One interpretation of the history of U.S. agricultural and food policy is that it has served the goals of social and economic stability and provided a producer and consumer safety net. Another interpretation is that it has served the self-interests of a few. Both might be considered accurate. Over the history of the planet, agricultural stability variously meant keeping rulers in power and preserving social order. In more recent history, U.S. farm policy has meant keeping farms profitable and people fed."[48] The legislation promoted by Henry A. Wallace laid the foundation of modern U.S. agricultural policies in subsequent periods. Though the agricultural laws were periodically revised and amended (every four to six years), all these revisions never strayed from the fundamental Ever-normal Granary program: without giving up either of the "two hands", the government dynamically adjusted the role of the two, so that their relationship was continuously adjusted according to the specific situations of agricultural development, ensuring the ever-normal development of agriculture while continuously increasing its productivity.

It is worth noting that the above discussion does not mean to exaggerate the influence of Chinese Ever-normal Granary to American agriculture. The American Ever-normal Granary was developed on the basis of the specific features of American agriculture, with focus on addressing the issue of surplus products in a market

---

of 1933. See: Zhang, Lin and Bi Zhi. 2010. Impact of Institutionalists on "New Deal". *Research Reports on Foreign Economics and China*. ed. Cheng, Enfu. Beijing: Social Sciences Academic Press. pp. 251-255.

[46] Ezekiel, M. 1966. Henry A. Wallace, agricultural economist. *Journal of Farm Economics*. 48(4): 789-802.

[47] Macdonald, D. 1948. *Henry Wallace: the Man and the Myth*. New York: The Vanguard Press. p. 62.

[48] James L Novak, et al. 2022.*Agricultural Policy in the United States: Evolution and Economics* (Second Edition). London and New York: Routledge. p.190.

economy. The Chinese Ever-normal Granary functioned as the "catalyst", which bridged the past and present and "introduced" a policy system different from the laissez-faire one. In the face of the unprecedented crisis of the 1920s and 1930s in the West, the Ever-normal Granary, which had a long history in China, was adopted to "smooth out" the economic fluctuations by way of government adjustments, thus highlighting its "modernity" in the new era. Of course, this was not a historical "coincidence". The two "great rivers" of civilization in the East and West, in their development process, had already developed a supplementary relationship by supplying each other with "fresh water". When and where they would encounter depends on the historical opportunities.

From the perspective of the general trend of economic thought and policy changes, the Western world in the 1920s and 30s was experiencing great transformation. In the United States, not only Henry A. Wallace and Franklin D. Roosevelt noticed the Ever-normal Granary, but also Graham, a famous investor, keenly recognized the contemporary value of this policy.

4.2.2 Multiple Buffer Stock in Industrial Society: Benjamin Graham's Application of **pingzhunfa** *in Modern Society*

Benjamin Graham (1894-1976), an American investor, is widely acknowledged to be the "Father of Modern Security Analysis". His name was known to all on the Wall Street. His ideas on financial analysis have influenced generations of investors. Warren Buffett, his student, is also one of the most successful investors in the world. It seems odd to associate such a man from the Wall Street, who seeks business opportunities and profits in the midst of ups and downs, with the Ever-normal Granary. However, a significant portion of his economic writings are pertaining to Ever-normal Granary.[49] Graham's work, *Storage and Stability*, was first published in 1937. In the "Preface" the author wrote:

> The Ever-normal Granary is a Chinese phrase, which has rather suddenly become a central issue in American economic policy. The first and most pressing business of the next session of Congress will be the passage of comprehensive farm relief legislation. By way of offset against the substantial benefits to be accorded by our government to the farmers, this legislation offers an Ever-normal Granary as a safeguard to the consuming population. The Granary idea, briefly, means the storage of reserve supplies of big crop years for use in time of crop failure.[50]

---

[49] Two of his representative works are as follows:Graham, B. 1937. *Storage and Stability: A Modern Ever-normal Granary*, New York and London: McGraw-Hill Book Company, Inc.; Graham, B. 1944. *The World Commodities and World Currency*, New York and London: McGraw-Hill Book Company, Inc.

[50] Graham, B. Preface. in Graham, B. 1937. *Storage and Stability: A Modern Ever-normal Granary*. New York and London: McGraw-Hill Book Company, Inc. p. v.

Graham was obviously inspired by the Chinese idea. He hoped to extend the agricultural Ever-normal Granary to a more comprehensive economic program which would contribute to the stability of macro-economy. He then continued:

> In this study we shall deal not only with the specific Ever-normal Granary proposals now before Congress, but — more comprehensively — with the general possibilities of storage of basic commodities as a source of stability and improvement in our national economy. Most attacks upon the problems of depression may be ranged under two distinct headings: those related to so-called overproduction, and those related to defects of our monetary and credit system. The concept of storage is unique in that it lies at the intersection of these two lines of difficulty, offering at once a synthesis and solution of both.[51]

In his opinion, storage is the intermediate stage between production and consumption. Its function has always been to absorb and level out disparities between supply and demand. At the macro level, it serves as an adequate remedy for the maladjustment between output and effective demand. There is an analogy between storage of staple commodities and storage of water in reservoirs: the reservoirs provide stable supplies of water and electricity, while the storage of commodities could prevent market speculation and periodic disturbance. Graham also stated the following points: as to the monetary field, storage of basic commodities suggests itself as the most suitable backing for a sound and adequate currency. The unique prestige of the gold standard has been deeply undermined by reason of the inadequacies. Silver vexes people as a lesser and more questionable gold. The alternative of "managed paper currency" bristles with dangers and difficulties as yet unexplored. A currency backed by, and actually redeemable in, stored basic commodities would possess an intrinsic soundness superior to that of gold and immeasurably beyond that of inconvertible paper,[52] as a group, or composite unit, of basic commodities rather than any single commodity (including gold) is used as the basis of currency emission. Thus the Storage mechanism, if skillfully employed, offers the solution of basic monetary problem. Graham also emphasized this point: reasonable price stability and general business stability go hand in hand. It may be demonstrated that the soundest price-control policy would be one that aims at stability of the general level of raw-materials prices, which exercise a determining influence over the price structure as

[51] Graham, B. Preface. in Graham, B. 1937. *Storage and Stability: A Modern Ever-normal Granary*. New York and London: McGraw-Hill Book Company, Inc. p. v.

[52] John M. Keynes classified money in three forms, namely commodity money, fiat money and managed money. The managed money, having a determinate value in terms of an objective standard, is the most generalized form of money. On one hand, when the managing authority holds against it 100 per cent of the objective standard (e.g. the gold), managed money may be considered to degenerate into commodity money (e.g. gold standard monetary system). On the other hand, when it loses its objective standard, the managed money may be considered to degenerate into fiat money. See: Keynes, J.M. 2013. *A Treatise on Money: the Pure Theory of Money*. New York: Cambridge University Press. pp. 6-7. Graham was worried about the unstable monetary system of the time: on one hand, the unique prestige of the gold standard has been deeply undermined by reason of the inadequacies revealed since the war; on the other hand, fiat money is not backed by reliable the objective standard. Graham held that money should resume the prestige backed by the objective standard. Therefore, storage of basic commodities suggests itself as the most suitable backing for a sound and adequate currency.

a whole. In the process the Storage mechanism plays a significant role. Based on the regulative or sales mechanism, Graham invented a whole system of storage for macro-economic governance. As Alvin Johnson (1874-1971), an American economist, praised him in the "preface" of Graham's work: "In economics no stone ever kills a single bird. Mr. Graham, like all economic inventors who know their job, kills several birds with one stone."[53]

Benjamin Graham named his storage program as "Modern Ever-normal Granary", which Alvin Johnson praised with the words "the invention is of such startling simplicity"[54]. There are three key points for the program[55]:

Firstly, commodity reserves are the foundation of the whole program. A number of primary commodities, or groups of staples, which reflect the overall market prices, are selected. On this basis, a Reservoir system under which a general surplus of basic commodities will flow into storage, without demoralizing the markets or business structure, and remain so mobilized until a consumptive demand develops for them.

Secondly, the monetization of reserve commodities is key to the program. The appropriate weighting of the different commodities in the groups are assigned, and then the Commodity Units and their prices are fixed at some appropriate level such as the average of 1921-1930, the base period. The price level for the component commodities *as a whole* will be fixed as equivalent to the value of dollars (Table 4.1). "According to a composite group of basic commodities exactly the same monetary status as was formerly given to gold" under the gold standard system, it is possible to create a monetary system based on basic commodity reserves. This will go far toward establishing a "dollar of constant purchasing power"[56].

Thirdly, the commodity-currency circulation mechanism transforms buffer reserves into stabilizers for the economic system. When the market demand decreases, the commodity units shall be acquired and reserved at a small discount below their established value. They shall be paid for in currency issued in exchange therefore (monetary expansion). If the market demand increases and the composite price of the commodities advances above the established standard, currency will be redeemed for commodity units (monetary contraction), thereby suppressing market speculation and excessive purchasing.

In this way, the commodity reserves, integrating fiscal policy and monetary policy through the two-way exchange between commodity units and commodity unit currency, forming a stabilizing mechanism where the product market and the monetary market complement each other. After analysis, Graham believes that this

---

[53] Johnson, Alvin. Foreword. in Graham, B. 1937. *Storage and Stability: A Modern Ever-normal Granary*. New York and London: McGraw-Hill Book Company, Inc. p. xvii.

[54] Johnson, Alvin. Foreword. in Graham, B.1937. *Storage and Stability: A Modern Ever-normal Granary*. New York and London: McGraw-Hill Book Company, Inc. p. xvi.

[55] Graham, B. 1937. *Storage and Stability: A Modern Ever-normal Granary*. New York and London: McGraw-Hill Book Company, Inc. pp. 47-68.

[56] Graham, B. 1937. *Storage and Stability: A Modern Ever-normal Granary*. New York and London: McGraw-Hill Book Company, Inc. p. 50

Table 4.1 The commodity unit

Commodity	Unit of quantity	Average production or consumption 1921-1930, millions	Weighted average price, 1921-1930, dollars	Average value of production or consumption 1921-1930, millions of dollars	Amount of commodity in 1000 one-dollar units	Value of commodity in 1000 commodity units, 1921-1930 average	Price, June 1937, cents	Value of commodity in 1000 commodity units, June 1937, dollars
Wheat	Bushel	824	1.24	1,022	84.4	104.9	123	103.8
Barley	Bushel	212	0.666	141	21.7	14.4	81	17
Cocoa	Pound	394	0.102	40	40.4	4.2	7.4	3
Coffee	Pound	1,421	0.172	244	145.5	25.1	10.9	15.8
Corn	Bushel	2,618	0.816	2,139	268	218.9	120	322
Cottonseed oil	Pound	1,258	0.1000.0.443	125	128.8	12.8	10	12.9
Oats	Bushel	1,220	0.908	540	125	55.6	48	60
Rye	Bushel	52	0.061	47	5.3	4.8	99	5.3
Sugar	Pound	12,670	0.205	771	1,297.20	78.9	4.6	59.7
Cotton	Pound	6,588	5.89	1,349	674.8	138.2	12.7	85.6
Silk	Pound	74	1.156	437	7.6	44.8	183	13.9
Wool	Pound	263	0.143	304	26.9	31.2	100	26.9
Copper	Pound	1,485	0.07	211	152.2	21.6	13.8	21
Lead	Pound	1,370	0.484	96	140.4	9.8	6	8.4
Tin	Pound	154	0.063	75	15.8	7.7	55.8	8.7
Zinc	Pound	1,003	0.018	63	102.7	6.5	6.8	7
Cottonseed meal	Pound	4,064	2.46	71	416	7.3	1.6	6.7
Flaxseed	Bushel	37	0.168	91	3.8	9.3	192	7.3
Hides	Pound	949	1.64	160	97.2	16.4	16.8	16.3
Petroleum	Barrel	772	0.308	1,265	79.1	129.5	36	107.5

(continued)

Table 4.1 (continued)

Commodity	Unit of quantity	Average production or consumption 1921-1930, millions	Weighted average price, 1921-1930, dollars	Average value of production or consumption 1921-1930, millions of dollars	Amount of commodity in 1000 one-dollar units	Value of commodity in 1000 commodity units, 1921-1930 average	Price, June 1937, cents	Value of commodity in 1000 commodity units, June 1937, dollars
Rubber	Pound	824	0.078	253	84.4	25.9	19.3	16.3
Tallow	Pound	510	0.21	40	52.2	4.2	8	4.2
Tobacco	Pound	1,346		283	137.9	29	25(est.)	34.5
Total				$9,767		$1,000		$964.40

Source: Graham, B. 1937. *Storage and Stability: A Modern Ever-normal Granary*. New York and London: McGraw-Hill Book Company, Inc. p. 57. There is slight adjustment to the headers of the table.

"reservoir system takes on a new stature as an essential regulatory mechanism for the normal systole and diastole of the breath of business. In other words, we set up not merely an emergency apparatus to deal with a sudden onrush of commodity surpluses, but rather a balance-wheel arrangement which can function as an integral and indispensable part of a smoothly operating business machine."[57]

The selection of commodity units is a key issue for the commodity reservoir plan. Benjamin Graham selected 23 products (Table 4.1), including foods, textiles, metals and miscellaneous products.[58] In Graham's opinion, a large change in one commodity will affect the others only slightly, because the one large change is absorbed by small changes of other commodities.[59]When the overall prices of the 23 products are comparatively stable, the appropriate weighting of each is assigned, hence the building of composite groups of basic commodities. Then the price level for the component commodities are fixed, at some appropriate level such as the average of 1921-1930, the base period, as equivalent to the value of dollars. (Table 4.1) Afterwards a monetary system based on basic commodity reserves may be created, hence the extension of the gold standard monetary system. In Graham's opinion, the monetary system based on basic commodity reserves may coexist with the gold standard monetary system, and the two would cooperate with each other to promote the stability of the currency and eventually the stability of the whole economic system.[60]

Benjamin Graham's "Modern Ever-normal Granary" is the expansion and application of "equalization policy" (*pingzhununfa*), the grain price adjustment in ancient China, in the modern industrial society, or the industrial version of agricultural Ever-normal Granary. Its novelty lies in the linkage of "equalization policy" to the monetary system, and thus a composite of commodity reserves is bestowed with the status similar to gold.[61] If Henry A. Wallace's greatest contribution was the establishment of ever-normal granaries for agricultural products as a solution to American agricultural problems, Graham went further in theoretical analysis by expanding the ancient Ever-normal Granary to establish composite reserves of basic commodities in order to stabilize the economy and currency. Graham held that Modern Ever-normal Granary was a better choice than the agricultural Ever-normal Granary. The reasons are as follows: firstly, Modern Ever-normal Granary stabilizes the overall price level rather than the price of a single commodity; secondly, Modern

[57] Graham, B. 1937. *Storage and Stability: A Modern Ever-normal Granary*. New York and London: McGraw-Hill Book Company, Inc. p. 89.

[58] Graham, B. 1937. *Storage and Stability: A Modern Ever-normal Granary*, New York and London: McGraw-Hill Book Company, Inc. pp. 53-54.

[59] Graham, B. 1937. *Storage and Stability: A Modern Ever-normal Granary*, New York and London: McGraw-Hill Book Company, Inc. p. 69.

[60] Graham, B. 1937. *Storage and Stability: A Modern Ever-normal Granary*, New York and London: McGraw-Hill Book Company, Inc. pp. 144-152.

[61] Benjamin Graham thought that it was W.S. Jevons, a British economist, who proposed currency convertible into a group of basic commodities. See: Graham, B. 1944. *World Commodities and World Currency*. New York and London: McGraw-Hill Book Company, Inc. pp. 70-71.

Ever-normal Granary is different from agricultural Ever-normal Granary which adopts production restrictions as the main adjustment method; thirdly, while agricultural Ever-normal Granary requires huge amounts of financial subsidies, the Modern Ever-normal Granary has commodity units as the currency reserves, realizing the self-financing and self-liquidating of currencies through the exchange between currency and commodities, with the cost of the reservation as the exception[62]; fourthly, compared with the complicated operations on agricultural Ever-normal Granary by the government, the Modern Ever-normal Granary is much easier to operate, with its focus mainly on determination of commodity units and their values in USD, as well as the storage and marketing of commodities and goods.[63]Graham's scheme for Modern Ever-normal Granary is undoubtedly a bold program that appears straightforward and feasible in theory, which is "an engineering mechanism applied to the field of economics"[64]. However, in reality, incorporating such a wide range of commodities into the buffer reserve is not a simple task. Even though the legislation for the Ever-normal Granary promoted by Wallace was limited to the agricultural sector, it had to face a lot of opposition, with critics arguing that it only served the interests of those agricultural interest groups. In Graham's Modern Ever-normalizing Granary plan, how to reach a consensus among producers on the determination of the weights of various commodities in the "commodity units" is likely to be a rather difficult issue.

Benjamin Graham, a man with keen insight, could always keep up with the times. When most Americans discussed the agricultural Ever-normal Granary, he proposed the Modern Ever-normal Granary; when international communities were discussing the post-war economic order, he introduced a new scheme in his book *World Commodities and World Currency* published in 1944, in which the Modern Ever-normal Granary was updated to a World Ever-normal Granary. He thought that, due to the increasing mutual dependence among the nations in their development of economy, these countries should work together to establish a worldwide Ever-normal Granary to achieve stability for the postwar economy. He proposed the establishment of an international agency, International Commodity Corporation (ICC), which would purchase and hold commodity units when the composite price fell below 95% of the base, and sell them out when the composite price rose above 105% of the base. The commodity unit would consist of 15 commodities from the fields of raw materials.[65]On this basis, an alternative international currency,

[62] Benjamin Graham thought that the storage cost "may be offset by various types of income arising from the operation of the Reservoir plan", such as the "seigniorage". See: Graham, B. 1937. *Storage and Stability: A Modern Ever-normal Granary*. New York and London: McGraw-Hill Book Company, Inc. p. 111.

[63] Graham, B. 1937. *Storage and Stability: A Modern Ever-normal Granary*. New York and London: McGraw-Hill Book Company, Inc. pp. 189-203.

[64] Graham, B. 1937. *Storage and Stability: A Modern Ever-normal Granary*. New York and London: McGraw-Hill Book Company, Inc. p. 232.

[65] The 15-commodity unit includes wheat, corn, cotton, wool, rubber, coffee, tea, sugar, tobacco, petroleum, coal, wood pulp, pig iron, copper and tin. See: Graham, B. 1944. *World Commodities*

Commodity Reserve Currency, would be created which functions as the equivalent of gold or the capital and deposit of the International Monetary Fund (IMF, similar to John M. Keynes' *Bancor* or Harry D. White's *Unita*[66]). Within the IMF framework, the new currency would be complementary to the international credit mechanism, stabilizing the world monetary system together. In this way, the World Ever-normal Granary would achieve the fourfold objectives of reasonable price stability, protective stockpiles, a balanced expansion of the world's output and consumption of goods, and foreign-exchange stability.[67]

With a foresight on possible problems of the post-war economy in the world, Benmamin Graham believed that the World Ever-normal Granary and the Commodity Reserve Currency would be effective mechanisms for the balance of economic development in various countries (including both the exporting countries and importing countries for basic raw materials). The World Ever-normal Granary was as significant as, or at least complementary to, *International Clearing Union* (or *the Keynes Plan*) proposed by John M. Keynes and *the White Plan* proposed by Harry D. White. That is because the Commodity Reserve Currency, similar to currency on the gold standard, is the extension of gold clearing and is strongly supported by reliable commodity reserves.[68] The Commodity Reserve Currency proposed by Graham is in fact a sort of "supranational currency", or "world currency" which is not tied to the sovereignty of any country or the sovereign credit currency. In Graham's opinion, such a currency would be free from political influences. However, such a "cosmopolitan" economic program overlooked the significant differences in resource endowments among countries, particularly the severe imbalance in their economic development, and it was not fit for the post-war world pattern which was different from the past. The historical fact was the formation of

and World Currency. New York and London: McGraw-Hill Book Company, Inc. p. 44.

[66] In the Keynes Plan, the value of the *Bancor*, the seemingly supranational world currency managed by the International Clearing Union, is to be fixed in terms of gold. However, the quota of the *Bancor* assigned to each country depends upon its average volume of international trade in the preceding three years before the Second World War. In this way, Britain and the British Commonwealth would take a higher share. Such allocation in Keynesian plan would help Britain to maintain the internationally dominant position of British pounds despite the country's depletion of gold reserves, and at the same time weaken the influence of U.S. dollars and U.S. gold reserves. The core of the White Plan is the establishment of an International Stabilization Fund, to which each member country would subscribe a prescribed share. A new unit of account, "*Unita*", is contemplated, which is pegged to the U.S. dollar or gold. Currencies of member countries are required to maintain a fixed ratio with the *Unita*. Since the share of the fund is determined by the member countries' gold reserves, international balance of payments, and national income, the White Plan is obviously a monetary scheme which is more beneficial to the United States.

[67] Graham, B. 1944. *World Commodities and World Currency*. New York and London: McGraw-Hill Book Company, Inc. pp. 91-105.

[68] Graham, B. 1944. *World Commodities and World Currency*. New York and London: McGraw-Hill Book Company, Inc. pp. 86-87.

the Bretton Woods system, a new monetary system which was based on U.S. dollars in line of *the White Plan*.[69]

Before Benjamin Graham's *World Commodities and World Currency* was published, some other people had put forward their proposals on building a World Ever-normal Granary. In an article published in January, 1942, Henry A. Wallace expressed his hope that "what might be called the 'ever normal granary principle' can be established for a number of commodities on a world-wide scale."[70]In May, 1944, Alvin H. Hansen published an article in *The New York Times*, suggesting the establishment of "an international commodity cooperation, designed to buy, store, and sell raw materials and to act as a buffer in the raw materials market."[71] On the other side of the Atlantic Ocean, John M. Keynes put forward his ideas on buffer stocks in his proposal on building the post-war economic order. In this trend for Ever-normal Granary, it is interesting that Keynes' proposal was closely linked with his revolutionary economic theories.

[69] In the "Preface" to *World Commodities and World Currency*, Graham stated, "The author's proposal for an international commodity reserve currency was not on the agenda of the conference (i.e. the International Monetary and Financial Conference held at Bretton Woods, New Hampshire), but it has claims on the attention of the commissions which are to continue its studies." See: Graham, B. 1944. *World Commodities and World Currency*. New York and London: McGraw-Hill Book Company, Inc. p. ix.

[70] Wallace, Henry A. 1942. Foundations of peace. *Atlantic Monthly*. January, p. 37. *qtd*. in: Bodde, D. 1946. Henry A. Wallace and the Ever-normal Granary. *The Far Eastern Quarterly*. 5(4): 423.

[71] Hansen further illustrated the operation mechanism and function of the ICC: "It would permit the free play of market forces between upper and lower limits for each commodity. Buying operations would be indicated as soon as the price pierced the lower limit, and selling operations as soon as it rose above the upper limit. These upper and lower limits should be the subject of continuous study by the corporation and should be adjusted from time to time according to fundamental trends of normal supply and demand. An important part of the corporation's function would be to search for new uses for basic raw materials, and to cooperate with the various national governments to facilitate the movement of resources out of submarginal areas in an effort to adjust normal supply to normal demand." *qtd*. in: Graham, B. 1944. *World Commodities and World Currency*. New York and London: McGraw-Hill Book Company, Inc. pp. 57-58.

Chapter 5

Buffer Stocks and Granary Formula: The Neglected Keynesian Economics Theory

The competitive system abhors the existence of stocks, with as strong a reflex as nature abhors a vacuum, because stocks yield a negative return in terms of themselves.
—*Keynes, J.M.*[1]

Classical economics was concerned with the logic of choice under conditions of scarcity; Keynes's economics with the logic of choice under conditions of uncertainty.
—*Skidelsky, R.*[2]

John M. Keynes provided a new interpretation of Ever-normal Granary in the context of modern macroeconomics. In *A Treatise on Money*, Keynes introduced the short-period prices theory and its equation expression $pq = xy$, which reveals the significant impact of clearing surplus products through market mechanisms on prices and output. If the government is introduced into the equation and affects the relevant variables through a buffer stock policy, a stable economic state will emerge. In the Chinese context, the theory of short-period prices can be referred to as the "Ever-normal Granary equation". Starting from investment practice, Keynes, as early as the 1920s, proposed the use of buffer stocks to address business cycles. And by the 1940s, he had elaborated a post-war global commodity control plan for the implementation of buffer stocks. After Keynes, Richard F. Kahn (1905–1989), a disciple of Keynes, further developed the idea of buffer stocks. Kahn believed that under conditions of limited funds, buffer stocks should play a dual role in speculation and assuming public responsibilities, and their buying and selling behaviors should be more flexible and proactive to prevent being exploited by the market. Keynes' short-period prices theory and the concept of buffer stocks are intrinsically coherent with his masterwork *The General Theory*. The essential policy in *The General Theory* is for the government to carry out organized investments based on

[1] Keynes, J. M. 1938. The policy of government storage of food-stuffs and raw materials. *The Economics Journal* 48 (191): 449.

[2] Skidelsky, Robert. 2003. *John Maynard Keynes: 1883–1946, Economist, Philosopher, Statesman*. New York: Penguin Books. p.529.

W. Xian, *Chinese Food Security Strategy*, Research Series on the Chinese Dream and China's Development Path,
https://doi.org/10.1007/978-981-95-7964-8_5

the "long-term marginal efficiency of capital"[3] (long-term MEC), or socialization of investment, the essence of which is to use buffer stocks to stabilize the macroeconomy. The macro-policy during a depression can be interpreted as follows: when market entities abandon various economic resources and hold money to avoid risks due to poor expectations (collapse of marginal efficiency of capital or MEC), the government should rely on buffer stocks or public works to implement the *pingdi* policy to stabilize the economy, either by storing or "employing" various resources, including labor, that have been discarded by the market (surplus resources). The government constructs an ever-normal stability mechanism by investing to compensate for investment, stabilize investment, and guide investment. A crucial component of this approach is achieving full employment, which has been further developed by the post-Keynesian school. This helps to deepen the concept of the "Ever-normal Granary" in macroeconomics.

5.1 Market Fluctuations and Theory of Short-period Prices

5.1.1 A Market Expert

In the history of economic theory, Keynesian Revolution and *The General Theory* are well-known terms. Although different interpretations and developments of Keynesian economics by later economists have resulted in various schools of thought on his groundbreaking macroeconomic theories, there are still some aspects of Keynes' contribution to economics that have been neglected, one of which is the concept of buffer stock.[4] When connecting this idea into Keynes' economic practice,

---

[3] Keynes defined "marginal efficiency of capital" with following words, "The relation between the prospective yield of a capital-asset and its supply price or replacement cost, *i.e.* the relation between the prospective yield of one more unit of that type of capital and the cost of producing that unit, furnishes us with the *marginal efficiency of capital* of that type. More precisely, I define the marginal efficiency of capital as being equal to that rate of discount which would make the present value of the series of annuities given by the returns expected from the capital-asset during its life just equal to its supply price." See: Keynes, J. M. 2013. *The General Theory of Employment, Interest and Money*. in *The Collected Writings of John Maynard Keynes,* vol. 7. ed. Moggridge, D. New York: Cambridge University Press. p. 135.

[4] For an earlier study of this issue, see: Dimand, R. and Dimand, M. A. 1990. J. M. Keynes on Buffer Stocks and commodity price stabilization. *History of Political Economy*. 22 (1): 113–123. For a recent systematic study from a different perspective, see: Fantacci, L. and Rosselli, A. 2009. Stabilizing Commodities. Buffer Stock Plans by Keynes and Kahn. *ESHET 13th Conference Paper*; Hirai, T. 2009. Aimed at the stabilization of commodity prices- Keynes's hopes betrayed and the transmutation process of the International Control Scheme. *ESHET 13th Conference Paper*; Kregel, J. A. 2010. Keynes's influence on modern economics: Some overlooked contributions of Keynes's theory of finance and economics policy. in *The Return to Keynes*. ed. Bateman, B. et al. Harvard: Harvard University Press. pp. 241–256; Fantacci, L. et al. 2012. Speculation and buffer stocks: The legacy of Keynes and Kahn. *The European Journal of the History of Economic Thought*. 19 (3): 453–473.

theories, and policies, we find that buffer stocks could clearly explains his macroeconomic theory from a rather unique perspective.

Keynes was not an economist confined to theoretical discussions. Since the early twentieth century, in addition to serving in government and conducting academic research, he also held a significant role as a market investor. Investment records show that Keynes began his investment activities as early as 1905. In his early investments, Keynes primarily engaged in speculative activities in the stock and foreign exchange markets, esp. with currencies like the US dollar, German mark, French franc, and Italian lira. After the 1920s, he ventured into the commodity futures market, with substantial transactions involving base metals such as lead, tin, and copper, as well as agricultural products like rubber, cotton, wheat, and sugar, etc. Moreover, Keynes was also engaged in the management of investment institutions. During his tenure as the Second Bursar at King's College, Cambridge (1919–1924), the college established the Chest Fund in June 1920, which managed investment in common stocks and commodity futures. Upon his promotion to the position of First Bursar (he took the position from 1924 till his death), the Chest Fund's activities became more active, encompassing not only steady and hedging investments but also a broader range of speculative activities. Following the outbreak of World War II, with the closure of relevant markets in Britain and restrictions on transactions in foreign markets, Keynes was forced to terminate his commodity investment activities.[5]

Keynes was well-versed in practical matters and had a comprehensive understanding and analysis of market information. A typical example is that from 1923 to 1930, Keynes collected a large amount of market information on raw material commodities and compiled it into a series of statistical and analytical materials titled "Stocks of Staple Commodities". These materials, all included in the "London and Cambridge Economic Service, Special Memorandum No.1 (April 1923)", occupied a total of 380 pages in vol. 12 of the "The Collected Writing of John Maynard Keynes".[6]

Keynes experienced personally the tremendous impact of significant price fluctuations on the market through his involvement in investment business, which brought him considerable profits as well as certain losses. At the same time, Keynes gained a profound understanding of the market. In an article titled "Some Aspects of the Commodity Markets" published in *The Manchester Guardian Commercial Supplement* on 12, April, 1923, Keynes analyzed the entire process of the significant fluctuations in raw material prices and production in the following order,

> (1) The high prices of the boom period over-stimulated production and eventually reached a point at which they somewhat retarded consumption. (2) The process of production being a lengthy one, the resulting fall of prices did not immediately curtail the delivery of new

[5] Fantacci, L. et al. 2010. Speculation in commodities: Keynes' "Practical Acquaintance" with future markets. *Journal of the History of Economic Thought*. 32 (3): 398–399.

[6] Keynes, J. M. 2013. *Economic articles and correspondence: investment and editorial*. in *The Collected Writings of John Maynard Keynes*, vol.12. ed. Moggridge, D. New York: Cambridge University Press. pp. 267–647.

> supplies of materials. (3) Since normal stocks (or, in the case of seasonal crops, 'carryover') bear, in general, a small proportion to annual production,—in most commodities three months' stocks (or carryover) are considered substantial,—the more rapid curtailment of consumption than of production led to the heaping up of stocks much beyond normal. (4) The sight of such heavy 'visible supplies' drove prices not merely below the exaggerated boom price but below all reasonable anticipations of normal cost of production, with the result that new production was greatly curtailed and brought, in some cases, almost to a standstill. (5) Thus, whereas consumption during the slump did not fall, in many cases, by more than 10–20 per cent, production fell off at the minimum by as much as 30–50 per cent. (6) Consequently the surplus stocks have been steadily eaten into, production had been so hard hit that it has been slow to revive except for certain prospects of a higher price, and we now find ourselves with the stocks disappearing and consumption proceeding at a substantially higher level than production. (7) Even when production revives under the stimulus of higher prices, an interval must elapse before this can have its full effect on supplies coming forward, so that consumers may be confronted for a time with a famine of raw materials.[7]

Then, amidst such fluctuations, is speculative behavior in the futures market a kind of inter-temporal adjustment mechanism for balance? Keynes points out in the article that speculative behavior might play such a role, "but it presumes that the speculator is better informed on the average than the producers and the consumers themselves, which, speaking generally, is rather a dubious proposition. The most important function of the speculator in the great organised 'futures' markets is, I think, somewhat different. He is not so much a prophet (though it may be a belief in his own gifts of prophecy that tempts him into the business), as a risk-bearer."[8] Keynes pointed out that, especially during times of falling prices, "political uncertainties", "weakened financial position", and the "recent memories of the disastrous slump" would cause them to hesitate.[9]

In Chap. 29 of the work *A Treatise on Money*, Keynes further analyzes three scenarios in the futures market. His intention is to demonstrate that the futures market cannot bring the prices of spot and futures to a state of equilibrium. For the first scenario, "If there are no redundant liquid stocks, the spot price may exceed the forward price (i.e. in the language of the market there is a 'backwardation'). If there is a shortage of supply capable of being remedied in six months but not at once, then the spot price can rise above the forward price to an extent which is only limited by the unwillingness of the buyer to pay the higher spot price rather than postpone the date of his purchase."[10] For the second scenario, "if supply and demand are balanced,

---

[7] Keynes, J. M. 2013. *Economic articles and correspondence: investment and editorial.*in *The Collected Writings of John Maynard Keynes*, vol.12. ed. Moggridge, D. New York: Cambridge University Press. p. 264.

[8] Keynes, J. M. 2013. *Economic articles and correspondence: investment and editorial.* in *The Collected Writings of John Maynard Keynes*, vol.12. ed. Moggridge, D. New York: Cambridge University Press. p.260.

[9] Keynes, J. M. 2013. *Economic articles and correspondence: investment and editorial.*in *The Collected Writings of John Maynard Keynes*, vol.12. ed. Moggridge, D. New York: Cambridge University Press. p.270.

[10] Keynes, J.M. 2013. *A Treatise on Money: the Applied Theory of Money*. in *The Collected Writings of John Maynard Keynes, vol.*6. ed. Moggridge, D. New York: Cambridge University Press. p. 128.

the spot price must exceed the forward price by the amount which the producer is ready to sacrifice in order to 'hedge' himself, i.e. to avoid the risk of price fluctuations during his production period.…In other words, the normal supply price on the spot includes remuneration for the risk of price fluctuations during the period of production, whilst the forward price excludes this."[11] For the third scenario, "What is the position in the case important to the argument of this chapter, namely where there exist redundant liquid stocks? In this case there cannot exist a backwardation; for if there was one, it would always pay to sell the stocks spot and buy them back forward rather than incur the warehousing and interest charges for carrying them during the intervening period. Indeed the existence of surplus stocks must cause the forward price to rise *above* the spot price, i.e. to establish, in the language of the market, a 'contango'; and this contango must be equal to the cost of the warehouse, depreciation and interest charges of carrying the stocks."[12] In Keynes' view, "the existence of a contango does not mean that a producer can hedge himself without paying the usual insurance against price changes. On the contrary, the additional element of uncertainty introduced by the existence of stocks and the additional supply of risk bearing which they require mean that he must pay more than usual. In other words, the quoted forward price, though above the present spot price, must fall below the anticipated future spot price by at least the amount of the normal backwardation; and the present spot price, since it is lower than the quoted forward price, must be much lower than the anticipated future spot price."[13]

Thus, Keynes revealed the "important factor of instability" in economic life, i.e., "Industry is extraordinarily sensitive to any excess or deficiency, even a slight one, in the flow of available output ready to be fed back into the productive process."[14] This is similar to adding or removing weights on a balance that was originally in equilibrium; even the slightest increase or decrease can lead to overall imbalance, and re-establishing the balance is a process that requires time. Compared to situations of supply shortage, Keynes was more concerned with the market conditions when there was surplus: "our present economic system abhors a stock of liquid goods. If such a stock comes into existence, strong forces are immediately brought into play to dissipate it."[15]To accurately analyze such situations, Keynes introduced the theory of short-period prices in Chap. 29 of *The General Theory*. This theory,

[11] Keynes, J.M. 2013. *A Treatise on Money: the Applied Theory of Money*. in *The Collected Writings of John Maynard Keynes*, vol.6. ed. Moggridge, D. New York: Cambridge University Press. p. 128.

[12] Keynes, J.M. 2013. *A Treatise on Money: the Applied Theory of Money*. in *The Collected Writings of John Maynard Keynes*, vol.6. ed. Moggridge, D. New York: Cambridge University Press. p. 129.

[13] Keynes, J.M. 2013. *A Treatise on Money: the Applied Theory of Money*. in *The Collected Writings of John Maynard Keynes*, vol.6. ed. Moggridge, D. New York: Cambridge University Press. p. 129.

[14] Keynes, J.M. 2013. *A Treatise on Money: the Applied Theory of Money*. in *The Collected Writings of John Maynard Keynes*, vol.6. ed. Moggridge, D. New York: Cambridge University Press. p. 130–131.

[15] Keynes, J.M. 2013. *A Treatise on Money: the Applied Theory of Money*. in *The Collected Writings of John Maynard Keynes*, vol.6. ed. Moggridge, D. New York: Cambridge University Press. p. 130.

expressed through equations, elucidates the significant impact that clearing the market of surplus goods has on prices and output.

5.1.2 The Equation of the Market Mechanism

Keynes stated as follows, "If x is the total cost per annum of carrying stocks measured as a proportion of the normal price; y is the proportion of the redundant stocks to a year's consumption; p the proportionate fall of prices below the normal at its maximum; and q the proportionate fall of new production below the normal (i.e. below the figure at which production and consumption are assumed to be balanced with a normal price) at its maximum, i.e. due to a proportionate fall p in prices; then p, the initial price fall, is given, subject to certain simplifying assumptions, by the equation

$pq = xy$."[16]

The equation is derived as follows:[17]

Let C represent the normal annual consumption, A represent the number of years required for the economy to return to a normal state, and S represent the excess storage. If output falls to zero, then the excess storage will be worked off in $y = S/C$ years. However, if current output remains positive then A > y, the surplus would be reduced during the adjustment period will be $C\text{-}(1 - q)Q$ in each period, where Q is the normal annual output. According to assumption 2, if the fall in prices leads to a proportional increase in consumption, then during the adjustment period the surplus would be reduced by $(1 + c)C{-}(1 - q)Q$, where c is the proportionate increase in consumption due to the fall in prices.

Assuming that $Q = C$ and $q = c$ and substituting according:

$$(1+c)C-(1-q)Q=(1+q)Q-(1-q)Q=Q(2q) \tag{5.1}$$

Thus, we have:

$$A=S/Q(2q) \tag{5.2}$$

---

[16] Keynes, J.M. 2013. *A Treatise on Money: the Applied Theory of Money*. in *The Collected Writings of John Maynard Keynes*, vol.6. ed. Moggridge, D. New York: Cambridge University Press. p. 125.

[17] Keynes gives some brief explanations of this equation in a footnote on page 126 of *A Treatise on Money: the Applied Theory of Money*. See: Keynes, J.M. 2013. *A Treatise on Money: the Applied Theory of Money*. in *The Collected Writings of John Maynard Keynes*, vol.6. ed. Moggridge, D. New York: Cambridge University Press. p. 126. For a complete derivation, see: Kregel, J. A. 1993. Keynesian stabilization policy and post-war economic performance. in *Explaining Economic Growth: Essays in Honour of Angus Maddison*. ed. Szimai, E. et al. Amsterdam: Elsevier Science Publishers B.V. pp. 432–433.

At the beginning of the adjustment period, the rate of reduction of stocks will be $2q$, and at the end zero; on average over the period it will be $2q/2$. Substituting $y = S/C$ into Eq. (5.2), we get:

$$A = y/(2q/2) = y/q \tag{5.3}$$

Let $p = (P_2 - P_1)/P_2$, where P_2 is the normal price of the commodity and P_1 is the lowest price of the commodity. Once the commodity price returns to its normal value, for market speculators engaging in buying low and selling high, the cost of carry must at least equal the profit obtained from the price difference. Let X be the annual carrying cost per unit of the commodity, then $p = A{\cdot}X/P_2$, which gives:

$$p = A{\cdot}x \tag{5.4}$$

Substituting Eq. (5.3) into Eq. (5.4) yields:

$$pq = xy \tag{5.5}$$

From the above equation, it can be seen that if we rely on spontaneous market adjustments, then the higher the storage costs, the more surplus products there are relative to normal consumption levels, which will lead to a greater downward adjustment in prices and output. Keynes analyzed this with the example of copper, "at the end of 1920, the redundant stocks of copper amounted to about 700,000 tons, or more than eight months' consumption. The estimate of the normal price, at the time, was about 14.5 cents per lb., and in 1921 the actual price fell to 11.7 cents per lb. In April 1921, the American producers took concerted action, and the bulk of the mines of the United States closed down and were only gradually restarted in the course of 1922. World production was thus reduced to less than 50 per cent of the normal, the bulk of the stocks was absorbed in 1921 and 1922, and by the end of 1922 the price had risen to a normal figure."[18] Keynes believed "*redundant stocks exercise a disproportionate effect on prices and therefore on new production: such stocks exercise a tremendous pressure on the market*".[19] One important factor is "the 'carrying' costs" represented by x in the equation, which includes "Allowance for deterioration in quality or in suitability", "Warehouse and insurance charg*es*", *"Interest charges" and "Remuneration against the risk of changes in the money value of the commodity during the time through which it has to be carried by means of borrowed money"*.[20] Keynes argued that this cost leaves the market with no

[18] Keynes, J.M. 2013. *A Treatise on Money: the Applied Theory of Money*. in *The Collected Writings of John Maynard Keynes*, vol.6. ed. Moggridge, D. New York: Cambridge University Press. p. 124–125.

[19] Keynes, J.M. 2013. *A Treatise on Money: the Applied Theory of Money*. in *The Collected Writings of John Maynard Keynes*, vol.6. ed. Moggridge, D. New York: Cambridge University Press. p. 125.

[20] Keynes, J.M. 2013. *A Treatise on Money: the Applied Theory of Money*. in *The Collected Writings of John Maynard Keynes*, vol.6. ed. Moggridge, D. New York: Cambridge University Press. p. 121.

incentive to create storage conditions for the stability of production, thus fluctuations in prices and even in the economic system were unavoidable in such conditions:

> Owing to the existence of high carrying charges of one kind or another, our present economic arrangements make no normal provision for looking after surplus liquid capital. If, as the result of a previous miscalculation, such stocks come into existence, the price of the goods continues to fall until either consumption increases or production falls off sufficiently to absorb them. In no case can surplus stocks exist alongside of normal production. Recovery - broadly speaking - cannot begin until stocks have been absorbed, with the result that the process of recovery cannot be much facilitated by the existence of stocks.[21]

J. Kregel pointed out that the theory of short-period prices reveal the depth and width of periodic recession and price fluctuations.[22] Therefore, it can be regarded as another macro-level interpretation of Alfred Marshall's cobweb theory (cobweb theorem). Keynes found, however, that people didn't have enough understanding to this point, "The theory of short-period prices has been so much neglected that this simple equation, which helps to explain the violence of the fluctuation of the relative prices of staple commodities, is, so far as I know, unfamiliar."[23] Of course, the economic society will not leave the market to develop on principles of *laissez-fair*. If some intervention mechanism is introduced into the equation to actively influence the relevant variables, thereby establishing a new equilibrium relationship, it is not difficult to obtain policy insights—if the cost of carrying are organized to be reduced or if consumption is increased to lower the values of x and y, the ranges of fluctuation in prices and output, namely the values of p and q, can be narrowed. Keynes specifically pointed out that "valorization schemes to provide by concerted action for the carrying of stocks are inevitable and defensible inevitable and defensible".[24] Once reserves are established, they can serve two functions: increased-price purchases (*pingdi*) to address surplus abundance, and reduced-price sales (*pingtiao*) to address shortages.

---

[21] Keynes, J.M. 2013. *A Treatise on Money: the Applied Theory of Money*. in *The Collected Writings of John Maynard Keynes*, vol.6. ed. Moggridge, D. New York: Cambridge University Press. p. 129–130.

[22] Kregel, J. A.1996. The theory of Value, Expectation and Chapter 17 of the General Theory. in Harcourt, G.C. and Riach, P. ed. *A Second Edition of the General Theory*. London: Routledge. p. 265.

[23] Keynes, J.M. 2013. *A Treatise on Money: the Applied Theory of Money*. in *The Collected Writings of John Maynard Keynes*, vol.6. ed. Moggridge, D. New York: Cambridge University Press. p. 126.

[24] Keynes, J.M. 2013. *A Treatise on Money: the Applied Theory of Money*. in *The Collected Writings of John Maynard Keynes*, vol.6. ed. Moggridge, D. New York: Cambridge University Press. p. 126.

5.2 Keynes' Buffer Stock Scheme

5.2.1 The Idea of Buffer Stock in the 1920s and 1930s

Since the 1920s, Keynes has continuously focused on and analyzed the price fluctuations of staple commodities, and proposed countermeasures which mainly included the establishment of buffer stocks for staple commodities. This idea gradually took shape and was further developed by Richard F. Kahn, Keynes's student, over a period of more than 30 years.

Through enquiry into inventory statistics of various commodities, Keynes realized that surplus stock levels could be seen as an important indicator of whether production is in excess relative to consumption and of price fluctuations. This determinant is closely related to the business cycle. As analyzed earlier, if there is surplus stock, output will be forced to adjust, as the market itself lacks a direct mechanism to stabilize output fluctuations. Therefore, in relation to the continuity of consumption, production will experience significant volatility. In April 1923, Keynes pointed out in the first issue of the special memorandum on "Stocks of Staple Commodities" that by maintaining a long-term observation of commodity inventory statistics, one could understand its intrinsic relationship with the business cycle. Therefore, "accurate information as to the volume from time to time of surplus stocks of staple commodities is of the utmost interest both to businessmen and to economists."[25] In June 1924, Keynes went further in its sixth issue of the special memorandum on "Stocks of Staple Commodities" that "it becomes remarkably apparent to anyone ...how sensitive the short-period price levels of many commodities are to maladjustments between the rates of production and of consumption of a comparatively small percentage amount." And he proposed a policy to address commodity price fluctuations by enhancing reserves, "It seems as if relative prices could be kept a good deal steadier if the organization for carrying stocks at a moderate cost were on a larger scale."[26]

In 1926, Keynes published an article titled "The Control of Raw Materials by Governments" in *The Nation and Athenaeum*, as a reaction to an earlier declaration by President Herbert Hoover and the Secretary of Commerce against control of the output or the price of particular raw materials. He stated, "In the long run this violent oscillation in price and in supply will be as injurious to the consumer as to the producer. Obviously the world will be better off on the whole if it can be prevented."[27]

---

[25] Keynes, J. M. 2013. *Economic articles and correspondence: investment and editorial.* in *The Collected Writings of John Maynard Keynes*, vol.12. ed. Moggridge, D. New York: Cambridge University Press. p. 267.

[26] Keynes, J. M. 2013. *Economic articles and correspondence: investment and editorial.* in *The Collected Writings of John Maynard Keynes*, vol.12. ed. Moggridge, D. New York: Cambridge University Press. p.315.

[27] Keynes, J. M. 2013. *Activities 1922–1929: the return to gold and industrial policy.* in *The Collected Writings of John Maynard Keynes*, vol.19. ed. Moggridge, D. New York: Cambridge University Press. p. 549.

Keynes believed that the violent fluctuations in prices were closely related to the inability of the market to carry surplus stocks and stated, "Market statistics indicate that a pure speculator will seldom run the risk of carrying stocks, particularly on a falling market, unless he has an expectation of profit of at least 10 per cent per annum…"[28] Thus, he argued that "it seems to me both inevitable and right that the government should intervene. It is *laissez-faire* gone crazy to maintain the contrary."[29] The specific action proposed for the government was that "it can supplement the deficient carrying power of the market by buying up stocks…Alternatively, it can restrict output or at any rate export,…The former class of action is, for obvious reasons, much more popular with producers, and sometimes it may prove the right course."[30]

In 1930, Keynes introduced the theory of short-period prices in *A Treatise on Money*, which can be seen as a summary and refinement of previous related thoughts. This theory, with concise and clear equations, reveals the significant impact of market mechanisms on prices when surplus commodities exist, and establishes a more apparent policy direction for reserves. A more systematic and mature exposition of the reserve ideas was primarily reflected in Keynes's paper "The Policy of Government Storage of Food-Stuffs and Raw Materials" published in September, 1938. This paper was initially written at the invitation of R.F. Harrod for a conference, but its far-reaching impact, as R.F. Harrod noted, was that "This paper was the basis of proposals which he elaborated in greater detail during the war, to be a subject for Anglo- American discussions on post-war reconstruction."[31] Keynes began by borrowing Aristotle's saying that "nature abhors a vacuum", to point out a significant flaw in the free competitive market:

> The competitive system abhors the existence of stocks, with as strong a reflex as nature abhors a vacuum, because stocks yield a *negative* return in terms of themselves. It is ready without remorse to tear the structure of output to pieces rather than admit them, and in the effort to rid itself of them.[32]

Keynes cited the price changes of four commodities—rubber, cotton, wheat, and lead—over a decade to illustrate the high instability of the staple commodities market. Building on his previous analysis, Keynes believed that the main causes for this

---

[28] Keynes, J. M. 2013. *Activities 1922–1929: the return to gold and industrial policy.* in *The Collected Writings of John Maynard Keynes*, vol.19. ed. Moggridge, D. New York: Cambridge University Press. p. 549.

[29] Keynes, J. M. 2013. *Activities 1922–1929: the return to gold and industrial policy.* in *The Collected Writings of John Maynard Keynes*, vol.19. ed. Moggridge, D. New York: Cambridge University Press. p. 550.

[30] Keynes, J. M. 2013. *Activities 1922–1929: the return to gold and industrial policy.* in *The Collected Writings of John Maynard Keynes*, vol.19. ed. Moggridge, D. New York: Cambridge University Press. p. 550.

[31] Harrod, R. F. 1969. *The Life of John Maynard Keynes*. New York: Augustus M. Kelley Publishers. p.485.

[32] Keynes, J. M. 1938. The policy of government storage of food-stuffs and raw materials. *The Economics Journal*. 48 (191): 449.

flaw were the high costs of storage and interest rates, as well as the market behaviors of speculators and producers trying to minimize unknown risks. The resulting significant fluctuations in prices and output indicated that the *laissez-faire* doctrine was unworkable. He suggested that, in addition to implementing restrictions on sales, quotas, and prices, establishing reserves was another viable solution. Notably, Keynes particularly praised the Ever-normal Granary established by Wallace, the U.S. Secretary of Agriculture, stating that compared to this, some ambitious plans were still in their initial stages. As to reserve policies, Keynes proposed two options: one was direct government purchases, and the other was government assistance to manufacturers in increasing reserves. He had a greater interest in the latter. Keynes' advice to the British government was,

> My proposal is, therefore, that the Government should offer storage to all Empire producers of specified raw materials, either free of warehouse charges and interest or for a nominal charge, provided they ship their surplus produce to approved warehouses in this country. The Government would not become the outright owners of the stocks in question, which would remain in the ownership of the depositors, who would run the risk of price changes and would be free to remove and dispose of the stocks at any time or to deal in them against warehouse warrants.[33]

Keynes emphasized that the reserve of raw materials should not be merely a wartime measure; it should develop into a long-term policy during peacetime, which not only would not interfere with normal economic activities but also would help create a sustained liquidity of commodities. The key point is that reserve services provided by the government would significantly reduce the private holding costs of surplus stocks, the charge for which would account for about 10 per cent per annum of the total value of commodities. If these reserve services were provided by the government, the cost would only be around 4 per cent per annum.[34] Keynes pointed out that the commodity reserve policy should not be understood in isolation; in addition to its positive impacts on imports and exports, foreign investment, and exchange rates, the commodity reserve, as a partial substitute for gold reserves, would contribute to safeguarding national security and economic interests, both in wartime and peacetime.[35]

---

[33] Keynes, J. M. 1938. The policy of government storage of food-stuffs and raw materials. *The Economics Journal* 48 (191): 455.

[34] Graham had also calculated this. "He feels justified, however, in venturing the statement that large-scale storage of commodity units can be effected, by one device or another, at a dollar cost not exceeding 31/2 per cent per annum of the value of the stored units,...In any event it would be entirely feasible to limit the cost to the government to 3 per cent, or a smaller figure, by requiring the producers of any commodity to bear that portion of its storage expense which exceeds, say, 3 per cent of its average value." See: Graham, B. 1937. *Storage and Stability: A Modern Ever-normal Granary*. New York and London: McGraw-Hill Book Company, Inc. p. 111.

[35] Keynes, J. M. 1938. The policy of government storage of food-stuffs and raw materials. *The Economics Journal*. 48 (191): 456–460.

5.2.2 Commodity Regulation: A Complete Buffer Stock Scheme

If Keynes's discussion of reserve policy in the 1920s and 1930s was more focused on domestic issues in the UK, by the end of 1941 he began to think more about constructing a global buffer stock scheme. This important shift originated from R.F. Harrod. In 1941, the UK and the US began discussing the reconstruction of the post-war world order. In *The Life of John Maynard Keynes*, Harrod wrote, "In the autumn of 1941 I subjected him to a bombardment of memoranda in favour of cooperation with the Americans, of a world bank, etc. In one of these I ventured to draw his attention to the paper which he had presented to the Economic Section of the British Association at Cambridge in 1938 advocating buffer stocks of commodities. ... Keynes took up the idea with zest and produced a full Memorandum on Buffer Stocks."[36] According to research by L. Fantacci et al., "By the end of 1941 Keynes was fully engaged in working on a scheme of international buffer stocks, the Commodity Control, drafting nine different versions between January 1942 and February 1943."[37] Among the nine versions, the fifth draft was a refined text, while the subsequent versions included a series of changes that reflected political concessions and compromises, rather than being the versions Keynes had hoped for.[38] Therefore, the fifth draft should be considered to more or less completely reflect Keynes's original design and inspiration.

The fifth draft, entitled "The International Control of Raw Materials" consists of four parts, with the core content for each as follows:[39]

Part I: "*The internationalisation of Vice-President Wallace's 'ever normal granary', in preference to restriction, is the basis of these proposals.*"[40] Viewing Wallace's Ever-normal Granary as a model, it indicates that Keynes not only understood but also highly recognized the United States' policy of Ever-normal Granary in the agricultural field. Keynes pointed out that the market was powerless in the face of severe fluctuations in prices of raw material, and the time has come to replace *laissez-faire* with effective means to achieve "stability". He stated that "an internationalisation of the 'Ever-normal Granary' proposals of Vice-President

[36] Harrod, R. F. 1969. *The Life of John Maynard Keynes*. New York: Augustus M. Kelley Publishers. p.531.

[37] Fantacci, L. et al. 2012. Speculation and buffer stocks: The legacy of Keynes and Kahn. *The European Journal of the History of Economic Thought*. 19(3): 461.

[38] Hirai, T. 2009. Aimed at the stabilization of commodity prices- Keynes's hopes betrayed and the transmutation process of the International Control Scheme. *ESHET 13th Conference Paper*.

[39] The contents of the fifth draft were all from following work: Keynes, J.M. 2013. *Activities 1940-1946: Shaping the Post-war World: Employment and Commodities*. in *The Collected Writings of John Maynard Keynes*, vol.27. ed. Moggridge, D. New York: Cambridge University Press. pp. 112–134.

[40] Keynes, J.M. 2013. *Activities 1940-1946: Shaping the Post-war World: Employment and Commodities*. in *The Collected Writings of John Maynard Keynes*, vol.27. ed. Moggridge, D. New York: Cambridge University Press. p.112.

Wallace… seem to go to the root of the matter and are likely to promote the *general* interest".[41] Keynes acknowledged that different commodities differ so widely that no plan can claim to be applicable to all commodities. However, some operational principles can be clearly defined and coordinated, while the essence of the plan is to pursue stable economic development.[42]

> The essence of the plan should be that prices are subject to gradual changes but are fixed within a reasonable range over short periods; … Thus we should aim at combining a short-period stabilisation of prices with a long-period price policy which balances supply and demand and allows a steady rate of expansion to the cheaper-cost producers.[43]

Part II: "*The outline of a plan*".[44] This part established the basic framework for the buffer reserve scheme. Keynes stated, "An international body would be set up called the Commod Control[45] on which the governments of the leading producing and consuming countries would be represented. The management would be independent and expert, and the interests of consumers equally represented with those of producers."[46] "Its object would be to stabilise the price of that part of world output which enters into international trade, and to maintain stocks adequate to cover fluctuations of supply and demand in the world market."[47] With the goal, "an initial basic price fixed c.i.f. at the principal centres of consumption…for commod would be fixed by the Commod Control at a reasonable level on the basis of current conditions".[48] The mechanism of the buffer reserve would go as follows: "the Commod Control would be prepared at all times to buy commod,… at a price (say) 10 per cent below the fixed basic price; and it would sell commod at all times at a

[41] Keynes, J.M. 2013. *Activities 1940-1946: Shaping the Post-war World: Employment and Commodities.* in *The Collected Writings of John Maynard Keynes*, vol.27. ed. Moggridge, D. New York: Cambridge University Press. p.113.

[42] Keynes, J.M. 2013. *Activities 1940-1946: Shaping the Post-war World: Employment and Commodities.* in *The Collected Writings of John Maynard Keynes*, vol.27. ed. Moggridge, D. New York: Cambridge University Press. p.113.

[43] Keynes, J.M.2013. *Activities 1940-1946: Shaping the Post-war World: Employment and Commodities.* in *The Collected Writings of John Maynard Keynes, vol.*27. ed. Moggridge, D. New York: Cambridge University Press, 2013, pp.114–115.

[44] Keynes, J.M.2013. *Activities 1940-1946: Shaping the Post-war World: Employment and Commodities.* in *The Collected Writings of John Maynard Keynes, vol.*27. ed. Moggridge, D. New York: Cambridge University Press. p.115.

[45] Keynes called the "typical commodity" as "*commod*". See: Keynes, J.M.2013. *Activities 1940-1946: Shaping the Post-war World: Employment and Commodities.* in *The Collected Writings of John Maynard Keynes*, vol.27. ed. Moggridge, D. New York: Cambridge University Press. p.115.

[46] Keynes, J.M. 2013. *Activities 1940-1946: Shaping the Post-war World: Employment and Commodities.* in *The Collected Writings of John Maynard Keynes, vol.*27. ed. Moggridge, D. New York: Cambridge University Press. p.115.

[47] Keynes, J.M.2013. *Activities 1940-1946: Shaping the Post-war World: Employment and Commodities.* in *The Collected Writings of John Maynard Keynes, vol.*27. ed. Moggridge, D. New York: Cambridge University Press. p.115.

[48] Keynes, J.M. 2013. *Activities 1940-1946: Shaping the Post-war World: Employment and Commodities.* in *The Collected Writings of John Maynard Keynes, vol.*27. ed. Moggridge, D. New York: Cambridge University Press. p.115.

price (say) 10 per cent above the fixed basic price."[49] Meanwhile, the fixed basic price is adjusted according to whether the inventory exceeds or falls below the specified quantity or ratio. Around this fundamental operation, Keynes outlined the management, organizational structure, and possible responses of the Commod Control: An initial basic price fixed c.i.f. at the principal centres of consumption for commod would be fixed by the Commod Control at a reasonable level on the basis of current conditions; the Commod Control would itself deal in the market or arrange with merchants so as to keep its stocks in motion; the quotas would be assigned when necessary; a General Council for Commodity Controls should be established which undertake certain duties; obtaining funds through the profits arising out of the difference between the buying and selling prices, export taxes, as well as the International Clearing Union, central banks of various countries, and national loans; publishing statistics of output, consumption and stocks and all other valuable information; and maintaining the potential productivity of commodities, etc.[50]

Part III: "*Commodity controls as a contributory measure to the prevention of the trade cycle*".[51] Keynes believed that buffer stocks have a preventive function, capable of halting the vicious cycle of the economy at its initial or nascent stage. He particularly emphasized, "The very fact that in the aggregate large sums of money may be involved in such storage schemes, though it aggravates the technical and financial problems, is of positive assistance when we come to the handling of the trade cycle. For we have at our disposal a weapon capable of producing large effects by rapid action, and of operating in the negative as well as in the positive direction, so that it can function as a stabilising factor both ways. By taking up or by releasing stocks, the complex of Commodity Controls can operate in both directions on a scale and with an immediacy which is quite impossible for projects of public works."[52]

Part IV. "*Some difficulties reviewed*". Keynes recognized that the buffer stock schemes would encounter numerous difficulties in the initial negotiations, and these questions are not easily answered. However, he emphasized that one should not stand still in order to introduce international trade into an orderly track, and should firmly reject defeatism. Keynes realized that differences in the level of development among countries, production costs, and standards of life would present challenges and difficulties in setting a fixed basic price. Thus, buffer stock schemes need to

[49] Keynes, J.M. 2013. *Activities 1940-1946: Shaping the Post-war World: Employment and Commodities*. in *The Collected Writings of John Maynard Keynes, vol.*27. ed. Moggridge, D. New York: Cambridge University Press. p.116.

[50] Keynes, J.M. 2013. *Activities 1940-1946: Shaping the Post-war World: Employment and Commodities*. in *The Collected Writings of John Maynard Keynes*, vol.27. ed. Moggridge, D. New York: Cambridge University Press. pp.115–119.

[51] Keynes, J.M. 2013. *Activities 1940-1946: Shaping the Post-war World: Employment and Commodities*. in *The Collected Writings of John Maynard Keynes*, vol.27. ed. Moggridge, D. New York: Cambridge University Press. p.121.

[52] Keynes, J.M.2013. *Activities 1940-1946: Shaping the Post-war World: Employment and Commodities*. in *The Collected Writings of John Maynard Keynes*, vol.27. ed. Moggridge, D. New York: Cambridge University Press. pp.121–122.

"leave each country free to give subsidies to their own producers",[53] but such subsidies should be "given on a substantial scale".[54] Establishing a price that is in line with long-term benefits, i.e., one that is progressively reduced, should be the ultimate goal. In response to the question of whether the Commod Control would degenerate into organization for restrictive schemes, Keynes believed that "stabilisation must not rest on the absurd assumption that conditions of demand and of supply are fixed."[55] Therefore, "Restriction schemes, when they *are* unavoidable to supplement the buffer stock arrangements, should be regarded as a means of temporary relief - not a normal or a persisting expedient." Keynes was a pragmatic action-oriented thinker; he believed that the entire scheme could not be achieved in one go. Although its advantages would only be fully realized after the systematic establishment of the Commod Control, a piecemeal approach, starting with buffer stocks for the most important or troubled commodities, is a more realistic and advantageous choice.

The fifth draft of the scheme of international buffer stocks, the Commodity Control, not only provided the overall framework but also delved into the meticulous contemplation of crucial issues involved in practical implementation. Keynes sought to extend his economic principles to international practice, "aiming at a plan which does take a middle course between unfettered competition under *laissez-faire* conditions and planned controls which try to freeze commerce into a fixed mould."[56] However, "his plan had been subjected to 'tens of thousands of minor or major criticisms from different Departments'"[57] As a result, "as is well known, Keynes's ideas, however, did not get through. At the World Food Conference, held at Hot Springs in May 1943, the British Delegation presented a document entitled 'Buffer Stocks', which was based on Keynes's plan. Nonetheless, the Conference on Trade and Employment in Washington in autumn 1945 took a position against the idea of buffer stocks, and a similar fate had its twin scheme (i.e. the International Clearing Union)". The "twin scheme" is none other than Keynes' proposal for establishment of the International Clearing Union.[58]

[53] Keynes, J.M.2013. *Activities 1940-1946: Shaping the Post-war World: Employment and Commodities*. in *The Collected Writings of John Maynard Keynes*, vol.27. ed. Moggridge, D. New York: Cambridge University Press. p.124.

[54] Keynes, J.M. 2013. *Activities 1940-1946: Shaping the Post-war World: Employment and Commodities*. in *The Collected Writings of John Maynard Keynes*, vol.27. ed. Moggridge, D. New York: Cambridge University Press. p.124.

[55] Keynes, J.M.2013. *Activities 1940-1946: Shaping the Post-war World: Employment and Commodities*. in *The Collected Writings of John Maynard Keynes*, vol.27. ed. Moggridge, D. New York: Cambridge University Press. p.126.

[56] Keynes, J.M.2013. *Activities 1940-1946: Shaping the Post-war World: Employment and Commodities*. in *The Collected Writings of John Maynard Keynes*, vol.27. ed. Moggridge, D. New York: Cambridge University Press. p.111.

[57] Skidelsky, Robert. 2003. *John Maynard Keynes: 1883–1946, Economist, Philosopher, Statesman*. New York: Penguin. p.693.

[58] Fantacci, L. et al. 2012. Speculation and buffer stocks: The legacy of Keynes and Kahn. *The European Journal of the History of Economic Thought*. 19(3): 464.

Looking back at the buffer stocks and ever-normal granaries in previous chapters, except in Benjamin Graham's proposal, we find that the shortage of capital was often the key constraint for the development of Ever-normal Granary program. The Ever-normal Granary in Chinese history encounters such a problem, so does Henry A. Wallace's. In order to raise funds, the government had to impose a special tax on downstream food processors, which drew their fierce opposition. Eventually the *Agricultural Adjustment Act of 1933* was judged by the court as unconstitutional and thus suspended. Keynes was acutely aware of the immense funds involved and the complexity of coordination required for applying buffer stocks internationally, hence he made special provisions in the second part of the fifth draft of the scheme. Echoing with this, Keynes, in his proposal for establishment of the International Clearing Union, also stated clearly as follows: "The Bank might set up an account in favour of international bodies charged with the management of a Commodity Control, ... By this means the financial problem of holding pools and 'ever-normal' granaries would be satisfactorily solved."[59]

However, to Kahn, a disciple of Keynes, capital is always a constraint that cannot be avoided. Buffer stocks cannot always rely on abundant financial support, and the solution lies in finding ways to manage to maintain its sustainability. It is here that Kahn pushes forward Keynes' ideas on buffer stocks.

5.2.3 *Kahn's Inheritance and Development*

From January 1943 to mid-1944, Richard F. Kahn, a disciple of Keynes, worked in the Raw Materials Division of the Ministry of Supply in London where his was interested with Keynes' international buffer stock scheme. In 1952, upon invitation, Kahn served as a consultant to the Food and Agriculture Organization of the United Nations (FAO), where he carried out research on buffer stock techniques. Unfortunately, the research was not completed due to various reasons, and Kahn had to abandon the project in 1959. But the notes, correspondence and unpublished manuscripts that have survived as archives give us a comprehensive view of his long-neglected economic thought.[60]

"Basically, Kahn believed that 'markets are good servants, but bad masters'."[61] This was the theoretical basis of his buffer stock idea. Kahn's greatest development

[59] Keynes, J. M. 2013. *Activities 1940–1944: Shaping the post-war world: the Cleaning Union.* in *The Collected Writings of John Maynard Keynes*, vol.25. ed. Moggridge, D. New York: Cambridge University Press. p. 91.

[60] For an earlier study on this issue, see: Palma, G. 1994. Kahn on Buffer Stock. *Cambridge Journal of Economics.* 18(1): 117–127. For A recent discussion, see: Fantacci, L. and Rosselli, A. 2009. Stabilizing commodities: Buffer Stock Plans by Keynes and Kahn. *ESHET 13th Conference Paper*; Fantacci, L., et al. 2012. Speculation and Buffer Stocks: The legacy of Keynes and Kahn. *The European Journal of the History of Economic Thought.* 19 (3): 453–473.

[61] Palma, G. 1994. Kahn on Buffer Stock. *Cambridge Journal of Economics.* 18(1): 117.

of Keynes' buffer stock idea was his understanding of how to manage and operate the buffer stock. "What makes Kahn's proposal interesting is that it is a true example of the Keynesian 'middle way'. Public intervention does not mean the introduction of rigidities against the market, but artful activities in the market. The buffer-stocks scheme is a middle way between 'unfettered competition' and planning, and the same mixed nature characterizes its management, which must behave partly like a private speculator and partly like a public body, combining public interest with the need to make a profit in order to survive."[62]

Kahn's judgment is based on his view that those opinions that "the buffer-stock can rely on unlimited resources" are "extremely unlikely". As was analyzed by Fantacci, L., et al., "It is only in this case that the trade-off between the two objectives of the buffer-stock – the aim of price stability and that of its own survival in the long- run – can be reconciled. Kahn is well aware that the buffer-stock authority operates in a market where there are not only individual agents who buy the commodity for their own use, but also other speculators who gain from temporary deviations of the price from its long-term trend. When the price gets close to the 'floor', speculators who are convinced that the buffer-stock authority will defend the 'floor', will be only happy to accumulate stocks of the commodity, relying on the hope of future increases in price and on the expectations that the buffer-stock will prevent them from incurring into any loss. By doing so and buying the commodity, they will help to stop the fall of its price. In this case, the buffer-stock performs its task of price stabilization very effectively, but it contributes to the profits of the speculators without any gain for itself. If traders are convinced instead that the 'floor' will be lowered, they will unload all their stocks to the buffer-stock authority who can go on buying only if its funds are unlimited. If they are not and in the end the 'floor' is lowered to avoid heavy losses, the buffer-stock authority will have saved itself at the cost of price instability…".[63]

Kahn suggested that the authorities should adopt a strategy which "can be summarized in 'sell early and buy late'" and that they should "take a long view and avoid or limit to a minimum operations based on a 'short view'".[64] In his mind, "when the market price is lower than the normal price, they must wait to buy. If the fall in the price is temporary, they give up the opportunity of a small profit, but if it is not, they preserve their ammunition for later intervention, and prevent catastrophic losses for the producers. When the price rises, they must sell out their stock immediately and be content with a small margin, without hoping for a further rise and higher profits. If their intervention stops the price rise, they have attained their

[62] Fantacci, L., et al. 2012. Speculation and Buffer Stocks: The legacy of Keynes and Kahn. *The European Journal of the History of Economic Thought*. 19(3): 465.

[63] Fantacci, L. and Rosselli, A. 2009. Stabilizing commodities: Buffer Stock Plans by Keynes and Kahn. *ESHET 13th Conference Paper*. p. 18.

[64] Fantacci, L., et al. 2012. Speculation and Buffer Stocks: The legacy of Keynes and Kahn. *The European Journal of the History of Economic Thought*. 19(3): 466–467.

goal; if it does not, they have done their best anyway by slowing down the rise."[65] Although the profits obtained from this may not be as much as those when the price increases further, in terms of effectiveness, it may either prevent or delay the increase of prices, thereby playing the role of buffer stock.

Kahn's design of the discretionary buffer policy, aims at avoiding a situation where, under the constraint of limited funds, reserve institutions find themselves unable to stabilize prices in the face of a complex market, leading to their unsustainability or being manipulated by the market. Once such a scenario arises, the buffer stock contradicts its original purpose of proactive adjustment and seeking a "middle way", thus making it difficult to survive in the market. Kahn illustrated this point with a vivid metaphor:

> It is bad enough if the market can guess which way the cat is going to jump if it jumps at all, it is fatal if they not only know this for certain but also how far it is going to jump and when.[66]

Therefore, "if the buffer-stock wants to survive in a speculative market, it must keep the market guessing",[67] making the speculators uncertain about the intentions of the authorities. In Kahn's design, the managers for the buffer stock, as a skillful quasi-speculative agent, "requires 'courage, skill and even a certain amount of low cunning'".[68] Reflecting on the practices of ancient Chinese, though the specifics may be lost to history, we know that Liu Yan of the mid-Tang dynasty actively implemented the equalization policy using limited financial resources to manage various materials. From the perspective of outcomes, Liu Yan achieving the dual goals of benefiting the nation and its people. Wasn't he the ideal manager and investor that Kahn would have approved of?

Viewed in isolation, the buffer stock ideas and policy designs of Keynes and Kahn seem to have been fruitless. However, from a different perspective, the fundamental principles of buffer stocks have been cleverly transformed into an important aspect of the "Keynesian Revolution", presenting itself to the world in a different form.

---

[65] Fantacci, L., et al. 2012. Speculation and Buffer Stocks: The legacy of Keynes and Kahn. *The European Journal of the History of Economic Thought*. 19(3): 467.

[66] Fantacci, L. and Rosselli, A. 2009. Stabilizing commodities: Buffer Stock Plans by Keynes and Kahn. *ESHET 13th Conference Paper*. p.19.

[67] Fantacci, L. and Rosselli, A. 2009. Stabilizing commodities: Buffer Stock Plans by Keynes and Kahn. *ESHET 13th Conference Paper*. p. 19.

[68] Fantacci, L., et al. 2012. Speculation and Buffer Stocks: The legacy of Keynes and Kahn. *The European Journal of the History of Economic Thought*. 19(3): 467.

5.3 Keynesian Macroeconomic Theory from a Buffer Stock Perspective

5.3.1 Marginal Efficiency of Capital and Organized Investment

Keynes conducted an in-depth analysis of the trade cycle in his work *The General Theory*. He believed that " the essential character of the trade cycle, and, especially, the regularity of time-sequence and of duration which justifies us in calling it a cycle, is mainly due to the way in which the marginal efficiency of capital fluctuates."[69] The level of marginal efficiency of capital "depends, not only on the existing abundance or scarcity of capital-goods and the current cost of production of capital-goods, but also on current expectations as to the future yield of capital-goods."[70] However, "the basis for such expectations is very precarious. Being based on shifting and unreliable evidence, they are subject to sudden and violent changes."[71] Therefore, he suggested that "a more typical, and often the predominant, explanation of the crisis is, not primarily a rise in the rate of interest, but a sudden collapse in the marginal efficiency of capital."[72]

In Keynes' opinion, "The later stages of the boom are characterized by optimistic expectations as to the future yield of capital-goods sufficiently strong to offset their growing abundance and their rising costs of production and, probably, a rise in the rate of interest also. It is of the nature of organized investment markets, under the influence of purchasers largely ignorant of what they are buying and of speculators who are more concerned with forecasting the next shift of market sentiment than with a reasonable estimate of the future yield of capital-assets, that, when disillusion falls upon an over-optimistic and over-bought market, it should fall with sudden and even catastrophic force. Moreover, the dismay and uncertainty as to the future which accompanies a collapse in the marginal efficiency of capital naturally precipitates a sharp increase in liquidity-preference — and hence a rise in the rate of interest. Thus the fact that a collapse in the marginal efficiency of capital tends to

---

[69] Keynes, J. M. 2013. *The General Theory of Employment, Interest and Money*. in *The Collected Writings of John Maynard Keynes, vol.7*. ed. Moggridge, D. New York: Cambridge University Press. p. 313.

[70] Keynes, J. M. 2013. *The General Theory of Employment, Interest and Money*. in *The Collected Writings of John Maynard Keynes, vol.7*. ed. Moggridge, D. New York: Cambridge University Press. p. 315.

[71] Keynes, J. M. 2013. *The General Theory of Employment, Interest and Money*. in *The Collected Writings of John Maynard Keynes, vol.7*. ed. Moggridge, D. New York: Cambridge University Press. p. 315.

[72] Keynes, J. M. 2013. *The General Theory of Employment, Interest and Money*. in *The Collected Writings of John Maynard Keynes, vol.7*. ed. Moggridge, D. New York: Cambridge University Press. p. 315.

be associated with a rise in the rate of interest may seriously aggravate the decline in investment. "[73]

Why is "an interval of time of a particular order of magnitude"[74] needed before the recovery from economic recession? Keynes believed there were two reasons. The first reason is "the length of life of durable assets": "Thus at the outset of the slump there is probably much capital of which the marginal efficiency has become negligible or even negative. But the interval of time, which will have to elapse before the shortage of capital through use, decay and obsolescence causes a sufficiently obvious scarcity to increase the marginal efficiency, may be a somewhat stable function of the average durability of capital in a given epoch."[75] The second reason is what was previously discussed in the theory of short-period prices in *A Treatise on Money* — the high carrying-costs of surplus stocks act like an "invisible hand" pushing surplus stocks onto the market, and the market mechanism then ruthlessly suppresses prices to gradually absorb the surplus commodities over time, while the affected production could simply recover slowly. Keynes reiterated this idea in *The General Theory* and particularly emphasized its impact on employment:

> The carrying-costs of these stocks will seldom be less than 10 per cent per annum. Thus the fall in their price needs to be sufficient to bring about a restriction which provides for their absorption within a period of, say, three to five years at the outside. Now the process of absorbing the stocks represents negative investment, which is a further deterrent to employment; and, when it is over, a manifest relief will be experienced.[76]

During a depression period, various capital-goods must undergo a painful process of consumption, causing overall shortage before the market confidence gradually restores. Consequently, a depression characterized by dashed expectations or a collapse in capital efficiency will inflict substantial economic losses and waste for the entire society. Keynes emphasized that the typical state of prosperity is not characterized by overinvestment in the true sense, meaning that capital is not so abundant to the extent that the entire society no longer has any reasonable use for it. This is because investment decisions are made under unstable conditions, and they cannot remain constant. Ultimately, investment is driven by market expectations, which are influenced by animal spirits and are therefore inherently unstable, leading to

[73] Keynes, J. M. 2013. *The General Theory of Employment, Interest and Money*. in *The Collected Writings of John Maynard Keynes, vol.7*. ed. Moggridge, D. New York: Cambridge University Press. pp. 315–316.

[74] Keynes, J. M. 2013. *The General Theory of Employment, Interest and Money*. in *The Collected Writings of John Maynard Keynes, vol.7*. ed. Moggridge, D. New York: Cambridge University Press. p. 317.

[75] Keynes, J. M. 2013. *The General Theory of Employment, Interest and Money*. in *The Collected Writings of John Maynard Keynes, vol.7*. ed. Moggridge, D. New York: Cambridge University Press. pp. 317–318.

[76] Keynes, J. M. 2013. *The General Theory of Employment, Interest and Money*. in *The Collected Writings of John Maynard Keynes, vol.7*. ed. Moggridge, D. New York: Cambridge University Press. p. 318.

eventual disappointment. At the same time, they may steer investment in the wrong direction. Based on this understanding, Keynes adjusted his previous thinking:

> For my own part I am now somewhat skeptical of the success of a merely monetary policy directed towards influencing the rate of interest. I expect to see the State, which is in a position to calculate the **marginal efficiency of capital-goods on long views** and on the basis of the general social advantage, taking an ever greater responsibility for directly **organizing investment**; since it seems likely that the fluctuations in the market estimation of the marginal efficiency of different types of capital, calculated on the principles I have described above, will be too great to be offset by any practicable changes in the rate of interest.[77]

When the market's expected marginal efficiency of capital experiences a significant decline, investors turn to holding money; when money is "hoarded" to a severe extent of suppressing investment, the unemployment of people becomes a prominent issue in the economic society. It is in such circumstances that "organized investment" or "socialization of investment" that replaces market investment becomes a policy choice in Keynesian macroeconomics. "I conceive, therefore, that a somewhat comprehensive socialisation of investment will prove the only means of securing an approximation to full employment."[78] However, the corresponding policies are not elaborated in *The General Theory*; the relevant content is only scattered here and there throughout the book. As Keynes himself said, the main purpose of *The General Theory* "is to deal with difficult questions of theory, and only in the second place with the applications of this theory to practice."[79] Of course, a comprehensive understanding of Keynesian economic theory and policy cannot be confined to *The General Theory*. The long-term depression of the British economy in the 1920s had already sown the seeds for Keynes to seek policy solutions:

> What started Keynes on the road to the Keynesian Revolution was the incomplete British recovery from the depression of 1920 to 1922. Nothing like the collapse of prices, output and employment had been seen since the end of the Napoleonic Wars. When the position was finally stabilized in 1923 it was on the basis of 10 per cent unemployment, which lasted for the rest of the decade.[80]

Viewed from this perspective, the ideas of buffer stocks and the theory of short-period prices that Keynes had already conceived in the 1920s take on a deeper significance. In fact, they have anticipated the "Keynesian revolution" in both theory and policy. Here, we can revisit the theory of short-period prices through *The*

---

[77] Keynes, J. M. 2013. *The General Theory of Employment, Interest and Money*. in *The Collected Writings of John Maynard Keynes, vol.7*. ed. Moggridge, D. New York: Cambridge University Press. p.164.

[78] Keynes, J. M. 2013. *The General Theory of Employment, Interest and Money*. in *The Collected Writings of John Maynard Keynes, vol.7*. ed. Moggridge, D. New York: Cambridge University Press. p.378.

[79] Keynes, J. M. 2013. *The General Theory of Employment, Interest and Money*. in *The Collected Writings of John Maynard Keynes, vol.7*. ed. Moggridge, D. New York: Cambridge University Press. p.xv.

[80] Skidelsky, Robert. 2003. *John Maynard Keynes: 1883–1946, Economist, Philosopher, Statesman*. New York: Penguin Books. p.316.

General Theory: if the state "is in a position to calculate the marginal efficiency of capital-goods on long views", and then, as an economic regulator, takes "an ever greater responsibility for directly organizing investment",[81] it can reduce the storage cost rate x of key commodities, increases the consumption rate to decrease y, and thereby decrease the price volatility p and output volatility q. In this way, market expectations can be effectively intervened, and the marginal efficiency of capital will acquire long-term stability, ensuring full employment accordingly. If such analysis is only a rough judgment, then the analysis of interest rates can more directly link *The General Theory* with the theory of short-period prices and buffer stock policy.

5.3.2 Theory of Interest Rate and "Ever-normal Granary Model"

The chapter "The Essential Properties of Interest and Money" is an important chapter in *The General Theory*. In this chapter, Keynes elucidates why the interest rate on money is higher than the marginal efficiency of capital in a different manner, by asserting that all goods have their own rates of interest. This, in turn, poses difficulties for investment and full employment.[82]

Keynes thinks that there are three attributes which different types of assets possess in different degrees: (i) the ability to produce a yield or output q, measured in terms of itself, by assisting some process of production or supplying services to a consumer; (ii) the suffering of some wastage or cost due to the mere passage of time, or the carrying cost c; (iii) the amount (measured in terms of itself) which people are willing to pay for the potential convenience or security given by this power of disposal, which is called liquidity-premium l.[83] Thus, the pure yield of a capital asset is equal to $q-c+l$. Keynes notes that "for every kind of capital-asset there must be an analogue of the rate of interest on money",[84] and $q-c+l$ represents their "interest rate" in terms of themselves, or the marginal efficiency of capital.

[81] Keynes, J. M. 2013. *The General Theory of Employment, Interest and Money*. in *The Collected Writings of John Maynard Keynes, vol.7*. ed. Moggridge, D. New York: Cambridge University Press. p.164.

[82] Translator's notes. See: Keynes, J. M. 1999. *The General Theory of Employment, Interest and Money*. trans. Gao Hongye. Beijing: The Commercial Press. p. 229.

[83] Keynes, J. M. 2013. *The General Theory of Employment, Interest and Money*. in *The Collected Writings of John Maynard Keynes, vol.7*. ed. Moggridge, D. New York: Cambridge University Press. pp. 225–226.

[84] Keynes, J. M. 2013. *The General Theory of Employment, Interest and Money*. in *The Collected Writings of John Maynard Keynes, vol.7*. ed. Moggridge, D. New York: Cambridge University Press. p.222.

Based on this, Keynes analyzed different types of interest rates.[85] It is characteristic of instrumental capital that is in use, that its yield (q) should normally exceed its carrying cost (c), while its liquidity-premium is probably negligible ($l = 0$). For money, its yield is *nil* ($q = 0$), and its carrying cost negligible ($c = 0$), but its liquidity-premium is substantial and not easily reduced, so the interest rate of money is equal to its liquidity-premium (l). Assume that the interest rate of money is l_1, and a certain capital-good has an interest rate of $q_2 - c_2 + l_2$ when expressed in its own terms, then its interest rate, when converted into money, is $a_2 + q_2 - c_2$ (ignoring the liquidity-premium). According to Keynes, the choice between holding the capital-good or money depends on the comparison between l_1 and $a_2 + q_2 - c_2$: if $a_2 + q_2 - c_2 > l_1$, they'd choose the capital-good; if $a_2 + q_2 - c_2 = l_1$, it is in a state of equilibrium; if $a_2 + q_2 - c_2 < l_1$, they'd choose money. It is obvious that as output increases, the yield (q) of capital-goods will continuously decline, and the carrying cost (c) becomes the key factor for the choice. Keynes specifically noted that that "what matters is the *difference* between the liquidity-premium and the carrying-costs; and in the case of most commodities, other than such assets as gold and silver and bank-notes, the carrying-costs are at least as high as the liquidity-premium ordinarily attaching to the standard in which contracts and wages are fixed".[86] This implies that the carrying cost largely determines the interest rate on capital goods, which is also known as the marginal efficiency of capital. This, in turn, influences the choice between capital-goods and money, and ultimately affects investment and employment levels.

From the above analysis, it can be seen that the "carrying cost" in *The General Theory* is closely related to the "carrying charges" in *A Treatise on Money*, as well as the variable x in the short-period prices equation $pq = xy$. One could even say that the former is developed from the latter. What is different is that the discussion of "carrying charges" in *A Treatise on Money* is limited to inventory, a special type of capital-goods, while the "carrying cost" in *The General Theory* should include a broader range of capital-goods. What is the same is that it is precisely at the crucial point where the high carrying costs are incurred for holding various capital-goods that Keynes potentially builds a bridge between the theory and policy. Thus the short-period prices equation, buffer stocks, and Keynesian macroeconomic thought are connected: from the perspective of *The General Theory*, buffer stock policy is actually a mechanism to lower the carrying cost (c) to maintain the stability of capital-goods' interest rates being higher than the interest rate on money, hence the establishment of buffer stocks by the government can be seen as Keynes' specific proposal for the socialization of investment. Behind the policy of reducing the carrying charges (x) to stabilize the volatility of important commodity prices (p) and

---

[85] Keynes, J. M. 2013. *The General Theory of Employment, Interest and Money*. in *The Collected Writings of John Maynard Keynes, vol.7*. ed. Moggridge, D. New York: Cambridge University Press. pp. 225–229.

[86] Keynes, J. M. 2013. *The General Theory of Employment, Interest and Money*. in *The Collected Writings of John Maynard Keynes, vol.7*. ed. Moggridge, D. New York: Cambridge University Press. p.237.

thus stabilize the volatility of output (q), this policy actually stabilizes the interest rate on capital-goods, i.e., the marginal efficiency of capital, to make it conform to the long-term development trend of the society and economy (long-term marginal efficiency of capital), preventing the economy from falling into significant fluctuations or even depression. In Keynes' view, the current price does not contain all the information needed to predict the future, and an important goal of the socialization of investment is "reducing the uncertainties associated with individualistic investment programs", so that "firms face an environment in which there is a much higher probability of economic success. Further, if the price level can be stabilized, …firms are in a much better position to estimate both future demand and costs, thus further reducing the risks attendant to uncertainty."[87]

However, traditional buffer stocks have a clear flaw in that they can only serve as static storage, failing to effectively utilize commodities to maximize their value and functionality immediately and fully. In fact, another solution proposed by Keynes for combatting depressions is more familiar to us, which is public works. The government directly participates in investment, transforming "dead material reserves" into "living projects". From the perspective of the short-period prices equation $pq = xy$, public works act as an intervention policy that reduces y, thereby minimizing fluctuations in prices and output (p, q). It's worth noting that public works can also be viewed as a special type of buffer stocks from another perspective. In the discussion of the ideas and policies of "labor relief" in Chinese history in Chap. 3, we analyzed how "large-scale public works" during famine years was a unique reserve with public works as the "granary" and "people" as the buffer objects, hence the Ever-normal Granary of labor force. From this perspective, Keynesian public works share a similar function: when investors, due to the anticipated unprofitability, abandon various capital-goods in favor of holding currency, they also relinquish the high "carrying cost" of labor (for investors, the "carrying cost" of labor includes at least wages and related benefits). This leads to widespread unemployment. Public works, in essence, create employment opportunities in "invisible" forms, building a buffer reserve that prevents labor from being discarded by the market. Therefore, the public works, when viewed through the lens of the short-period prices equation $pq = xy$, not only affect y, but also have significant impact on x.

With a broad understanding of the equation $pq = xy$, it seems that this simple expression is also an "Ever-normal Granary equation". From the Keynesian perspective, the market operates on the left side of the equation, while the government operates on the right side. In the dynamic development process of the economic society, the fluctuations of the marginal efficiency of capital are largely attributed to the expected instability of the future. In the process of the economic transition from stability to instability due to changes in the marginal efficiency of capital, the government should play the role of an "Ever-normal Granary" with reverse regulation: when investors in the market, due to poor expectations and high carrying costs, give

[87] Henry, J. F. 2001. Keynes' economic program, social institutions, ideology, and property rights. *Journal of Economics Issues*. 35(3): 640.

up various resources including labor and turn to holding money to avoid possible risks, the government should establish physical granaries or the intangible "granary" of public works to store and utilize these resources, which is the strategy of "*pingdi*"; conversely, when investors, due to improved market conditions and expectations, rush to acquire various resources (which may lead to inflation), the government should release the above resources, which is the strategy of "*pingtiao*". The government constructs an ever-normal stability mechanism by investing to compensate for investment, stabilize investment, and guide investment, thus forming a coordinated complementary and interactive relationship with the market. This simple yet smart "coordination" process ensures the full utilization of resources through the buffer mechanism of purchasing and selling, promotes the formation of reasonable and stable expectations in the market, and thus keeps effective demand at a high and stable level. It seems that the "Ever-normal Granary equation" can explain Keynes' complex macroeconomic thoughts in a simple way. In J.A. Kregel's words, there is "the genesis of the dynamics of *The General Theory* in the short-period theory of prices",[88] however it is often generally overlooked.

From a comparative perspective between the West and China, Keynes' macroeconomic theory seems to have little in common with the ever-normal granaries in ancient China. However, upon closer examination of the evolution of Keynesian economic theory and policy, one can uncover a buffer mechanism of purchasing and selling for stability underlying. The short-period prices theory, which may be called "Ever-normal Granary equation", is a crucial but overlooked thread in the development of Keynesian economics. This seems to echo with Keynes' statement in the preface of *The General Theory*: "The ideas which are here expressed so laboriously are extremely simple and should be obvious."[89] The Ever-normal Granary, a clever simplification of Keynesian economics, not only revives the ancient Chinese principles of purchase and sale for stability, but also imbues them with new and abundant implications.

Keynes was both an economist and a humanist. As Skidelsky firmly asserts, "Keynes's student allegiance to G. E. Moore's ethical standpoint was not a youthful aberration but a lifelong commitment."[90] In this context, it is easy to understand Minsky's view that "in fact, *The General Theory* can be viewed as giving an economic theoretic rationalization for views that Keynes's ethics and intuition had led him to, even as he was a practicing 'classical' economist."[91] Keynes' theoretical system encompasses profound reflections on social justice and public welfare, along

[88] Kregel, J. A. 1996. The theory of value, expectation and Chapter 17 of the General Theory. in *A Second Edition of the General Theory*. ed. Harcourt, G. C. and Riach, P. London: Routledge. p.264.

[89] Keynes, J. M. 2013. *The General Theory of Employment, Interest and Money*. in *The Collected Writings of John Maynard Keynes, vol.7*. ed. Moggridge, D. New York: Cambridge University Press. pp. xvi-xvii.

[90] Skidelsky, Robert. 2005. *John Maynard Keynes: 1883–1946, Economist, Philosopher, Statesman*. New York: Penguin Books. p. xxix.

[91] Minsky, H. P. 2008. *John Maynard Keynes*. New York: McGraw-Hill. p. 143.

with a blueprint for social reform,[92] in which achieving full employment is a crucial component. In Keynes' opinion, under free-market conditions, "the evidence indicates that full, or even approximately full, employment is of rare and short-lived occurrence",[93] and "its failure to provide for full employment" was an outstanding fault of the capitalist society in which he lived.[94] Unemployment became a separator that disrupted efficiency and fairness. In terms of solutions, as is discussed earlier, public works could allow the unemployed to enter the labor buffer stock "without leakage", thereby making full employment a sustainable state rather than a fleeting occurrence. However, in Keynes' policy proposals, we do not see him explicitly treating labor as a special category of buffer stock and elaborating on it. This task was left to his successors—the post-Keynesian economists. Some post-Keynesian economists recognized this "policy crux" and innovatively developed the "Buffer Stock Employment" (BSE) model, where the government, as the "Employer of Last Resort" (ELR), incorporated workers into the buffer mechanism. This theory revitalized the ancient ideas of "labor relief" (Ever-normal Granary of labor force), allowing it to enter a new stage of development after surpassing Keynesian theory.

[92] Elliott, J. E. and Clark, B.S.1987. Keynes's "General Theory" and social justice. *Journal of Post Keynesian Economics*. 9(3): 381–394; Davis, J.B. 1994. *Keynes's Philosophical Development*. Cambridge: Cambridge University Press.

[93] Keynes, J. M. 2013. *The General Theory of Employment, Interest and Money*. in *The Collected Writings of John Maynard Keynes, vol.7*. ed. Moggridge, D. New York: Cambridge University Press. pp. 249–250.

[94] Keynes, J. M. 2013. *The General Theory of Employment, Interest and Money*. in *The Collected Writings of John Maynard Keynes, vol.7*. ed. Moggridge, D. New York: Cambridge University Press. p. 372.

Chapter 6

Buffer Stock Employment: "Ever-normal Granary of Labor Force" and the Kalecki Dilemma

> Society simply does not find its equilibrium until it revolves around the sun of labour.
> —*Marx, Karl*[1]

> Work can exercise human nature and sharpen the will. Work is the most noble, important, and valuable behavior in life.
> —*Kazuo, Inamori*[2]

Economic depressions mean general "unemployment": dashed expectations (or the collapse of the marginal efficiency of capital) would bring monetary "unemployment" (investment preferences shifting towards liquidity preference), leading to a widespread "unemployment" state where people are out of work and goods are left unused. In this situation, the government acts as "the Employer of Last Resort" that does not pursue commercial profits but is committed to maintaining the long-term marginal efficiency of capital. This allows for the re-employment of the "unemployed" people, capital, and goods in the market. The question then arises: who enjoys the priority for "employment"? If macroeconomic policies focus more on top-down management of total demand, emphasizing investment, growth, and closing output gaps (i.e., focusing on employment of "goods"), then it is difficult to achieve full employment due to structural constraints within the economy and society. This can prevent the macro-economy from achieving sustainable endogenous stability. Following Keynes' idea that public works are programs for "permanent on-the-spot job creation", post-Keynesian economists suggest a bottom-up approach which prioritizes the employment of workers, and further developing the "Buffer Stock Employment" (BSE) model: the government creates public employment opportunities for "buffer stock" which absorbs or releases workers in a

[1] Marx, Karl. 2010. Epilogue to revelations concerning the communist trial in Cologne. in Marx, Karl and Frederick Engels. *Marx &Engels Collected Works*, vol.24. London: Lawrence & Wishart. pp. 53–54.

[2] Kazuo, Inamori. 2015. The Way to Work (働き方). trans. Cao Xiuyun. Beijing: Machinery Industry Press. p. 5.

W. Xian, *Chinese Food Security Strategy*, Research Series on the Chinese Dream and China's Development Path,
https://doi.org/10.1007/978-981-95-7964-8_6

counter-economic-cyclical manner, forming a complementary and interactive coordination mechanism with the market. This plays the role of an economic stabilizer. The model of "buffer stock employment" is the theoretical extension of the ideas and policies of "labor relief" in ancient China and in Franklin D. Roosevelt's New Deal. Post-Keynesian economists' unique interpretation of fiscal functions provides theoretical support for the government to expand spending to create buffer stock employment, thus unlocking the "deadlock" of fiscal deficit constraints. However, from the perspective of Marxian political economy, the theory of "buffer stock employment" overlooks the variable of social institution, revealing the discontinuity in the "Kalecki's dilemma" that capitalist systems and full employment are incompatible. If the focus is on "capital" rather than "people", the "knack" of this model may be difficult to be implemented and transformed into a long-term sustainable mechanism.

6.1 Returning from Aggregate Demand Management to for Employment Demand Management

Keynes' emphasis on demand overturned the tenet of Say's Law, which was steadfast in its belief in supply. The Keynesianism, with modification of Keynesian economics, therefore became obsessed with aggregate demand management, believing that as long as expenditure could be increased or stimulated to ensure economic growth and fill the output gap (as analyzed in Okun's Law), everything would go smoothly (including the eventual achievement of full employment). Although this macroeconomic policy has an immediate and visible effect when demand is weak, adhering to it over the long term can lead to many social and economic problems. For example, the "growth fever" in the 1950s and 1960s in the major Western capitalist countries introduced the "stagflation" of the 1970s; and in subsequent economic fluctuations up to the twenty-first century, there were signs of recovery with insignificant employment growth; at the same time, issues such as income distribution and poverty not only did not receive better solutions but became more severe.

Keynesian aggregate demand management policies have been criticized by post-Keynesian economics, to which Pavlina analyzes and summarizes the key point, indicating that effective demand, as one of Keynes' main theoretical contributions, is distinct from the aggregate demand of Keynesianism and the two should not be confused. The latter is a theory about expanding government and private sector expenditures to achieve certain economic output targets, while the former is a theory about the factors determining investment (marginal propensity to consume, marginal efficiency of capital, interest rates). Although aggregate demand management can, to some extent, address the issue of insufficient effective demand by influencing these factors, it is difficult to truly achieve full employment due to the constraints of the economic structure. In Keynesian economics, the key to macro governance is to accurately target demand and focus on job creation rather than output creation. Deficient effective demand ultimately boils down to underemployment or unsatisfied job demand, instead of deficient aggregate demand.[3] Aggregate demand management focuses on "things" such as investment and GDP, while ignoring the "people" emphasized by Keynesian demand management. Okun's Law,[4] which posit a regular relationship between the rate of growth of output and unemployment, seems to provide a standard guideline for aggregate demand management. However, reality shows that the law often proves incorrect, and its conclusion based on empirical relationship is weak and difficult to become a genuine "law".[5] It should be noted that Keynes did believe that "it may require a large increment of investment to produce full employment."[6] Keynes, however, assumed that the *investment multiplier* k was equal to the *employment multiplier* k' proposed by Kahn.[7] He stated that "there is no reason in general to suppose that $k = k'$", "but to elucidate the ideas involved, it will be convenient to deal with the simplified case where $k = k'$".[8] Yet this simplification unintentionally obscures k' and amplifies k, opening the way for aggregate demand management. However, with ignorance of k', the aggregate demand management looks more like a "hormone" prescription for the economic and social organism. This "prescription" may have some effect in the short term, especially when the economy is in recession. But the root cause of the disease cannot be eradicated, and the economic and social organism will be hyperactive and have great side effects in the long term.

Therefore, from the perspective of policy, although aggregate demand management has the original intention and measures (such as unemployment insurance and income redistribution) to solve problems of unemployment and income inequality, etc., on the whole its mechanism and effect are fraught with many drawbacks. First and foremost, aggregate demand management cannot achieve full employment because its theoretical foundation—the Trickle-Down Mechanism[9]—already has

---

[3] Tcherneva, P. R. 2008. Keynes's approach to full employment: aggregate or targeted demand? *Working Paper No.542*. pp. 6–8. https://www.econstor.eu/bitstream/10419/31663/1/585087695.pdf

[4] The law states that a 1 per cent increase in unemployment would bring about approximately a 2 per cent decline in GDP growth. The relationship varies depending on the country and time period under consideration.

[5] Cai, Fang. 2007. Why doesn't Okun's Law work in China: a second discussion of relationship between economic growth and employment? *Macroeconomic Research*. (1): 11–14.

[6] Keynes, J. M. 2013. *The General Theory of Employment, Interest and Money*. in *The Collected Writings of John Maynard Keynes*, vol.7. ed. Moggridge, D. New York: Cambridge University Press. p.118.

[7] Kahn, R. F. 1931. The relation of home investment to unemployment. *Economic Journal*. 41 (162): 173–198.

[8] Keynes, J. M. 2013. *The General Theory of Employment, Interest and Money*. in *The Collected Writings of John Maynard Keynes*, vol.7. ed. Moggridge, D. New York: Cambridge University Press. p. 115–116.

[9] The Trickle-Down Mechanism, also known as Trickle-Down Economics, is a policy theory that suggests that economic benefits (like tax cuts, deregulation, and other business-friendly policies) given to wealthy individuals and corporations will eventually "trickle down" to the lower and middle classes. The idea is that these benefits will lead to economic growth, job creation, and

defects. On the surface, injecting more aggregate demand into the economic society through a top-down transmission mechanism can ultimately benefit the lower class of society. However, as was pointed out by Minsky, H. P., the trickle-down mechanism could only occasionally ensure that aggregate demand is precisely directed to the right place and the right people, creating enough employment and wages sufficient for the employees to support their families. On the other hand, as we approach full employment, any increase in spending will lead to greater inflationary pressure. Facing such dilemma, policy makers will be forced to abandon policies to stimulate aggregate demand and will ultimately fail to achieve the goal of employment. Second, aggregate demand management exacerbates income inequality. Aggregate demand management, oriented for growth and investment, includes various policies favorable to capital, which makes the already unequal capital-labor income distribution even worse, thereby reinforcing the favorable conditions for capital investment and financing. The resulting cumulative effect further intensifies inequality.[10] Third, unattainable full employment and widening income gap will eventually lead to institutionalization of poverty. Aggregate demand management cannot benefit all the people at the lower class of society. Therefore, while relief policies may appear to be the right approach to tackling poverty, the failure of the economic society to provide true employment means that it is impossible for the poor to climb up from the bottom of the society, hence artificial barriers for their self-improvement.[11]

It must be recognized that the economic society is structural in nature, and the distribution of aggregate demand is not equal, symmetrical, or even "preference-free". These important factors will cause the structural decomposition of aggregate demand to generate various problems and contradictions characterized by "uneven heat and cold" among different groups, industries, and regions. This ultimately makes it difficult to benefit more people, achieve more employment, and thus bring the effective demand to a sufficient and stable level. Aggregate demand management policies treat the symptoms but not the root cause, and are contrary to Keynes' economic philosophy—in Keynes' view, "the outstanding faults of the economic society in which we live are its failure to provide for full employment and its arbitrary and inequitable distribution of wealth and incomes."[12] The aggregate demand

increased consumer spending, which will then benefit the entire economy. The theory is based on the assumption that the wealthy will invest their additional income, hire more workers, and spend more, thereby stimulating economic activity and creating jobs. This, in turn, is supposed to lead to increased wages and improved living standards for everyone.

[10] Piketty's research reveals the trend of income inequality in the major capitalist countries: there was a significant improvement in income distribution after World War II, but it has gradually worsened since the 1970s. When the histories of the major capitalist countries are analyzed in sequence, the pattern of income distribution shows a U-shaped curve. See: Pikett, T. 2014. *Capital in the Twenty-First Century*. trans. Arthur Goldhammer. Cambridge: Belknap Press. p.118.

[11] Tcherneva, P. R. 2011. Fiscal policy: Why aggregate demand management fail and what to do about it. *Working Paper No.650*. pp. 5–9. https://www.econstor.eu/bitstream/10419/57004/1/654831750.pdf

[12] Keynes, J. M. 2013. *The General Theory of Employment, Interest and Money*. in *The Collected Writings of John Maynard Keynes*, vol.7. ed. Moggridge, D. New York: Cambridge University

management will artificially create these two problems in a "regulated" market economy, so we still have to resort to Keynes, "Here is a real problem, fundamental yet essentially simple, which it is important for all of us to try to understand. The first task is to make sure that there is enough demand to provide employment for everyone."[13] With this cognition, Keynes proposed the well-known solution of socialization of investment, along with its important policy means: public works.

We know that Keynes' elaboration of policies is quite scattered in his various writings. Post-Keynesian economists have joined together Keynes' fragmented expressions regarding public works, and through comprehensive analysis they have summarized the essence of public works as "permanent on-the-spot job creation". They point out that this key point has not been paid due attention by mainstream economics, hence "the missing Keynes Plan".[14] The term "permanent" aims to emphasize that public works in the Keynesian economics is a kind of "all-weather" mechanism, meaning it lays stress not only on the "cure" during economic cycles but also on the "prevention": "if the bulk of investment is under public or semi-public control and we go in for a stable long-term programme, serious fluctuations are enormously less likely to occur." Therefore, we cannot "do a little less than justice to investment under public auspices by emphasizing the deficiencies of this method in the short period, whilst under-estimating their efficacy for preventative purposes and as a means of avoiding the sharp fluctuations which, once they have occurred, it is so difficult to offset."[15] Keynes wants to clarify that private investment is unstable, and measures for socialization of investment like public works should be a continuously implemented policy rather than a temporary solution to cyclical fluctuations. The term "on the spot" as noted by commentators, originates from Keynes phrase "man-year of employment on the spot",[16] indicating that employment can be created immediately and without obstacles. The extreme employment example that Keynes cited in *The General Theory*, which involves "burying jars with money for the unemployed to dig out", is used "largely to emphasize the importance of 'on-the-spot' employment programs".[17]

From Keynes' standpoint, economic processes and goals should serve people and enhance overall social welfare. The transition from "growth demand" and

---

Press. p. 372.

[13] Keynes, J.M. 2013. *Activities 1940-1946: Shaping the Post-war World: Employment and Commodities*. in *The Collected Writings of John Maynard Keynes*, vol.27. ed. Moggridge, D. New York: Cambridge University Press. p. 267.

[14] Tcherneva, P. R. 2012. Permanent on-the-spot job creation-the missing Keynes Plan for full employment and economic transformation. *Review of Social Economy*. 70 (1): 57–80.

[15] Keynes, J.M. 2013. *Activities 1940-1946: Shaping the Post-war World: Employment and Commodities*. in *The Collected Writings of John Maynard Keynes*, vol.27. ed. Moggridge, D.New York: Cambridge University Press. p. 326.

[16] Keynes, J. M. 2013. *Activities 1931–1939: World Crisis and Policies in Britain and America*. in *The Collected Writings of John Maynard Keynes*.vol.21. ed. Moggridge, D. New York: Cambridge University Press. p. 171.

[17] Tcherneva, P. R. 2012. Permanent on-the-spot job creation-the missing Keynes Plan for full employment and economic transformation. *Review of Social Economy*. 70 (1):65.

"output demand" to "employment demand" becomes an inevitable choice for optimizing demand management policies, the latter one characterized by bottom-up, people-centered endogenous driving forces. In the long term, economic development should be firmly based on a fundamental concept: emphasizing the protection of labor and employment rights for all workers in society, and prioritizing the satisfaction and strengthening of employment demand as the major macroeconomic goals. This approach will allow full employment to generate a sustained stability that curbs fluctuations and unleash ever-lasting momentum for a virtuous cycle.

According to this reasoning, we can further reinforce a judgment made in the previous chapter, which views the short-period prices equation $pq = xy$ as a more generalized expression of buffer stocks. Public works, if understood as means for "permanent on-the-spot job creation" to address the issue of unemployment "at any time", indeed serve as a buffer stock specifically for "people" (the "surplus labor commodity"), just as buffer stocks for "commodities" that could be used to store surplus commodities (i.e., "unemployment") at any time. Although Keynes did not explicitly propose a buffer stock scheme for labor, his thoughts clearly encompass such content. It is here that post-Keynesian economists demonstrate their inheritance and development of Keynesian economics, and the theory of "buffer stock employment" emerges prominently.

6.2 "Employment Buffer Stocks": Macroeconomic Stabilizers

6.2.1 Stabilization Mechanism for the Buffer Stock Employment

The policy of aggregate demand management cannot "float all boats", especially for full employment. Hyman P. Minsky pointed out the shortcomings of the macroeconomic policies in the United States at that time when discussing employment issues in his book *Stabilizing an Unstable Economy* published in the 1980s, and proposed an alternative plan to achieve full employment:

> The current strategy seeks to achieve full employment by way of subsidizing demand. The instruments are financing conditions, fiscal inducements to invest, government contracts, transfer payments, and taxes. This policy strategy now leads to chronic inflation and periodic investment booms that culminate in financial crises and serious instability. The policy problem is to develop a strategy for full employment that does not lead to instability, inflation, and unemployment.
>
> The main instrument of such a policy is the creation of **an infinitely elastic demand** for labor at a floor or minimum wage that does not depend upon long- and short-run profit expectations of business. Since only government can divorce the offering of employment

from the profitability of hiring workers, the infinitely elastic demand for labor must be created by government.[18]

Minsky's employment proposal was summarized in the 1990s as the "Employer of Last Resort" (ELR).[19] Coincidentally, Mitchell also proposed the "Buffer Stock Employment" (BSE) scheme to achieve the goal of full employment.[20] Similarly, some scholars have subsequently proposed policy that guarantee government support for employment demand and named them "Job Guarantee" (JG) and "Public Service Employment" (PSE).[21] It is worth noting that in recent studies, the terms "Employer of Last Resort", "Buffer Stock Employment" and "Job Guarantee" are often discussed in parallel and used to explain each other.[22] Therefore, for the convenience of writing and discussion, we will also use these terms interchangeably in the following analysis without making specific distinctions.

The goal of the "Employer of Last Resort" (ELR) is to create "an infinitely elastic demand for labor", aiming for a more comprehensive goal of full employment. It sounds quite "bold". As was stated by Mosler, the government's plan to act as the Employer of Last Resort is "an entirely different policy option where the government assumes the role of employer of last resort (ELR), eliminating involuntary unemployment, while it maintains price stability by fixing the price it pays for the proposed supplementary ELR labor pool."[23] In Mosler's opinion, "Any government can achieve full employment by offering a public service job to anyone who wants one at a fixed market wage. The cost of employing those hired in the ELR pool will be a supplement to the current budget. Moreover, by fixing the wage paid under this ELR program at a level that does not disrupt existing labor markets—that is, a wage level close to the existing minimum wage—substantive price stability can be expected."[24]

[18] Minsky, H. P. 2008. *Stabilizing an Unstable Economy*. New York: McGraw- Hill. p. 343.

[19] Wray, L.R. 1998. *Understanding Modern Money: A Key to Full Employment and Price Stability*. Northampton: Edward Edgar. Post-Keynesian economists believe there is an earlier version of this idea. See: Beveridge, W. H. 1944. *Full Employment in a Free Society*. New York: W. W. Norton & Company, Inc.; Pierson, J. H. G.1964. *Insuring Full Employment: A United States Policy for Domestic Prosperity and World Development*. New York: The Viking Press.

[20] Michell, W. F. 1998. The Buffer Stock Employment model and the NAIRU: The path to full employment. *Journal of Economics Issues*. 32 (2): 547–555.

[21] Harvey, P. 1989. *Securing the Right to Employment*. Princeton: Princeton University Press; Gordon, W. 1997. Job assurance: The job guarantee revisited. *Journal of Economic Issues*. 31 (3): 826–834; Ramsay, T. 2002–2003.The jobs guarantee: A post Keynesian analysis. *Journal of Post Keynesian Economics*. 25 (2): 273–291.

[22] Wray, L.R. 1998. *Understanding Modern Money: A Key to Full Employment and Price Stability*. Northampton: Edward Edgar; Tcherneva, P.R. 2020. *The Case for a Job Guarantee*. Cambridge: Polity Press.

[23] Mosler, W. 1997–1998. Full employment and price stability. *Journal of Post Keynesian Economics*. 20(2): 167.

[24] Mosler, W. 1997–1998. Full employment and price stability. *Journal of Post Keynesian Economics*. 20(2): 168.

To gain a better understanding on the price-stabilizing mechanism of the Employer of Last Resort (ELR) policy, we can analyze from the perspective of buffer stock. As was discussed in previous chapters, the government can establish a price-stabilizing mechanism through the creation of a buffer stock. The gold standard, a monetary system anchored by gold reserves, serves as a classic example of a price anchor. However, "gold is a relatively minor commodity in the modem economy",[25] and its limited supply means its capacity to stabilize prices has waned. "Stabilizing the price of gold does not create strong forces to stabilize the prices of other commodities. It would be much more preferable to select a more significant commodity as the foundation for a buffer stock policy. For instance, petroleum products are integral to the production of most other commodities, making oil a strong candidate for such a policy. Stabilizing the price of oil would exert a far greater stabilizing influence on the modern economy than returning to a gold standard or a gold buffer stock regime."[26] By setting up a petroleum buffer stock, the government could be poised to buy or sell oil at predetermined prices. Given the widespread use of oil in both production and daily life, as well as in the processing of related products, the establishment of an oil buffer stock can exert a stabilizing influence akin to that of the gold standard. "There is, however, an even better commodity to serve as a buffer stock, and that commodity is labour."[27]

In Mitchell's analysis, "Suppose we characterize an economy with two labor markets: A (primary) and B (secondary) broadly corresponding to the dual labor market depictions. Wage setting in A is contractual and responds in an inverse and lagged fashion to relative wage growth (*A/B*)...A government stimulus to this economy increases output and employment in both sectors immediately. Wages are relatively flexible upwards in Sector B and respond immediately. The compression of the *A/B* relativity stimulates wage growth in Sector A after a time....... A combination of wage-wage and wage-price mechanisms in a soft product market can then drive inflation. This is a Phillips curve world. To stop inflation, the government has to repress demand. The higher unemployment brings the real income expectations of workers and firms into line with the available real income, and inflation stabilizes-a typical NAIRU story."[28] Mitchell believes that the introduction of buffer stock employment (BSE) can achieve true full employment while also providing greater economic stability. During economic downturns, the government employs unemployed labor at a fixed wage level (primarily in the B market), which means that a buffer stock employment is established in the B market. "This sets a floor in

[25] Wray, L.R. 1998. *Understanding Modern Money: A Key to Full Employment and Price Stability*. Northampton: Edward Edgar. p. 8.

[26] Wray, L.R. 1998. *Understanding Modern Money: A Key to Full Employment and Price Stability*. Northampton: Edward Edgar. p. 8.

[27] Wray, L. R. 1998.*Understanding Modern Money: A Key to Full Employment and Price Stability*. Northampton: Edward Edgar. p. 9.

[28] Michell, W. F. 1998. The Buffer Stock Employment model and the NAIRU: The path to full employment. *Journal of Economics Issues*. 32 (2): 550–551. Here NAIRU refers to the Non-Accelerating Inflation Rate of Unemployment.

the economy's cost structure for given productivity levels",[29] without affecting the wage structure in the market (A/B). In the economic upswing when total demand increases, the buffer stock employment provides a buffer mechanism based on a wage floor, with an abundant supply of labor, effectively suppressing inflationary pressures driven by wage increases in the A and B labor markets. Mitchell further argues that the size of the buffer stock can be measured by the Buffer Employment Ratio (BER), which is "the ratio of buffer stock employment to total employment".[30] "The BSE/ELR policy generates inflation stability ... This leads to the definition of a new concept, the Non-Accelerating Inflation Buffer Employment Ratio (NAIBER), which, in the buffer stock economy, replaces the NAIRU/ MRU as an inflation control mechanism."[31]

Comparing "buffer stock employment" with those discussed in the previous chapters, it becomes evident that regardless of the type of buffer stock, the government essentially serves as the "market maker" in maintaining socio-economic stability. The key difference lies in that in buffer stock employment (BSE) the government is not dealing with ordinary commodities but rather with labor. On one hand, the government creates employment demand by providing public sector jobs and stands ready to hire the unemployed at the predetermined basic public sector wage (BPSW).[32] On the other hand, the government is equally prepared to supply labor to the market, effectively alleviating inflationary pressures that arise from labor market tightness. Through a "stock-release" cycle, the government ensures that labor is always in a state of being "fully employed". The most important reason why buffer stock employment can also function as a tool for price stabilization is as follows: since labor is a special commodity that is essential in nearly all production processes and is even more important than gold or oil, the government effectively sets the value of the currency by setting the wage of the buffer stock. "If the wage demands of workers in the private sector exceed by too great a margin the employer's calculations of their productivity, the alternative is to obtain BPSE[33] workers at a mark-up over the BPSW."[34] Thus, as long as the BPSW remains relatively stable, it becomes a price anchor and provides a benchmark for other wages. In this sense, buffer stock employment creates a "labor standard", achieving the dual

---

[29] Michell, W. F. 1998. The Buffer Stock Employment model and the NAIRU: The path to full employment. *Journal of Economics Issues*. 32 (2): 551.

[30] Michell, W. F. 1998. The Buffer Stock Employment model and the NAIRU: The path to full employment. *Journal of Economics Issues*. 32 (2): 552.

[31] Michell, W. F. 1998. The Buffer Stock Employment model and the NAIRU: The path to full employment. *Journal of Economics Issues*. 32 (2): 552.

[32] In relevant discussions, the wage obtained is called the basic public sector wage (BPSW). See: Wray, L. R. 1998. *Understanding Modern Money: A Key to Full Employment and Price Stability*. Northampton: Edward Edgar. p. 126.

[33] BPSE refers to the basic public sector employment.

[34] Wray, L. R. 1998. *Understanding Modern Money: A Key to Full Employment and Price Stability*. Northampton: Edward Edgar. p. 132.

macroeconomic objectives of full employment and price stability. In Wary's mind, this is clearly a superior policy choice:

> Under ELR, the government would 'monetize' labour just as it 'monetizes' gold under the gold standard. The question is: Do we prefer to have gold 'fully employed', or is it preferable to have labour 'fully employed'? Should we attempt to stabilize prices by reestablishing the gold standard, or should we move to a BPSW standard? Or should we simply continue on the present path, which requires unemployment of labour to try to minimize inflation?[35]

Labor maintains the "liquidity" throughout the dynamic process of being fully employed. The buffer stock acts like a "buffer pool", allowing labor to flow in and out like a stream of "living water", enabling people to engage in various socially necessary work rather than waiting idly for welfare. This undoubtedly injects more positive stability and growth into the economy and society. Of course, within buffer stock employment, there will inevitably be some "sediment", meaning that some labor may remain in the reserve pool for extended periods either because they have not been hired in the competitive market or for other reasons. However, Gorden emphasize that for those who are "ready, willing, and able to work" without health barriers, the government has the responsibility to provide job assurance. Even for those "handicapped", as long as they can, the government should offer them suitable jobs.[36]Thus, at the policy level, the Employer of Last Resort (ELR) program aims not only to maintain macroeconomic stability but also to achieve true "zero unemployment" through an effective minimum wage under the principle of employment fairness.[37] In fact, the government's prescribed minimum wage is significant only when zero unemployment is achieved. That is to say, if there are people who are willing to work but stay unemployed, the minimum wage is substantially devalued—in essence, it means nothing in that case.

When workers become unemployed, their labor capacity (and even their willingness to work) would decline over time. The lower their capacity, the harder it is for them to achieve reemployment, creating a vicious cycle that ultimately leads to the loss of work habits and their exit from the labor market, thereby reducing the labor participation rate. The cost of unemployment is very high, and the losses caused by unemployment are not limited in economic aspects. The weariness of personal willpower and the various negative impacts on society brought about by unemployment are not easy to notice in the short term, but the potential harm can be substantial in the long run. In this light, the government's establishment of buffer stock employment addresses not only economic issues but also social ones. By allowing individuals to "learn while working" in public sector jobs, people's labor abilities, mental well-being, and self-esteem are protected and nurtured, providing a buffer platform for their future self-development. Additionally, it's important to note that labor hired

---

[35] Wray, L. R. 1998. *Understanding Modern Money: A Key to Full Employment and Price Stability*. Northampton: Edward Edgar. p. 136.

[36] Gordon, W. 1997. Job assurance: The job guarantee revisited. *Journal of Economics Issues*. 31(3): 826.

[37] Wray, L. R. 1998. Zero unemployment and stable price. *Journal of Economics Issues*. 32(2): 539–545.

through the buffer stock provides more and better public goods, which clearly enhances the efficiency of the economic and social system.

In a market economy, "unemployment" has become a persistent issue in macroeconomic management. The government's establishment of buffer stocks to ensure full employment is undoubtedly of positive significance. In addition to its stabilizing function, the Employer of Last Resort (ELR) scheme is a much more proactive economic policy compared to passive unemployment relief, encouraging individuals not to abandon their responsibilities toward themselves and the society. This policy reinforces the view that labor is both a fundamental right and a basic duty for everyone, ensuring fairness and justice through concrete measures.

With the above discussion, the mechanism of buffer stock employment for full employment can be further illustrated in Fig. 6.1. In face with unemployed individuals who have demands for employment, a government responsible for the welfare of its people has no reason to withhold assistance. Generally, workers are arranged in a pyramid structure according to their education level, abilities, and skills. In the context of market mechanisms, the market which prioritize efficiency, tends to employ workers in the way from the top down. Mainstream economics posits the existence of a "Non-Accelerating Inflation Rate of Unemployment" (NAIRU). However, the natural rate of unemployment described by NAIRU is not really "natural". In the world of NAIRU, most of the unemployed are located at the lower end of the pyramid. In the rapidly changing modern society, frictional and structural unemployment can more easily push workers out of the labor market, leading to a continuous decline in labor participation, which exacts a high cost on both individuals and society. The government's Employer of Last Resort (ELR) policy, however, guarantees employment by hiring labor from the bottom up, counter to the market's top-down mechanism, without competing with or excluding the market. This approach achieves greater employment and higher labor participation rates.

Here, we can refer to the mechanisms of labor hiring by the market (from the top down) and by the government (from the bottom up) as the "dual convection" model, where both play opposite wax-and-wane roles in employment. During economic recessions, the market demand for labor experiences a "falling tide", leading to increased unemployment. At this point, the government's supply of public sector jobs accordingly experience a "rising tide". The Buffer Employment Ratio (BER), as described by Mitchell, reaches a high level at BER2. As the Employer of Last

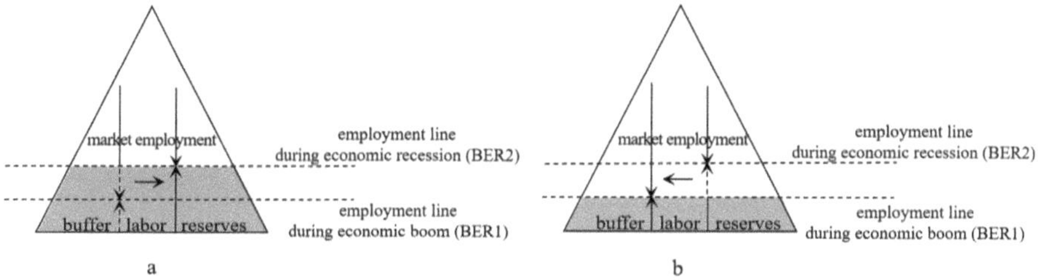

Fig. 6.1 Public employment countercyclical buffer reserve

Resort (ELR), the government provides employment security by absorbing the unemployed labor force through Keynesian public works projects (see Fig. 6.1a). At the level of BER2, effective demand is stabilized. Conversely, when the market demand for labor experiences a "rising tide", the government's buffer stock appropriately experiences a "falling tide" (see Fig. 6.1b), and the Buffer Employment Ratio (BER) falls to a low level at BER1. In the transition from BER2 to BER1, the buffer stock releases labor into the market at a basic public sector wage (BPSW), which is determined by productivity levels and does not disrupt the wage structure, thereby suppressing inflation. At the same time, the buffer stock acts as a stabilizer, ensuring that the economy achieves real full employment that is not based on the Non-Accelerating Inflation Rate of Unemployment (NAIRU) (BER1 is what Mitchell describes as NAIBER, Non-Accelerating Inflation Buffer Employment Ratio). Throughout this process, the buffer stock pool expands and contracts against the economic cycle, mitigating market fluctuations and functioning as an automatic stabilizer for the economy. Obviously, buffer stock employment serves as a special kind of "Ever-normal Granary of the labor force". However, unlike traditional ever-normal granaries, during times of *pingdi*, the government "purchases" labor by employing and training workers. In times of *pingtiao*, the government supplies labor to the market without charge. As is shown in Fig. 6.1, the productivity of labor employed through the buffer stock fluctuates dynamically with economic cycles. In transition from BER1 to BER2, the relatively high productivity of the buffer stock labor exerts a positive incentive on market-employed labor, and the reverse is also true. Thus, the changing productivity of the buffer stock becomes a key component of its role in stabilizing both production and prices.[38]

6.2.2 *Historical Practice of the New Deal*

Can the government, the Employer of Last Resort, provide enough public sector jobs to meet the employment demand of the involuntary unemployed? In response to this question, Minsky used the employment strategy of Franklin D. Roosevelt's New Deal as an example to provide the answer:

> An employment strategy must deal with youth and adult unemployment as well as the provision of jobs for older adults. The instruments of an employment strategy can be identified by labels drawn from the 1930s: The Civilian Conservation Corps (CCC), the National Youth Administration (NYA), and the Works Progress Administration (WPA). In the New Deal days these programs were viewed as transitory, but in the light of the inherent instability of capitalism and the chronic shortage of jobs, they will be conceived of here as permanent.[39]

[38] Wray, L. R. 1998. *Understanding Modern Money: A Key to Full Employment and Price Stability*. Northampton: Edward Edgar. p. 139.

[39] Minsky, H. P. 2008. *Stabilizing an Unstable Economy*. New York: McGraw- Hill. p. 345.

According to Minsky, the employment policies promoted by the Franklin D. Roosevelt administration can be seen as a typical government initiative to create "an infinitely elastic demand for labor" through a work guarantee program known as the Employer of Last Resort (ELR). As evident from the second "fireside chat" on September 30, 1934, Franklin D. Roosevelt was unequivocal about the government's responsibility to ensure high-level full employment:

> … the program of public works …designed to put more men back to work… I answer that no country, however rich, can afford the waste of its human resources. … Some people try to tell me that we must make up our minds that for the future we shall permanently have millions of unemployed just as other countries have had them for over a decade. … But as for this country, I stand or fall by my refusal to accept as a necessary condition of our future a permanent army of unemployed. On the contrary, we must make it a national principle that we will not tolerate a large army of unemployed and that we will arrange our national economy to end our present unemployment as soon as we can and then to take wise measures against its return.[40]

The Great Depression caused millions of Americans to lose their jobs. In response to this unprecedented crisis, the U.S. government initiated large-scale unemployment relief programs. However, President Franklin D. Roosevelt believed that such passive relief efforts were ineffective. He described them as "a narcotic, a subtle destroyer of the human spirit…the vitality of our people be further sapped by the giving," and therefore, "the Federal Government must and shall quit this business of relief."[41] As a result, Franklin D. Roosevelt adjusted the policy, stating that "direct giving shall, wherever possible, be supplemented by provision for useful and remunerative work."[42]Following this principle, the U.S. government shifted from passive assistance to a more proactive work relief program. This program created jobs through various public works projects, and these projects followed the guideline that "Projects shall be of a nature that a considerable proportion of the money spent will go into wages for labor".[43] As a result, the government employed millions of workers within just a few years. Among the many work relief programs, there were several creative initiatives that not only provided targeted employment opportunities for specialized or professional groups but also planted the seeds for long-term economic and social development in the United States.

---

[40] Roosevelt, Franklin D. 1938. Second "Fireside Chat" of 1934—"We Are Moving Forward to Greater Freedom, to Greater Security for the Average Man". in *The Public Papers and Addresses of Franklin D. Roosevelt, vol.3: The Advance of Recovery and Reform, 1934.* ed. Roseman, Samuel I. New York: Random House. p.420.

[41] Leuchtenburg, William E. 2009. *Frankin D. Roosevelt and the New Deal: 1932–1940.* New York: Harper Perennial. p.124.

[42] Roosevelt, Franklin D. 1938. The First "Fireside Chat" of 1934 - "Are You Better Off Than You Were Last Year?". in *The Public Papers and Addresses of Franklin D. Roosevelt, vol.3: The Advance of Recovery and Reform, 1934.* ed. Roseman, Samuel I. New York: Random House. p.313.

[43] Roosevelt, Franklin D. 1938. The First "Fireside Chat" of 1935—"Fear Is Vanishing, Confidence Is Growing … Faith Is Being Renewed in the Democratic Form of Government". in *The Public Papers and Addresses of Franklin D. Roosevelt, vol.4: The Court Disapproves, 1935.* ed. Roseman, Samuel I. New York: Random House. p. 135.

In 1933, the U.S. government established the Civilian Conservation Corps (CCC) to implement soil erosion control projects under Sections 202 and 203 of the National Industrial Recovery Act. The CCC recruited unemployed urban youth, aged 18 to 25, to participate in environmental engineering projects. Over a period of 9 years, hundreds of thousands of CCC members set up camps across the country, engaging in diverse tasks such as soil conservation, reforestation, forest and pasture protection and restoration, wildlife conservation, maintenance of historical sites, construction of outdoor facilities, and various rescue, flood control, and recycling efforts. By 1941, "the CCC had employed almost 3.5 million men. Some estimates are that they planted 2.5 billion trees, protected 40 million acres of farmland from erosion, drained 248,000 acres of swamp land, replanted almost a million acres of grazing land, built 125,000 miles of roads, fought fires, and created 800 state parks".[44] Because the CCC directly addressed the issue of unemployment, the government became the "Employer of Last Resort" for many young people. Franklin D. Roosevelt stated, "One of the great values to this work is the fact that it is direct and requires the intervention of very little machinery." He further emphasized, "In creating this civilian conservation corps, we are killing two birds with one stone. … We are conserving not only our natural resources, but our human resources."[45] The CCC offered young people more than just protection from unemployment, hunger, and idleness. It also allowed them to leave the troubled urban cities and immerse themselves in the vast natural and rural landscapes, where they gained physical and mental practice through hard work. The benefits of such "practice" were long-lasting. A recent empirical study shows that the CCC program had positive impact on CCC participants' long-term development, including improvements in health, employment, and income. The longer participants were involved in the program, the more significant these impacts became.[46] In addition to its immediate impacts, the CCC left behind an invaluable intangible asset: by engaging young participants in hands-on conservation work, it broadened the public base for environmental conservation in the U.S., and raised awareness of the importance of protecting and scientifically utilizing natural resources, laying the foundation for the post-war environmental movement in America.[47]

The Great Depression devastated various industries, and the art market was no exception. When Franklin D. Roosevelt was the president, there were 10,000 unemployed artists in the U.S. During the years of New Deal, the U.S. government implemented cultural programs such as the Public Works of Art Project (PWAP), the

[44] Ganzel, Bill. *CCC, Civilian Conservation Corps, 2003* [EB/OL]. http://www.livinghistoryfarm.org/farminginthe30s/water_12.html

[45] Roosevelt, Franklin D. 1938. The Second "Fireside Chat"—"What We have Been Doing and What We Are Planning to Do". in *The Public Papers and Addresses of Franklin D. Roosevelt, Vol.2: The Year of Crisis, 1933*. ed. Roseman, Samuel I. ed. New York: Random House. p.162

[46] Aizer, A. et al. 2020. Do youth employment programs work? Evidence from the New Deal. *NBER Working Paper No.27103*.

[47] Teng, Haijian. 2006. Origin and Status of Civilian Conservation Corps in the history of America. *Journal of Historical Science*. (10): 57–64.

Section of Painting and Sculpture (later renamed Section of Fine Arts) in Department of the Treasury, and the Federal Art Project (FAP), which employed large numbers of jobless artists. To promote the development of public art, these artists explored and preserved traditional American art, organized workshops to teach the public skills in painting, weaving, and art design, and created murals and sculptures for public buildings—some of which still adorn municipal facilities across the country today. Though not all of these works were great masterpieces, they significantly strengthened the links between American citizens and art appreciation. Jobs provided by the government saved artists from unemployment, expanded the spaces of public art, and helped lay the foundation for the eventual dominance of Abstract Expressionism in Western art. The New Deal also employed overlooked groups for forgotten tasks in various employment programs. For instance, the Federal Writers' Project (FWP) hired writers to publish nearly a thousand books, including public books, and the Federal Theatre Project (FTP) employed new talents to innovate performance arts, bringing theater to the masses.[48]

Although the employment programs in Franklin D. Roosevelt's New Deal were part of extraordinary measures in extraordinary times, the fact that the government was able to create tens of millions of public sector jobs in just a few years just shows that the economic society harbored a large number of valuable, yet overlooked, jobs. On this point, Keynes had the same standpoint as Franklin D. Roosevelt. In the face of skepticism, Keynes said, with an unconventional and encouraging tone, "There are innumerable schemes pigeonholed in government offices, the children of the most active and progressive brains in the country, which only have to be fished out to provide a great quantity of employment widely distributed in kind and locality." Thus, the solutions to the employment problem calls for "a new atmosphere of *doing things,* instead of one of smothering negation".[49]

The ideas and actions of Keynes, Roosevelt, and Minsky are certainly inspiring. However, if we look further back in history, we might, with surprise, find that ancient China was perhaps one of the earliest implementers of employment guarantees. As was discussed in Chap. 3, during normal years in ancient China, small-scale farmers would settle on their land, the agricultural production remained relatively stable, and people of various sectors including scholars, farmers, artisans and merchants could live and work in peace. However, during years of natural disasters, agricultural production was interrupted, leading to the dispersal of small farmers, which in turn caused severe "unemployment" problems that could easily trigger social crises. The labor relief policy, a kind of "Ever-normal Granary of labor force" adopted by successive dynasties, absorbed displaced people and became an effective measure for economic stabilization. Thus, we can see that the ancient Chinese government already played the role of "the Employer of Last Resort", revealing

[48] Liu, Xuyi and Li, Cunxun. 2002. *General History of the United States*, vol.5. Beijing: People's Publishing House. pp. 120–121; Zhao, Lisha. 2014. Patronized art project in the New Deal. *Public Art.* (4): 5–9.

[49] Keynes, J. M. 2013.*Essays in Persuasion.* in *The Collected Writings of John Maynard Keynes, vol.*9. ed. Moggridge, D. New York: Cambridge University Press. p. 99.

modern qualities in its approach. This assessment is not unfounded or contrived. Guo Moruo (1892–1978), a Chinese poet, historian, archaeologist and government official, when analyzing the *chimi* (on extravagance in spending) chapter of *Guanzi*, in which there was a sentence "rather than giving them food, it is better to avoid taking them away from production",[50] stated that "the author is advocating for full employment rather than passive relief aid."[51] Hu Jichuang, when discussing Wang Fuzhi's ideas on organizing public works during years of famine to "gather the unemployed", pointed out that if we expand the concept of "unemployment" caused by famine to general "unemployment", Wang Fuzhi's ideas to solve unemployment problem through large-scale public works projects was later advocated by Keynes in the 1930s.[52] In our discussion of labor relief policies in Chap. 3, we cited a passage from the *Qing Shilu* (Factual Records of Qing Dynasty): as to the public works projects, "governors and lieutenant-governors of each province should conduct detailed investigations, prioritize tasks based on urgency, make preliminary estimates, and compile registers to be submitted to the ministry. ..., if labor relief is to be implemented, it can be quickly executed by referring to these records, preventing delays and significantly benefiting the people's livelihood."[53] From a modern perspective, isn't this essentially an ancient Chinese version of "permanent on-the-spot job creation"? This institutional innovation of ancient China was rediscovered and applied in Western industrial societies. Although separated by a thousand years of history and different socio-cultural backgrounds, the two civilizations had subtle connections which are worth deep reflection. From the perspective of the "Ever-normal Granary", Franklin D. Roosevelt's New Deal, in addition to promoting agricultural ever-normal granaries, also created an "Ever-normal Granary of labor force" through public works projects. Since the program of public works were "closely allied to the N.R.A" (National Industrial Recovery Act),[54] this "Ever-normal Granary of labor force" was also crucial in restoring and stabilizing industrial development. During special periods, the agricultural granary and "Ever-normal Granary of labor force" complemented each other and made a historic contribution to pulling the United States out of the mire of depression.

[50] Guanzi. 1985. *Political, Economic, and Philosophical Essays from Early China*, vol. 1. trans. W. Allyn Rickett. Princeton: Princeton University Press. p.327

[51] Guo, Moruo. 1954. A study of the chapter "on Extravagance in Spending". *Historical Research*. (3): 35, 37.

[52] Hu, Jichuang. 1998. *History of Chinese Economic Thought*, vol.2. Shanghai: Shanghai University of Finance and Economics Press. p. 501. Continuing the ideological tradition of labor relief, Wang Fuzhi also specifically discussed how to implement the policy of labor relief according to local conditions. See: Wang, Fuzhi.1996. *Nightmare*. in *Complete Works of Wang Fuzhi*, vol.12. Changsha: Yuelu Publishing House. p. 577.

[53] Qing, Gui and Dong Gao et al. 1985. *Factual Record of Qing Dynasty: Records of Emperor Gaozong*, vol.46. Beijing: Zhonghua Book Company. p. 795.

[54] Roosevelt, Franklin D. 1938. Second "Fireside Chat" of 1934—"We Are Moving Forward to Greater Freedom, to Greater Security for the Average Man". in *The Public Papers and Addresses of Franklin D. Roosevelt, vol.3: The Advance of Recovery and Reform, 1934*. ed. Roseman, Samuel I. New York: Random House. p. 420.

Let us return to theoretical analysis. It is now necessary to conduct a comprehensive review of the Keynesian—post-Keynesian buffer stock approach. In *The General Theory*, after introducing a series of complex economic analyses, Keynes presents a macroeconomic picture where, due to unstable expectations, investors alternately "hold" and "expend" money and other factors of production, giving rise to endogenous macroeconomic cyclical fluctuations. This implies that in an economy filled with uncertainty, in the face of dashed expectations or the collapsed marginal efficiency of capital, investors, in an attempt to avoid risk, will choose to hold money. At this point, money becomes "unemployed" due to an increase in liquidity preference. Since one of the important functions of money is to facilitate the employment of various factors of production in the whole social system, the "unemployment" of money can cause the market to fall into a general state of "unemployment" where people lose their jobs and resources are left unused. As a result, the social organism enters a pathological state. Keynes recognized that this pathological unemployment is not caused by over-investment, where capital no longer has any reasonable place for use. It is caused by the fact that investments are made under conditions of unstable expectations, which will inevitably fail to be realized sooner or later. In this situation, the government is to act as the "Employer of Last Resort," which is not driven by the pursuit of commercial profit but is firmly committed to maintaining the long-term marginal efficiency of capital. Through "organized investment," the government employs the "unemployed money,"[55] thereby re-employing the unemployed labor and resources in the market, ensuring the full circulation of factors of production and achieving healthy and stable macroeconomic development. The question then arises: who should be employed first?

Here, the government, as the "Employer of Last Resort," offers a clear answer by establishing the "buffer stock employment" system: employing people first can effectively drive the "employment" of other factors of production. Activating the labor force and setting it into motion provides the most fundamental guarantee for effective demand and overall macroeconomic stability. This explains why Keynes used the level of employment as a crucial indicator of economic performance. In fact, once we recognize in Keynes' opinion, "the outstanding faults of the economic society in which we live are its failure to provide for full employment",[56] then it is easy to understand the core position of "people" in Keynes' economic theory. Though Keynes placed money in a prominent position within macroeconomic analysis, he attached even greater emphasis on the role of people as the central actors in the economy, thus in essence inheriting the Marshallian welfare tradition. However,

[55] In Fan Li's words, "The principle of storing goods is to try to get commodities which can be preserved for a long time without damage or depreciation". See: Sima, Qian. 1993. Biographies of Money-Makers. *Records of the Grand Historian: Han Dynasty*, vol.2. trans. Burton Watson. Hong Kong and New York: Columbia University Press. p. 437. There is similarity between the two principles.

[56] Keynes, J. M. 2013. *The General Theory of Employment, Interest and Money*. in *The Collected Writings of John Maynard Keynes, vol.7*. ed. Moggridge, D. New York: Cambridge University Press. p. 372.

unlike Pigou's welfare economics, Keynes took a different path, shifting welfare economics at the macro level towards unemployment and full employment, highlighting a distinctive macro-welfare dimension. In the specific era, Keynes had a profound understanding of unemployment: he called it "the monstrous evil of Unemployment", and thought that "Unemployment is an infectious illness. It multiplies itself and spreads from house to house …."[57] Therefore, "His received view of the world was of a society in which each man had his appointed place, and it was an injustice for him not to be allowed to feed his family and retain his self-respect in fulfilling the task ordained for him."[58] It is in this context that some post-Keynesian economists, when discussing macroeconomic policy, emphasize that Keynes' macro-stabilization policies should be understood more as applying socialized investment to achieve full employment. In the long term, addressing the basic needs of people—specifically, the demand for employment to fill the employment gap—rather than simply using stimulus policies to meet growth and investment needs to fill the output gap, is the fundamental solution to macroeconomic stability. This understanding undoubtedly captures the essence of Keynesian macroeconomics, giving prominence to the primary importance of full-employment-oriented economic policies.

The theory and policy of the "Employer of Last Resort" or "buffer stock employment" in Post-Keynesian economics sparked intense debate when it was proposed in the 1990s, gaining both support and criticism. Proponents argue that this idea brings a breath of fresh air to economics. Although it presents a bold policy proposal, its theoretical foundation is carefully built upon the intellectual lines of earlier economists, and its value orientation reflects a positive approach toward addressing deep-seated economic ailments. On the other hand, the criticisms are more varied but generally revolve around a few key issues: many issues in economics involve trade-offs, and whether it is possible to achieve full employment while maintaining price stability remains a significant question; even setting that aside, the Employer of Last Resort plan could face numerous practical challenges in its implementation, and a more pressing concern might be whether the plan can actually provide sufficient jobs as designed; furthermore, even if the plan is successfully implemented, the government's fiscal budget may not only run into deficits but also remain at a high level due to long-term accumulation, raising questions about the program's sustainability under fiscal constraints.

The aforementioned doubts are issues that the proponents of the theory and policy cannot avoid and must address. In fact, they have indeed discussed many

---

[57] Keynes, J. M. 2013. *Activities 1922–1929: the return to gold and industrial policy.* in *The Collected Writings of John Maynard Keynes*, vol.19. ed. Moggridge, D. New York: Cambridge University Press. p.826.

[58] Johnson, Elizabeth. 1973. John Maynard Keynes: Scientist or Politician? in *After Keynes: Papers Presented to Section F (Economics) at the 1972 Annual Meeting of the British Association for the Advancement of Science*. ed. Joan Robinson. Oxford: Basil Blackwell. pp. 20–21.

specific plans and practical cases to demonstrate the feasibility of the policy.[59] Here, our focus is on whether the policy is theoretically feasible. In response to the criticisms, the proponents systematically addressed the issue of fiscal constraints. From a traditional fiscal perspective, the buffer stock employment policy would generate significant fiscal deficits[60] —raising concerns that this modern "Ever-normal Granary of labor force" may still face the historical problem encountered by ever-normal granaries in ancient China, namely the difficulty of consistently securing sufficient "stock". However, Post-Keynesian economists, based on the theory of "New Functional Finance", provide the following answer: deficits do not constitute a real "constraint" on the buffer stock employment policy, and this employment strategy can indeed be sustainably implemented.

6.3 Functional Finance: A Mechanism for Maintaining Buffer Stock Employment

6.3.1 Lerner's Law and Endogenous Finance

Why is it said that the buffer stock employment policy does not face fiscal budget constraints? To answer this question, we need to firstly clarify the different understandings people have regarding fiscal policy and national debt.

In the history of economic thought, people's attitude to various economic issues typically fall into three categories: conservative, radical and moderate. However, in the realm of fiscal theory and policy, there is a widely held belief that national finances are akin to household finances—consistently spending more than is earned and relying on borrowing will inevitably lead to "bankruptcy". From this, two mainstream views on fiscal thought have emerged: the first view holds that fiscal deficits and national debt always have negative impacts on the economic society. Deficit spending leads to inflation, raises interest rates, crowds out private investment, and leaves a heavy burden of national debt for future generations. The second view, a moderate one, suggests that under specific economic conditions (such as economic recession), increasing deficits and national debt is a reasonable choice. Fiscal balance should be achieved over the economic cycle, rather than within a single fiscal

---

[59] A case in point is the Jefes program in Argentina. See: Tcherneva, P. R. and Wray, L. R. 2005. Employer of last resort: A case study of Argentina's *Jefes* Program. *Working Paper No.43, Center for Full Employment and Price Stability of the University of Missour-Kansas City*. For more case studies, see: Murray, M. J. and Forstater, M., ed. 2013. *Employment Guarantee Schemes*. New York: Palgrave Macmillan; Tcherneva, P. R. 2020. *The Case for a Job Guarantee*. Cambridge: Polity Press.

[60] It should not be overlooked that by directly creating public employment positions to hire the unemployed, the government will correspondingly reduce a significant amount of passive welfare expenditures, such as unemployment relief.

year. While deficits may increase burdens, the assets (such as infrastructure) created through deficit policies are beneficial for long-term economic development.

In addition to these two mainstream views, there is another non-mainstream understanding of fiscal deficits: Abba Lerner's "Functional Finance" theory, and the macroeconomic proposals of some Post-Keynesian economists that may be called "New Functional Finance". They argue that taxes are not the source of government revenue, and that the issuance of government bonds is not a means of financing fiscal expenditure. Therefore, fiscal policy need not be constrained by the self-imposed limits of balancing revenue and expenditure but should instead focus on achieving economic stability. This view, which runs counter to "common sense of economics", may seem fantastic. However, by carefully analyzing this non-mainstream economic thought that developed in the twentieth century, we can gain valuable insights and a unique perspective for observing the macroeconomy.

"Abba P. Lerner was one of the most original and imaginative economists of his generation."[61] He proposed the theory of "functional finance", which posed a significant challenge to mainstream economics and had a profound influence on an important school of heterodox economics, namely Post-Keynesian economics. The basic idea of functional finance was introduced in the article "The Economic Steering Wheel",[62] but it was formally named "functional finance" in his paper "Functional Finance and the Federal Debt". In that paper, Lerner stated, "Fundamentally the new theory, like almost every important discovery, is extremely simple. Indeed it is this simplicity which makes the public suspect it as too slick. Even learned professors who find it hard to abandon ingrained habits of thought have complained that it is "merely logical" when they could find no flaw in it."[63] Afterwards, Lerner proposed a revolutionary view of fiscal policy, arguing that the primary focus of government fiscal policy should be on the "results", "effects" or "functions":

> The central idea is that government fiscal policy, its spending and taxing, its borrowing and repayment of loans, its issue of new money and its withdrawal of money, shall all be undertaken with an eye only to the *results* of these actions on the economy and not to any established traditional doctrine about what is sound or unsound. This principle of judging only by *effects* has been applied in many other fields of human activity, where it is known as the method of science as opposed to scholasticism. The principle of judging fiscal measures by the way they work or function in the economy we may call *Functional Finance*.[64]

In Lerner's view, the core principle of fiscal policy lies in the effectiveness of its outcomes, and whether the budget is "balanced" or not during the process should not be a constraint. In other words, the foundation of fiscal policy should be the "effect" it produces, rather than the "surplus or deficit" in revenue and expenditure.

---

[61] Scitovky, T. 1984. Lerner's Contribution to economics. *Journal of Economic Literature.* 22(4): 1547.

[62] Lerner, A. P. 1983. The economic steering wheel. in *Selected Economic Writings of Abba P. Lerner.* ed. Colander, D. New York: New York University Press. pp. 271–277.

[63] Lerner, A. P. 1943. Functional finance and the federal debt. *Social Research.* 10 (1): 39.

[64] Lerner, A. P. 1943. Functional finance and the federal debt. *Social Research.* 10 (1): 39.

If a policy remains entangled in the debate over surplus versus deficit and ignores the objectives it aims to achieve, it would be a case of putting the cart before the horse. So, what are the functions of fiscal policy, and what are the effects that it should achieve?

For the first law of functional finance, Lerner stated, "The first financial responsibility of the government (since no-body else can undertake that responsibility) is to keep the total rate of spending in the country on goods and services neither greater nor less than that rate which at the current prices would buy all the goods that it is possible to produce. If total spending is allowed to go above this there will be inflation, and if it is allowed to go below this there will be unemployment."[65] Thus, fiscal instruments are inherently prescribed: "the adjustment of total spending (by everybody in the economy, including the government) in order to eliminate both unemployment and inflation, using government spending when total spending is too low and taxation when total spending is too high."[66] Based on this understanding, Lerner clearly stated, "Functional Finance rejects completely the traditional doctrines of "sound finance" and the principle of trying to balance the budget over a solar year or any other arbitrary period."[67] Why did Lerner emphasize the effects of fiscal policy to such importance, discarding the fiscal traditions long established in classical political economy?

Like Keynes, Lerner, an economist of his contemporary time, recognized that laissez-faire capitalism is an unstable system. In his article "The Economic Steering Wheel", Lerner depicted an economic scene in which the capitalist economy resembles a car driving down a highway without a driver or a steering wheel. "What appears to be a runaway car is speeding along the road and veering off to one side. As it approaches the rising edge of the highway its front wheels are turned so that it gets back onto the road and goes off at an angle making for the other side where the wheels are turned again."[68] Lerner used this metaphor to illustrate the cyclical fluctuations of the capitalist economy between "recession - unemployment" and "boom – inflation". Fiscal policy, in this metaphor, should act as the steering wheel of the economy, with the sole aim of keeping the macroeconomy moving smoothly. To achieve this goal, the precondition of balancing revenue and expenditure should not be regarded as a "driving standard".

Based on this understanding, Lerner's theory of functional finance can be understood as a form of "endogenous fiscal theory". It is termed endogenous because the economic fluctuations in capitalist systems stem from inherent instability, and fiscal policy is therefore endogenously assigned the role of eliminating unemployment and maintaining macroeconomic stability. However, in Lerner's view, Keynes' deficit policy had not completely overturned traditional fiscal doctrines. In other words,

[65] Lerner, A. P. 1943. Functional finance and the federal debt. *Social Research.* 10 (1): 39.

[66] Lerner, A. P. 1943. Functional finance and the federal debt. *Social Research.* 10 (1): 41.

[67] Lerner, A. P. 1943. Functional finance and the federal debt. *Social Research.* 10 (1): 41.

[68] Lerner, A. P. 1983. The economic steering wheel. in *Selected Economic Writings of Abba P. Lerner.* ed. Colander, D. New York: New York University Press. p. 271.

while Keynes opened the door to deficit policies, he only went halfway.[69] Lerner, on the other hand, advanced further along the path that Keynes had paved, decisively breaking with traditional doctrines. Lerner was clearly more radical in his approach. He fundamentally broke the doctrine of budget balance, proposing a new fiscal view that explicitly judged the quality of fiscal policy based on its effectiveness rather than on the amount of spending or the balance of revenues and expenditures. However, this radical proposition initially seemed so inconceivable that functional finance became somewhat of a forgotten corner of macroeconomics for a time. It wasn't until a group of Post-Keynesian economists revived it that it gained renewed attention.[70] For the sake of discussion and differentiation, we can refer to this recent development in thought as "New Functional Finance".

Theories of Functional Finance and New Functional Finance (hereinafter collectively referred to as "(New) Functional Finance") are closely connected with Keynesian economics, as it continues the Keynesian revolution. Therefore, strictly speaking, Keynes is a significant originator of this theoretical framework. However, as a theoretical system rooted in Keynes but with its own innovations, (New) Functional Finance, in its critical "construction", inherently requires a logical "deconstruction", which involves reinterpreting a series of issues, the most crucial one being how to understand the functions of government bonds and taxation.

For the second law of Functional Finance, Lerner stated, "The second law of Functional Finance is that the government should borrow money only if it is desirable that the public should have less money and more government bonds, for these are the effects of government borrowing. This might be desirable if otherwise the rate of interest would be reduced too low (by attempts on the part of the holders of the cash to lend it out) and induce too much investment, thus bringing about inflation. Conversely, the government should lend money (or repay some of its debt) only if it is desirable to increase the money or to reduce the quantity of government bonds in the hands of the public."[71] This law indicates that the issuance or repayment of government bonds by the government is, to a large extent, a monetary policy. The goal is "to achieve the rate of interest which results in the most desirable level of investment."[72]

[69] According to Lerner's recollection, Keynes referred to Lerner's fiscal views as a deceptive lie during a speech in Washington in 1944. However, a month later, Keynes retracted his criticism. See: Colander, D. 1984. Was Keynes a Keynesian or a Lernerian? *Journal of Economic Literature* 22 (4): 1572–1573.

[70] Wray, L.R. 1998. *Understanding Modern Money: A Key to Full Employment and Price Stability.* Northampton: Edward Edgar; Forstater, M. 1999. Functional finance and full employment: Lesson from Lerner for today. *Journal of Economic Issues.* 33(2): 475–482; Bell, S. 1999. Functional finance: what, why, and how? *Working Paper No. 287, Levy Economics Institutes of Bard College*; Bell, S. 2000. Do taxes bonds finance government spending? *Journal of Economic Issues.* 34(3): 603–620; Arestis, P. and Sawyer, M. 2004. *Re-examining Monetary and Fiscal Policies in the Twenty-First Century.* Cheltenham: Edward Elgar.

[71] Lerner, A. P. 1943. Functional finance and the federal debt. *Social Research.* 10 (1): 40–41.

[72] Lerner, A. P. 1943. Functional finance and the federal debt. *Social Research.* 10 (1): 41.

Following Lerner's ideas, the New Functional Finance theory further asserts that the real purpose of government bond issuance is to provide the public with an alternative monetary asset to reduce bank reserves, thereby stabilizing the interbank lending rate at a target level. Bell argues that government deficit spending increases the reserves in the banking system, producing what is known as the "reserve effect": when there is an excess of reserves, the supply of money in the interbank market will exceed demand, inevitably causing the interbank rate to decline possibly even to zero. Since the interbank rate is a wholesale funding rate, its fluctuations directly influence various market interest rates through arbitrage mechanisms. Therefore, the real objective of government bond issuance is to regulate the reserve levels, ensuring that this critical interest rate remains within a reasonable range around the target.[73] Traditional views hold that government deficit spending leads to higher interest rates, crowding out private investment. However, based on the aforementioned analysis, New Functional Finance draws a conclusion entirely opposite to mainstream economics. It suggests that deficit policy not only does not lead to a "crowding out effect" but actually results in lower interest rates, thereby encouraging investment through a "crowding in effect". As a result, it is impossible to reach what Lerner described as the "the most desirable level of investment". The proposed solution is for the government to replace bank reserves by issuing bonds, guiding the public to reduce the net reserve balance by purchasing interest-bearing assets. In this understanding, government bond issuance is a post-operational activity relative to deficit spending, not an ex-ante financing measure. Additionally, Bell points out that when the public pays taxes to the government, bank reserves are transferred to the central bank's Treasury account, which also absorbs the reserves increased by government spending, producing an effect similar to government bond issuance. Therefore, fiscal policy has a more significant impact on the money supply than what is traditionally understood. This implies that, in order to maintain relatively stable interest rates, monetary policy calls for close coordination with fiscal policy.[74]

6.3.2 "Taxes-Drive-Money" (TDM) and Endogenous Deficits

If the interpretation of bonds in (New) Functional Finance theory already goes beyond convention, its understanding of the nature of taxation is even more radical. Based on the first law of Functional Finance, Lerner derived "an interesting, and to many, shocking corollary" that "taxation should never be undertaken merely because the government needs to make money payments. According to the principles of

[73] Bell, S. 1999. Functional finance: what, why, and how? *Working Paper No. 287, Levy Economics Institutes of Bard College*; Bell, S. 2000. Do taxes bonds finance government spending? *Journal of Economic Issues*. 34(3): 603–620.

[74] Bell, S. 2000. Do taxes bonds finance government spending? *Journal of Economic Issues*. 34(3): 603–620.

Functional Finance, taxation must be judged only by its effects."[75] This effect is achieving the goal stated in the first law, i.e., "to keep the total rate of spending in the country on goods and services neither greater nor less than that rate which at the current prices would buy all the goods that it is possible to produce" by regulating taxpayers' spending. Why did Lerner, in contrast to traditional views, assert that taxation is not a general condition for government expenditure? The answer becomes clearer when we connect Lerner's understanding of money with this issue. In the 14th edition of the *Encyclopaedia Britannica*, under the entry "Money", Lerner made the following interpretation to the nature of money:

> But it only means that general acceptability is not easily established. General acceptability may come about gradually. If a growing number of people are willing to accept payment in a particular form, this makes others willing to accept that kind of payment. General acceptability may be established rapidly if very important sellers or creditors are willing to accept payment in a particular form of money. For example, if the government announces its readiness to accept a certain means of payment in settlement of taxes, taxpayers will be willing to accept this means of payment because they can use it to pay taxes. Everyone else will then be willing to accept it because they can use it to buy things from the taxpayers, or to pay debts to them, or to make payments to others who have to make payments to the taxpayers, and so on.[76]

Lerner's somewhat circumlocutious explanation emphasizes that the acceptability of money is the fundamental condition for money to be money, and that the government's tax system creates a special mechanism that allows money to be widely accepted. If the government requires taxes to be paid in a particular currency, taxpayers need to obtain that currency through economic activities, spreading demand for that currency throughout the economy. Lerner's unique understanding of money was influenced by The State Theory of Money[77] advocated by the economist Georg Friedrich Knapp from the German Historical School, which left him a deep impression during his time at the London School of Economics.[78] In Lerner's view, modern money is a creature of the state, and the key to establishing a mechanism for the widespread circulation of money lies in taxation.[79] That is, money is created by the state through its tax system, and the purpose of taxation is purely to sustain the demand for money and regulate spending. Under this framework, fiscal policy completely breaks free from the dogmatic understanding of taxation in traditional theory.

Post-Keynesian economists, who emphasize monetary and financial theory, were inspired by Lerner's unique understanding of money, leading to the development of New Functional Finance. They delved into the history of money and monetary

---

[75] Lerner, A. P. 1943. Functional finance and the federal debt. *Social Research.* 10 (1): 40.

[76] Lerner, A. P. 1946. Money. in *Encyclopedia Britannica: A New Survey of Universal Knowledge,* 14th Edition, vol.15. London: Encyclopedia Britannica, Inc. p. 693.

[77] Knapp, G.F. 1924. *The State Theory of Money*. London: Macmillan.

[78] Lerner, A. P. 1947. Money as a creature of the state. *The American Economic Review. Papers and Proceedings of the Fifty-ninth Annual Meeting of the American Economic Association.* 37(2): 312.

[79] Lerner, A. P. 1947. Money as a creature of the state. *The American Economic Review. Papers and Proceedings of the Fifty-ninth Annual Meeting of the American Economic Association.* 37(2): 313.

theory[80] and offered a new understanding of the essence of modern money: modern money is a unit of account, essentially a special institutional arrangement reflecting creditor-debtor relationships.[81] If money is understood as a relationship between creditor and debtor, it can be seen as equivalent to an IOU. The key to turn IOU into money is to ensure that they are accepted by others through some form of commitment — when the IOU holder owes a debt to the IOU issuer and demands that the latter settle the debt using IOU, the latter must accept the IOU "issued" by himself as a means of payment.[82] Expanding on this example explains the nature of modern money: it is a standardized IOU issued by the state, denominated in units of account, and representing the state's liability. How does the state ensure that its IOUs are widely accepted by the public? This is where Lerner and Knapp's insight comes in: the state, by virtue of its sovereignty, can levy taxes and require them to be paid in the currency it issues. This ensures that the currency is widely accepted within the whole state. However, this does not imply that only taxpayers need money or that only those with tax obligations would accept it. As Lerner analyzed in the entry on "Money" in *Encyclopaedia Britannica*, since taxpayers must use the designated currency to pay taxes, they will require that currency in transactions with those who do not owe taxes, who will, in turn, accept that currency for payment. Through this cascading process, demand for money spreads throughout the economic society, and it becomes the standard medium of exchange for everyday transactions. This is the essence of the "Taxes-drive-money" (TDM) theory proposed by New Functional Finance.

Under this interpretation, modern money becomes a standardized unit of account for credit-debt relationships backed by state credit and the tax system, along with the corresponding arrangements for settlement and clearing. When the logical relationship between money and taxation is reversed as that "taxes drive money", from the state's perspective taxation becomes the tool that "makes money into money" rather than a means to generate revenue. On one hand, the ripple effect of taxation leads people to willingly accept this IOU in various transactions. On the other hand, before issuing the IOU, the state does not need other IOUs to finance the issuance. According to this logic, proponents of New Functional Finance derive the following conclusions: when government spending is less than taxation, the public lacks sufficient money to pay taxes; when government spending equals taxation, the public can just meet their tax obligations but has no net savings; only when government spending exceeds taxation, i.e., when a deficit occurs, will the public have net monetary assets.

---

[80] In the early twentieth century, in addition to Knapp's theory of "Money as a Creature of the State", the Credit Theory of Money proposed by Innes had a great influence on post-Keynesian economics and the new functional fiscal theory. See: Innes, A. M. 1913. What is Money? *The Banking Law Journal* 30(5): 377–408; Innes, A. M. 1914. The Credit Theory of Money? *The Banking Law Journal*. 31(2): 151–168.

[81] Wray, L. R. 1998. *Understanding Modern Money: A Key to Full Employment and Price Stability*. Northampton: Edward Edgar. pp. 18–73.

[82] For example, if A issues an IOU to B to borrow a bag of grain from B, then when B owes A a debt of equal value, B can use this IOU issued by A to settle the debt. At this point, A must promise to accept the previously issued IOUs from Bas "money" for repayment. Such commitment thus become an important condition for the transformation of IOUs into "money".

This can be further explained by the following equation, which diverges from mainstream economics[83]:

$$G_t + Tr_t + iB_t = M_t = T_t + \triangle B_t + \triangle H_t$$

Here G_t represents government spending, *Tr* denotes transfer payments, and *iB* refers to government bond interest payments. These three combined equal total expenditure of the government. Through spending, the government injects high-powered money (i.e., reserves *M*) into the economy, among which part is reclaimed through taxes *T*, another part is swapped back through bond issuance $\triangle B$, and the remaining part becomes net monetary assets $\triangle H$ held by the public. It should be noted that the private sector cannot create net monetary surpluses because any asset in the private sector is offset by a corresponding liability, meaning that the private sector's net monetary surplus must stem from the government's deficit spending.[84] This implies that if the government seeks to "store wealth among the people" (*cang fu yumin*) ($\triangle H>0$), deficits are the norm.[85] Further analysis reveals that without bond issuance, government deficit spending will inevitably lead to an increase in $\triangle H$. Linking this to the previous analysis, the reserve effects become evident: government bond issuance becomes the means for adjusting the balance of net monetary assets $\triangle H$, i.e., the stock of reserves, directly influencing interest rate control within monetary policy.

Following Lerner's line of reasoning, New Functional Finance builds a comprehensive theoretical system based on the "reserve effects" and the "taxes-drive-money" view. It must be recognized that while New Functional Finance, following the Lerner tradition, exposes the policy fallacy of "being caught in one's own trap" in the pursuit of budget balance, this does not imply an absence of constraints. As Lerner's First Law stipulates, full employment and price stability are both the goals and constraints of functional finance. Government spending must be aimed at employment, otherwise macroeconomic stability and the general improvement of welfare will be difficult to achieve. Once full employment is achieved, further deficit spending or tax cuts will generate more income and demand, leading to inflation, at which point price stability again becomes a constraint of functional finance.

---

83 Mehrling, P. 2000. Modern Money: Fiat or Credit? *Journal of Post Keynesian Economics*. 22(3): 398–400; Kadmos, G. and O' Hara P. A. 2000. The Taxes-Drive-Money and employer of last resort approach to government policy. *Journal of Economics and Social Policy*. 5(1): 4.

84 Mosler, W. 1997–1998. Full employment and price stability. *Journal of Post Keynesian Economics*. 20(2): 170–172.

85 This can also be explained with the help of the familiar three-sector constant. If we assume that (M-X) = 0, then in the three-sector constant (G-T) = (S-I) + (M-X), the government deficit on the left side of the equation must necessarily manifest itself as a net surplus in the domestic private sector on the right side of the equation. There is another issue that needs to be noted here, i.e., the relationship between bank money and national money. For more information, see: Xian, wen and Feng Xiaoying. 2012. Loan-created deposits and endogenous supply of money: from the perspective of the nature of money. *Journal of Finance and Economics*. (1): 14–23.

The disruptive recognition of Functional Finance ultimately is to be implemented in macroeconomic management. Lerner keenly grasped Keynes' key contribution, pushing forward the development of the Economics of Employment.[86] He emphasized that unemployment would cause greater economic loss than other forms of resource misallocation, and that full employment could yield substantial societal benefits, including increased economic efficiency, individual economic security, weakening of racial and other discrimination, and social stability.[87] Proponents of New Functional Finance have inherited the Keynes-Lerner tradition, arguing that the failure to achieve full employment is both a consequence and a cause of capitalist economic fluctuations. They further criticize Keynesian aggregate demand management policies, asserting that they not only fail to achieve full employment but also have significant side effects detrimental to macroeconomic stability. Accordingly, these scholars argue that government spending should directly target at employment demand to achieve true "zero unemployment rate". The marginal efficiency of capital fluctuates with unstable expectations, so the responsibility of achieving high-level full employment should not be undertaken by the market. Therefore, the government must break free from deficit constraints to address the unemployment issue, employing all the unemployed who are willing and able to work. When the deficit is tasked with achieving full employment, it takes on an "endogenous" nature. Since deficiency of effective demand is endogenous to the market economy, the government's use of fiscal policy to correct imbalances and steer the economy toward equilibrium becomes the inevitable choice. Thus, the traditional view of fiscal policy, which exogenously imposes so-called prudent and balanced "constraints", is entirely a way of "putting first things last and last things first".

Each individual at microeconomic level has macroeconomic value, and if full employment is not used to activate the labor force—the most dynamic production factor—long-term macroeconomic stability and development will be unattainable. In this sense, deficit policies can be good or bad, with the distinguishing factor being whether they are people-centered. If deficit spending addresses fundamental needs such as employment, it provides the economy and society with sustainable endogenous momentum and stability, forming a virtuous cycle and a positive feedback mechanism. Conversely, if deficits are primarily aimed at ensuring output growth, then aggregate demand management policies will, in the long run, erode stability and development, possibly leading to coexistence of stagnation, inflation, high unemployment rate, and income inequality.

Following the above logic, the buffer stock employment model establishes a complete system from policy to theory. According to New Functional Finance, if the government is willing to establish the buffer stock, an endogenous deficit policy can fully support an "Ever-normal Granary of labor force". This makes the solution seem simple, but in reality capitalist societies face an inescapable "Kalecki's Dilemma".

---

[86] Lerner, A. P. 1951. *Economics of Employment*. New York: McGraw-Hill.

[87] Forstater, M. 1999. Functional finance and full employment: Lesson from Lerner for today. *Journal of Economic Issues*. 33(2): 475–482.

6.4 The Kalecki Dilemma

New Functional Finance seeks to break away from traditional dogmas and theoretically unlock the "deadlock" of fiscal constraints, focusing instead on the macroeconomic effects of fiscal policy. This approach provides a fresh perspective for expanding government expenditure to build an Ever-normal Granary of labor force, so as to solve the persistent unemployment problem under capitalism and stabilize the inherently unstable economy. From this viewpoint, capitalism might use "fiscal new policies" to significantly escape the cyclical crises and achieve sustainable healthy development. However, upon deeper reflection, one could find that the analytical framework of New Functional Finance overlooks a key element. As previously analyzed, one of its important premises lies in a unique interpretation of "money". Specifically, Lerner's redefinition of the relationship between money and taxation, including the assertion of "money as a creature of the state", was further developed by New Functional Finance into the taxes-drive-money view. Consequently, the "state" becomes the institutional foundation upon which the entire theory and policy are established. However, while New Functional Finance explores the essence of money, there is little discussion on the theory of the state. This may stem from the proponents' view that the state's macro responsibilities are self-evident, assuming that any government could achieve full employment and price stability through functional finance.[88] In reality, however, full employment and price stability, especially the former one, are not policy objectives that can be easily realized.

Michal Kalecki had profound insights into this issue. "When the latter author (Michal Kalecki) firstly put forward his version of the principle of effective demand, he immediately gave a prominent place to government spending as an additional source of demand..."[89] On one hand, Kalecki believed that developed capitalist nations could theoretically achieve full employment through deficit policies, and enterprises could, under conditions of full employment, achieve higher profits, thus reaching an ideal state. Before Lerner's proposal of Functional Finance, Kalecki already "considered that budget deficits might be necessary as a permanent feature of full employment capitalism, and not merely as a last resort instrument used only under circumstances of crises."[90] This coincidence of thought led scholars to realize that Kalecki had put forward the theory of Functional Finance earlier than Lerner.

But on the other hand, deeply influenced by Karl Marx's ideas, Kalecki insightfully realized that full employment and capitalism are fundamentally incompatible: full employment achieved through deficit policies would shift the control of

---

[88] Mosler, W. 1997–1998. Full employment and price stability. *Journal of Post Keynesian Economics*. 20(2): 168.

[89] Julio López G. and Michaël Assous. 2010. *Michal Kalecki*. London and New York: Palgrave Macmillan. p.129.

[90] Julio López G. and Michaël Assous. 2010. *Michal Kalecki*. London and New York: Palgrave Macmillan. p.130.

economic society from capitalists to laborers. As a result, "'discipline in the factories' and 'political stability' are more appreciated by the business leaders than profits. Their class instinct tells them that lasting full employment is unsound from their point of view and that unemployment is an integral part of the 'normal' capitalist system."[91] Acknowledging this reveals the paradox that New Functional Finance faces: A seemingly logical policy proves difficult to implement or sustain in reality. To achieve the desired effects, institutional reform becomes inevitable, as Kalecki incisively pointed out:

> Full employment capitalism" will have, of course, to develop new social and political institutions which will reflect the increased power of the working class. If capitalism can adjust itself to full employment a fundamental reform will have been incorporated in it. If not, it will show itself in outmoded system which must be scrapped.[92]

This assertion is referred to by scholars as "Kalecki's Dilemma".[93] The dilemma between either persistent unemployment or institutional reform led Kalecki to recognize the existence of the "political business cycle" in developed capitalist countries: a state of permanently high employment through deficit policies would alter power equilibrium within society.[94] Then, "in this situation a powerful alliance is likely to be formed between big business and rentier interests, and they would probably find more than one economist to declare that the situation was manifestly unsound. The pressure of all these forces, and in particular of big business – as a rule influential in government departments – would induce the government to return to the orthodox policy of cutting down the budget deficit."[95] Government spending on improving employment rises and falls with political bargaining, triggering "resonance" in the economic society. In this way Kalecki revealed a deep institutional dilemma in the Keynes-Lerner-Post Keynesian theoretical trajectory. As Joan Robinson stated, "The great trouble with Keynes was that he was an idealist. He thought that when people could understand his theory, could understand how the capitalistic system actually works, they would then behave in a reasonable manner and operate the system in such a way as to produce favourable results, to produce in particular a high and stable level of employment."[96] Indeed, Keynes believed that in the society he lived in, "If two-thirds or three-quarters of total investment is carried out or can be influenced by public or semi public bodies, a long-term programme of a stable character should, be capable of reducing the potential range of fluctuation

---

[91] Kalecki, M. 1943. Political aspects of full employment. *Political Quarterly*. 14 (4): 326.

[92] Kalecki, M. 1943. Political aspects of full employment. *Political Quarterly*. 14 (4): 331.

[93] Sotiropoulos, D. P. 2011.Kalecki's dilemma: toward a Marxian political economy of neoliberalism. *Rethinking Marxism*. 23(1): 106.

[94] Julio López G. and Michaël Assous. 2010. *Michal Kalecki*. London and New York: Palgrave Macmillan. p.220.

[95] Julio López G. and Michaël Assous. 2010. *Michal Kalecki*. London and New York: Palgrave Macmillan. p.221.

[96] Kahn, R. F. 1984.*The Making of Keynes' General Theory*. London and New York: Cambridge University Press. p. 203.

to much narrower limits than formerly, ..."[97] However, this has not become the norm in reality, because capitalist macro-control policies cannot achieve a neutral balance. Mandel analyzed this by stating: "state intervention in economic life, managed economy, economic programming, indicative planning, are not the least bit neutral from the social point of view. They are instruments of intervention into the economy which lie in the hands of the bourgeois class or of the ruling groups in the bourgeois class, and are in no sense arbitrators between the bourgeoisie and the proletariat."[98]

From the perspective of Marx-Kalecki, unemployment is an inherent characteristic of the capitalist system. This makes it clear that New Functional Finance seems to face an insurmountable obstacle, and Kalecki's "political business cycle" appears to prove this: "Capitalist production constantly strives to overcome these immanent barriers, but it overcomes them only by means that set up the barriers afresh and on a more powerful scale."[99] Interestingly, we can observe another form of "functional finance" in reality. During the financial crisis of 2008, the U.S. government spent massive amounts of money to bail out too-big-to-fail financial institutions, while unemployment increased at the same time. This illustrates how "the treasury became a powerful pump... providing various subsidies and assistance to monopoly capital groups."[100] Who does a nation's currency serve? Who does a nation's functional finance serve? The answers to these questions reveal the deeper "non-neutrality" of money and functional finance.

New Functional Finance belongs to the non-mainstream tradition of Western economics. It breaks away from traditional dogma and stands out as a unique theory. Upon further examination, we find that its proposals are not baseless but have solid academic roots. It logically follows Keynes and Lerner, extending the Keynesian revolution. However, the Kalecki Dilemma reveals a crossroads that this theoretical path has to face: it must either move closer to Marxism or revert to the old paths of mainstream economics, finding an unnatural "natural rate of unemployment" between full employment and unemployment to explain the "natural" state of the economic society. Ignoring the importance of productive relations and institutions, these seemingly beneficial policies will eventually fail to be implemented or transformed into long-term mechanisms.

With the above analysis, we can briefly summarize the evolution of the Ever-normal Granary. The Ever-normal Granary in Franklin D. Roosevelt's New Deal from the 1930s to 1940s (including Wallace's agricultural Ever-normal Granary, and labor-relief Ever-normal Granary of labor force), Keynesian macroeconomics,

---

[97] Keynes, J.M. 2013. *Activities 1940-1946: Shaping the Post-war World: Employment and Commodities*. in *The Collected Writings of John Maynard Keynes*, vol.27. ed. Moggridge, D. New York: Cambridge University Press. p. 322.

[98] Mandel, E. 1967. *An Introduction to Marxist Economic Theory*. New York: Pathfinder Press. p. 76.

[99] Marx, Karl. 1981. *Capital: A Critique of Political Economy*, vol.3. trans. David Fernbach. London: Penguin Books. p.358.

[100] Liu, Diyuan. 1997. *Review of Keynesian Economic Doctrine*. Wuhan: Wuhan University Press. p. 303.

and Graham's modern "equalization policy" (*pingzhunfa*), could collectively be called "Modern Ever-normal Granary". These concepts are interconnected, offering mutual inspiration and lessons. Notably, the first two promoted the development of macroeconomic intervention policies in the Western world with a far-reaching impact. With this Modern Ever-normal Granary, the Ever-normal Granary in ancient China can be called the classical Ever-normal Granary. From Geng Shouchang's original design to the various ever-normal granaries of the Northern and Southern Song dynasties, the Chinese people systematically explored and practiced the mechanism of buffer grain storage. The labor relief system embedded in this mechanism holds special significance from the perspective of Keynesian and Post-Keynesian economics. Post-Keynesian economists' buffer stock employment theory, rooted in the Keynesian revolution and surpassing both classical and modern ever-normal granaries, develops into what can be called "the new Ever-normal Granary". It is termed "new" because it integrates the buffer stock principle with the economic theories of Keynes and Lerner, making progress in two key areas: First, it explicitly incorporates labor into the buffer stock mechanism, presenting a wholly new concept of full employment in the strictest sense and defining money more closely in terms of labor, viewing full employment as the foundation of economic stability. Second, from the perspective of fiscal function and the nature of money, it breaks through the barrier of budget constraints and proposes the unorthodox theory of New Functional Finance, providing financial support for the implementation of the buffer stock employment policy. In this way, from the standpoint of the Ever-normal Granary, the new Ever-normal Granary in Post-Keynesian economics represents a great historical leap. However, this leap has its limits—the institutional constraints discussed earlier. If budget constraint is a "false constraint", then institutional constraint is a "real constraint". Ultimately, the buffer stock employment program will face the Kalecki Dilemma, making it difficult to truly implement or become the norm in capitalist society. Of course, the Kalecki Dilemma does not invalidate New Functional Finance. Rather, it provides new perspectives and possibilities for macroeconomic stability, particularly for achieving full employment.

The comprehensive development of the new Ever-normal Granary theory and policy reflects the deeper implications in political economics. Who does a nation's currency serve? Who does its fiscal policy serve? What is the foundation of economic stability? These questions lead us to understand that only when money and fiscal policy are centered on people and grassroots could they help establish a stable Ever-normal Granary mechanism with employment as basic goal and welfare. This approach upholds the profound understanding of labor in the saying "He who does not work, neither shall he eat", which views labor as the essence of human being and human nature. In connection with the economic theory and practice of socialism with Chinese characteristics in the new era, the new Ever-normal Granary offers important insights on how to comprehend the essence of fiscal policy and deficits, and how to properly manage the relationship between government and the market, as well as between full employment and macroeconomic stability. Moreover, it organically links China's economic tradition with modern economic theory, uniting Western and Chinese economic thought and bringing economics and ethics together.

The buffer stock employment model of the new Ever-normal Granary vividly illustrates that economic stability, in essence, cannot be separated from humanistic care. It must fundamentally safeguard and uphold the value of labor through a people-centered approach. Thus, Marx's words take on deeper meaning when viewed from this perspective:

> Society simply does not find its **equilibrium** until it revolves around the sun of **labour**.
> —Marx, Karl[101]

[101] Marx, Karl. 2010. Epilogue to revelations concerning the communist trial in Cologne. in Marx, Karl and Frederick Engels. *Marx &Engels Collected Works*, vol.24. London: Lawrence & Wishart. pp. 53–54.

Chapter 7

Changing Tradition and Historical Transcendence: Dialectical Equilibrium and the "Ever-normal Law"

The myriad things constitute one aspect of the Way, and a single thing constitutes one aspect of the myriad things. The stupid who act on the basis of one aspect of one thing, considering that therein they know the Way, are ignorant.
—Xunzi (Warring States Period)[1]

The Judgment unfolds how the principles of things are the same, so as to shed light on the moment and function of the Split hexagram. The way of sages is to align what has split apart. Seeing the sameness in things that are the same is the knowledge of the customs of the times. The sages shed light on how the principles of things are the same at their root, and so they can bring sameness to the world, harmonizing and aligning the ten thousand kinds of thing.
—Cheng Yi (Northern Song Dynasty)[2]

The principle of economic stability underlying the Ever-normal Granary—its countercyclical purchase and sale of grain, and intertemporal allocation of resources—is followed from ancient to modern times, and in both China and the West, manifesting the vitality of this economic tradition in ancient China. The theoretical essence of this economic model is the identification of dominant economic resources or factors of production, including labor, as the economic base. By establishing a buffering purchase and sale mechanism, the economic base stays in a state of "full employment", effectively guiding the full utilization of other resources and production factors and thus exerting a stabilizing force on the economic society. The Ever-normal Granary has its "application". When we trace the mode of thinking behind this application, we find its "principle" and "essence". As *Guanzi* states, "Now all things are born of the two, Yin and Yang, so that a third comes into being." This philosophical essence, along with the economic principle of "*qing* and *zhong* give

[1] Knoblock, John. 1994. *Xunzi: A Translation and Study of the Complete Works*, vol.3. Stanford: Stanford University Press. p.22.

[2] Cheng, Yi. 2019. Split (*Kui*). in *The Yi River Commentary on the Book of Changes*. trans. L. Michael Harrington. New Haven and London: Yale University Press. pp. 302–303.

W. Xian, *Chinese Food Security Strategy*, Research Series on the Chinese Dream and China's Development Path,
https://doi.org/10.1007/978-981-95-7964-8_7

birth to balance"[3] and the four modes of specific application—primary-secondary coordination ("A but B"), excess being just as bad as deficiency ("A (B) but not A+ (B+)"), impartiality ("neither A nor B"), and flexible adaptation ("both A and B")—lay the foundation for the dialectical nature of Chinese economic thinking. Its essence is to seek dynamic equilibrium or ever-normal development in the economic society. The essence, principle, and application of economic thoughts in *Guanzi* shaped the economic worldview of the Chinese—maintaining balance through the mean. Like an "invisible hand", it has profoundly influenced economic cognition and practice in later generations. To this day, from economic systems and basic economic institutions to major economic policies, all are concrete examples of the modern transformation of such economic tradition. The A-B model, based on dialectical thinking, forms a rigorously logical and mutually supportive framework in accordance with the "doctrine of the mean". We have reason to call this "ever-normal principle" in Chinese economic thought. In the new environment, the Chinese people unify theoretical logic and historical logic together in the practice, and, with a more inclusive and open holistic view, endow the "ever-normal principle" with fresh meaning. The modern transformation of this economic tradition represents a significant historical transcendence.

[3] Walter. A. Rickett explains the term "*qing zhong*" with the following words, "*Qing* means 'light', and by extension 'unimportant', 'inconsequential', or 'cheap'. As a verb, it means to accord little or no value to something. *Zhong* means 'heavy', and by extension 'important', 'serious', or 'expensive'. As a verb, it means to value something. As a compound the two characters together usually mean 'weight', and in economic writings *qing* and *zhong* are often used to refer to the weight of coins. Thus, *qing* and *zhong* may be used to refer to the value of money in relation to goods or to the relationship between supply and demand. When supply is greater than demand, it is because things are not valued or *qing*; when the opposite is true, it is because things are valued or *zhong*. As the compound appears in the title of this section, however, *qing zhong* refers to a wide range of policies that were based on the *qing zhong zhi fa*, '*qing zhong method*', said to have originated with Guan Zhong. This method involved using money to acquire grain and other critical commodities when they were plentiful and cheap (*qing*), and to sell them when they were in short supply and expensive (*zhong*) in order to control the profits of merchants and gain income for the state. Thus in this section *qing zhong* may refer merely to taking advantage of market conditions to manipulate prices, or it may refer to a broad range of economic policies involving such things as government monopolies, loans to producers, foreign trade and territorial expansion, currency control, and work incentives." See: Guanzi. 1998. *Political, Economic, and Philosophical Essays from Early China*, vol. 2. trans. W. Allyn Rickett. Princeton: Princeton University Press. pp.338–339.

7.1 Ever-normal Granary in China and the West in Ancient and Modern Times

In ancient China, all good governance was people-oriented, and the essence of this principle lay in nourishing the people (*yang min*). How can the people be nourished? "It lies in none other than farming and planting."[4] The concept of "nourishing the people" (*yang min*), when combined with the small-scale peasant economy, fostered a deep-rooted tradition of prioritizing agriculture. This tradition developed into a mature system of agricultural economic management, with a simple and clear objective: to ensure that the large amounts of small-scale farmers remained dedicated to farming and planting. Therefore, when fluctuations in agricultural production went against this objective, the national Ever-normal Granary system, which allowed the allocation of grain across time and space, became an indispensable institutional part within this economic management system.

From a modern perspective, the Ever-normal Granary system contains several elements of modernity. First, there was the concept that "Heaven gives birth to the multitude of people".[5] "Heaven" bestows upon the ruler the responsibility of nourishing the people (*yang min*). "Heaven sees as my people see; Heaven hears as my people hear.[6]" Heaven becomes the superior "people", while people are specific representatives of "Heaven". This unity of Heaven and humanity imbues the principles of "respecting Heaven" (*jing tian*) and "nourishing the people" (*yang min*)' with both economic and institutional rationality. Second, the fragile small-scale peasant economy created an unstable economic base, and the goal of "nourishing the people" (*yang min*) became the core objective of national governance, and "stabilizing an unstable economy" became the modern macroeconomic goal. Third, the buffering mechanism of the Ever-normal Granary, which involved the purchase and sale of grain, included multiple economic aspects, such as maintaining supply and demand equilibrium (economic base), stabilizing prices, and ensuring full employment. These goals are nearly identical to those of modern macroeconomic policies.

However, these comments do not imply an overly high evaluation of Ever-normal Granary's function in ancient Chinese economic society. The implementation of the system was constrained by various factors, and reformers throughout Chinese history continually sought to modify and improve it. In the resource-scarce environment of ancient society, particularly in terms of grain production, the functions of purchasing grain at increased prices (*pingdi*) and selling at reduced prices (*pingtiao*) were often asymmetrical. Disaster relief and famine mitigation became the primary roles of the Ever-normal Granary in stabilizing the economic society under extreme

[4] Qiu, Jun. 2012. Property of the people. *Supplement to Great Learning*, vol.14. ed. Jing, Liangnian. Shanghai: Shanghai Bookstore Publishing House. p. 133.

[5] Waley, Arthur. 1960. *The Book of Songs, The Ancient Chinese Classic of Poetry*. New York: Grove Press. p.252.

[6] Legge, J. (trans.) 1865. *The Shoo King, or The Book of Historical Documents*, vol.2. London: Tuübner & Co. p.292.

conditions. When considering the involvement of different types of granaries, from central to village levels, in increased-price purchases (*pingdi*) and reduced-price sales (*pingtiao*) of grains, the Ever-normal Granary system throughout Chinese history could be seen as a woven network for stability. In this context, the key to effective ever-normal regulation was determining the proper boundaries for government intervention. This would ensure that the government did not exceed its duties, while coordinating the efforts of the market and various aspects of the society to utilize resources effectively.

The functionality of the Ever-normal Granary system varied in visibility depending on the strength of the state. During the mid-Qing dynasty, the central and local governments demonstrated unprecedented management capabilities in stabilizing fluctuations in economic society. As China's traditional agrarian society entered a period of decline in the modern era, the Ever-normal Granary system seemed to reach its endpoint. However, the economic crisis faced by Western capitalist societies in the 1920s and 1930s presented a historical opportunity for the westward transmission and modern transformation of this system. It is particularly important to remember the historical contribution of Chen Huan-chang's doctoral dissertation, *The Economic Principles of Confucius and His School*, written and published during his studies in the United States. Chen Huan-chang's discussions on the Ever-normal Granary and Wang Anshi's Green Sprouts Act inspired Henry A. Wallace, the U.S. Secretary of Agriculture, and provided a historical foundation and institutional blueprint for American agricultural reform in the 1930s. As a result, the Agricultural Adjustment Act of 1938 was even referred to as legislation for "Ever-normal Granary". Wallace's agricultural Ever-normal Granary encompassed many aspects, including production control, price support, environmental protection, and efficiency promotion, with buffer stock management of agricultural products being just one key component. Thus, Wallace's agricultural Ever-normal Granary was essentially a comprehensive agricultural regulation system in the context of industrialization. The new concept embedded within this system—"government + market = ever-normal stability"—went beyond agriculture itself. During Franklin D. Roosevelt's New Deal, the market economy model with government's intervention came onto the historical stage in the industrial age through agricultural reforms. Reflecting on this period, we are struck by the fact that, after Adam Smith's revolution, another revolution in Western economics had an unrecognized connection to traditional Chinese economics.

The Ever-normal Granary system and the equalization policy (*pingzhunfa*) differ in names, but both are forms of buffer stock systems, with the main distinction being the target of government purchases and sales. Due to various constraints, the equalization policy (*pingzhunfa*) was more often implemented in urban areas with highly-developed commerce in ancient China. In middle Tang dynasty, Liu Yan implemented the equalization policy and "controlled the prices of all goods", promoting the policy to a new height. During the Northern Song dynasty, Wang Anshi's implemented the Market Exchange Law (*shiyifa*), which sought to replace commercial monopolies with government monopolies. It proved to be a less successful adaptation of the equalization policy. In the 1930s in the U.S., as Wallace promoted agricultural reforms based on the Ever-normal Granary, Benjamin Graham, inspired by the equalization policy, proposed the establishment of "Modern Ever-normal Granary". His mechanism integrated fiscal and monetary policies into a buffer stock system of a basket of commodities, positioning this basket alongside gold as a new standard to stabilize currency, prices, and supply-demand relationship. The Ever-normal Granary system in ancient China also implicitly contained elements of monetary policy: as grain served as a widely accepted commodity, it performed many monetary functions in the ancient time. Therefore, China's historical Ever-normal Granary can be viewed, to some extent, as a currency regulation system based on grain. Graham sought to adapt to the expanded range of basic commodities in an industrial society by converting a single standard into a multi-commodity standard under the framework of a "Modern Ever-normal Granary". To extend this concept globally, Graham envisioned a more reliable global currency, making his ideas a pioneer to the notion of a "supra-sovereign currency".

From the 1920s to the 1940s, research literature on buffer stock theories proliferated, giving rise to a trend of economic thought on buffer stocks.[7] Among these, Keynes' research was undoubtedly the most theoretically valuable. His participation in market speculation led him to recognize the close relationship between commodity inventories and business cycles, which he elaborated in *A Treatise on Money* as the theory of short-period prices. The equation for short-period prices, $pq = xy$, demonstrated the substantial impact of surplus products on prices, output, and markets, with the policy implication that governments should establish buffer stocks to stabilize markets. In this way, Keynes provided a concise economic explanation for the Ever-normal Granary system in ancient China. The main difference between Keynes, Wallace, and Graham lay in that Keynes' theories offered more general guidance for policies, with greater flexibility in practice. When the economy experienced recession and the market was stagnant, the government could intervene through increased public spending—an approach akin to the "increased-price purchase" (*pingdi*) in ancient China. In economic terms, this reflected a situation where the collapse of the marginal efficiency of capital obstructed private investment, leading to the economic depression characterized by idle capital, unused resources and widespread unemployment, which necessitated government intervention to stabilize effective demand. When government's public investment was directed toward public works projects, the mechanism of "*pingdi*" took on another type of meaning—mobilizing "unemployed" capital to employ both unemployed works and surplus goods. Keynes' economic theory should not be simplistically interpreted as a theory of depression economics. Keynes believed that preventing the waste of labor resources through public investment to achieve full employment should serve as a long-term mechanism for stabilizing the economy. This idea laid the groundwork for the "buffer stock employment" theory in Post-Keynesian economics. Traditional buffer stock systems was still important in Keynes's thought, and his scheme of

[7] Graham, B. 1944. *World Commodities and World Currency*. New York and London: McGraw-Hill Book Company, Inc. p.110.

international buffer stocks, after several revisions, aimed at establishment of ever-normal granaries for staple commodities to stabilize global economies, although it was never implemented.

Keynes had a high regard for Wallace's agricultural Ever-normal Granary. Then how did he view Graham's proposal? In 1943, Friedrich A. Hayek revisited Graham's ideas and submitted his essay "A Commodity Reserve Currency" to *The Economic Journal*, for which Keynes was the editor-in-chief at the time. Although the article was accepted and published,[8] Keynes expressed skepticism about the practicability of such a commodity-backed currency.[9] One year later, Frank D. Graham from Princeton University commented on views of Keynes and Hayek on commodity-backed currency.[10] Keynes explained further in "Note by Lord Keynes", acknowledging that he did not oppose the idea of monetary mechanism with commodity standard, which should be the "visions" to be realized in the future. However, at the specific time and in the specific situation, it would be difficult to have the plan implemented. Therefore, he suggested a gradual approach which started with establishment of international buffer stocks. When people master the technique, it will be time to think about the implementation. He stated, "On buffer stocks I can enthusiastically join forces with Professor Frank Graham and Mr. Benjamin Graham. Though even here I am beginning to feel a slight reserve about whether just this moment…".[11]

Keynes's theory implicitly contained humanitarian concern and ethical orientation. His goal was to establish a stable capitalist system, with sustainable full employment as a primary means to that end. After Keynes, macroeconomics branched into different schools of thought that had divergent views. Keynesians believed that the effective means for economic regulation was aggregate demand management. However, non-mainstream schools of thought, represented by Post-Keynesian economics, argued that due to complex structural constraints within the economic society, aggregate demand management could not effectively stabilize the macroeconomy or achieve full employment. Instead, they could lead to inflation and exacerbate income inequality. Inheriting Keynes' tradition, Post-Keynesian economists believed that aggregate demand management should be more precise, focusing directly on employment by constructing a bottom-up buffer stock system that targets labor as the object of stabilization, or "buffer stock employment". In doing so, Post-Keynesian economists gave the Ever-normal Granary system new implication, emphasizing the importance of achieving strict, non-NAIRU full employment

[8] Hayek, F. A. 1943. A commodity reserve currency. *The Economic Journal*. 53(210/211): 176–184.

[9] Keynes, J. M. 1943.The objective of international price stability. *The Economic Journal*. 53(210/211): 185–187.

[10] Graham, F. D.1944. Keynes vs. Hayek on a commodity reserve currency. *The Economic Journal*. 54 (215/216): 422–429. Frank D. Graham, in his book *Social Goals and Economic Institutions* published in 1943, discussed Benjamin Graham's ideas on commodity money. See: Graham, F. D. 1942. *Social Goals and Economic Institutions*. Princeton: Princeton University Press. pp. 94–103.

[11] Keynes, J.M. 1944. Note by Lord Keynes. *The Economic Journal*. 54(215/216): 429–430.

for macroeconomic stability. In their view, no economic policy was more crucial than maintaining stable employment for stabilizing the economy.

Full employment was not a new concept in traditional Chinese agricultural society. It was often expressed as the social ideal of "making full use of manpower" and "employment for the able-bodied".[12] Within this framework, labor relief was an important institutional invention, where public works projects, especially agricultural infrastructure like irrigation, served as an invisible granary, while labor became the object for the Ever-normal Granary system. This approach protected labor, maintained stability, and boosted productivity, achieving multiple goals at once. During the Great Depression, echoing Wallace's agricultural Ever-normal Granary, labor relief as a special "Ever-normal Granary of labor force" became a key component of Franklin D. Roosevelt's New Deal. As a successful public employment policy, it was implemented with unprecedented scale and duration in twentieth-century capitalist society.

In thousands of years and different social systems, the Ever-normal Granary system has gone through fascinating evolution, both in ancient and modern times and between East and West. Despite numerous changes, its basic theoretical logic remains consistent: in a world with much uncertainty and the unpredictable fluctuations of economic systems, people have sought, according to the economic features of different eras, a core mechanism capable of stabilizing the economy. By establishing a buffer stock system for key resources, people could keep these resources in a state of "full utilization" or "full employment", thus efficiently guiding the use of production factors and other resources, releasing stabilizing forces that mitigate economic volatility, and achieving a dynamic balance in economic development. At its core, regardless of the type of Ever-normal Granary established, the ultimate goal is the well-being of "people". Only by prioritizing people, safeguarding them, and ensuring that labor resources are fully utilized, can the stability of the economic society be reliably secured. However, in the historical practice of the Ever-normal Granary system, the employment effects of various granaries have differed significantly. In ancient China, granaries established at the prefecture and county levels often couldn't fully cover villages and communities, undermining the goal of stabilizing the labor force and ensuring that people remained engaged in agriculture. To address this issue, Zhu Xi created the community granary system rooted in grassroots villages and communities, which largely compensated for the shortcomings of the traditional Ever-normal Granary system. Similarly, Post-Keynesian economists recognized that while top-down aggregate demand management may, on the surface, fill the output gap and achieve

[12] In the chapter "The Li Yun" of classic work *The Li Ki*, there are following words: "Thus men did not love their parents only, nor treat as children only their own sons. A competent provision was secured for the aged till their death, employment for the able-bodied, and the means of growing up to the young. They showed kindness and compassion to widows, orphans, childless men, and those who were disabled by disease, so that they were all sufficiently maintained." See: Legge, J. (trans.) 1885. *The Sacred Books of China: The Texts of Confucianism, Part 3–4, The Li Ki*. Oxford: Clarendon Press. p.365.

economic growth, it does not necessarily achieve the goal of full employment. This means that behind economic growth, if there is no solid foundation of full employment rooted in the broader grassroots economy, sustainable and stable development cannot be achieved. Although the economic analysis here may seem complex, it reflects a simple and profound truth that the ancient Chinese already understood—"nourishing the people" (*yang min*) is an enduring economic theme that transcends time and space. If laborers, out of reasons other than their own, are unable to sustain themselves, the government should assume the role of the Employer of Last Resort and support every worker who is able and willing to work through a buffer stock employment system. This policy upholds labor as a fundamental human need, reinforces the responsibility and obligation of work, and affirms the value of labor as an essential aspect of human existence, embodying a more proactive vision of economic welfare in modern society. However, if a capitalist society were to implement a more rigorous policy of full employment as a basic principle, the balance between labor and capital would inevitably tilt in favor of the former. However, widespread unemployment would run counter to the interests of capital. This dilemma, known as the Kalecki Dilemma, highlights the inherent institutional constraint: while buffer stock employment may be considered a fiscal remedy for economic stabilization, it is inevitably hindered by systemic limitations, making its full or lasting implementation very difficult.

The greatest truths are the simplest. Ancient Chinese people did not put forward complex economic theories, but their wisdom gave birth to an important system invention— the Ever-normal Granary, with the flexible use of the buffer stocks, maintained the stable development of the economic society. This simple yet profound and wise contribution of originality continues to inspire and guide the later generations to creatively have it transformed. To this day, although modern economics has constructed a variety of subtle theories, the simple buffer principle of buying grains in good years and selling stored grains in bad years still occupies an important position.

Through the twists and turns in history, it seems that the "story" of the Ever-normal Granary should come to an end here. But we may ask further questions, like "how could the ancient Chinese have possibly invented this?", and "what is the native way by which such thinking was created?". If these deeper questions are answered, we may be able to further explore the intangible cultural codes hidden behind the Ever-normal Granary.

Then, where should we begin? Through the analysis in the first chapter, we know that "light and heavy principles" in *Guanzi* theoretically demonstrates the mechanism of buffer stock, which serves as the ideological foundation for the Ever-normal Granary system and its practices. The "light and heavy principles" symbolize a peak in the history of Chinese economic thought. Contemporary historians of economic thought have extensively studied and highly praise it. Hu Jichuang remarks that the thoroughness of its theoretical framework, depth of its analysis and flexibility of its application has reached an amazing level,[13] and there must be a whole set of philosophical reflections backing the proposal of such "amazing" economic theories. This judgment should be accurate because, although *Guanzi* appears to blend various ideas, they are in fact integrated into a cohesive whole through mutual embedding and support. For example, in the "law" (*fa*) of *Guanzi*, one can see "ritualistic principles" or "propriety" (*li*); in "profit" (*li*), one can see "righteous conduct" or "a sense of duty"(*yi*); and in "hegemony" (*ba*), one can see "kingly authority" (*wang*). Therefore, behind the "buffer stock — Light and Heavy Principles", there should also be more information awaiting discovery, which is precisely what is needed to answer the above questions. It seems that we must still trace back to *Guanzi*, and discover the rationale behind the economic thoughts through text analysis of this work. By doing so, we can explore the unique mode of thinking supporting the Ever-normal Granary, a distinctive tradition in Chinese economics.

7.2 The Economic-Philosophical Origins of the Ever-normal Granary: The Economic Worldview of *Guanzi*

7.2.1 Cardinal Sayings

In the chapter "Cardinal Sayings" (*shuyao*) of *Guanzi*, many short philosophical sentences serve as the central guiding principles of the text. One such sentence states: "Now all things are born of the two, *Yin* and *Yang*, with reciprocal reference to each other, so that a third comes into being. Because of this third aspect, the former kings were careful to observe both what went in and what came out."[14] According to commentator, all things in the world can be divided into two aspects, with such "two aspects" representing the mutually dependent yet opposing contradictions between *Yin* and *Yang*. This is why it is said "all things are born of the two, *Yin* and *Yang*,[15] with reciprocal reference to each other, so that a third comes into

[13] Hu, Jichuang. 1998. *History of Chinese Economic Thought*, vol.1. Shanghai: Shanghai University of Finance and Economics Press. p. 334.

[14] The quotation is adapted from Walter. A. Rickett's translation, "Now all things are born of the two, *Yin* and *Yang*, so that a third comes into being. Because of this third aspect, the former kings were careful [to observe] both what went in and what came out." See: Guanzi. 1985. *Guanzi: Political, Economic, and Philosophical Essays from Early China*, vol. 1. trans. W. Allyn Rickett. Princeton: Princeton University Press. p. 219. The Chinese scholar Zhai Jiangyue translated the sentences as follows, "As for tens of thousands of things of the world, they are products of the cooperation of the Yin and Yang. Ancient kings knew it, so they would master both the positive and negative sides of things scrupulously." See: Zhai, Jiangyue. (trans.) 2005. *Guanzi*, vol.1. Nanning: Guangxi Normal University Press. p.285.

[15] *Yin* and *Yang*: The primary meaning of *yin* and *yang* is the orientation of things in relation to the sun, with *yang* meaning the sunny side and *yin* the shady side. There are two extended meanings: 1) two opposite kinds of *qi* (气) in nature; and 2) two basic contrary forces or qualities that coexist, thus the active, hot, upward, outward, bright, forward, and strong are *yang*, while the passive, cold,

being." In this sentence, the word "reciprocal" (参, *can*)[16] is a key concept. The famous Chinese scholar Guo Moruo interprets this sentence with following words, "*Yin* and *Yang* represent the 'two' entities. When they unite, they are transformed with each other and thus give birth to 'the third' (or 'synthesis'). This reflects the dialectical idea of thesis, antithesis, and synthesis."[17] Based on this understanding, the word "reciprocal" (*can*) here carries the meaning of dialectical synthesis. The contemporary Chinese scholar Pang Pu further explains the meaning of the word with reference from Pre-Qin historical documents. He argues that the word "reciprocal" (参, *can*), associated with "two", should generally be interpreted as "three" (叁,*san*), or "the third entity" derived from the "two". Hence, the "third" dependent on the two is not simply the number three but the dialectical logic of synthesis, encompassing three aspects: first, the object of cognition consists of two aspects, wherein a contradiction is introduced through the opposition of one side, feature or characteristic against another, thereby exposing and revealing the whole contradiction; second, the process of practice involves comparing and contrasting the opposing sides, mediating and reconciling them to achieve unity; three, the ideal outcome of cognition and practice is the birth of "the third", which is different from the original yet still connected to it. Since "the third" inherits the essence of the original, it leads to the harmonious development.[18]

Thus, the phrase "born of the two, *Yin* and *Yang*" in the saying does not represent a simple dichotomy. The birth of "the third" is the result of harmonizing and unifying *Yin* and *Yang*, bringing the whole matter into a state of equilibrium. The saying indeed serves as a cardinal saying. With limited number of words, it encompasses both an ontological theory and a methodological approach, with the word "reciprocal" (*can*) being particularly crucial. This explains why the latter half of the sentence emphasizes "the third" and "careful": "Because of this third aspect, the former kings were careful to observe both what went in and what came out."

---

downward, inward, dark, backward, and weak are *yin*. The interaction between *yin* and *yang*, or *yin qi* and *yang qi*, determines the formation and existence of all things. The theory of *yin* and *yang* later became the basis for ancient Chinese to explain and understand the universe and everything in it, social order, and human relations. For example, heaven is *yang* and earth is *yin*, ruler is *yang* and subordinates are *yin*, husband is *yang* and wife is *yin*, noble is *yang* and ignoble is *yin*, leading is *yang* and following is *yin*. For example, in the Chinese classic work Laozi there is a saying, "All things stand, facing *yang* and against *yin*. The interaction between *yin* and *yang* creates a state of harmony." in Dong Zhongshu's work Luxuriant Gems of The Spring and Autumn Annals (*chunqiu fanlu*) there is a saying, "*Yin* and *yang* cannot work without each other." See: "Yin and Yang", Key Concepts in Chinese Thought and Culture, https://www.chinesethought.cn/EN/shuyu_show.aspx?shuyu_id=2172.

[16] In classic Chinese, the character for "reciprocal" (*can*) is interchangeable with that for "three" (*san*).

[17] Guo, Moruo et al. 1984. *Commentary on Guanzi.* in *The Complete Works of Guo Moruo: History*, vol.5. Beijing: People's Publishing House. p. 323.

[18] Pang, Pu. 2009. S*tudies on the Dialectics of Confucianism.* Beijing: Zhonghua Book Company. pp. 102–109.

The dialectical logic of "dividing one into three" contained in the word "reciprocal" (*can*) or "three" (*san*) — first dividing into two and then merging into one, resulting in a superior third — is considered the key to interpreting the Confucian Doctrine of the Mean, which advocates "grasping these ideas at both ends, he would exercise impartiality (*zhong*)".[19] However, this dialectical logic is not exclusive to Confucian thought. In "Cardinal Sayings" of *Guanzi*, the saying "all things are born of the two, *Yin* and *Yang*, with reciprocal reference to each other, so that a third comes into being" represents another profound expression of dialectical "impartiality". *Guanzi* lays emphasis on practical effectiveness, and the philosophical ideas in the above saying finds widespread application, one typical example being the discussion of the balance between light and heavy in the economic domain.

*7.2.2 The Substance (*ti*) and Principle (*li*) of Economic Thought in* Guanzi

The *qing zhong* economic policies (light and heavy principles) abstracted a pair of categories, "light" and "heavy", from economic phenomena. It argues that any commodity may develop a "light-heavy" dynamic due to either human intervention or spontaneous factors, and this dynamic is reflected in currency prices as being "cheap" or "expensive". Thus, the *qing zhong* economic policies contain both theoretical analysis and application of currency, prices, and the law of supply and demand. It must be noted that the scope of the *qing zhong* economic policies extends far beyond these issues. In the chapters "Calculations and Measures" (*kui du*) and "*Qing Zhong* Economic Policies, Part E" (*qing zhong wu*), historical examples are quoted to show that the governance of the world also follow the principles of the *qing zhong* policies.[20] While such approach of emphasizing the significance of the *qing zhong* policies with historical examples is akin to, in Marx's words, summoning

[19] Ames, Roger T. and David L. Hall. 2001. *Focusing the Familiar: A Translation and Philosophical Interpretation of the Zhongyong*. Honolulu: University of Hawai'i Press. p. 91. The theory of "dividing one into three" is an important theoretical contribution of Pang Pu, which has a far-reaching impact on the study of Confucianism. Pang Pu's in-depth study of "dividing one into three" has resulted in a series of mutually complementary important achievements, the most important of which are *Commentary on Doctrine of the Mean* (*Chinese Social Sciences*, 1980) and *Studies on the Dialectic Methods of Confucianism* (Zhonghua Book Company, 1984).

[20] In the chapter "Calculations and Measures" there are following words, "Since the time of Sui Ren there has never been anyone who did not employ *qing zhong* economic policies in ruling the empire." See: Guanzi. 1998. *Political, Economic, and Philosophical Essays from Early China*, vol. 2. trans. W. Allyn Rickett. Princeton: Princeton University Press. p. 431. Sui Ren is one of the three mythical sovereigns who are supposed to have preceded the five emperors. In the chapter "*Qing zhong* Economic Policies, Part E", there are following words, "Since the first organization of a state in the time of Fu Xi", replied Guanzi, "there has never been anyone who was able to be successful in his reign without utilizing *qing zhong* economic policies." See: Guanzi. 1998. *Political, Economic, and Philosophical Essays from Early China*, vol. 2. trans. W. Allyn Rickett. Princeton: Princeton University Press. p.499.

the spirits of the past to serve one's own ends,[21] the illustrations in *Guanzi* can also be understood as the proof that the *qing zhong* policies were adopted as the guiding directive for state-level management design and practice, as was stated in "The Best Methods for Insuring Fiscal Control" (*shan zhi shu*), "to manage the empire using *qing zhong* economic policies".[22] Economic issues naturally fall under this directive and are not limited to any single domain. Hu Jichuang pointed out that viewing the *qing zhong* economic policies solely as "a unique theory of Chinese monetary economics" is a severe misunderstanding. A more accurate interpretation instead is that "if the theory of value is the foundational theory of political economy, then the *qing zhong* economic theory is the cornerstone of the whole economic thoughts of *Guanzi*."[23] Therefore, "the *qing zhong* economic policies has a wide range of applications, encompassing fiscal matters of feudal states, land policies, economic systems, currency, prices, storage, as well as various economic policies or measures, including domestic and foreign trade policies, agricultural and industrial production incentives, etc…"[24] Ma Feibai, a Chinese historian and economist, also held a similar view. He divided the *qing zhong* theory into that in the narrow sense and that in broad senses. In the narrow sense, the *qing zhong* theory refers to the law of supply and demand, while in the broad sense, it encompasses various economic measures and even extends into political, legal, military, educational, and national competitiveness domains.[25]

The above analysis and the previous discussion of the "Cardinal Sayings" clearly show that there is a relationship of "substance" (*ti*) and "principle" (*li*) between *Yin-Yang* view in *Guanzi* and the *qing zhong* theory. Since all things can be abstracted into the duality of Yin and Yang, economic matters are naturally no exception. However, in the realm of economic theory, the philosophical duality of Yin and Yang is transformed into the duality of *qing* and *zhong*. It is worth noting that the transformation from Yin-Yang duality to *qing zhong* duality in *Guanzi* is not isolated. The logic that "the interplay between *Yin* and *Yang* gives rise to a third" holds universal significance in *Guanzi*. When applied to different issues, the abstract categories of *Yin* and *Yang* are rendered into various dialectical relationships (for convenience, let us designate them as A and B hereinafter). In addition to the *qing-zhong* dynamic in economics, many other A-B pairings are formulated in *Guanzi*, such as "peace vs. danger", "order vs. chaos", and "prosperity vs. decline" in politics, or "giving vs. taking", "rewarding vs. punishing" and "opening vs. closing" in state

[21] Hu, Jichuang. 1998. *A History of Chinese Economic Thought*. Shanghai University of Finance and Economics Press. p. 319.

[22] Guanzi. 1998. *Political, Economic, and Philosophical Essays from Early China*, vol. 2. trans. W. Allyn Rickett. Princeton: Princeton University Press. p.412.

[23] Hu, Jichuang. 1998. *A History of Chinese Economic Thought*. Shanghai University of Finance and Economics Press. p. 319.

[24] Hu, Jichuang. 1998. *A History of Chinese Economic Thought*. Shanghai University of Finance and Economics Press. p. 323.

[25] Ma, Feibai. 1979. *New Interpretation of the qing-zhong Chapters in Guanzi*. Beijing: Zhonghua Book Company. pp. 53–54.

governance. Since these relationships are dual in nature, the seemingly opposing A and B are in fact interdependent to each other, thus forming a whole. What *Guanzi* focuses on is how to harmonize and unify A and B, creating a state or action C that accounts for both A and B while transcending them. This is reflected in ideas such as being prepared for danger in times of peace, the ruler's sense of crisis that he should never forget the danger of downfall, as well as the governance philosophy of having the worthy serve the unworthy.[26]The transformation of A-B to C can be theoretically expressed as that "the interplay between *Yin* and *Yang* gives rise to a third".

Back to economic issues, if the interplay between *Yin* and *Yang* is transformed into that between *qing* and *zhong* in economic thought of *Guanzi*, then is there a corresponding category of "reciprocal reference to each other" in the *qing zhong* economic policies? Or, to put it another way, if we apply "reciprocal reference" between "*qing*" (A) and "*zhong*" (B), what kind of state or action (C) could be achieved? The logic of *qing zhong* economic theory includes two key aspects. First, since economic affairs follow both the principle of "the interplay between *qing* and

[26]When discussing important issues from the perspective of "all things are born of the two", *Guanzi* often keep high alert against potential risks and problems. In the chapter "On the Cultivation of Political Power" (*Quan Xiu*) there are words, "if there is proper measure in taking from the people and limits are placed on their employment, even a small state is certain to be safe. But if proper measure is not exercised in taking from the people, and no limits are placed on their employment, even a large state is certain to be in danger." See: Guanzi. 1985. *Guanzi: Political, Economic, and Philosophical Essays from Early China*, vol.1. trans. W. Allyn Rickett. Princeton: Princeton University Press. p. 94. In the chapter "Cardinal Sayings" (*Shu Yan*) there are following words, "The treasure of the kingly ruler is spent on his people, while that of the lord protector is spent on his generals and troops. The treasure of the weak ruler is spent on those in high positions, while that of the ruler who is about to perish is spent on/ women and precious stones. Therefore the former kings were careful with their treasure." See: Guanzi. 1985. *Guanzi: Political, Economic, and Philosophical Essays from Early China*, vol.1. trans. W. Allyn Rickett. Princeton: Princeton University Press. p.218. In the chapter "The Best Methods for Insuring Fiscal Control" (*Shan Zhi Shu*) it was again emphasized that "True kings entrust their wealth to their people, lord protectors (*ba*) entrust theirs to great officers, while decrepit states a families doomed to perish entrust theirs to a money chest." See: Guanzi. 1998. *Political, Economic, and Philosophical Essays from Early China*, vol. 2. trans. W. Allyn Rickett. Princeton: Princeton University Press. p. 412. The author carefully watches the societal transition from "peace" to "crisis" and the shift from a ruler's "reign" to "downfall". In his view, while such transformations seem evident in hindsight, they easily occur unintentionally in the course of events, hence the particular emphasis on being "careful". The key lies in the following: to keep "peace" for long, people must view and act upon from the perspective of its opposite, "crisis"; if a ruler wants to maintain his "reign" for long, he must think and act from the perspective of its opposite, "downfall". Such notion is more explicitly expressed in another discussion in *Guanzi*: "what makes the honored truly honored is that they use their honored [position] to serve the lowly. What makes the worthy truly worthy is that they use their worthiness to serve the less worthy." See: Guanzi. 1985. *Guanzi: Political, Economic, and Philosophical Essays from Early China*, vol.1. trans. W. Allyn Rickett. Princeton: Princeton University Press. p. 221. The author intends to clarify that, in order to prevent things from being transformed into opposites that are not conducive to their development, it is necessary to find a third type of action that is not only in harmony and coordination with A and B, but also transcends them. This ideal state is exemplified by being prepared for danger in times of peace, the ruler's sense of crisis that he should never forget the danger of downfall, the honored serving the lowly, and the worthy serving the unworthy.

zhong" and the law that "if your standard price is cheaper (*qing*) than that of others, your goods flow abroad. If it is more expensive (*zhong*), goods will be dumped on you",[27] then they are in a constant state of mutual transformation between *qing* and *zhong*. As was recorded in the chapter "Calculations and Measures" (*kui du*) in *Guanzi*, "Duke Huan questioned Guanzi, saying, 'How can the use of methods involving the manipulation of prices (*qing zhong*) be brought to an end?' 'It is like the repetition of the four seasons', replied Guanzi, 'there is no end...'"[28] Second, the phrase "there is no end" does not mean that the activities are not guided by principles, directions, or purposes. In the eyes of narrators, economic practice should be conducted with reference to the theory of *qing* and *zhong*, so as to harmonize and unify the two and find "the third" that contributes to the development of the economy and the prosperity of the state. This third is an important concept introduced by the theory of *qing* and *zhong*—balance (*heng*). With focus on the concept of "balance", in the chapter "*Qing zhong* Economic Policies, Part B" (*qing zhong yi*) of *Guanzi* there is a conversation between Duke Huan and Guanzi:

> Duke Huan questioned Guanzi saying, "Is there a specific figure at which one may maintain a proper balance in the economy?"
>
> "No, there is not," replied Guanzi. "To maintain a proper balance, one must cause prices to go up or down. It is impossible to keep them constantly steady."
>
> "So, we can't set such a figure?" asked Duke Huan.
>
> "No, we can't," replied Guanzi. "If we were to try, there would be no movement. If there were no movement, prices would remain constant. If they were to remain constant, there would be no fluctuation in price differential, and if there were no fluctuation in price differential, goods could not be obtained and utilized."
>
> "Then," said Duke Ruan, "how does one take advantage of the seasons?"
>
> "Now," replied Guanzi, "...the year has its four harvests and is divided into four seasons. Once one grasps the sequence of these four, one may issue orders and commands that will cause prices to rise or fall ten or a hundredfold. Consequently, the supply of goods cannot be kept constantly steady, and it was for this reason that I said there can be no specific figure for maintaining a proper balance in the economy."[29]

With the above discussion, the main content of "balance" is revealed. We may briefly summarize the two key points as follows.

Firstly, "balance" is the essence behind economic phenomena. Although *qing* and *zhong* are opposite concepts, they do not mean negation to each other. If *qing* is eliminated, there would be no so-called *zhong*, and the economic system would fall into a stagnant state in which "there would be no fluctuation in price differential" and "goods could not be obtained and utilized". This implies that *qing* and *zhong* endow economic affairs with the attribute of value, and the functions of *qing* and *zhong* are manifested due to the existence and role of the other. Therefore, *qing* and

[27] Guanzi. 1998. *Political, Economic, and Philosophical Essays from Early China*, vol. 2. trans. W. Allyn Rickett. Princeton: Princeton University Press. p.366.

[28] Guanzi. 1998. *Political, Economic, and Philosophical Essays from Early China*, vol. 2. trans. W. Allyn Rickett. Princeton: Princeton University Press. p.436

[29] Guanzi. 1998. *Political, Economic, and Philosophical Essays from Early China*, vol. 2. trans. W. Allyn Rickett. Princeton: Princeton University Press. p. 478–479.

zhong are opposite yet complementary and supportive to each other as a unified whole, making it possible to coordinate the two to arrive at a better state—— "balance" (*heng*). Since "balance" encompasses both *qing* and *zhong*, allowing each to manifest its utility while rejecting the either/or relationship of the two, it avoids the problem of one-sidedness. Thus "balance" transcends the superficiality of *qing* and *zhong*, and reveals the essential connotation conducive to economic and social development.

Secondly, "balance" implies dynamic equilibrium. The *qing-zhong* category constitutes the internal heterogeneity and evolution of economic affairs. Therefore, while the third "balance" that emerges from the interplay of *qing* and *zhong* is a desirable state, it is not a static one. The fact that "to maintain a proper balance, one must cause prices to go up or down" indicates that "balance" also contains the potential trend towards "imbalance", and "it is impossible to keep them constantly steady" further shows that "balance" is simply temporary and transient. The goal of the *qing* and *zhong* economic policies in the real economic society is to continuously find the equilibrium point between the two according to changing situations. Consequently, the economic society witnesses a continuous process of balance from "*qing* 1-*zhong*1- *qing* 1" to "*qing* 2-*zhong* 2- *qing* 2" and then to "*qing* 3-*zhong* 3-*qing* 3", etc.... This is a historical process with endless change and continuous efforts towards balance. This means that the "balance" in the theory of *qing* and *zhong* is not a natural equilibrium state or sequence but a dynamic equilibrium achieved through constant adjustment under the fundamental premise of the continuous "change" driven by *qing* and *zhong*. Thus "balance" resides in "change", thus Guanzi stated that "there can be no specific figure for maintaining a proper balance in the economy" and "it is impossible to keep them constantly steady." Guanzi particularly emphasize that if one should like to manually "adjust" to achieve an absolute state of balance, the economic system will fall into rigidities due to stasis state (static balance). Without the change between *qing* and *zhong*, "when administering the country, if prices are always the same, there will be no way to make a profit.".[30] Without profits, then the economy would lose its motive force of development.

It is evident that the theory of *qing* and *zhong* simplifies economic affairs to the *qing*—*zhong* relationship, and explains the perpetual motion of the economic system through the endless interactions between the two. It is not difficult to recognize the attribute of "change", but the challenge lies in how to explain it through a simple model and further apply this model to understand the nature and laws of the economic society. The theory of *qing* and *zhong* in *Guanzi* has undoubtedly made a creative contribution in this regard by clarifying a dialectical relationship between *qing* and *zhong*. Within the changing dynamics of *qing* and *zhong* which mutually promote each other, the concepts of *qing* and *zhong* are coordinated and unified, thus achieving a balance that is conducive to the development of economic society.

[30] Guanzi. 1998. *Political, Economic, and Philosophical Essays from Early China*, vol. 2. trans. W. Allyn Rickett. Princeton: Princeton University Press. p.497.

From this perspective, the theory of *qing* and *zhong* implies a logical process from one to two—there is *qing* and *zhong* within all things, and then from two to three—there is balance between *qing* and *zhong*. In particular, while balance is the optimal state, it is not static; moreover, balance cannot be predetermined in advance. In other words, "The policies suitable for a specific reign can never be foreseen in advance.[31]" Guanzi realized that "uncertainty" is a fundamental attribute of change. In a historical timeline filled with variables, "empowering" according to the specific "time" becomes a key factor in achieving a state of balance. Hence, there are sayings "observing the seasons and establishing policy standards"[32] and "when the proper time arrives, they must act; when it is past, they must let go.[33]" According to the theory of *qing* and *zhong*, in the economic society with various possibilities, "balance" (*heng*) could never be simplified, mechanized, or unified into a single model. It must change with the specific "time" and "circumstances", thus embodying the characteristics of a comprehensive historical materialism.

In correspondence with "balance" (*heng*), the theory of *qing* and *zhong* also contains a concept with a roughly similar meaning — "stability" (*zhun*).[34] The difference of the two concepts lies in that "stability" (*zhun*) is mainly used in discussion of specific economic policies, while "balance" (*heng*) is more of a theoretical category, and "balance" (*heng*) does not appear so frequently as "stability" (*zhun*) in the chapters of "*qing zhong* Economic Policies" in *Guanzi* (see Table 7.1). However, the extensive use of "stabilizing" (*zhun*) as a verb makes it clear that, according to the theory of *qing* and *zhong*, the state of balance is difficult to reach spontaneously. Therefore, Guanzi emphasizes that organized actions need to be taken at the right moment, with application of the "controlling" (*yu*) method to achieve desire "balance" (*heng*). Specifically speaking, "when things develop, one acts accordingly; when one hears news, one takes advantage of it",[35] and "therefore the supply (*qing zhong*) must be set at a certain figure and kept there."[36] In this way, "if he (the prince) controls the rise and fall of prices all around him, his country will have no

---

[31] Guanzi. 1998. *Political, Economic, and Philosophical Essays from Early China*, vol. 2. trans. W. Allyn Rickett. Princeton: Princeton University Press. p. 445.

[32] Guanzi. 1998. *Political, Economic, and Philosophical Essays from Early China*, vol. 2. trans. W. Allyn Rickett. Princeton: Princeton University Press. p. 443.

[33] Guanzi. 1998. *Political, Economic, and Philosophical Essays from Early China*, vol. 2. trans. W. Allyn Rickett. Princeton: Princeton University Press. p. 445.

[34] *Zhun*, "to equalize" or "stabilize" the money or grain supply. As was illustrated in *Guanzi*, "Zhunis an abbreviation for pingzhun, a term that literally means 'level' but was used especially during the Han to indicate a standard, happy-medium price set by the government for various commodities as well as a balance in the weight of coins. Pingzhunis the title of chapter 30 of the Shi ji, which deals with money and the economy." See: Guanzi. 1998. *Political, Economic, and Philosophical Essays from Early China*, vol. 2. trans. W. Allyn Rickett. Princeton: Princeton University Press. p.365.

[35] Guanzi. 1998. *Political, Economic, and Philosophical Essays from Early China*, vol. 2. trans. W. Allyn Rickett. Princeton: Princeton University Press. p.447.

[36] Guanzi. 1998. *Political, Economic, and Philosophical Essays from Early China*, vol. 2. trans. W. Allyn Rickett. Princeton: Princeton University Press. p.437.

Table 7.1 Frequency of keywords related to economic regulation in the *qing zhong* chapters

Chapter titles	Stability (*zhun*)	Balance (*heng*)	Controlling (*yu*)	Adjusting (*tiao*)
Introduction to the *Qing Zhong* Section(*Ju Cheng Ma*)	1	2	–	–
The Art of Fiscal Management (*Cheng Ma Shu*)	3	–	–	–
Discourse on Economic Matters (*Shi Yu*)	1	–	–	–
Kingship Based on the Sea (*Hai Wang*)	–	–	–	–
The State's Store of Grain (*Guo Xu*)	5	1	7	4
Using Statistics to Control State Finance (*Shan Guo Gui*)	4	–	–	3
Methods for Coping with Change (*Shan Quan Shu*)	4	–	2	2
The Best Methods for Insuring Fiscal Control (*Shan Zhi Shu*)	6	2	1	1
Methods for Exploiting the Earth (*Di Shu*)	1	2	–	–
Calculations and Measures (*Kui Du*)	6	2	–	4
Maintaining Stability in State Finances (*Guo Zhun*)	3	–	–	–
Qing Zhong Economic Policies, Part A (*Qing Zhong Jia*)	4	3	–	2
Qing Zhong Economic Policies, Part B (*Qing Zhong Yi*)	–	8	1	3
Qing Zhong Economic Policies, Part D (*Qing Zhong Ding*)	6	1	3	–
Qing Zhong Economic Policies, Part E (*Qing Zhong Wu*)	–	–	–	–
Qing Zhong Economic Policies, Part F (*Qing Zhong Ji*)	–	–	–	–
Total	44	21	14	19

itinerant traders and prices will be appropriate", then he could "maintain a proper balance in the nation's economy."[37] Therefore, in the theory of *qing* and *zhong*, the achievement of "balance" (*heng*) requires the active participation of people. The term "balance" (*heng*) has the connotations of "making it balanced" (actions that lead to steady development of the economic society) and "taking it as balanced" (regarding the harmonious development of the economic society as the optimal

[37] Guanzi. 1998. *Political, Economic, and Philosophical Essays from Early China*, vol. 2. trans. W. Allyn Rickett. Princeton: Princeton University Press. p.435.

state). Consequently, both "balance" (*heng*) and "stability" (*zhun*) serve as nouns indicating a state or category, and verbs indicating action.[38]

In summary of the above analysis, within the ideological system of *Guanzi*, the philosophical discourse of "all things are born of the two, *Yin* and *Yang*, with reciprocal reference to each other, so that a third comes into being", could logically extend to the economic discourse of "*qing* and *zhong* give birth to balance (*heng*)". It means that the later economic principle is founded upon the ontological basis of the former philosophical principle, both stemming from the dialectical logic of dividing one into three and the dialectical way of thinking behind. It is particularly noteworthy that if we consider "balance" (*heng*) as a dynamic state, then semantically there is no essential difference between "balance" (*heng*) and the "equilibrium" (*changping*) of the Ever-normal Granary system. The grain buffer stock mechanism in the theory of *qing* and *zhong* proposed in *Guanzi*, which is the theoretical precursor to the Ever-normal Granary, could then be seen as a typical application of the idea "balance" (*heng*). This is achieved through dynamic buying and selling of grain [e.g. "formation of *qing-zhong* relationship 1 between grain and currency—buffer buying and selling (or no intervention)—achieving balance 1"; "formation of *qing-zhong* relationship 2 between grain and currency—buffer buying and selling (or no intervention)—achieving balance 2"; "formation of *qing-zhong* relationship 3 between grain and currency—buffer buying and selling (or no intervention)—achieving balance 3";...] to maintain the long-term stability between grain supply and demand as well as the prices.

It can be seen that the progression from the idea that "all things are born of the two, *Yin* and *Yang*, with reciprocal reference to each other, so that a third comes into being", to the idea that "*qing* and *zhong* give birth to balance (*heng*)", and to the maintenance of ever-normal equilibrium through buffer buying and selling, is a logical process from substance (*ti*) to principle (*li*), and further from principle (*li*) to application (*yong*). Although the economic ideas in *Guanzi* might seem loosely organized, they are in fact meticulously related with each other intrinsically. Of

[38] If we compare the "balance" (*heng*) of the theory of *qing* and *zhong* with the idea of balance in Western economics, we will find the significant differences between them. According to the theory of *qing* and *zhong*, "change" comes first, and "balance" (*heng*) second. Balance is a kind of dynamic and relative equilibrium achieved through "controlling" (*yu*), "adjusting" (*tiao*) or "stabilizing" (*zhun*). It focuses on the coordination of organized forces (of the government) and spontaneous forces (of the market) - not only to give full play to the subjective initiative of people, but also to make the best use of the situation. Western economics, since its classical origins, has maintained a mainstream view that the economic system can spontaneously reach equilibrium under free market conditions. This state is considered the natural and authentic feature of the economic system, and an excellent "natural order." Artificial intervention or regulation would only disrupt this order. Marx criticized this by saying, "The economists have a singular way of proceeding. For them, there are only two kinds of institutions, artificial and natural. The institutions of feudalism are artificial institutions, those of the bourgeoisie are natural institutions. In this they resemble the theologians, who likewise establish two kinds of religion. Every religion which is not heirs is an invention of men, while their own is an emanation of God ... Thus there has been history, but there is no longer any." See: Marx, Karl. 1976. *Capital: A Critique of Political Economy*, vol.1. trans. Ben Fowkes. London: Penguin Books. p.175.

course, buffer buying and selling is only one direction in which the economic thought of *Guanzi* extends from substance (*ti*) to application (*yong*). In the face of different problems and situations in the economic and social spheres, to achieve dynamic equilibrium or constant equilibrium, *Guanzi* proposes a variety of policy models.

7.3 Economic Policy Models in *Guanzi* and Maintaining Balance Through the Mean[39]

Through his in-depth study of Confucian dialectical thought, the contemporary Chinese scholar Pang Pu believes that the core of Confucian political ethics is to maintain balance, achieve coordination, and pursue harmony. However, the status of balance, coordination and harmony between individuals and groups are differentiated and even fundamentally opposed. Therefore, seeking harmony between opposite sides is an important aspect of Confucian philosophy.[40] With this as the basis, Pang Pu established four logical formulas for the coordination and unification of opposing sides A and B, which are used to analyze the dialectical logic of "dividing one into three" in Confucian thought (both ends A and B giving birth to the third, i.e. the state of balance). This provides an effective analytical tool for grasping the doctrine of the mean (*zhongyong*).[41] As was pointed out in the previous section, the economic thought in *Guanzi* is also guided by the dialectical logic of "*qing-zhong*-balance" at the theoretical level, which serves as the fundamental principle for the economic and social development. Hence, there is a consistency in the mode of thinking between *Guanzi* and Confucianism. Next, the author will apply the dialectical thinking of "*qing-zhong*-balance" to various economic issues discussed in *Guanzi*, attempting to explore the focal points of economic thought in *Guanzi* from the perspective of the A-B schema. On this basis, the author will summarize the economic views of "maintaining balance through the mean" in *Guanzi*.

---

[39] *zhong* (the mean), or *zhongyong* (golden mean), was considered to be the highest level of virtue by Confucius (551–479 BC) and Confucian scholars. *Zhong* means moderate in one's words and deeds. Everything has its limits, and neither exceeding nor falling short of the limits is desirable. *Yong* has two meanings. One is common or ordinary and the other is unchanging. Moderation can be maintained for over a long time constantly only when one practices it in everyday life. *Zhongyong* means the standard of moderation that one should follow in dealing with others and in one's everyday conduct. See: "*zhongyong*", Key Concepts in Chinese Thought and Culture, https://www.chinesethought.cn/EN/shuyu_show.aspx?shuyu_id=2179.

[40] Pang, Pu. 2009. *Studies on the Dialectics of Confucianism*. Beijing: Zhonghua Book Company. pp.14–15.

[41] The four concise logical formulas are as follows: A yet B; A but not A'; neither A nor B; both A and B. The relevant discussions are primarily reflected in Pang Pu's research on the theory of "division of one into three". For further details, please refer to the notes on Pang Pu's theory of "division of one into three"

7.3.1 *Four Methods for Application of the Mean*

Primary-Secondary Coordination

In ancient Chinese society, agriculture which created wealth, and commerce which facilitated exchange of goods, were two critical sectors influencing economic and social stability and development. Determination of their relative significance, and the coordination of the "concrete-abstract" relationship of the two, were focal points of *Guanzi*. The work *Guanzi* strongly advocates agricultural fundamentalism, repeatedly emphasizing that state wealth originates from agricultural production on the land: "Unless the people have grain, they will have nothing to eat. Unless there is land, grain will not be produced. Unless there are people, the land will not be worked. Unless people have the energy to work, there will be no way to acquire the resources required by the state."[42] "When people serve in agriculture, fields will be well cultivated. If fields are well cultivated, grain will become plentiful. If grain is plentiful, the state will prosper."[43] "Expend effort on the land and act in accordance with the seasons. Then the country will be certain to prosper."[44] While emphasizing the fundamental status of agriculture, *Guanzi* does not ignore the irreplaceable role of commerce in resource allocation: "Since merchants were made to assemble and dwell together, they came to watch out for times of poor harvest and famine and paid careful attention to the changes within the country. They took note of the four seasons and examined the products of their districts in order to know their market value. They assumed burdens and bore responsibilities. They yoked oxen and harnessed horses in order to encompass the four quarters of the realm. They calculated the supply and then estimated prices in order to exchange that which they had for that which they had not. They bought cheaply and sold dearly."[45]

Although *Guanzi* acknowledges the significance of commerce, it decisively advocates restraining powerful merchants and their speculative profiteering, showing a clear anti-commercial stance. Putting agriculture and commerce together, how does *Guanzi* handle their relationship? In essence, *Guanzi* adheres to a cognitive model: if agriculture (A) and commerce (B) are set as distinct categories, then their relationship is that of "A yet B" (i.e. A is significant, yet B is indispensable). Agriculture is the mainstay of the national economy. Prioritizing agriculture and agricultural administration are fundamental state policies. "Land is the basic of government."[46] This principle is immutable. However, the belief that prioritizing

---

[42] Guanzi. 1985. *Guanzi: Political, Economic, and Philosophical Essays from Early China*, vol.1. trans. W. Allyn Rickett. Princeton: Princeton University Press. p.230.

[43] Guanzi. 1998. *Political, Economic, and Philosophical Essays from Early China*, vol. 2. trans. W. Allyn Rickett. Princeton: Princeton University Press. p.177.

[44] Guanzi. 1998. *Political, Economic, and Philosophical Essays from Early China*, vol. 2. trans. W. Allyn Rickett. Princeton: Princeton University Press. p.187.

[45] Guanzi. 1985. *Guanzi: Political, Economic, and Philosophical Essays from Early China*, vol.1. trans. W. Allyn Rickett. Princeton: Princeton University Press. p.327.

[46] Guanzi. 1985. *Guanzi: Political, Economic, and Philosophical Essays from Early China*, vol.1. trans. W. Allyn Rickett. Princeton: Princeton University Press. p.116.

agriculture has no disadvantage at all is overly simplistic. Instead, there should be primary-secondary coordination in industrial polices such as developing commerce to assist agriculture. *Guanzi* recognizes that "markets" as venues for commercial transactions, though unable to bring about wealth like agriculture (i.e. "it is incapable of bringing about abundance or scarcity on its own"[47]), could benefit people by alleviating shortages (i.e. "Each subdistrict should have a marketplace. If it does not, the people will suffer shortages."[48]), regulate prices (i.e. "The marketplace determines the value of goods"[49]), and even serve as indicators of order and disorder (i.e. "the marketplace may know order or disorder, abundance or scarcity"[50]). The book *Guanzi* recognizes that the market has the capacity of generating and transmitting information, arguing that without understanding information such as supply, demand and prices, one cannot act effectively or optimize their actions. By integrating agricultural production into a continuous reproduction process, it upholds that the development and prosperity of agriculture are inseparable from commercial activities. Thus, the "abstract" knowledge of "abundance or scarcity" in the market and the "concrete" action to "bring about abundance or scarcity" are separate but interdependent. With agriculture as the foundation, the "abstract" commerce is used to support the "concrete" agriculture. "A yet B" (i.e. A is significant, yet B is indispensable) represents the dialectical relationship between agriculture and commerce according to the book *Guanzi*.[51]

---

[47] Guanzi. 1985. *Guanzi: Political, Economic, and Philosophical Essays from Early China*, vol.1. trans. W. Allyn Rickett. Princeton: Princeton University Press. p.118.

[48] Guanzi. 1985. *Guanzi: Political, Economic, and Philosophical Essays from Early China*, vol.1. trans. W. Allyn Rickett. Princeton: Princeton University Press. p.119.

[49] Guanzi. 1985. *Guanzi: Political, Economic, and Philosophical Essays from Early China*, vol.1. trans. W. Allyn Rickett. Princeton: Princeton University Press. p.118.

[50] Guanzi. 1985. *Guanzi: Political, Economic, and Philosophical Essays from Early China*, vol.1. trans. W. Allyn Rickett. Princeton: Princeton University Press. p.118.

[51] A dialectical view of the relationship between enriching the people (*fu min*) and enriching the state (*fu guo*) is another typical application of "A yet B". We know that *Guanzi* emphasizes the necessity for the state to accumulate various important resources, which is often largely interpreted as advocating for methods such as cunning acquisition and plundering to achieve the goal of wealth accumulation for the state. However, the people-centric values and the theory of enriching the people (*fu min*), which are often seen as conflicting with the above proposals, are also frequently expressed in *Guanzi*. In fact, people tend to become fixated on one side while overlooking dialectical analysis in *Guanzi* of the relationship between a wealthy state and its citizens. It can be said that the fundamental judgment of *Guanzi* is that both the people and the state should both be wealthy ("A yet B"). Firstly, enriching the people is the logical starting point for governing the state; the statement "the way to maintain good order in a state is to be certain, first of all, to make its people prosperous" in *Guanzi* clearly indicates that state wealth cannot supersede enriching the people, and state wealth cannot come at the expense of the impoverished people. Secondly, enriching the people doesn't mean to let the individuals do as they wish; it requires participation and intervention from the state. *Guanzi* recognizes that fluctuations in agricultural production and intense competition between states could do harm to the people. Only when the state possesses sufficient resources (such as critical strategic resources like grain) can it respond adequately and solidify the foundation for enriching the people. Therefore, *Guanzi* attaches importance to both enriching the people (*fu min*) and enriching the state (*fu guo*); the harmonious combination of

Excess Being Just as Bad as Deficiency

The primary-secondary relationship between agriculture and commerce as narrated in *Guanzi* has further implication: agriculture and commerce are not of equal significance; instead the "concrete" agriculture could constrain the "abstract" commerce. The text profoundly analyzes the inherent risks of commerce. In the chapter "On Extravagance in Spending" (*chi mi*), *Guanzi* analyzes the function of markets: the markets could promote the production of agriculture; however, if there is excessive consumption from the markets, the agricultural production could not stand long. In other words, if a society experiences excessive prosperity in commerce leading to extravagance and ostentation, the dominant position of agriculture will be undermined. Rather than the "unbalance" state of commerce, *Guanzi* is more concerned about the crisis that the "abstract" commerce might undermine the "concrete" agriculture. That is to say, if the market is dominated by merchants, the monopolists would seize the opportunity to unscrupulously acquire wealth through cunning and plunder. Then "it will lead to large-scale traders roaming the markets and taking advantage of the people's lack of things to increase their capital a hundredfold."[52] "They are also the times when prices fluctuate and when the people can most easily be gathered together."[53] Such exploitation can undoubtedly devastate the fragile peasant economy, destabilizing the economic foundation of the whole society. In this context, the harmonious relationship between commerce and agriculture, i.e. the "abstract" commerce promoting the "concrete" agriculture, shifts to one of sharp conflict, threatening the fundamental agriculture-centric policy. Highly vigilant about this issue, *Guanzi* takes a clear stance with following words: "Thus big traders and families engaged in hoarding are unable to force exactions from our people."[54] Therefore, *Guanzi* adopts a model of "B but not B+" for the governance of commerce, where B+ represents the immoderate or excessive development of commerce. "B but not B+" reflects an awareness and governance orientation aimed at preventing extremes, including policies for commercial control and market regulation. *Guanzi* advocates for placing a portion of production and circulation closely related to the national economy and people's livelihood under state control, which is largely out of consideration from this perspective. However, this does not mean that *Guanzi* supports a shift to another extreme, namely endorsing government monopolies while excluding private merchants and, consequently, the market. If that were the case, the various functions that the market is supposed to fulfill as discussed in *Guanzi* would be out of the question.

enriching the people and enriching the state constitutes the complete ideas of strength and prosperity in *Guanzi*.

[52] Guanzi. 1998. *Political, Economic, and Philosophical Essays from Early China*, vol. 2. trans. W. Allyn Rickett. Princeton: Princeton University Press. p.379.

[53] Guanzi. 1998. *Political, Economic, and Philosophical Essays from Early China*, vol. 2. trans. W. Allyn Rickett. Princeton: Princeton University Press. p.392.

[54] Guanzi. 1998. *Political, Economic, and Philosophical Essays from Early China*, vol. 2. trans. W. Allyn Rickett. Princeton: Princeton University Press. p.382.

In the relationship of "A yet B" (i.e., A is significant, yet B is indispensable) between agriculture and commerce, the "concrete" A (agriculture) and the "abstract" B (commerce) respectively play the primary and secondary roles, but they complement each other without bringing harm to the other. Specifically, B is employed to better maintain the dominant position of A, achieving the goal of "harmony" by supporting agriculture through commerce. The mode "B but not B+" aims to curb the excessive development of commerce which might do harm to agriculture at the primary position. It would ensure that A and B do not fall into a mutually harmful, irreconcilable, or chaotic state as the saying goes "excess being just as bad as deficiency". From the perspective of economic governance objectives, the combination of modes "A yet B" and "B but not B+" is a rational and moderate choice for maintaining industrial balance in a traditional agricultural society.

The policy model advocated in *Guanzi* for managing the relationship between agriculture and commerce can be said to have had a profound influence on later generations. Although it seems contradictory, it is essentially aimed at unifying and coordinating agriculture and commerce, while maintaining a subtle *qing-zhong* balance between the two. It is embodiment of the concept "harmony", rather than simply a method of restraining commerce. Therefore, the so-called "restraining commerce" in *Guanzi* should be understood within the context of prioritizing agriculture and with analysis of the dialectical relationship between agriculture and commerce. The key lies in how to dynamically regulate commerce so that it aligns with the broader direction of coordinated industrial development. Wang Anshi, a prominent politician, poet, essayist and philosopher during the Northern Song dynasty stated: "It is probably due to the desire to limit the merchants' prosperity. If the merchants' business are prosperous, more and more people would abandon their original professions (such as agriculture). However, there is also a fear of commercial decline, because if commerce declines too much, goods will no longer be circulated. Therefore, laws are applied to maintain a balance."[55] This is a succinct expression of the idea of prioritizing agriculture and weighing the relative importance of agriculture and commerce.

Setting aside the discussion of commerce in terms of "B but not B+" in analysis of the relationship between agriculture and commerce, if we examine a specific economic affair (designated as A) in isolation, *Guanzi* also shows a high level of vigilance toward its extreme development (designated as A+). As mentioned earlier in the chapter "On the Cultivation of Political Power" (*quan xiu*) of *Guanzi*, "if there is proper measure in taking from the people and limits are placed on their employment, even a small state is certain to be safe. But if proper measure is not exercised in taking from the people, and no limits are placed on their employment, even a large state is certain to be in danger."[56] This reflects the economic thought in *Guanzi*,

[55] Wang, Anshi. 2017. Reply to Han Qiuren. *The Collected Works of Master Linchuan*, vol. 72. in *Complete Works of Wang Anshi*, vol. 7. ed. Wang, Shuizhao. Shanghai: Fudan University Press. p. 1292.

[56] Guanzi. 1985. *Guanzi: Political, Economic, and Philosophical Essays from Early China*, vol.1. trans. W. Allyn Rickett. Princeton: Princeton University Press. p. 94.

which advocates for "proper measure" and opposes the practice of "no limits". Here the idea of "A but not A+" is shown. For another example, in the chapters "On Extravagance in Spending" (*chi mi*) and "The Five Aids" (*wu fu*) in *Guanzi*, there are following words, "It is said that the very rich cannot be employed and the very poor know no shame",[57] therefore "should the poor and rich lack proper measure, excesses will prevail. "[58] Moderate poverty and wealth are normal phenomena. However, if poverty or wealth reaches extremes, it will bring about various problems. To avoid a situation in which there is extreme disparity between the rich and the poor (A+), it is advised in *Guanzi* to implement policies "to take from the rich to give to the poor",[59] thus achieving the distribution goal "to disperse these hoards, bring surpluses and shortages into balance, and divide up wealth that has been accumulated".[60] This is an important goal for economic governance in *Guanzi*.

Impartiality

"Impartiality" here refers to another dialectical mode "neither A nor B". The typical application of this mode is found in Ever-normal Granary system. It should be noted that there is some overlap between this part and Chap. 2. In order to maintain logical coherence and the continuity of the argument, it is necessary to provide some supplementary analysis in this part.

Guanzi reveals the relationship between price and supply-and-demand through the *qing-zhong* principle, which has been highly regarded by later generations. However, *Guanzi* does not stop at this point; it goes further to discuss the practical application of these theories in policies. The author of the work particularly noted the significant impact of the two opposing forces that arise in the market on people's livelihoods. The first is that "when goods are so cheap, they cannot be sold for even half their cost of production, and for their efforts, people are not even able to recoup their original investment."[61] The second is that "when goods become expensive, they cannot be had for ten times their normal price, and the needs of the people cannot be satisfied."[62] "The five grains and rice are the people's Masters of Destiny."[63]*Guanzi* has grain as a typical example in its analysis of the significant impact that fluctuations in production and prices have on the economy and society:

[57] Guanzi. 1985. *Guanzi: Political, Economic, and Philosophical Essays from Early China*, vol.1. trans. W. Allyn Rickett. Princeton: Princeton University Press. p.308.

[58] Guanzi. 1985. *Guanzi: Political, Economic, and Philosophical Essays from Early China*, vol.1. trans. W. Allyn Rickett. Princeton: Princeton University Press. p.197.

[59] Guanzi. 1998. *Political, Economic, and Philosophical Essays from Early China*, vol. 2. trans. W. Allyn Rickett. Princeton: Princeton University Press. p.436.

[60] Guanzi. 1998. *Political, Economic, and Philosophical Essays from Early China*, vol. 2. trans. W. Allyn Rickett. Princeton: Princeton University Press. p.380

[61] Guanzi. 1998. *Political, Economic, and Philosophical Essays from Early China*, vol. 2. trans. W. Allyn Rickett. Princeton: Princeton University Press. p.381.

[62] Guanzi. 1998. *Political, Economic, and Philosophical Essays from Early China*, vol. 2. trans. W. Allyn Rickett. Princeton: Princeton University Press. p.381.

[63] Guanzi. 1998. *Political, Economic, and Philosophical Essays from Early China*, vol. 2. trans. W. Allyn Rickett. Princeton: Princeton University Press. p.377.

"When there is a bumper harvest, no one can sell grain in the market, and dogs and pigs eat the food of people. When there is a bad harvest, grain is sold in the market for ten strings of cash per *fu* and the roads are filled with starving people."[64] In the face of such problems, what solutions does *Guanzi* propose?

If the state that "when there is a bumper harvest, no one can sell grain in the market"[65] is referred to as A, and the state that "when there is a bad harvest, grain is sold in the market for ten strings of cash per *fu*"[66] as B, then maintaining grain prices at the state of "neither A nor B", i.e., instituting "controls in order to maintain stable prices",[67] becomes another dialectical and moderate goal of *Guanzi*. This is achieved by establishing a grain buffer stock, which later evolved into the Ever-normal Granary system. Although humans cannot control the weather so as to control agricultural production, *Guanzi* argues that the government holds a critical regulatory tool — currency. Currency serves as the "mediums of exchange" (*tong shi*), "means of circulation" (*tong huo*) and "channel for exchange" (*gou du*). Then, it is usual that "knife and spade money (*daobi* and *bubi*) is being kept in the government treasury, the counterfeiting of coins and manipulation of prices is completely in the hands of merchants."[68] The *qing-zhong* economic theory asserts that money and grain follows the basic principle of "cheap money" and "expensive grain", or "cheap grain" and "valued money". This provides a key mechanism for adjusting the *qing-zhong* of grain and thus influencing its supply. It follows the operational principle to "make use of what is valued to acquire what is not valued and what has been acquired cheaply to ease the price of what has become too expensive."[69] The policy establishes a buffer stock mechanism: when grain is cheap, the state purchases it at higher prices; when it is expensive, the state sells it at lower prices. Specifically, in years of abundant harvest, when there is a surplus of grain, there would be a relationship of "cheap grain" and "valued money" in the market, which at its extreme leads to the phenomenon that "dogs and pigs eat the food of people".[70] At the time, the state issues currency to purchase the surplus grain ("make use of what is valued to acquire what is not valued"). As the currency supply in the markets and the supply-demand relationship of grain shift, the extreme situation of "cheap grain"

[64] Guanzi. 1998. *Political, Economic, and Philosophical Essays from Early China*, vol. 2. trans. W. Allyn Rickett. Princeton: Princeton University Press. pp. 380–381.

[65] Guanzi. 1998. *Political, Economic, and Philosophical Essays from Early China*, vol. 2. trans. W. Allyn Rickett. Princeton: Princeton University Press. p.380.

[66] Guanzi. 1998. *Political, Economic, and Philosophical Essays from Early China*, vol. 2. trans. W. Allyn Rickett. Princeton: Princeton University Press. p.380.

[67] Guanzi. 1998. *Political, Economic, and Philosophical Essays from Early China*, vol. 2. trans. W. Allyn Rickett. Princeton: Princeton University Press. p.382.

[68] Guanzi. 1998. *Political, Economic, and Philosophical Essays from Early China*, vol. 2. trans. W. Allyn Rickett. Princeton: Princeton University Press. p.417.

[69] Guanzi. 1998. *Political, Economic, and Philosophical Essays from Early China*, vol. 2. trans. W. Allyn Rickett. Princeton: Princeton University Press. pp. 381–382.

[70] Guanzi. 1998. *Political, Economic, and Philosophical Essays from Early China*, vol. 2. trans. W. Allyn Rickett. Princeton: Princeton University Press. p.380.

and "valued money" is under control. Conversely, in years of bad harvest when grain is scarce, there would be a relationship of "cheap money" and "expensive grain" in the markets, which at its extreme results in the fact that "grain is sold in the market for ten strings of cash per *fu*".[71] In this situation, the state sells reserved grain at prices lower than market ones ("make use of ...what has been acquired cheaply to ease the price of what has become too expensive"), thereby controlling the extreme situation of "cheap money" and "expensive grain". In short, the state establishes a grain buffer stock by leveraging monetary expansion and contraction so as to adjust the *qing-zhong* relationship between money and grain, stabilizing grain prices within a reasonable range. It is also noted that "in general the five grains determine the value of all other things. Should grain be expensive, other things will be cheap; should grain be cheap, other things will be expensive".[72] The regulation policy of "neither A nor B" for grain price, thus has a macroeconomic impact: "Therefore the prince controls the alternating superiority of grain and other things by intervening in the market when prices are unstable."[73] This policy is frequently discussed in the *qing-zhong* chapters, reflecting its significance.

In the dialectical model "A yet B" (i.e., A is significant, yet B is indispensable) between agriculture and commerce, A is the main part, while B serves to complement A's deficiencies, thus developing a relationship of "harmony". For the dialectical model "neither A+ nor B+" (A+ and B+ symbolize two extremes), it aims at avoiding extremes of A or B ("excess being just as bad as deficiency"), so as to avoid scenarios where economic conditions beneficial to development are transformed into their opposites. In the regulation principle of "neither A nor B", the objective is to remain between the extremes instead of going towards the extreme of either one, hence the limitation of grain prices within a reasonable range. This more intuitively reflects the approach of holding both ends and exercising impartiality (*zhong*) so as to achieve equilibrium (or "ever-normal" state).

Flexible Adaptation

The chapter "On Extravagance in Spending" (*Chi Mi*) in *Guanzi* analyzes the role of "extravagance" from the perspective of stimulating production through consumption. It argues that for the wealthy, if "the wealth of the prince and his ministers need not be hidden away",[74] but rather is spent in a way of "extravagance", then impoverished workers, craftsmen, and female laborers will find employment and secure their livelihoods. The chapter "The Art of Fiscal Management" (*Cheng Ma Shu*) further applies the idea of extravagance to economic regulation: "Then, if there is a

[71] Guanzi. 1998. *Political, Economic, and Philosophical Essays from Early China*, vol. 2. trans. W. Allyn Rickett. Princeton: Princeton University Press. p.380.

[72] Guanzi. 1998. *Political, Economic, and Philosophical Essays from Early China*, vol. 2. trans. W. Allyn Rickett. Princeton: Princeton University Press. p.382.

[73] Guanzi. 1998. *Political, Economic, and Philosophical Essays from Early China*, vol. 2. trans. W. Allyn Rickett. Princeton: Princeton University Press. p.382.

[74] Guanzi. 1998. *Political, Economic, and Philosophical Essays from Early China*, vol. 2. trans. W. Allyn Rickett. Princeton: Princeton University Press. p.380.

year of severe droughts or floods and the people lose their primary source of income, he builds palaces and pavilions, thereby providing employment for those households so poor that they have neither a dog in front nor a pig behind. Thus, his building of palaces and pavilions is not to gratify his pleasure, but to maintain equilibrium in the economic policies of the state."[75] Obviously the author believes that the more serious the famine and economic hardship is, the more necessary it is for the state to play the role of a "wealthy man" who carries out seemingly extravagant consumption activities to help the impoverished laborers escape their plight. This idea aligns with the modern concept of labor relief.

The theory of Extravagance in Spending is elaborated in several chapters of *Guanzi*.[76] Therefore, it is not "occasional" idea in *Guanzi*. Conversely, in other chapters, *Guanzi* also advocates for the principle of "frugality" (*Jian*). In the chapter *On Conforming to the Law* (*Fa Fa*) there are following words:

> The enlightened prince builds his ancestral temple just adequate enough to provide for the guests at sacrificial feasts, but does not strive for lavish beauty. He erects palaces and pavilions just adequate enough to avoid dryness and dampness, cold and heat, but does not strive for grandiosity. He sees that their carvings and engravings are just adequate enough to differentiate between the honored and lowly, but does not strive for ostentatiousness. Thus, the peasants do not neglect their seasonal occupations, the various artisans do not neglect their work, the merchants do not lose their profits, the people have no idle days, and wealth is not hoarded.
>
> Therefore it is said: "Frugality is the way."[77]

The coexistence of the ideas of extravagance in spending and frugality in *Guanzi* may puzzle newcomers. How should we interpret this apparent "self-contradiction"? If we consider *Guanzi* not as the work of a single author at a specific era, then the "self-contradiction" between various chapters can be easily reconciled. However, economic historians argue that extravagance and frugality are not fundamentally contradictory. *Guanzi* advocates for a balanced approach that varies under different conditions: frugality is the norm during normal years that could promote development through accumulation, and extravagance is advocated for years of famine-stricken years that could stimulate the economy with "money spending" and "extravagance" such as labor relief.[78] To sum up, *Guanzi's* views on consumption reflect a situation-dependent dialectical model of "both A and B".

---

[75] Guanzi. 1998. *Political, Economic, and Philosophical Essays from Early China*, vol. 2. trans. W. Allyn Rickett. Princeton: Princeton University Press. p.365.

[76] In addition to the chapter "On Extravagance in Spending" (*Chi Mi*), *the idea may also be found in chapters like "Canonical Statements" (Jing Yan), "On Military Taxes" (Cheng Ma), Ban Fa, "Explanation of the Ban Fa" (Ban Fa Jie), "Discourse on Economic Matters" (Shi Yu),* "The Art of Fiscal Management" *(Cheng Ma Shu),* "Methods for Coping with Change" *(Shan Quan Shu)*, etc.

[77] Guanzi. 1985. *Guanzi: Political, Economic, and Philosophical Essays from Early China*, vol.1. trans. W. Allyn Rickett. Princeton: Princeton University Press. pp. 255–256.

[78] See: Hu, Jichuang. 1988. *History of Chinese Economic Thought*, vol.1. Shanghai University of Finance and Economics Press. p. 315; Wu, Baosan. 1989. *Research on Guanzi's Economic Thought*. Beijing: China Social Sciences Press. pp. 159–160.

Guanzi emphasizes adaptability, stressing that "when establishing their even-handedness, they did not long for the past or remain stuck in the present. They changed with the times and developed along with customs."[79] It urges flexibility in addressing issues:

> Now in ancient times there was more than one so-called enlightened prince. The rewards they instituted might be meager or substantial, the prohibitions they established might be light or severe, and the accomplishments they left behind were certainly not the same, but it was not a case of deliberately trying to be different. Everything changed in accordance with the times and was determined by the prevailing customs.[80]

Therefore, the model "both A and B" embodies the principle of changing as time and circumstances change. The chapter "*Qing Zhong* Economic Policies, Part B" (*Qing Zhong Yi*) also illustrates this point: "Accordingly, in order to be good at running a state, when the world lowers its prices, we should raise ours. When it treats something lightly, we should value it. When they enlarge their supply, we should curtail ours. Then we will be able to bring the rest of the world to court."[81] The foreign economic policy must adapt to external changes, fluctuating between high and low, light and heavy, abundant and scarce, thus maintaining initiative status. While this may superficially seem to go to extremes, such flexibility — which allows for adjustments according to the changing situations and imbalances — is a rational and effective strategy that seeks to balance one aspect against another over temporal and spatial dimensions.

The dialectical model of "both A and B" not only takes into account that the opposites in economic affairs can be unified in different times and spaces, but also notes their mutual coordination within the same time and space. For example, in *Guanzi* there is the well-known utilitarianism, holding that "it is the nature of men that whenever they see profit, they cannot help chasing after it."[82]*Guanzi* compares profit-seeking as running water in a metaphor: "People follow after benefits just as water runs downhill."[83] Therefore, "success in government lies in following the hearts of the people",[84] and "the people hate poverty and low position, so the prince

---

[79] Guanzi. 1998. *Political, Economic, and Philosophical Essays from Early China*, vol. 2. trans. W. Allyn Rickett. Princeton: Princeton University Press. p.173.

[80] Guanzi. 1998. *Political, Economic, and Philosophical Essays from Early China*, vol. 2. trans. W. Allyn Rickett. Princeton: Princeton University Press. p.172.

[81] Guanzi. 1998. *Political, Economic, and Philosophical Essays from Early China*, vol. 2. trans. W. Allyn Rickett. Princeton: Princeton University Press. p.472.

[82] Guanzi. 1998. *Political, Economic, and Philosophical Essays from Early China*, vol. 2. trans. W. Allyn Rickett. Princeton: Princeton University Press. p.219.

[83] Guanzi. 1985. *Guanzi: Political, Economic, and Philosophical Essays from Early China*, vol.1. trans. W. Allyn Rickett. Princeton: Princeton University Press. p.71.

[84] Guanzi. 1985. *Guanzi: Political, Economic, and Philosophical Essays from Early China*, vol.1. trans. W. Allyn Rickett. Princeton: Princeton University Press.p.54. Here "heart of the people" or "will of the people" (*min xin*) refers to the evaluative judgment or view of the people in a country or region, on an issue, phenomenon or incident which touches on their common interest and which has broad societal meaning. Ancient Chinese often took the "mandate of heaven" to be the basis and highest concept for the legitimacy of political authority and for policymaking, but in fact they

should provide them with riches and honor."[85] Yet, *Guanzi* seemingly contradicts itself by emphasizing that the way to rule the country lies in countering the people's inclinations: "Whoever would rule a country must act to counter the natural tendencies of the people; only then can he draw close to them."[86] Here, "to counter the natural tendencies of the people" means to teach people with morality. *Guanzi* asserts that "the goals of government and education...are the same, but their methods differ."[87] Therefore *Guanzi* discusses profit-seeking while addressing the significance of morality. Economic strategies for governing the state lie in following the people in their pursuit of "benefits", while educational strategies lie in enlightening the people with "morality".[88] This interplay of following the people in their pursuit of "benefits" and enlightening the people for their "morality" (in the model of "both A and B"), allows the people to achieve a rational unity between being economically minded and morally principled.[89]

The previous text discussed how the relationship "A yet B" (i.e., A is significant, yet B is indispensable) shows the property of "harmony" between the opposites. Here the relationship "both A and B" also embody the property of "harmony". Both restrains A and B in a way of ""harmony" so as to prevent economic behaviors from developing excessively towards one end, thereby maintaining balance and avoiding disorder. Of course, in "both A and B" there is no distinction between the primary and secondary elements as in "A yet B"; instead, it treats A and B as equal elements. Furthermore, it particularly highlights the mutual complementarity of A and B in different times and spaces. This indicates that being unaware of "flexible

often regarded the "will of the people" to be the principal source, content, and manifestation of the "mandate of heaven." They also considered it to be the fundamental principle of a country's governance, and thought that having or losing the will of the people determined the rise or fall of a country and political power as well as the development of state affairs. It is the core of the Chinese concept of the people as the foundation of the state. All enlightened Chinese statesmen past and present have regarded the "will of the people" to be the most important factor in governance. See: https://www.chinesethought.cn/EN/shuyu_show.aspx?shuyu_id=3988

[85] Guanzi. 1985. *Guanzi: Political, Economic, and Philosophical Essays from Early China*, vol.1. trans. W. Allyn Rickett. Princeton: Princeton University Press. p.54.

[86] Guanzi. 1998. *Political, Economic, and Philosophical Essays from Early China*, vol. 2. trans. W. Allyn Rickett. Princeton: Princeton University Press. p.312.

[87] Guanzi. 1998. *Political, Economic, and Philosophical Essays from Early China*, vol. 2. trans. W. Allyn Rickett. Princeton: Princeton University Press. p.307.

[88] For example, in the first chapter of Guanzi, "On Shepherding the People" (*mu min*), the four cardinal virtues or four guiding principles that support the state: propriety (li), righteousness (yi), integrity (lian) and a sense of shame (chi): "The primary measure for preserving the state is to promote the four cardinal virtues." Guanzi. 1985. *Guanzi: Political, Economic, and Philosophical Essays from Early China*, vol.1. trans. W. Allyn Rickett. Princeton: Princeton University Press. p.52.

[89] Another example that can be elaborated on this is that *Guanzi* not only respects the spontaneous forces of the market, or the "causes" (*yin*), but also attaches emphasis on the intervention of the government, or the "controlling" (*yu*) and "adjusting" (*tiao*). The previous text discussed how the government utilizes grain buffer reserves to adjust grain prices, ensuring that they are neither too high nor too low ("neither A nor B"). This is achieved through the interplay of the two forces of the market and the government ("both A and B").

adaptability" represents another kind of stubborn bias,[90] while the true path to moderation lies in responding flexibly to changing circumstances. The chapter "All-embracing Unity" (*zhou he*) of *Guanzi* there are following words: "The great worthy is able to be shallow or deep, to sink or float, to be bent or straight, to speak or be silent",[91] and "Heaven has more than a single season, Earth more than a single source of benefit, and man more than a single activity."[92] In reality, time waits for no man, therefore "opportunity is crucial in handling affairs. It cannot be stored up or set aside."[93] Thus, being adept at adaptability, proactively acting according to the times and responding actively to circumstances is advocated as superb practice in *Guanzi*: "The true king takes advantage of the situation, and the sage takes advantage of the principle of change",[94] and "a small country may wish to become a large one and a large one may wish to rule the world, but such a thing will never be possible unless they both come to understand planning designed to cope with change."[95] The timing of decision-making is a decisive factor for economic success or failure. The *qing-zhong* chapter of *Guanzi* repeatedly emphasizes the necessity to seize opportunities in "controlling" (*yu*) and "adjusting" (*tiao*) economy according to specific circumstances. The chapter "The State's Store of Grain" (*Guo Xu*) explicitly states the importance to "take advantage of the rise and fall of prices during the four seasons, and control them by utilizing the stabilizing features of *qing zhong* economic policies."[96]

7.3.2 Unity of Essence, Principle and Application

In the four dialectical relationships discussed above, agriculture versus commerce, moderation versus extremity of wealth and poverty, years with bad harvests versus those with abundant harvests, extravagance versus frugality, and the economically minded man versus morally principled man, constitute multiple opposing aspects within the economic system. These represent specific extensions of the *qing-zhong*

---

[90] There are following words in Chap. 8 of *Mencius*, "But holding to the Mean without allowing for exigencies resembles their holding to one point." Bloom, Irene (trans.) 2009. *Mencius*. New York: Columbia University Press. p.150.

[91] Guanzi. 1985. *Guanzi: Political, Economic, and Philosophical Essays from Early China*, vol.1. trans. W. Allyn Rickett. Princeton: Princeton University Press. p.203.

[92] Guanzi. 1985. *Guanzi: Political, Economic, and Philosophical Essays from Early China*, vol.1. trans. W. Allyn Rickett. Princeton: Princeton University Press.p.203.

[93] Guanzi. 1985. *Guanzi: Political, Economic, and Philosophical Essays from Early China*, vol.1. trans. W. Allyn Rickett. Princeton: Princeton University Press. p.124.

[94] Guanzi. 1998. *Political, Economic, and Philosophical Essays from Early China*, vol. 2. trans. W. Allyn Rickett. Princeton: Princeton University Press. pp. 414–415.

[95] Guanzi. 1998. *Political, Economic, and Philosophical Essays from Early China*, vol. 2. trans. W. Allyn Rickett. Princeton: Princeton University Press. p.399.

[96] Guanzi. 1998. *Political, Economic, and Philosophical Essays from Early China*, vol. 2. trans. W. Allyn Rickett. Princeton: Princeton University Press. p.385.

relationship in the realm of economics under the paradigm that "all things are born of the two, *Yin* and *Yang*, with reciprocal reference to each other". To be more specific, the practice of coordinating agricultural and commercial relationships through "A yet B" and "B but not B+", preventing the extremes of wealth and poverty via "A but not A+", seeking a balance between years of bad harvest and abundant harvest with "neither A nor B", and being extravagant in some years while frugal in other years by adopting "both A and B", all clearly indicates that *Guanzi* strives to find an optimal state that can harmonize and coordinate these contradictions and oppositions in economic matters, thereby benefiting economic stability and development. This reflects the idea that "all things are born of the two, *Yin* and *Yang*, with reciprocal reference to each other, so that a third comes into being", and the idea that "*qing* and *zhong* give birth to balance (*heng*)".

Within a singular cultural system, the unique value of economic ideas in *Guanzi* may be difficult to be acknowledged. However, through horizontal comparisons across different cultural systems worldwide, the essential features of economic ideas in *Guanzi* can be more clearly identified. Here, the concept of "Axial Period" provides a good reference frame. We know that Karl Jaspers introduced the concept of the "Axial Period" in his book *The Origin and Goal of History*. Karl Jaspers believed that from 800 B.C. to 200 B.C., various human civilizations, while isolated from one another, experienced a spiritual breakthrough initiated by wise philosophers. In China, representatives are Laozi, Confucius and Mozi, etc.; in India, the Buddha; in the Middle East, Elijah and Isaiah; and in Greece, Homer, Heraclitus and Plato.[97] The profound significance of the spiritual breakthroughs during the Axial Period lies in the fact that they shaped the spiritual character of various civilizations, giving rise to distinct cultural systems that played a guiding role in later historical developments. Thus, an important question arises: how did the sages of different regions during the Axial Period develop significantly different cultural systems based on their unique cognitions and modes of thinking? Karl Jaspers did not provide further analysis in *The Origin and Goal of History*, while Joseph Needham, in a somewhat overlooked footnote in volume 3 "*Mathematics and the Sciences of the Heavens and the Earth*" of the work "Science and Civilisation in China", sheds light on the core issue:

> While the Greeks and Indians paid early and detailed attention to formal logic, the Chinese (as we saw many times invol.2) showed a constant tendency to develop dialectical logic. The corresponding Chinese philosophy of organism paralleled Greek and Indian mechanical atomism.[98]

In Joseph Needham's view, the ancient Chinese, Indians, and Greeks have their own traditions and strengths in thinking modes. The "early" period in his words, when the distinctive features were formed, should be appropriately the "Axial Period" in

[97] Jaspers, Karl. 1953. *The Origin and Goal of History*. New Haven and London: Yale University Press. p. 2.

[98] Needham, Joseph. 1959. *Science and Civilisation in China,* vol.3. Cambridge: Cambridge University Press. p.151.

Karl Jaspers' words. If this judgment is generally accurate, then the "dialectical logic" that Joseph Needham refers to is a distinctive way of thinking that was formed among the Chinese during the Axial Period, setting it apart from other civilizations. Examining the history of thought before the Qin dynasty, we find that dialectical thinking has undergone a long-term process as a cognitive mode that profoundly influenced later generations. During the process, scholars from various schools of thought made their own significant contributions, each expressing some laws and characteristics of dialectics in their unique ways and terminologies. Although there was much debate among them, this did not hinder the existence of commonalities in their dialectical thoughts, thereby forming a comprehensive chain for understanding dialectics.[99]The final and most crucial link in this chain is that the thinkers adapted to the trend of academic integration at the end of the Warring States period. They summarized the cultural creations of the Axial Period with the inclusive principle of "all roads leading to Rome" that helped eliminate biases between schools of thought. Centered on the highest category of "the Way"(*dao*), they established a philosophical system of *yin* and *yang* that spans heaven, earth and man.[100] The fundamental theme of this system is what we know as "the reciprocal process of *yin* and *yang* is called the Dao".[101] The proposition of "the reciprocal process of *yin* and *yang* is called the Dao" represents the "crowning ceremony" in the construction of the ontological edifice in ancient Chinese philosophical culture, marking the completion of a breakthrough during the Axial Period by the Chinese.

From the materialist historical perspective, the construction of metaphysical ontology during the Axial Period was rooted in social life. The philosophers of the Pre-Qin period, based on social life and concerns, actively participated in the rational contemplation and theoretical construction of the concept of "Dao". Through the interaction between the material world and spiritual world, they ultimately distilled the wisdom in the book *I Ching* (*Book of Changes*) which states that "the reciprocal process of *yin* and *yang* is called the Dao". From this perspective, the view that "the reciprocal process of *yin* and *yang* is called the Dao" aligns with the

[99] Pang, Pu. 2009. *Studies on the Dialectics of Confucianism*. Beijing: Zhonghua Book Company. p.7.

[100] Yu, Dunkang. 2016. *The Past and Present of Philosophy of Changes*. Beijing: China Renmin University Press. pp. 30–31.

[101] Lynn, R. J.1994. *The Classic of Changes: A New Translation of the I Ching as Interpreted by Wang Bi*. New York: Columbia University Press. p.53. In its original meaning, *dao* (道) is the way or path taken by people. It has three extended meanings: (1) the general laws followed by things in different spheres, e.g. the natural order by which the sun, moon and stars move is called the way of heaven; the rules that govern human activities are the way of man; (2) the universal patterns followed by all things and beings; and (3) the original source or ontological existence of things, which transcends form and constitutes the basis for the birth and existence of all things, and for the activities of human beings. In their respective discussions of Dao, Confucianism, Daoism, and Buddhism imbue it with very different connotations. While benevolence, righteousness, social norms, and music education form the basic content of the Confucian Dao, the Buddhist and Daoist Dao tends to emphasize *kong* (空 emptiness) and *wu* (无 void). See: "Dao (Way)", https://www.chinesethought.cn/EN/shuyu_show.aspx?shuyu_id=2127.

philosophic idea articulated in *Guanzi* that "all things are born of the two, Yin and Yang, so that a third comes into being"; the latter even more comprehensively expresses the theoretical structure, logical process, and value orientation of dialectical thinking, which is a significant contribution of *Guanzi*. Moreover, of particular significance is that the authors of *Guanzi* made creative transformations based on this idea by uniquely developing the theory of *qing* and *zhong* in the economic realm along with a set of policy frameworks. It can be observed that the economic thought in *Guanzi* adeptly reveals the essence of economic phenomena by showcasing their oppositional aspects, while also analyzing the economic society from a holistic perspective that does not lean towards one side, thereby coordinating various contradictions under the harmonious development goal of mutual generation and integration.[102]

Economy is the material foundation of social development. When discussing the Axial Priod and Axial Breakthrough in Chinese history, we must not only remember the sages like Laozi, Confucius and Mozi, but also acknowledge a group of thinkers who pioneered the exploration of the "Dao" of economics and their significant achievements. Therefore, we have reason to assert that *Guanzi* aligns with the trends and currents of its time. Unlike other schools that delved deeply into economic issues, *Guanzi*, based on the ontology of "all things are born of the two, Yin and Yang, so that a third comes into being", formed the "Dao" of economics and achieved an "Axial Breakthrough" in the realm of economic thought. Even if *Guanzi* is not the only contributor to this breakthrough, it is certainly the most important

[102] It should be noted that the fundamental characteristics of the theory of *qing* and *zhong* in *Guanzi* can be summarized as follows "three *yi*": simplicity (*jian yi*), variability (*bian yi*) and invariability (*bu yi*). The theory of *qing* and *zhong* is highly abstracted with the two concepts *qing* and *zhong*, which represents simplicity; it reveals the development of the economic society between dynamic changes in *qing* and *zhong*, which signifies variability; and it adheres to the principle and goal of balance (*heng*) for economic development, which indicates invariability. These three characteristics align with the general features of *I Ching*, which are also summarized as "three *yi*" (simplicity, variability, and invariability) in dialectical thinking of *yin* and *yang*. However, such alignment is not coincidental. We know that the dating of *I Ching* is also an unresolved issue, but most scholars believe that the main body of *I Ching* was completed in the pre-Qin period, specifically during the Warring States period. The earliest version of *Guanzi* was came into being no later than the late Warring States period. Therefore, it is well possible that *Guanzi* absorbs and integrates various schools of thought, including those from *I Ching*. For further reference, see the article: Xian, Wen. 2017. The view of "Three *yi*" and dialectical reasoning: A brief exploration of the economic theory of *qing* and *zhong* in *Guanzi*. *The Ideological Front* (*Yunnan University's Journal of Social Sciences*). 43(4): 98–107. Additionally, the theory of *yin* and *yang* of the Zou Yan (324 B.C.-240 B.C.), a scholar in the Warring States period, influenced the ideas of *I Ching*. The Jixia Academy, where Zou Yan once served as a teacher, played an important role for the formation of *Guanzi*. Therefore, it is logical that the theory of *yin* and *yang* becomes a shared part in both *I Ching* and *Guanzi*, providing a convenient pathway for *Guanzi* to absorb and develop the philosophical concepts of *I Ching*. In this light, the connection between the "three *yi*" of *qing* and *zhong* in *Guanzi* and the "three *yi*" in *I Ching* is obvious. Therefore, it can be concluded that in both the philosophical proposition "all things are born of the two, Yin and Yang, so that a third comes into being" and the economic theory based on the principle of *qing* and *zhong*, *Guanzi* encompasses the philosophy and thinking of *I Ching*.

one. Its profound significance lies in the fact that the economic theoretical framework constructed in *Guanzi* has largely shaped the unique economic thinking or worldview of the Chinese people, which can be further summarized as "maintaining balance through the mean".

"Maintaining balance through the mean" can be interpreted as, from the overall perspective, emphasis is laid on the function of the economic system and the various dialectical relationships closely related to it, which involves the broad aspects of production, exchange, distribution and consumption, and the various relationships behind such as the relationship of the government the market, the ruler and his people, the taking and the giving, the righteousness and profits, and even the deeper relationship of peace and danger, governance and disorder. Thus it has led to the construction of "political economics" with "productive relations" as the object of investigation. The core objective of this system is to achieve dynamic balance in economic development through the harmonization of productive relations, and its basic principle is the dialectical logic of "dividing one into three". Here the "three" is the result of turning disorder into order and turning contradiction into harmony on the basis of the epistemology of *yin* and *yang*, the *qing* and the *zhong*. Philosophically, the "three" is obtained through "the mean", which is termed "balance" (*heng*) in *Guanzi*. Dynamically "balance" (*heng*) itself implies that "there can be no specific figure for maintaining a proper balance in the economy". In other words, we should creatively achieve the dynamic balance in the changing economic society. Another figurative expression of such dynamic balance is "ever-normal balance" (*chang-ping*). In terms of policy application, *Guanzi* expands the concept of "maintaining balance through the mean" into four modes between A and B, which are complementary to each other, thus constituting a complete combinations of policies. From this point of view, although the economic thought of *Guanzi* seems to be varied and elusive, it has its roots, namely "all things are born of the two, Yin and Yang, so that a third comes into being", its principle namely ""*qing* and *zhong* give birth to balance (*heng*)", as well as its practical applications in the four modes between A and B, thus constituting a rigorous system of the trinity. It can be seen that the economic thought of *Guanzi* is a system of doctrines that is internally coherent in essence and can be grasped as a whole. It should be noted in particular that although in theory the essence of the ideas derives from "the mean" and "balance", in practice it is always directed to the concrete "people". Therefore, the people-oriented principle that includes "protecting the people", "drawing close to the people", "spending for the people" and "entrusting the king's wealth to their people" is the integral component of *Guanzi's* economic thought, i.e. "maintaining balance through the mean". It is a fundamental feature of *Guanzi* to implement the *qing-zhong* theory in a humane way.

The economic idea of "maintaining balance through the mean" in *Guanzi* has had a profound influence on the later generations, and has laid down the distinct dialectical quality of traditional Chinese economic thinking. Examining the thinking, debates and practices on major economic issues in various historical periods, we may easily find that most of them were consciously developed in a dialectical way, such as the state's choice between "taking from the people" and "giving to the people", the industrial balance between agriculture and commerce, the ethical discernment between righteousness and profit, the dispute between extravagance and frugality, and the policy choices between governmental intervention and laissez-faire, etc. Among them the most valuable thoughts and practices is to keep balance among the seemingly contradictory but interdependent "relations of production" and looking for moderate methods that meets the needs of the times according to the dialectical logic of the "dividing one into three".[103]

It is interesting to note that when we turn our attention again to the history of Western economic thought, we will find that several major theoretical revolutions have also been devoted to coordinate the contradictions, aiming to achieve ever-normal development in a "harmonious" way with moderate methods.

7.4 The Ever-normal Views in Western Economic Thought

Keynes and his followers resurrected the Ever-normal Law of ancient China, and such "inheritance" suggests that there might be a subtle connection between Keynesian economics and the economic thought of *Guanzi*, which is based on the principle of "maintaining balance through the mean". Keynes argued that if the interest rate on money was the only significant interest rate, money would become a safe haven from uncertainty when people make asset choices. The view has hit the mark of the modern monetary economy and captured *qing* and *zhong* of monetary economy.

For an investor, the choice of investment is decided by the comparison of interest rates on various capital goods. Keynes believed that this comparison is measured against the interest rate on money. Since the interest rate on money is characterized by relative stability, while the interest rates of non-monetary assets are based on unstable expectations, Keynes identified the relationship of *qing* and *zhong* between the money and various types of capital goods through the rate of interest (it is an important theoretical contribution of the *qing-zhong* theory in *Guanzi* to extract a key point from the complex *qing-zhong* relationships of all things — the *qing-zhong* relationship between money and all other goods). The significance of this analysis lies in its ability to dynamically observe the following aspects: the *qing* and *zhong*

[103] From the long period of history, the economy and society are always in the midst of structural changes. With the entry into modern era, there was the rise of the western industrial and commercial civilization. In the context of the eastward expansion of western power, the traditional relationship between agriculture and commence gradually was transformed. To adapt to the historical trend, the dialectic model of "A yet B" needs to be dynamically converted to the model "both A and B" (i.e. both agriculture and commerce are significant). The emergence of "mercantilism" in the late Qing dynasty can be regarded as a progressive trend of thinking that seeks to change the traditional economic model in order to be in line with the general trend.

conversion between money and capital goods, which can be further used to analyze the inner mechanism of macroeconomic fluctuations; another important relationship underlying the *qing* and *zhong* conversion between money and capital goods, i.e., the *qing-zhong* relationship between money and labor.

In this way, we can reconstruct Keynes' "general theory" of "employment, interest and money" from the perspective of the *qing-zhong* theory. In macroeconomics, investment is based on the expected benefits, which are measured in terms of the marginal efficiency of an unstable capital good, and the decision for investment depends on the gap between the marginal efficiency of capitals and the interest rate on money. As a result, there are investment fluctuations that revolve around the interest rate on money, which has direct influence on employment. The logical relationship among them is as follows: when money is "light" (yielding lower returns), all goods (capital goods) are "heavy" (yielding higher returns), and people will choose to hold goods (including labor power) because they offer higher returns, hence near or temporary full employment; conversely, when money is "heavy" (yielding higher returns), all goods (capital goods) are "light" (yielding lower returns), and people will choose not to hold goods (including labor power) because they offer lower returns, hence involuntary unemployment.

Since the *qing-zhong* theory can theoretically clarify Keynes' main view on macroeconomic fluctuations, then the regulatory law of *Guanzi*, or the proposal to "make use of what is valued to acquire what is not valued and what has been acquired cheaply to ease the price of what has become too expensive",[104] should have corresponding propositions in Keynes' works. Indeed, this is the case. In the discussions in Chaps. 5 and 6, we find that the macroeconomic regulatory means proposed by Keynes is the socialized investment based on the principle of "making use of what is valued to acquire what is not valued". In other words, when people and goods are "not valued" while money is "valued" in the market, the government should operate inversely by taking people and goods as "valued" and money as "not valued", and establish a general buffer stock through active fiscal policies. Post-Keynesian economists have continued Keynes' emphasis on macroeconomic welfare, specifically employment, and further analyzed the significance of buffer stock employment for macroeconomic stability. Though there is no concept analogous to *qing* or *zhong* in Keynes' economic works, his unique analysis of money has already revealed the distinctions between *qing* and *zhong* and their relationships in economic affairs with money as the reference standard. Moreover, it particularly demonstrates the followings points: the relationship between *qing* and *zhong* is in constant change and endogenous to the economic society; the concepts of *qing* and *zhong* are unified, in that without the difference between *qing* and *zhong* there would be no investment and economic development; and the concepts of *qing* and *zhong* are also contradictory, in that imbalance between the two would lead to macroeconomic fluctuations and involuntary unemployment.

---

[104] Guanzi. 1998. *Guanzi: Political, Economic, and Philosophical Essays from Early China*, vol. 2. trans. W. Allyn Rickett. Princeton: Princeton University Press. pp. 381–382.

The book *Guanzi* embraces the view of change, stating that "Heaven and Earth cannot remain static. Therefore they move, and they transform the old into the new."[105] It further asserts that in the world the rise and fall of prices cannot be stabilized "in an entire lifetime",[106] implying that there is continuous variation between *qing* and *zhong*. Consequently, it is of significance for "observing the seasons and establishing policy standards",[107] meaning that policies should be flexible and responsive to changing conditions. The text also emphasizes, "When the proper time arrives, they must act; when it is past, they must let go. The policies suitable for a specific reign can never be foreseen in advance."[108] Such views are consistent with the ideas in Xici chapter of *I Ching* (*Book of Changes*), which states that "The Yi …as a Way it is always shifting. It fluctuates and moves without rest, revolving and flowing through the six vacancies, rising and falling with no constancy, the firm and yielding [lines] changing into each other. They cannot be considered fixed essences, as they simply change along with circumstances."[109]In the view of commentators, the reasons for changes between *qing* and *zhong* are diverse (see Fig. 2.1). Among them, changes in the "Four Seasons", particularly the unpredictable climate changes which lead to shifts between good harvests and bad harvests in agricultural production, serve as a typical inducement. Compared to the agricultural era, human economic activities in an omnipotent industrial society seem to have become more autonomous and controllable. And once the "rational economic man" activates the "market mechanism", which is regarded by many mainstream economists as the most ingenious device, the economy will exhibit a perfectly balanced state akin to that described by Newtonian mechanics. So, does this mean that the "devil" of "unpredictability" has been successfully "expelled" from the modern economy? Keynes's answer to the question is "no". He states that "the theory we devise in the study of how we behave in the market place should not itself submit to market-place idols. I accuse the classical economic theory of being itself … which tries to deal with the present by abstracting from the fact that we know very little about the future."[110] He also emphasizes that "the outstanding fact is the extreme

[105] Guanzi. 1998. *Political, Economic, and Philosophical Essays from Early China*, vol. 2. trans. W. Allyn Rickett. Princeton: Princeton University Press. p.328.

[106] Guanzi. 1998. *Political, Economic, and Philosophical Essays from Early China*, vol. 2. trans. W. Allyn Rickett. Princeton: Princeton University Press. p.466.

[107] Guanzi. 1998. *Political, Economic, and Philosophical Essays from Early China*, vol. 2. trans. W. Allyn Rickett. Princeton: Princeton University Press. p.443.

[108] Guanzi. 1998. *Political, Economic, and Philosophical Essays from Early China*, vol. 2. trans. W. Allyn Rickett. Princeton: Princeton University Press. p. 445.

[109] Zhu, Xi. 2020. *The Original Meaning of the Yijing: Commentary on the Scripture of Change*. trans. Joseph A. Adler. New York: Columbia University Press. p.296.

[110] Keynes, J. M. 1937. The general theory of employment. *Quarterly Journal of Economics*. 51 (2): 215.

precariousness of the basis of knowledge on which our estimates of prospective yield have to be made."[111] Therefore, "most, probably, of our decisions to do something positive, … can only be taken as a result of animal spirits…, and not as the outcome of a weighted average of quantitative benefits multiplied by quantitative probabilities."[112] These crucial insights reveal the truth of the economic world, which, like the seasons and climate, is forever subject to unpredictable change. This, as Robinson summarized, is the true revolutionary aspect of the Keynesian Revolution—a shift from an equilibrium perspective to a historical perspective:

> Once we admit that an economy exists in time, that history goes one way, from the irrevocable past into the unknown future, the conception of equilibrium based on the mechanical analogy of a pendulum swinging to and fro in space becomes untenable.[113]

In the work of Davidson, a post-Keynesian economist, the characteristic of "calendar time" is articulated as "non-ergodicity".[114] The economic and social system is an open and evolving one, exhibiting continuous and qualitative changes that distinguish it from ergodic processes. It is precisely for this reason that the necessity of discretionary government regulation to achieve dynamic equilibrium is highlighted. Understanding this allows us to recognize the trans-temporal "tacit agreement" between the most fundamental economic philosophy of the Keynesian Revolution and the concept of change in the *qing-zhong* theory in ancient China. There are "astonishing similarities" in Ever-normal Granary systems in ancient and modern times, and in the East and the West. Although in the *qing-zhong* theory as presented in *Guanzi*, economic fluctuations are primarily attributed to supply shocks, whereas in Keynes' theory, they are mainly caused by demand shocks, we believe that *Guanzi* and Keynes would still reach a consensus at a deeper level: the world develops forward amidst change, and uncertainty permeates the whole historical process.

Precisely because of this, Keynes pointed out that capitalist societies were not perpetually in a state of full employment, as classical economics had insisted. Unpredictable economic fluctuations lead to involuntary unemployment, and therefore, economies cannot be allowed to develop purely on principles of laissez-faire. Instead, government intervention is necessary, with specific policies and actions to address uncertainty and achieve sustainable full employment. Similar to *Guanzi* which advocates the *qing-zhong* theory to "make use of what is valued to acquire

---

[111] Keynes, J. M. 2013. *The General Theory of Employment, Interest and Money*. in *The Collected Writings of John Maynard Keynes, vol.*7. ed. Moggridge, D. New York: Cambridge University Press. p.149.

[112] Keynes, J. M. 2013. *The General Theory of Employment, Interest and Money*. in *The Collected Writings of John Maynard Keynes, vol.*7. ed. Moggridge, D. New York: Cambridge University Press. p.161.

[113] Robinson, Joan. 1973. What has become of the Keynesian Revolution? In *After Keynes: Papers Presented to Section F (Economics) at the 1972 Annual Meeting of the British Association for the Advancement of Science*. ed. Joan Robinson. Oxford: Basil Blackwell. p.5.

[114] Davidson, P. 1982. Rational expectation: a fallacious foundation for studying crucial decision making processes. *Journal of Post Keynesian Economics*. 5 (2): 182–198.

what is not valued and what has been acquired cheaply to ease the price of what has become too expensive",[115] Keynes and his followers hoped that the government would establish a broader buffer stock so as to dynamically achieve "balance" (*heng*) in economy.

From the perspective of traditional Chinese discourse, the goal of the Keynesian Revolution was to bring the capitalist economy into an "ever-normal" state, a concept expressed in *qing-zhong* theory of *Guanzi* as "*qing-zhong*-balance". Recognizing the limitations of the market, Keynes advocated for organized government regulation to complement and counterbalance the spontaneous forces of the market, amid the polarity between economic hyperactivity and economic depression. Therefore, Keynes advocated for coordinating the two extremes to utilize "the mean" (*zhong*), which he termed the "middle way". His fundamental stance was as follows:

> I conceive, therefore, that a somewhat comprehensive socialisation of investment will prove the only means of securing an approximation to full employment; though this need not exclude all manner of compromises and of devices by which public authority will co-operate with private initiative.[116]

And further:

> ...the free play of economic forces may need to be curbed or guided. But there will still remain a wide field for the exercise of private initiative and responsibility. Within this field the traditional advantages of individualism will still hold good.[117]

Keynes' ideal was to achieve a unified "harmony" between economic efficiency and social justice, with full employment serving as the intersection of the two. However, in the logical framework of Marx-Kalecki, Keynes' regulatory approach of striking a balance between *qing* and *zhong*, in the long run, is deemed unviable. This hits the nail on the head, pointing to a more fundamental "*qing-zhong*" relationship: if in the *qing-zhong* relationship of social structure there is consistent tilting towards capital, resulting in the alienation of human labor as an object and tool of capital control, then no matter what economic regulatory policies are implemented, the chronic problem of unemployment cannot be solved. Even governance "tricks" like functional finance and buffer stock employment will find it difficult to break through the constraints of underlying institutional barriers.

In Marx's system of political economy, the "imbalance between *qing* and *zhong*" in the field of distribution, manifested in the acquisition of surplus value in capitalist

---

[115] Guanzi. 1998. *Political, Economic, and Philosophical Essays from Early China*, vol. 2. trans. W. Allyn Rickett. Princeton: Princeton University Press. pp. 381–382.

[116] Keynes, J. M. 2013. *The General Theory of Employment, Interest and Money*. in *The Collected Writings of John Maynard Keynes*, vol.7. ed. Moggridge, D. New York: Cambridge University Press. p.378.

[117] Keynes, J. M. 2013. *The General Theory of Employment, Interest and Money*. in *The Collected Writings of John Maynard Keynes*, vol.7. ed. Moggridge, D. New York: Cambridge University Press. pp. 379–380.

production, is the source of economic fluctuations. And it is significantly externalized through the disparity between production and consumption. Compared to John Maynard Keynes, Marx conducted an earlier and deeper analysis of capitalist economic crises, with his logical approach grounded in the labor theory of value. Marx believed that the contradiction in distribution under capitalism, expressed as the opposition between profits and wages, is a profound cause of the inherent instability of the capitalist system. Marx stated, "the society's power of consumption… is determined neither by the absolute power of production nor by the absolute power of consumption but rather by the power of consumption within a given framework of antagonistic conditions of distribution, which reduce the consumption of the vast majority of society to a minimum level, only capable of varying within more or less narrow limits. It is further restricted by the drive for accumulation, the drive to expand capital and produce surplus-value on a larger scale….The market, therefore, must be continually extended…The internal contradiction seeks resolution by extending the external field of production. But the more productivity develops, the more it comes into conflict with the narrow basis on which the relations of consumption rest."[118] Therefore, "the ultimate reason for all real crises always remains the poverty and restricted consumption…[119] "In Marx's view, the solution to problem is to apply "the mean" between the two poles of *qing* and *zhong* in the distribution of labor and capital, by realizing the socialization of the ownership of the means of production. That is to say, it is by unifying the laborers with the means of production so that "everyone is only a worker like everyone else".[120] By doing so, the distributional relationship between various people turns harmonious and the relationship between productive forces and consumption is coordinated, thereby avoiding a fundamental conflict between productive forces and consumption and leading to sustainable economic development.

Let's trace back to Adam Smith. We know that Smith revealed the economic principle in "An Inquiry into the Nature and Causes of the Wealth of Nations" that individuals, guided by "an invisible hand", could enhance social welfare. However, in another important work, "The Theory of Moral Sentiments", Smith emphasizes the importance to "feel for others", rather than "for themselves". Based on moral norms of compassion and justice, people could also achieve the "happy situation of our fellow-citizens".[121] The "conflict" between these two viewpoints have been summarized by German historical-school economists as "Das Adam Smith

[118] Marx, Karl. 1981. *Capital: A Critique of Political Economy*, vol.3. trans. David Fernbach. London: Penguin Books. pp. 352–353.

[119] Marx, Karl. 1981. *Capital: A Critique of Political Economy*, vol.3. trans. David Fernbach. London: Penguin Books. p.615.

[120] Marx, Karl. 1972. *Critique of the Gotha Program*. Beijing: Foreign Languages Press. p.15.

[121] Smith, Adam. 1976. *The Theory of Moral Sentiments*. Oxford: Oxford University Press. p.231.

Problem".[122] Such a "paradox" has led scholars to debate whether the economic man and the moral man should be separated and whether economics should "speak of morality".[123]

However, from the perspective of the alternating creation and revision of "The Theory of Moral Sentiments" and "An Inquiry into the Nature and Causes of the Wealth of Nations", as well as Adam Smith's entire research and writing plan, his ideological system is fundamentally consistent. As a matter of fact, Smith did not intentionally create a personality split between the "economic man" and the "moral man". In fact, the work "An Inquiry into the Nature and Causes of the Wealth of Nations" does not abandon compassion and justice, nor does "The Theory of Moral Sentiments" abandon the self-interest nature of human beings. Therefore, it is more accurate to say that Smith sought to transcend both and allow them to complement, constrain, and coexist harmoniously[124] rather than that he foresaw the tension and conflict of the opposing poles of human nature in commercial society. This means that Adam Smith stands between the economic man and the moral man, holding both ends to find a "middle ground". The reason why the "Adam Smith Revolution" is called a "revolution" may lie in his attempt to move from the "two" (the "new moral man" developed from the Renaissance and Enlightenment, and the "new economic man" shaped by the progress of commerce and the formation of a market economy) to the "three" (coordinating and transcending of the two). How to move towards the "three"? This is a major issue for modern society. Unfortunately, the highly valuable topic that Adam Smith implicitly raised has been more often disassembled later, regressing from moving towards the "three" to a dichotomy that is contrary and diverging, turning people into "one-dimensional" desire-driven atoms.

The above analysis demonstrates that these three thinkers, based on the realities and conflicts of their respective times, analyzed economic and social issues holistically rather than in isolation, and comprehensively rather than uni-dimensionally. Whether Smith's denial of monism in human nature, Keynes' opposition to the laissez-faire theory of classical economics, or Marx's critique of capitalism, all aimed to illustrate that economic analysis, which focuses only on one aspect while ignoring the whole, or which, though seeing the whole, still persists in one aspect, will inevitably fall into a crisis of theory and reality.[125] Ironically, the financial crisis

[122] Montes, L. 2003. Das Adam Smith problem: its origins, the stages of the current debate, and one implication for our understanding of sympathy. *Journal of the History of Economic Thought*. 25 (1): 63–90.

[123] Wan, Junren. 2000. On the moral dimension of the market economy. *Chinese Social Sciences*. (2): 5. Also in: Wan, Junren. 2000. *The Dimension of Morality: An Introduction to Modern Economic Ethics*. Guangzhou: Guangdong People's Publishing House.

[124] White, Jonathan B. 2002. *Saving Adam Smith: a Tale of Wealth, Transformation, and Virtue*. Upper Saddle River: Prentice Hall.

[125] Although Karl Marx and Keynes are economists with completely different temperaments, from Smith's perspective there is one point in common between the two: their economic theories both contain a strong humanistic concern. Specifically speaking, they are both responding to the moder-

that erupted in 2008 provides a vivid footnote to the theoretical crisis: weren't the lessons summarized in the post-crisis era, like the blindly trust of economic rationality, free markets, and capitalism as the end of history, already warned about or predicted by thinkers in the history?

7.5 Changing Tradition and the "Ever-normal Law"

7.5.1 The Path of Holistic and Coordinated Reform

For a long period of time, due to the belief that "socialism—planned economy" and "capitalism—market economy" are logically independent from each other, people firmly believed that these two economic categories are irreconcilable opposites. However, with practical exploration, the Chinese gradually discovered that the binary judgment of "socialism with planned economy" and "capitalism with market economy" is a dogmatic and one-sided understanding. For example, if "socialism" is studied within the context of its developmental history, its "primary stage" has its obvious shortcomings. Since there are shortcomings, effective means are needed to compensate for, enrich, and strengthen it, for which the market economy is a good means. In the view of Deng Xiaoping, the chief architect of the reform and opening-up in China, socialism and market economy can be fully coordinated, and there is no fundamental conflict between the two. He made the famous assertion that contemporary Chinese people are familiar with during his "Southern Tour":

> The proportion of planning to market forces is not the essential difference between socialism and capitalism. A planned economy is not equivalent to socialism, because there is planning under capitalism too; a market economy is not capitalism, because there are markets under socialism too. Planning and market forces are both means of controlling economic activity. The essence of socialism is liberation and development of the productive forces, elimination of exploitation and polarization, and the ultimate achievement of prosperity for all.[126]

Engels, in his comments of Marx's worldview, said that "his way of viewing things is not a doctrine but a method. It does not provide ready-made dogmas, but criteria for further research and the method for this research."[127] Abandoning dogmatism and bookishness, contemporary China has designated "socialist market economy" as the fundamental economic system for its primary stage because Deng Xiaoping,

---

nity issue raised by Adam Smith, i.e. how to unify the economic man and the moral man in modern society.

[126] Deng, Xiaoping. 1994. *Selected Works of Deng Xiaoping, vol.*3. Beijing: Foreign Languages Press. p.361.

[127] Engels, Frederick. 1976. Engels to W. Sombark, March 11, 1895. in Marx, Karl and Frederick Engels. *Karl Marx and Frederick Engels: Selected Works*, vol.3. Moscow: Progress Publishers. p.506.

the wise designers, guided by historical materialism and dialectical methodology, recognized that a market economy can support and strengthen socialism at this stage. Although socialism and market economy may seem contradictory, they are actually fully compatible and unifiable. The tremendous achievements in China's economic development demonstrate that such "combination of the two" — an economic system that acknowledges opposition yet strikes a balance of the two — has provided China with vast spaces for economic innovation and development without losing the fundamental principles or direction.

If we further abstract the dialectical logic of the "socialist market economy", we can still reduce it to an A-B model, namely, "A yet B" (i.e. A is significant, yet B is indispensable). Here, A represents "socialism" and B "market economy". Socialism (A) is the main body, while the market economy (B) can effectively assist in the development of socialism. Socialism is a good system, but single socialism may have limitations under specific historical conditions. Especially when China's socialism is still in its primary stage, it is necessary to have the seemingly opposing B to support and assist A, compensating for A's deficiencies while maintaining A's dominant position. In 1991, when inspecting Shanghai, Deng Xiaoping clearly stated, "Don't think that any planned economy is socialist and any market economy is capitalist. That's not the way things are. In fact, planning and regulation by the market are both means of controlling economic activity, and the market can also serve socialism."[128] This means that although socialism (A) is the main body, the market economy (B) is indispensable, because without the market economy the essence and superiority of socialism cannot be manifested in its primary stage. Therefore, in the dialectical model of "socialist market economy" (A yet B), the institutional rationality of A requires it to modestly adopt B. Of course, in the model of "A yet B", it is also necessary to restrain and balance B with A to prevent B from trending towards profit-seeking extremes (which can be expressed as "B but not B+"). China's market economy must be based on the premise of the basic system of socialism, and the market economy must serve the general direction of socialism.

However, such a system cannot find its basis in mainstream Western economic theories, the "classical" dogmas of which still hold that socialism, public ownership and market economy cannot coexist with or even mutually repel each other. For the Chinese, the wisdom of applying "the mean" has revealed the compatibility that exists between seemingly contradictory objects. The rationale of "the mean" coordinates and unifies socialism and market economy by means of integration, forming a distinctive characteristic of the Chinese path.[129]

---

[128] Deng, Xiaoping. 1994. *Selected Works of Deng Xiaoping*, vol.3. Beijing: Foreign Languages Press. p. 354.

[129] In the 1930s, the Polish economist Oskar Ryszard Lange (1904–1965) combined Western mainstream economics with Marxist political economy, theoretically breaking through the dogmatic model of their mutual opposition at the early stage. Lange believed that market competition and public ownership were not only not contradictory but also compatible; a competitive market and centralized planning could complement and integrate with each other in resource allocation; and

Following this logic, we can further sum up some typical A-B models in China's contemporary economy, which are hereby illustrated with examples.

The first is concerned with the choice of the basic economic system. If public ownership is A and multiple forms of ownership are B, then the basic economic system that develops multiple forms of ownership with public ownership as the main body is "A yet B". This is a dialectical model that is compatible with the "socialist market economy". Here, public ownership (A) serves as the fundamental guarantee of the social system, while multiple forms of ownership (B) are the inherently required for a market economy. The joint development of public ownership (A) as the main body and multiple forms of ownership (B) is the suitable path for ever-normal development of China after its constant exploration and summarization of economic transformation. At the beginning of the reform and opening-up, facing the large-scale but low-efficiency state-owned economy, China did not rush to promote stock reform but instead actively introduced and developed various forms of ownership outside the system in a gradual manner. Through incremental reforms, the monism economy was transformed into dualism economy, improving the operational efficiency and stability of the economy and cultivating the soil for the development of a new system. After reducing the risks of reform, China, under favorable conditions for system transformation, compelled a series of reforms for state-owned enterprises to adapt to marketization. The reform for joint development of public ownership as the main body and multiple forms of ownership effectively illustrates the dialectical logic of "A yet B": by introducing B, applying B to support A, and promoting A with B, the state could draw forth a driving force beneficial to economic development between the seemingly contradictory parts, allowing A and B to perform in a mutually competitive, complementary and vibrant market, and further consolidating the dominant position of A, thereby strengthening the socialist system.

In the ownership model of "A yet B", another coordinated policy that China has consistently adhered to is encouraging the development of the non-public sectors of economy. By implementing and refining policies that support the growth of the private economy, eliminating unreasonable obstacles that hinder its development, and broadening and advancing access for private enterprises into various sectors, China has promoted the development of private economy and private enterprises which have been growing and thriving for the past four decades, becoming a crucial pillar and integral part of national economy. Consequently, during the theoretical and practical exploration of reform and opening-up, China has established a fundamental economic system with distinctive characteristics, namely the "two unswervinglys" (unswervingly to consolidate and develop the public sector, and to encourage, support, and guide development of the non-public sector).

the principle of resource allocation through competitive markets could be combined with the socialist principle of distribution according to work. See: Luo, Weidong and Jiang Ziqiang. 1994. The Lange model and the theory of socialist market economy: The historical origins of the theory of socialist market economy. *Academic Monthly*. (5): 41–46. Although the exploration of China's socialist market economy has drawn on theories like Lange's, we believe that the Chinese traditional dialectical thinking is a more fundamental reason.

The "two unswervinglys" represent the two principal lines of ownership, but this "two" is a coordinated and symbiotic whole. For instance, the market competitiveness formed by the non-state-owned economy cannot be separated from the basic products and infrastructure provided by the state-owned economy. The expansion policies of the state-owned economy during economic downturns create a relatively stable market environment for market entities, including those in the non-state-owned economy, while private economy's participation in state-owned enterprises optimizes the latter's governance. Throughout the history of the People's Republic of China, the evolution of the ownership structure as the economic foundation can be summarized as follows: "developing from none to one"—establishing public ownership through socialist transformation to lay the economic foundation of the socialist system; "developing from one to two"—developing the non-public economy outside the planned system and fostering a market economy through transformation; "developing from two to three" or "converging two into one"—achieving binary coordination between public and non-public ownership to create a new form of ownership suitable for the primary stage of socialism, thus promoting stable economic and social development. Starting from one, progressing to two, and then dialectically integrating them into a whole, this is a continuous and indivisible process that reflects Chinese social practice under the dialectical materialism viewpoint, achieving a unity between theoretical logic and historical logic.

The second is concerned with adhering to the fundamental functions of an industry to prevent its excessive or abnormal development. If A represents the normal state of economic affairs, and A+ signifies an extreme deviation, then the model "A but not A+" means avoiding "excess being just as bad as deficiency", embodying a policy choice that "the wise stay far from all extremes, all surfeit, all grandeur".[130] For instance, the fundamental role of finance is to serve the real economy, using virtual means to support and enhance the real. However, due to the potential risks in finance, speculative activities in financial markets can easily push A towards A+. This is manifested as highly leveraged financial "euphoria", self-inflation, and the continuous creation of financial bubbles through "idle spinning" detached from the real economy, ultimately evolving into systemic crises. There is warning for this in the book *I Ching (Book of Changes)*, "The word haughty indicates knowing to advance but not to retreat, knowing to maintain existence but not to let perish, and knowing to gain but not to lose."[131] The 2008 financial crisis stands as a typical lesson of greedy financial capital going from A to A+. Therefore, while actively developing financial markets in recent years, China has continually strengthened financial regulation and vigilance against industries (such as real estate) shifting from real to virtual economy due to financialization.[132] By suppressing speculation,

---

[130] Laozi. 2001. *Dao De Jing: the Book of the Way*. trans. Moss Roberts. Berkeley, Los Angeles and London: University of California Press. p.90.

[131] Huang, Alfred. 1998. *The Complete I Ching*. Vermont: Inner Traditions. p.37.

[132] As is reported by Xi Jinping, the Chinese president and general secretary of the Communist Party of China Central Committee, it is a fundamental policy of the Chinese government "adhering to the principle that housing is for living in and not for speculation". See: Xi, Jinping. 2017. *Secure*

deleveraging, and squeezing out bubbles, we aim to eliminate potential risks and maintain a healthy state of "being A but not A+". If "A yet B" (i.e., A is significant, yet B is indispensable) embodies the compatibility of contemporary China's dialectical view of economy under socialism, then "A but not A+" well demonstrates its awareness of potential risks. Emphasizing a prudent and cautious approach to economic development and a "bottom-line thinking" by preparing for the worst, is essentially a reverse cognition of "A but not A+", which is to view A from the perspective of A+. This is aimed both at preventing problems before they arise and at better understanding the essence of A. "A but not A+" is a governance model in the economic field that is difficult to control. It requires a deep analysis of the economic and financial crises in capitalist societies, a profound understanding of the nature of currency and finance under market economy conditions, and the ability to discern subtle signs in policy practice. This involves taking proactive measures to build a robust financial and monetary system while maintaining "A but not A+". It is a significant task for ensuring the stable development of the contemporary Chinese economy. As the saying goes, "a humbling is spared by few wants, a miscarriage by knowing the limits; Thus one can abide and endure."[133] "Deepening the reform of the financial system, enhancing the ability of financial services to support the real economy… Improving the financial regulatory system and safeguarding the bottom line of not allowing systemic financial risks"[134] have set the basic principles for the model of "A but not A+" in the financial industry.

The third involves interval regulation of economic fluctuations. If excessive economic prosperity is designated as A and economic depression as B, then "neither A nor B" represents "the mean" of interval regulation. This is often expressed in China's macroeconomic policies as "preventing large fluctuations in the economy" and "keeping the macroeconomic operation within a reasonable range." "Neither A nor B" is the negation of "A yet B". In the model of "A yet B", A is the main body, and B is used to assist and develop A, and maintain A's dominant position. In the model "A but not A+", A remains the main body, while "not A+" is aimed at preventing A from sliding into extremes. However, in the model "neither A nor B", the requirement is to avoid leaning toward either side. Compared to the previous two models, "neither A nor B" more intuitively reflects the balanced view of dialectical thinking, allowing both A and B to be moderated. Since the reform and opening-up, with the continuous enhancement of China's macroeconomic regulation

a Decisive Victory in Building a Moderately Prosperous Society in All Respects and Strive for the Great Success of Socialism with Chinese Characteristics for a New Era: Report to the 19th National Congress of the Communist Party of China. Beijing: People's Publishing House. p. 47.

[133] Laozi. 2001. *Dao De Jing: the Book of the Way*. trans. Moss Roberts. Berkeley, Los Angeles and London: University of California Press. p.121

[134] Xi, Jinping. 2017. *Secure a Decisive Victory in Building a Moderately Prosperous Society in All Respects and Strive for the Great Success of Socialism with Chinese Characteristics for a New Era: Report to the 19th National Congress of the Communist Party of China*. Beijing: People's Publishing House. p. 34.

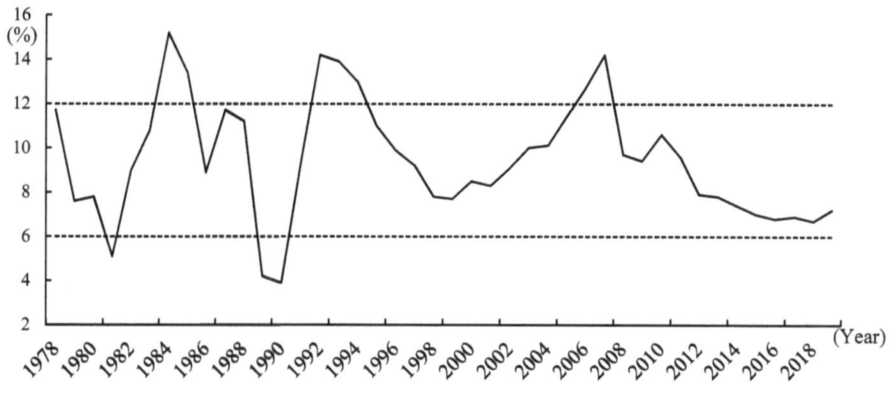

Fig. 7.1 China's annual GDP growth rate. Source: website of The National Bureau of Statistics, P. R. China. https://data.stats.gov.cn/easyquery.htm?cn=C01&zb=A0208&sj=2019

capabilities, the economy has adjusted in a timely manner in response to institutional transformations and ever-changing domestic and international situations. Overall, macroeconomic policies have neither been too tight nor too loose, nor have they fluctuated erratically, thus ensuring a smooth transition between different stages of economic development. (See Fig. 7.1).

The fourth addresses the relationship between economic development and environmental protection. Environmental protection is A, and economic development is B, giving rise to the model of "both A and B". President Xi Jinping's "Two Mountains Theory"—"lucid waters and lush mountains are invaluable assets" and "we need both green mountains and clear waters and mountains of gold and silver"—exemplifies the model of "both A and B". It views environmental protection and economic development, as well as short-term economic benefits and long-term social and resource-environmental benefits, as an integrated whole. "Both A and B" is the negation of "neither A nor B". If the aforementioned "neither A nor B" best represents the concept of "the mean" (*zhong*), then "both A and B" best expresses the concept of "harmony" (*he*). In other words, it aims to create a positive interaction between economic development and environmental protection, achieving the goal of mutual benefits and promotion. "Only through mutual respect can there be mutual benefit."

"Both A and B" is a further development of "A yet B". In "A yet B", only A is the main body, while in "both A and B" both A and B are the main bodies holding equal status. This means that in formulation of policies, both economic development and environmental protection should be taken into consideration equally. However, if A and B cannot coordinate their relationship well to achieve "harmony" (*he*) under present conditions, such as in areas facing ecological fragility where the ecosystem is difficult to restore once damaged during economic development, then obviously "both A and B" cannot be achieved for such prominent contradictions under current capabilities and technological conditions. If A and B cannot be reconciled, it is necessary to appeal to the overall principle of national well-being and general philosophy of development—"socialism". The conclusion is that overall and long-term interests are superior to partial and short-term interests, rejecting the practice of sacrificing the ecological environment for temporary economic growth. In other words, we need "rather green mountains and clear waters than mountains of gold and silver". From this perspective, "both A and B" also contains the inherent requirement to prioritize "A" or "B" according to specific time and place. It adheres to the principle of "analyzing specific issues in a specific context, with everything dependent on time, place, and conditions", and "both emphasizing the dialectical relationship and focusing on key points".[135] In the "Two Mountains Theory", the focus on "rather green mountains and clear waters than mountains of gold and silver", although seemingly biased towards one end ("green mountains and clear waters"), is actually based on the holistic perspective of harmonizing A and B, ultimately preserving the other end ("mountains of gold and silver") in the long run.

In the path of economic development with Chinese characteristics, the model "both A and B" is presented in another typical example. We know that comparative advantage and the strategies of comprehensive catch-up (reverse comparative advantage) are two industrial paths that late-developing countries can adopt for industrialization. The former selectively develops cost-advantage industries through market mechanisms, while the latter relies more on national power to build an industrial system. On a comprehensive evaluation, both industrial strategies have their respective advantages and disadvantages.[136] Since the reform and opening-up, China has drew lessons from the planned economy era for its industrial strategy while not completely relying on market selection of industries. Instead, it has combined comparative advantage with reverse comparative advantage, achieving a complementary relationship between their strengths and a mutual elimination of their weaknesses. This has led to an industrial development path that can be termed "appropriate catch-up", characterized by the "both A and B" approach.[137] It has formed a "dual structure" in the industrial system, where some enterprises participate in the global value chain and industrial division of labor, while others pursue an independent development path. This "mixed" industrial policy, which emphasizes unleashing the creativity of the main entities while fully utilizing market laws

[135] Publicity Department of the CPC Central Committee. 2018. *Thirty Lectures on Xi Jinping's Thought on Socialism with Chinese Characteristics for a New Era.* Beijing: Xuexi Chuban She (Learning Press). pp. 112, 332.

[136] Although comparative advantage follows market principles, it can easily fall into the "comparative advantage trap", which hinders industrial upgrading in the context of national competition. While comprehensive catching up can avoid the "comparative advantage trap" through government intervention, the industrial system established in this way is largely isolated from the market, resulting in a lack of "self-generating capacity" and making sustainable industrial development difficult.

[137] Xian, Wen and Li Dawei. 2016. The development strategy of late-developing countries: from comparative advantage to appropriate catch-up. *Social Sciences in Ningxia.* (5): 76–83.

to adapt to circumstances, has not only endowed industrial development with "self-generating capacity" but has also seized opportunities in some key areas, taking the initiative and achieving significant breakthroughs through self-reliance.

The dialectical model of "both A and B" has been practiced in many other ways in China's reform. The following are some examples: the dual-track pricing system implemented during the transition from a planned economy to a market economy, where state-controlled prices and market-regulated prices coexisted; balancing the relationship between development and stability in the reform and opening up; leveraging the initiatives of both central and local governments in macroeconomic management; and coordinating the economic and social development of different regions.

It should be noted that the above examples do not imply that there are no problems in China's overall path of coordinated development. We must recognize that the drawbacks of one-size-fits-all, one-sided, and mechanical approaches to economic issues are still prevalent in various fields. As reforms deepen, the various structural problems and contradictions that originally existed in economic development become more prominent. This requires us to consciously upgrade the gradually maturing economic thoughts and practices with Chinese characteristics into fundamental methodologies or principles, in order to better serve economic development.

7.5.2 "The Ever-normal Principle"

The Chinese have applied dialectical thinking in determining the economic system and addressing major economic issues in the process of reform. By connecting these elements, one can observe their uniqueness: viewing the economy and society as an organic system with first focus on the whole. When confronted with problems and conflicts, they do not resolve them in a simplistic either-or manner, as focusing solely on "this end" would lead to the loss of "the other", making it difficult for "this end" to sustain itself in the long run. The approach adopted is to embrace opposing views inclusively, collaborate with all parties, adapt to changing circumstances, avoid extremism, embrace the moderate way of inclusiveness, and form an economic system and policy framework characterized by comprehensive balance, coordination, and integrated policy implementation.

In this way, it is possible to grasp the complementarity and unity of the various aspects in the economy and society, to take into consideration "the big picture" and "the overall account", to grasp the reasonable "degree" of economic development, and to dynamically and flexibly determine optimal policies from a higher level. This ensures that the economic layout is comprehensive and strategic, and that economic development maintains stability, flexibility, adaptability and resilience. It effectively prevents transitions from stability to crisis, creating significant enormous upward potential for economic growth and providing maneuvering space for economic

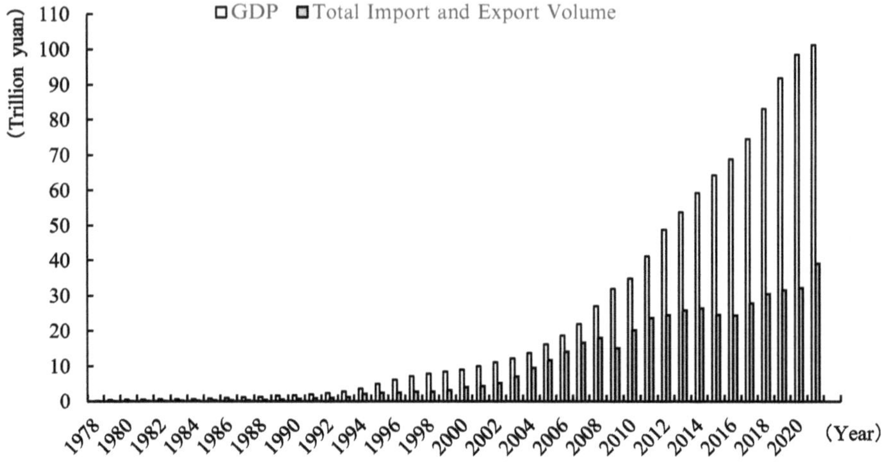

Fig. 7.2 China's GDP and total import and export volume. Source: website of National Bureau of Statistics, P. R. China https://data.stats.gov.cn/easyquery.htm?cn=C01

adjustments. Consequently, it can effectively dissolve, buffer and avoid various negative impacts, turning large waves into small fluctuations and turning crises into opportunities, thereby ensuring decades of stable development of the Chinese economy. Although it is gradual from the perspective of the development process, in terms of the medium-and-long-term outcomes (see Figs. 7.2 and 7.3), it demonstrates a steady and far-reaching trajectory, accumulating what has astonished the world as the "Chinese miracle".

Throughout the economic development path of China since the reform and opening up, the reason for China's remarkable economic achievements lies mainly in "maintaining balance through the mean" under the overarching direction of socialism. This principle can explain why the Chinese economy been able to maintain stability and achieve long-term success. When the logic of both history and reality is presented together, it may come as a surprise. The economic tradition of "maintaining balance through the mean" is consistent between ancient and modern times; it has always been embedded in the thinking of the Chinese people and remains vibrant.

Vibrant traditions inevitably contain elements of regularity. Based on the above discussion, we can make the following summary.

In the twentieth century, one of the easily overlooked yet crucial reasons why China chose Marxism (economics), which upholds dialectical materialism, as the backbone of its theoretical framework among various Western economic ideas is its "commensurability" with China's (economic) tradition in the sense of T. Kuhn's "paradigm". In other words, Marxism (economics) found its grounding, rooting and reconstruction in China through an inherent "link" originating from the primary ideological and cultural system of the Axial Age. The core of this primary ideological and cultural system is the dialectical mode of thinking discussed in detail in

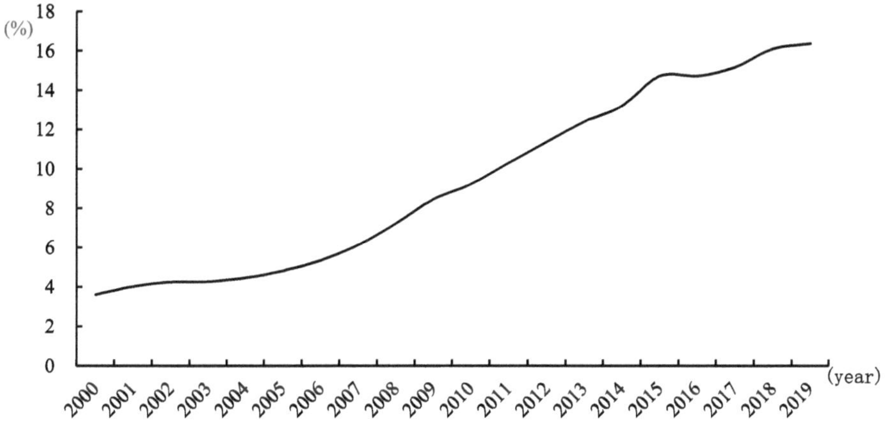

Fig. 7.3 The proportion of China's GDP in the world. Source: website of World Bank, https://data.worldbank.org.cn/indicator/NY.GDP.MKTP.CD?end=2019&name_desc=false&start=1960&view=chart

Sect. 7.3 of this chapter. In the Chinese context, simple expressions of this mode include "the reciprocal process of *yin* and *yang* is called the Dao", "now all things are born of the two, *yin* and *yang*, with reciprocal reference to each other, so that a third comes into being", "one object has two forms", and "pairs of contradictory objects".[138] Thus, it can be concluded that the dialectical thinking, epistemological foundation of "maintaining balance through the mean", is consistent between ancient and modern China. In the twentieth century, Chinese people invented, inherited and developed this excellent cultural tradition through the modern theoretical system of Marxism (economics), which in turn localized Marxism (economics) and was creatively transformed for their own use.

China's traditional dialectical thinking recognizes that things have opposing sides or contradictions, yet they also constitute an inseparable unity. "Opposition" here does not mean "standing opposite each other" or "opponent" but rather signifies a "pair" or "mutual rooting of *yin* and *yang*". Laozi stated, "bend to not break, wrong leads to right, depletion to expansion, ruin to revival."[139] Marx clearly articulated this through the relationship between production and consumption: "Each of them is not only directly the other, nor does it merely mediate the other, but each of

[138] Cheng Hao stated, "All things have their counterparts—*yin* and *yang*, good and evil... This principle, when extrapolated, reaches far and wide. Does it not?" See: Cheng, Hao and Cheng Yi. 2004. *The Collected works of Cheng Hao and Cheng Yi*, vol.11. ed. Wang, Xiaoyu. Beijing: Zhonghua Book Company. p. 123.

[139] Laozi. 2001. *Dao De Jing: the Book of the Way*. trans. Moss Roberts. Berkeley, Los Angeles and London: University of California Press. p.76.

the two, by the fact of its taking place, creates the other, creates itself as the other."[140] In China today, a typical expression of this same way of thinking is "lucid waters and lush mountains are invaluable assets." Such unity or identity requires the cognitive subject to "hold fast to oneness",[141] meaning that only by focusing on a holistic view rather than isolated or partial view can one deeply grasp the essence of things. Therefore, the harmonious unity of evolving from two to three—achieving an internal balance of the whole to facilitate its development—becomes an important methodology. This is the "underlying principle" in maintaining balance through the mean. The "underlying principle" is the unchanging "one". But when applied, it exhibits "differentiation" according to different issues and situations. Thus, "the mean" in "maintaining balance through the mean" is far from being a simple midpoint or median in geometric or algebraic terms. In practice, "the mean" is transforms into four A-B models. When the four models namely "A yet B", "A(B) but not A+(B+)", "neither A nor B" and "both A and B" are put together, it is found that "the mean" represents any one point or two points (or even several points) between the opposing sides A and B,[142] flexibly adapted to different problems and situations. At the same time, it is a balanced state that conforms to "the mean" in specific time and space. It is not a unprincipled compromise or a fixed or rigid state. In other words, the four A-B models encompass all possibilities for unifying and coordinating A and B. Although these countless possibilities lie between A and B, they transcend A and B, representing a series of higher-level balances — dynamic balances that adapt to circumstances and progress with the times. Their economic manifestation is "ever-normal balance".

Collectively, these four A-B models constitute a logically rigorous, complementary and mutually supportive combination of "the mean", giving us ample reason to collectively refer to them as the "ever-normal principle". The ever-normal principle, through dialectical thinking, points out a practical path for development of the economic society, emphasizing the need to focus on the whole and to systematically promote it. Only in this way can reasonable development goals be set and the pace of development controlled within a comprehensive perspective, effectively addressing uncertainties. In terms of epistemology and methodology, the ever-normal principle abandons the black-or-white cognition and unifies conflicting parties with an approach of "harmony" (*he*). The unity is achieved through "the mean". In the seemingly chaotic "gray" state, it effectively utilizes, guides and regulates the "potential differences" and "energy" endogenous to conflicts so that "harmony

[140] Marx, Karl and Frederick Engels. 1986. *Karl Marx and Frederick Engels: Selected Works*, vol.3. Moscow: Progress Publishers. p.30.

[141] Laozi. 2001. *Dao De Jing: the Book of the Way*. trans. Moss Roberts. Berkeley, Los Angeles and London: University of California Press. p. 76.

[142] Currently, the regional development policy that coordinates development among regions with different levels of economic development is a typical example of the "multi-point theory". It takes into account all regions of China, including the eastern, western, central and northeastern regions.

begets new things",[143] allowing the economic society to maintain vitality and resilience through inclusiveness and acceptance. This creates a stable structure that avoids exclusivity while enabling all parties and elements to promote and constrain each other, thereby preventing extremes, ensuring long-term development, and accumulating remarkable development achievements. Application of "the mean" relies on various aspects of economic affairs while transcending them, and only by transcending them can the ever-normal state be achieved. Therefore, "maintaining balance through the mean" reveals a law of causation in the economic field, which decomposes into four A-B models for different problems and situations, representing the specific manifestation of the ever-normal principle. Among them, "A yet B" is particularly difficult to understand and grasp. While recognizing the value of A and adhering to it, one must also deeply recognize A's limitations under specific temporal and spatial conditions and using its opposite B to assist and enrich it. This completely frees oneself from the metaphysical and dogmatic understanding of certain economic ideas or affairs—as Marx succinctly pointed out the key point: "it (the dialectic) does not let itself be impressed by anything, being in its very essence critical and revolutionary."[144] The model "A yet B" breaks through the sharp dichotomy and opens up a path of critical and innovative understanding through the cognition of "the mean" and the approach of "harmony", demonstrating the distinctive characteristics of Chinese economic thought and practice.

Strictly speaking, the four dialectical modes of the ever-normal principle are not parallel but have an inherent hierarchy and structure. Among them, "A yet B" holds a foundational and decisive position in determining the basic economic forms. For example, the dialectical modes of contemporary Chinese economy are governed and constrained by the overarching principle of the socialist market economy ("A yet B"). Without the unity of socialism and market economy, the unity of value rationality and instrumental rationality, and the unity of righteousness and profit, the various practices of "the mean" we discuss herein (such as the basic economic system with public ownership as the mainstay and diverse forms of ownership developing alongside it, and the macro policies combining market regulation and government control) would be inconceivable. Furthermore, when coordinating major economic relationships and handling the contradictions, it is essential to start from the fundamental requirements and core values of socialism and adhere to the ultimate value rationality of socialism, which serves as the basic program and commanding height

[143] The notion that harmony begets new things was advanced by Grand Astrologer Shibo in the late Western Zhou dynasty. He believed different things, when coexisting in harmony, would complement each other and beget new things. When applied to political governance, this concept requires those in power to preserve the particular features of different people and things and allow them to flourish. This nurtures the growth of new things and promotes the development of society. See: "Harmony Begets New Things", https://www.chinesethought.cn/EN/shuyu_show.aspx?shuyu_id=4475.

[144] Marx, Karl. 1976. Postface to the Second Edition. Marx, Karl. *Capital: A Critique of Political Economy*, vol.1. trans. Ben Fowkes. London: Penguin Books. p.103.

for addressing economic and social issues. Therefore, the ever-normal principle is flexible in response to changes in time and space, while also maintaining certain constant amidst change; this constant is "the mean", implicitly encompassing the grand idea that "the world belongs to all" (*tianxia weigong*).[145] Why does "the mean" entail "all" (*gong*, public)? Laozi stated, "Acceptance (means) magnanimity".[146] It is with magnanimity that one can uphold "the mean", displaying a mindset of publicness. Conversely, it is easier to understand that without "a mindset of publicness", how can one transcend the narrow confines of personal and group interests to genuinely perceive the entirety of economic affairs and apply "the mean" dialectically?

If we regard the philosophical view and methodology embodied in "maintaining balance through the mean" as a "principle", then then the phrase "ever-normal" (*chang*) cannot simply be interpreted as "frequently" (*jingchang*) or "always" (*changhyou*). It also includes Laozi's understanding of *chang* at the level of "Dao", i.e. the unchanging "natural order". Laozi stated, "Returning life, call natural order; To know this order, inner vision. Not to know it is delusion. Delusion will produce misfortune."[147] The ever-normal principle, which emerges from dialectical thinking, represents a unique creation of the Chinese in the field of economics and constitutes a significant contribution of the Chinese to economic theory.

Historically examined, the economic connotations of A and B are continuously evolving, undergoing a dynamic process from A1-B1 to A2-B2, and further to A3-B3, and so on. Therefore, the ever-normal principle is a dynamic theoretical system that is capable of self-transformation. In the *qing-zhong* theory of *Guanzi*, it is asserted that in the process of "*qing-zhong*-balance (*heng*)" "there can be no specific figure for maintaining a proper balance in the economy." This not only signifies

---

[145] The World Belongs to All (*tianxia weigong*): The world is a public realm and therefore belongs to all the people. *Tianxia*, which literally means everything under heaven, used to refer to the monarch, state power, or the nation; later it extended to mean the whole world. In the narrow sense, *gong* refers to figures with both integrity and competence, while in the broad sense it refers to all the people of a country, or everyone in the world. This term has two meanings. The first is that the position of a ruler is not the private property of just one person or his family, but rather belongs to all people of virtue and ability. Hence, the throne should be passed on to people according to their merit rather than through bloodline. The second meaning is that a country does not belong to a single individual or family, but belongs to the public. This is a people-centered vision, which opposes hereditary rule and believes that people with virtue and competence should be selected to exercise power. Ancient Chinese held this to be the foundation and guarantee for people to enjoy a happy life and realize universal harmony. In modern times, it evolved into a key concept calling for overthrowing autocracy and realizing democracy and later into a longing for an ideal society. In *Li Ji* (The Book of Rites), there are following words: "When the Great Way prevails, the world belongs to all the people. People of virtue and competence are chosen to govern the country; honesty is valued and people live in harmony."

See: "The World Belongs to All": http://www.chinesethought.cn/EN/shuyu_show.aspx?shuyu_id=4006.

[146] Laozi. 2001. *Dao De Jing: the Book of the Way*. trans. Moss Roberts. Berkeley, Los Angeles and London: University of California Press. p.64.

[147] Laozi. 2001. *Dao De Jing: the Book of the Way*. trans. Moss Roberts. Berkeley, Los Angeles and London: University of California Press. p.64.

that the quantity of balance is boundless but also indicates that the content and structure of balance are in a grand process of constant change. Hence, people must keep pace with the times by "observing the seasons and establishing policy standards".[148] In the context of globalization, under new historical conditions and in the new era of socialism, the Chinese people stand at the intersection of past and present, as well as East and West, unifying theoretical and historical logic in practice. With a more inclusive and open view, they have endowed the ever-normal principle with new connotations. The self-renewal and revival of the ever-normal principle have unleashed tremendous energy, and the modern transformation of economic traditions has enabled it to achieve a significant historical transcendence.

Going through twists and turns, we have come a long way from Ever-normal Granary to ever-normal principle. And the next chapter will return to Ever-normal Granary to propose a clear policy system based on the intrinsic requirements of the development of the socialist economy with Chinese characteristics in the new era.

[148] Guanzi. 1998. *Political, Economic, and Philosophical Essays from Early China*, vol. 2. trans. W. Allyn Rickett. Princeton: Princeton University Press. p. 443.

Chapter 8

Constructing a Modern Large Ever-normal Granary

Confucius said, "What is danger? It arises when one is satisfied with his security and neglects danger. What is to perish? It arises when one is satisfied with his survival and neglects death. What is disorder? It arises when one is satisfied with things in order and neglects disorder. Therefore the superior person does not forget danger when he is in security, nor does he forget death when he is well, nor does he forget disorder when his affairs are in order. In this way he gains personal safety and is able to protect the empire. Thus, the I says, 'Forget not! Forget not! Tying up to the trunks of mulberry trees.'"
—*I Ching (Book of Changes)*[1]

Accordingly, the wise know how to salvage men
And make sure none go to waste;
They know how to salvage things
And make sure none go to waste;
This is called far-reaching insight.
—*Laozi (Spring and Autumn Period)*[2]

As socialism with Chinese characteristics has entered a new era, the principal contradiction in Chinese society has evolved into that between unbalanced and inadequate development and the people's ever-growing needs for a better life. A series of issues and challenges, such as economic structural transformation, rural revitalization, and constraints imposed by resources and the environment, need to be addressed and solved one by one within a certain period to achieve high-quality economic and social development. The insights and enlightenment from the evolution and transcendence of Ever-normal Granary from past and present and from China to the West provide a feasible approach for China to promote high-quality development. Specifically, starting from China's national conditions, we should comprehensively and systematically integrate population, agricultural and

[1] Huang, Alfred. 1998. *The Complete I Ching*. Vermont: Inner Traditions. p.130.

[2] Laozi. *Dao De Jing: the Book of the Way*. 2001. trans. Moss Roberts. Berkeley, Los Angeles and London: University of California Press. p86.

W. Xian, *Chinese Food Security Strategy*, Research Series on the Chinese Dream and China's Development Path,
https://doi.org/10.1007/978-981-95-7964-8_8

industrial bulk products, and basic resources into the policy framework of "Modern Grand Ever-normal Granary". By flexibly applying the principle of buffer buying and selling, we can establish a socialist modern grand Ever-normal Granary with Chinese characteristics in the new era, which is based on full employment and stable supply of bulk products, guaranteed by sustainable utilization of basic resources, with inclusive, stable, secure and sustainable development as its basic requirements.

8.1 People Orientation: Ever-normal Granary of Labor Force

The socialist Ever-normal Granary of Labor Force is a people-oriented buffer and stabilizing system aimed at achieving full employment. It coordinates the efforts of the government, market and society, relying on public products to reserve, cultivate and release labor force. The "Report to the 20th National Congress of the Communist Party of China" states, "Implementing the employment-first strategy. Employment is the most basic component of the people's wellbeing. We need to intensify efforts to implement the employment-first policy and improve related mechanisms to promote high-quality and full employment. We will refine the public services system for employment and the system of providing employment support for key groups and do more to help those in difficulty find employment and meet their basic needs…In this way, we will ensure that everyone has the opportunity to pursue a career through hard work."[3] The clear arrangements for full employment, fair employment, and making the best use of everyone's abilities provide tremendous potential for the development and construction of the Ever-normal Granary of Labor Force.

Since the entry into the twenty-first century, with the continuous expansion of its economic volume, China's economic development philosophy has undergone significant adjustments. "In the context of an underdeveloped economic level, the main task for a period of time is to run fast. However, after covering a certain distance, we should pay attention adjusting relationships and focusing on the overall effectiveness of development. Otherwise, the 'barrel effect' will become increasingly apparent, and a series of social contradictions will continue to deepen."[4] From the 2010s to the present, the central government has introduced a series of top-level designs in the economic field, aiming to enable China's economy to switch to a path of

[3] Xi, Jinping. 2022. *Hold High the Great Banner of Socialism with Chinese Characteristics and Strive in Unity to Build a Modern Socialist Country in All Respects*: *Report to the 20th National Congress of the Communist Party of China*. Beijing: People's Publishing House. p.47.

[4] Publicity Department of the CPC Central Committee. 2018. *Thirty Lectures on Xi Jinping's Thought on Socialism with Chinese Characteristics for a New Era*. Beijing: *Xuexi Chuban She* (Learning Press). p.108.

high-quality development through comprehensive structural transformation.[5] Among these, "employment-first", "stable employment" and "full employment" are not only important guarantees for the successful transformation and upgrading of the economy, but also challenges that need to be addressed.

As a populous country, China faces considerable pressure to meet employment demand. In addition, its economy is at a crucial stage of transformation and upgrading, it is encountering new situations and challenges for employment. However, by shifting perspectives, it becomes apparent that this issue can largely be addressed through resolving another problem. China is currently in a stage of development where urbanization and rural revitalization are advancing together, and the prominent contradictions between the supply and demand of public goods have become a bottleneck restricting economic and social development. Key areas closely related to urban and rural production and life, such as childcare, education, healthcare, elderly care, transportation, water conservancy, energy, ecological and environmental protection, agriculture and rural affairs, social management, emergency management, and disaster prevention and mitigation, all require continuous increases in investment. Therefore, while supply-side reform optimizes market supply, it also has an important task of increasing and optimizing the supply of public goods. Contradictions present opportunities; there are numerous potential and valuable job opportunities within the field of public goods in China. If effectively developed, they can not only continuously create employment but also address the shortfalls in public goods, thus unleashing development potential.

At present, China's employment structure is undergoing a significant historical transition. From the perspective of high-quality development, it exhibits three fundamental characteristics. First, backward industries have minimal or even negative contribution to economic and social development. Consequently, labor will gradually be withdrawn from these sectors over a period of time, leading to a substantial creation of new employment demand. Second, in contrast, there is a significant labor gap in the development of emerging industries and the upgrading of traditional industries, with the market's demand for higher-quality laborers continuously expanding. Third, at the same time, the contradiction between the supply and demand of public goods in urban and rural areas has become an important factor constraining supply-side reform. However, dialectically, this contradiction also indicates that various public positions with huge demand urgently need to be developed. Therefore, to ensure a comprehensive shift towards high-quality development of the national economy, it is essential to vigorously tap into the employment potential in the public sector. By establishing a dynamic flow mechanism between market employment and public employment, the latter can function as a buffer and stabilizer akin to Ever-normal Granary. On the one hand, this ensures that labor force displaced due to

[5] From a macro perspective, China's economy has completed and is currently undergoing two major transformations since the reform and opening up in 1978, namely the transformation of the economic system and the transformation of the economic structure. The latter is to further transform China into a country with high-quality development after its successful transformation to the socialist market economy system.

structural and cyclical economic adjustments can smoothly transition into the public employment sector, which possesses significant absorption capacity. This not only addresses employment issues but also enhances the quantity, quality and efficiency of public goods supply in urban and rural areas. On the other hand, public employment can be developed into a reservoir of human resources, a training pool, and a development zone, continuously nurturing and releasing competitive laborers for the ongoing transformation and upgrading of the economy and society. In summary, China is at an opportune moment to systematically establish an Ever-normal Granary of labor force. This can effectively address new problems and contradictions arising in the employment sector due to structural transformation, catering to real-world demands and fulfilling critical functions of safeguarding employment, promoting stability, and facilitating high-quality development.

In terms of their direct impact on job creation, public goods can be divided into two categories: hard products and soft products. Comparatively, hard products are more tangible products characterized by "more raw materials and less labor" (such as public infrastructure), while soft products primarily consist of intangible products with "more labor and less raw materials" (such as various public services). Soft products not only have considerable potential for job creation but also meet substantial social demands, yielding immediate employment effects. Therefore, in the process of establishing the Ever-normal Granary of labor force, sufficient attention should be paid to the development and management of public service positions. Two examples will illustrate this point hereinafter.

In rural areas of China, while the material conditions for production and living have continuously improved, the development in the cultural sector has relatively lagged behind. A thriving culture is essential for the revitalization of rural communities, and enhancing the quantity and quality of cultural public goods is a fundamental requirement for rural revitalization. In recent years, many regions have implemented public projects such as "rural reading rooms" to build cultural infrastructure in rural areas. However, despite significant improvements in hardware conditions, problems such as inadequate staffing and weak service functions still persist. If we targetedly develop relevant jobs and integrate hardware construction with software services, rural cultural infrastructure (such as rural reading rooms, rural cultural stations and cultural halls) can be transformed into comprehensive platforms integrating various "micro-initiatives" like educational and cultural promotion and training, the development and implementation of cultural and sports activities, as well as the exploration and preservation of local resources. Through dynamic optimization, it can effectively address the shortcomings in the public cultural sector at the grassroots level in rural areas.

After successfully completing the task of poverty alleviation, rural areas in China have comprehensively transitioned into a new stage of rural revitalization. Accelerating the extension of public goods to towns and villages, achieving comprehensive coverage of basic public services in rural areas, and further realizing the equalization of urban and rural public services are important policies for rural revitalization. In 2018, the "Thousand Villages Demonstration and Ten Thousand Villages Renovation" project (abbreviated as "Thousand-Ten Thousand Project") in

Zhejiang Province was awarded the "Inspiration and Action Award" by the United Nations as part of the "Champions of the Earth".[6] From the project of "Thousand Villages Demonstration and Ten Thousand Villages Renovation" to "Thousand Elite Villages, Ten Thousand Beautiful Villages", and then to "Thousand Future Villages, Ten Thousand Prosperous Villages", Zhejiang has explored a development path for comprehensive rural revitalization, starting with the improvement of the rural living environment and continuously iterating policies. Accompanying this progress is the continuous improvement and optimization of the rural living environment, followed by the corresponding development of public sector jobs, which in turn attracts more people to start businesses in rural areas. The "Thousand-Ten Thousand Project" has achieved a "multiplier effect" on employment. Nowadays, the "Thousand-Ten Thousand Project" is being promoted in an orderly manner across vast rural areas in China based on the local conditions. Since it is a long-term project that requires sustained efforts, the ongoing governance of the living environment and its continuous upgrades will inevitably generate a significant demand for public services, providing an important historical opportunity for developing Ever-normal Granary for public employment in rural areas. Therefore, during the promotion of the "Thousand-Ten Thousand Project" in various regions, it is essential to establish Ever-normal Granary for public employment in rural areas. This not only helps address the shortfall in the supply of public goods across vast rural areas, but also nurtures and develops human resources that serve rural revitalization. Furthermore, improvements in the socio-economic conditions in rural areas can attract more employment opportunities, yielding multiple benefits. Examples of public job creation in rural areas in China that accompanies rural revitalization are shown in the table below (Table 8.1).

College graduates have become the focus of newly emerging labor force in China in recent years. As the market increasingly demands comprehensive qualities and professional experience from workers, the pressure for college graduates to enter the workforce continues to rise. In response, the government and society have been exploring and implementing various strategies. Among them, the sub-projects under the "Grassroots Training Program for College Graduates", such as the "Program of College Graduates as Village Officials", the "Special Posts Plan for Teachers in Rural Compulsory Education", the "Program to Take Community-level Posts in Education, Agriculture, Health Care, and Poverty Relief" (commonly known as "Three Supports and One Assistance"), and the "College Graduates 'Go West'

[6] This award category recognizes individuals or organizations who have taken bold environmental action in urging and creating decisive positive change on behalf of the planet and its inhabitants. Their leadership and example inspires and motivates others. The Champions of the Earth laureates are selected by a global jury following a public nomination process. The high volume of nominations reflects how an increasing number of people understand what is possible and see the opportunities in protecting and restoring nature. The Champions of the Earth face down adversity and affirm that humanity has the ingenuity and the ambition to protect and restore our environment. Their initiatives confront the triple planetary crisis of climate change, biodiversity loss and pollution, and they remind us environmental sustainability is key to achieving sustainable development. For more information, see: https://www.unep.org/championsofearth/award/inspiration-and-action?%2Fzh-hans%2Faward%2Fjiliyuxingdongjiang=

Table 8.1 Examples of public job creation in rural areas

Jobs	Responsibilities
Maintenance and upkeep of rural infrastructure	The construction of infrastructure in rural areas is continuously increasing, and subsequent long-term maintenance work needs to be promptly followed up.
Basic health care and health services in rural areas	Build and improve a comprehensive health care infrastructure and supporting service system that covers grassroots areas in rural regions.
Cultural and sports development and management in rural areas	Build and improve a comprehensive cultural and sports infrastructure and supporting service system that covers grassroots areas in rural regions.
Comprehensive elderly and childcare service system in rural areas	Build and improve a comprehensive elderly care and childcare infrastructure and supporting service system that covers grassroots areas in rural regions.
Comprehensive emergency rescue services in rural areas	Establish a networked and easily accessible comprehensive emergency rescue system, especially in remote rural areas.
Resource, environment, and natural disaster surveys	Conduct dynamic surveys of land resources, natural environments, and natural disasters in rural areas to provide first-hand data for government policymaking.
Economic and social surveys in rural areas	Conduct dynamic field surveys of the economy and society in rural areas to provide first-hand data for government policymaking.

Volunteer Program" are relatively mature and successful cases of the government's efforts to address employment of college graduates, talent cultivation and selection (see Table 8.2). In fact, these programs can be seen as the "Ever-normal Granary of labor force". On the one hand, they promote the development of public services in specific regions through designated job positions; on the other hand, they alleviate employment pressure and provide grassroots training for college graduates. After a "incubation" process, the young labor force released by the "Grassroots Training Program for College Graduates" becomes more competitive and has a clearer understanding of their social positioning and career development. Therefore, as long as the job design is reasonable, a buffer stock pool for human resource development can be established, characterized by "being able to go down to the grassroots, staying at the grassroots, performing well, having mobility, and having prospects for development". This pool can continuously nurture and provide fresh talent to the society, supplying a strong workforce for various industries.[7]

[7] The Program of College Graduates as Village Officials has recently become a focal point of attention. A number of extensive and in-depth studies have concluded that, although there are some problems for the program in its implementation, its far-reaching significance cannot be underestimated. Therefore, through institutional redesign, the Program of College Graduates as Village Officials should have better development prospects. For reference, see: Luo, Jiangling. 2017. *Research on the Program of College Graduates as Village Officials and Relevant Problems*. Beijing: China Social Sciences Press; She, Yu. 2013. *Minor Policies on "Village Officials", Grand Strategy for Talents: Evaluation of Program of College Graduates as Village Officials*. Beijing: China Development Press.

Table 8.2 Sub-projects of "Grassroots Training Program for College Graduates"

Name	Main content	Working years
Program of college graduates as village officials	Recruiting and assigning college graduates to serve in rural grassroots positions, fulfilling responsibilities such as promoting and implementing policies, fostering economic development, serving and connecting with the masses, popularizing science and technology, participating in village affairs management, and strengthening the construction of grassroots organizations.	Over 2 years
Special posts plan for teachers in rural compulsory education	Recruiting college graduates to teach in rural schools for compulsory education below the county level in western regions that are focusing on achieving the "Two Basic Goals" (nine-year compulsory education and basic literacy for rural adults), gradually addressing issues such as the overall shortage and improper structure of rural teachers, and improving the overall quality of the rural teaching staffs.	3 years
Program to take community-level posts in education, agriculture, health care, and poverty relief	Recruiting college graduates to work in the townships in education, agriculture, health care and poverty alleviation. Upon completion of their service, they will enter the market and freely choose their employment.	2 years
College graduates "Go West" volunteer program	Recruiting college graduates or graduate students to carry out volunteer service at the grass-roots level in the west, and encouraging them to take root in local employment and entrepreneurship upon completion of their service. The services are divided into seven aspects: Basic education, service to agriculture, rural areas and farmers, health care, grass-roots youth work, grass-roots social management, service to Xinjiang, and service to Xizang.	1–3 years

Source: "Implementation Plan for Grassroots Training Program for College Graduates", website of the Ministry of Education of the People's Republic of China, http://www.moe.gov.cn/jyb_xxgk/moe_1777/moe_1779/201105/t20110530_124093.html, and websites of relevant sub-projects

In fact, the Grassroots Training Program for College Graduates can be further expanded and upgraded in terms of job types and numbers of positions available (for instance, by incorporating the "Thousand-Ten Thousand Project" into this program). Therefore, the government and social forces should work together vigorously to systematically plan and develop public sector jobs and establish a buffer stock system for college students' employment. On the one hand, the central and provincial governments should set up special funds for public employment of college graduates and formulate corresponding national and provincial grassroots service programs, grassroots growth plans, and grassroots training programs for college graduates. Based on actual needs, local regions should develop and reserve public sector jobs that are fundamentally rooted in grassroots work, aligning them precisely with the aforementioned programs from the bottom up to ensure that college graduates can take up positions immediately when facing employment difficulties. On the other hand, mechanisms for incentive and restraint, assessment and selection, transition, or long-term residence should be established to effectively manage the public sector employment of college graduates both during and after their tenure, contributing to their growth and better career development in the future. It should be noted that some college graduates may choose to stay in public sector jobs for an extended period not because they lack the competitive power to move to other positions, but because they have found their own value in these jobs.[8]

The structural transformation that the Chinese economy is undergoing necessitates adaptive adjustments in the top-level design of employment policies, with the Ever-normal Granary of labor force serving as an important option. The "government purchase of public services" initiative promoted by the state in recent years has laid the groundwork for establishing the Ever-normal Granary of labor force. Its advantage lies in the government's ability to accurately and flexibly create jobs in response to actual demands in the public sector by collaborating with market and social forces, thereby enhancing the efficiency of public services and public sector employment. Additionally, social enterprises, characterized by both profitability (without pursuit of maximum profits) and public welfare (undertaking social responsibility), cannot be overlooked in the construction of the Ever-normal Granary of labor force. The prototype of social enterprises can be traced back to Zhu Xi's community granary (*shecang*) in ancient China, which leveraged government and private funding and mutual aid to provide relief and assistance in rural communities while ensuring operational sustainability through minimal profits. With creative transformation of the traditional Zhu Xi's community granary, social enterprises with Chinese characteristics (such as community elderly care institutions) can be developed to create employment opportunities for more labor force (including the disabled), playing a pivotal role in the Ever-normal Granary of labor force.

In summary, a vast Ever-normal Granary of labor force exists within the public sector of our country. If it is properly established and operated, the stability it provides and the economic and social value it generates will be immeasurable. In the face of China's enormous economic volume, macro policies must focus intently on "people" and ensure that they revolve around the "sun of labor". Only then can fundamental guarantees for the stable development of the economy and society be maintained.

---

[8] The "Program to Take Community-level Posts in Education, Agriculture, Health Care, and Poverty Relief" (Three Supports and One Assistance) listed in Table 8.2 has cultivated and trained a large number of college graduates. Feng Jiang, a graduate of Huazhong Agricultural University, joined the program in 2008 and has been working on wetland conservation in Chenhu Wetland Reserve in Wuhan until now (typically, the service period for this program is 2 years). He has made significant contributions to the protection of bird habitats and was featured as the cover story of Yangtze River Daily in 2022 for his efforts. This highlights the great significance of the Grassroots Training Program for College Graduates: jobs are available at the grassroots level, these jobs are valuable, and they provide opportunities for personal growth. After 2–3 years of experience, young people will become more competitive in the labor market or in their current positions, and they will be better equipped to fulfill their life values.

8.2 Economic Security Barriers: Ever-normal Granaries for Agriculture, Industry and Basic Resources

Since the beginning of the twenty-first century, especially after 2008, the price volatility of major commodities in the world has significantly increased (see Figs. 8.1 and 8.2). In the face of an uncertain global economy and resource and environmental constraints, it is imperative for China to establish and improve its Ever-normal Granary system. At the beginning of the twenty-first century, Zhang Qing, a Chinese scholar, conducted a comprehensive and systematic study on the issue of national commodity reserves, and presciently proposed the specific concept for establishing China's "grand reserve system", which aligns closely with our vision of constructing a large-scale Ever-normal Granary. In the new stage of development, to meet new demands, it is necessary to answer the questions such as "what should be stored?", "who should store it?", and "how should it be stored?" Among these, the issue "what to store" is clearly the primary one that needs to be addressed. Here, we divide ever-normal granaries of non-labor-force into three categories: agricultural ever-normal granaries, industrial ever-normal granaries, and basic resource ever-normal granaries.

Agricultural Ever-normal Granaries

China has a population of 1.4 billion, and agriculture is the foundation of the national economy and people's livelihood. The stability of grain supply and prices is an important basis for national security. For a long time, the Chinese government has been promoting the construction and development of ever-normal granaries for

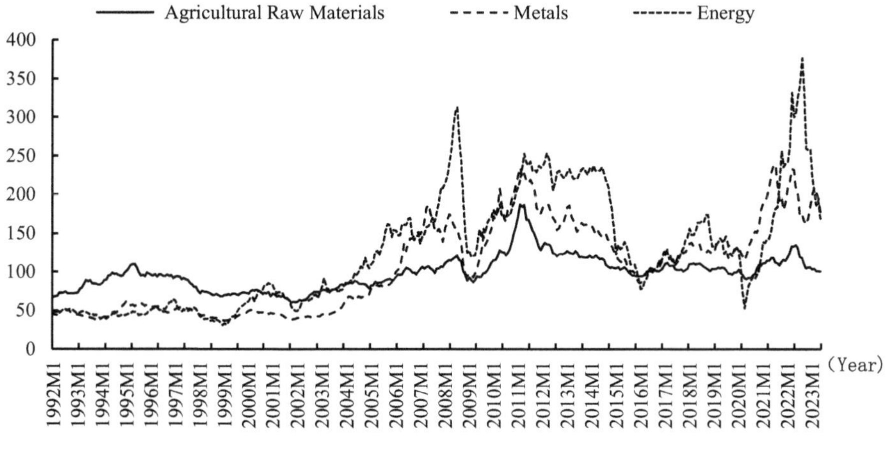

Fig. 8.1 Indices of primary commodity prices in the international markets. *Source: website of the International Monetary Fund, https: //*www.imf.org/en/Research/commodity-prices. *In the year 2016, the index number is designated as 100. Agricultural raw materials include timber, cotton, wool, rubber and leather; primary metals include aluminum, cobalt, copper, iron ore, lead, molybdenum, nickel, tin, uranium and zinc; and energy resources includes petroleum, natural gas, coal and propane*

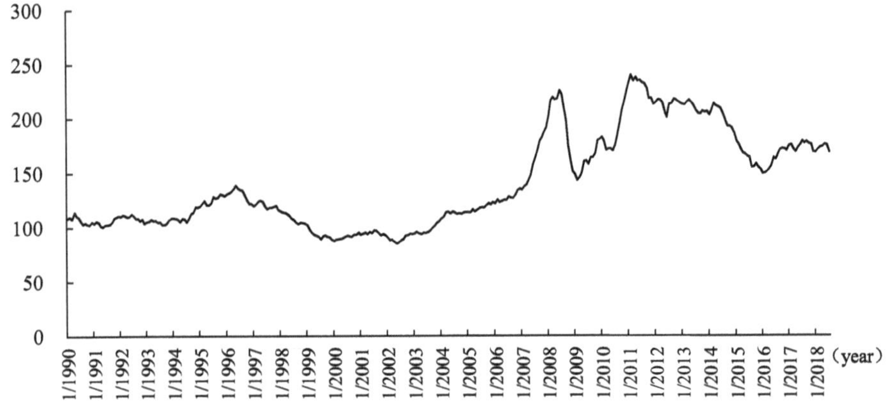

Fig. 8.2 World food price index. *Source: Website of the Food and Agriculture Organization of the United Nations, http:* http://www.fao.org/worldfoodsituation/foodpricesindex/zh/

grains. The white paper "Food Security in China" released in 2019 indicates that China's grain reserve capacity has been significantly enhanced, evidenced by the following aspects: Food storage is further modernized, logistics capacity has increased markedly, and rain reserves and emergency response systems are improving. The government has a rational process for determining the functions of central and local reserves: the central grain reserves are mainly used to maintain basic needs, respond to disasters and stabilize expectations, which is the "ballast stone" of national food security. Local grain reserves are mainly used in the regional market to meet emergencies, stabilize grain prices and guarantee supply, which is the first line of defense of national food security. While improving the grain reserve capacity, China is continuously innovating and improving the food market system, and furthering reform of the grain collection and storage system and the price formation mechanism.[9] By allowing the market to function as the market should and Ever-normal Granary to operate as it is intended, both can complement each other and better ensure national food security.

In today's world, extreme weather conditions and the various disasters they trigger are increasingly frequent, posing long-term challenges to global food security. The white paper "Food Security in China" states, "In the medium to long term, China's grain production and demand will remain closely aligned, which means China must not slacken its efforts to ensure food security for a moment."[10] Therefore, the construction of agricultural ever-normal granaries should focus on creating "large granaries" that incorporate more elements, rather than being limited to merely "storing grain in containers". The agricultural Ever-normal Granary promoted by

[9] State Council Information Office of the People's Republic of China. 2019-10-14. *Food Security in China*. http://www.scio.gov.cn/zfbps/ndhf/2019n/202207/t20220704_130642.html

[10] State Council Information Office of the People's Republic of China. 2019-10-14. *Food Security in China*. http://www.scio.gov.cn/zfbps/ndhf/2019n/202207/t20220704_130642.html

Wallace encompasses "granaries" of land, finance and technology. "Stored grain is susceptible to decay, while the yield from farmland is inexhaustible."[11] Nurturing and reserving farmland means establishing a coordinated system of intangible ever-normal granaries of farmland and tangible ever-normal granaries of grain. Hence, policies for "storing grain in the land" such as the continuous improvement of low-and-medium-productivity farmland, the construction and permanent protection of high-standard farmland, the permanent protection of high-quality land (e.g., black soil), and the implementation of crop rotation and fallow systems, are indispensable to the construction of China's agricultural ever-normal granaries. At the same time, "storing grain in technology" (addressing the technological shortcomings throughout the entire industrial chain from breeding to storage, transportation and processing), "storing grain in currency" (fully utilizing fiscal, financial and insurance policies to support agricultural product prices, farmers' incomes and the agricultural economy), and "storing grain in water conservancy" (ensuring a balanced water supply and demand for agriculture across time and space through construction of various levels of water networks) should all be integral parts in the construction of agricultural ever-normal granaries.

The Report to the 20th National Congress of the Communist Party of China states, "We will adopt an all-encompassing approach to food... and build a diversified food supply system."[12] This implies that the agricultural Ever-normal Granary discussed above is still limited to the traditional view of grain. Since ecological resources such as mountains, rivers (and oceans), forests, farmlands, lakes, grasslands and deserts can all provide food supplies to humans, from a more inclusive and forward-looking perspective, "storing food in the ecology" should be regarded as the establishment of a grand agricultural Ever-normal Granary in China over a longer period of time (Fig. 8.3).

Industrial Ever-normal Granaries and Basic Resource Ever-normal Granaries

The "industrial ever-normal granaries" refer to the Ever-normal Granary system established for non-renewable energy sources and important industrial raw materials. Industrial ever-normal granaries hold a crucial position in national economic development and strategic security layout. In addition to bulk industrial resources such as petroleum, natural gas, coal and iron, it is essential to enhance the construction of ever-normal granaries for strategic and critical industrial raw materials. In recent years, China has been continuously enhancing resource protection and regulation efforts within the rare earth industry, improving the development and utilization capabilities. Establishing strategic ever-normal granaries for rare earth resources

[11] Lin, Xiyi. 1986. Sequel to the Eleven Drafts of *Lin Xiyi*, vol.11. in *Complete Library in the Four Branches of Literature (Wenyuange Edition)*, *Ji* section, vol.1185. Taibei: Commercial Press of Taiwan. p. 679.

[12] Xi, Jinping. 2022. *Hold High the Great Banner of Socialism with Chinese Characteristics and Strive in Unity to Build a Modern Socialist Country in All Respects*: *Report to the 20th National Congress of the Communist Party of China*. Beijing: People's Publishing House. p.31.

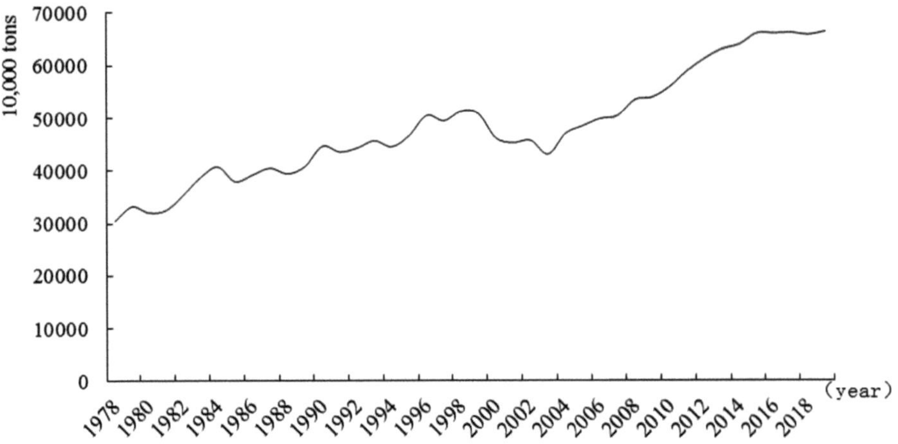

Fig. 8.3 Total grain output of China

can provide an effective means for the further advancement of relevant policies. World history repeatedly proves that a country, despite possessing certain abundant resources, may fall victim to the "resource curse" or even a poverty trap if these resources are exploited carelessly and undervalued. However, if used prudently and wisely, these resources can become powerful boosters for a country's development and rise.[13] China's economy and society are currently undergoing a comprehensive transition towards high-quality development, where rare earth resources undoubtedly provide critical support for technological revolutions and industrial upgrades. Therefore, intensively developing and utilizing important industrial raw material resources, while independently extending the industrial chain and moving towards high-end production, is a way to better protect and reserve these resources. As more and more high-tech materials and products increasingly rely on rare earths—the "industrial vitamins", constructing ever-normal granaries for rare earth that integrate protection, reserves, development, utilization and market regulation, is key to constructing the nation's future core competitiveness.

Resource constraints are a bottleneck that restricts the sustainable development of China's economy and society. As fundamental resources, both land and freshwater are at relatively low levels of per capital availability in China, leading to a prominent contradiction between their protection and utilization. (Fig. 8.4). A long-term strategy to address this is the establishment of ever-normal granaries of land resources and water resources. The ever-normal granaries of land resources primarily focus on the conservation, restoration, and comprehensive management of undeveloped, inefficiently developed, overdeveloped, or abandoned forest, grassland, arable land, and other types of land resources due to various reasons. This forms a

[13] Jia, Genliang and Liu Lin. 2011. Rare-earth issues in China: A perspective from economic history and an analysis of evolutionary economics. *Journal of Peking University (Philosophy and Social Science).* (4): 138–146.

permanent reserve or reserve-release mechanism to ensure the continuous improvement of the land resource environment and the steady supply of land resources needed for economic and social development. The ever-normal granaries of water resources mainly treats various water resources as subjects for conservation, restoration and comprehensive management, forming a permanent reserve or reserve-release mechanism to ensure the continuous improvement of the water resource environment and the steady supply of water resources needed for economic and social development.

The cross-temporal and cross-spatial regulation and allocation of water resources is a crucial function of the ever-normal granaries of water resources. In addition to reservoirs, water diversion projects such as the "South-to-North Water Diversion Project" are also typical examples of ever-normal granaries of water resources. The central and eastern regions along the route of the "South-to-North Water Diversion Project" are vital industrial and agricultural areas in China. Through this project, water resources along the route are effectively integrated, achieving cross-spatial and cross-temporal "balanced distribution" and "stabilization". From this perspective, the national water network that China is implementing is a higher-level Ever-normal Granary of water resources, encompassing projects like the "South-to-North Water Diversion Project". "The national water network is a comprehensive system based on natural rivers and lakes, with diversion and drainage projects as channels, storage and regulation projects as nodes, and smart regulation as the means. It integrates functions such as optimized allocation of water resources, flood control and disaster reduction in river basins, and protection of water ecosystems."[14] The

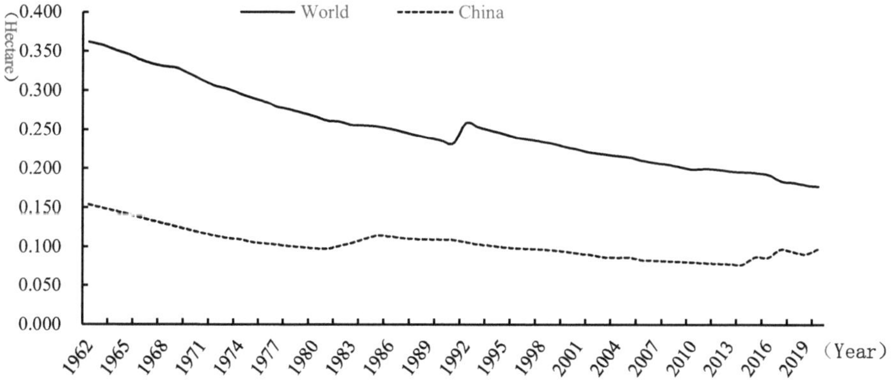

Fig. 8.4 Per Captia arable land in the World and China. Source: website of the World Bank, https://data.worldbank.org.cn/indicator/AG.LND.ARBL.HA.PC?locations=CN&name_desc=true&view=chart

[14] See: *Guideline on the National Water Network Construction*. 2023-5-25. https://www.gov.cn/zhengce/202305/content_6876214.htm

national water network is an Ever-normal Granary constructed in response to China's water resource challenges, including scarcity and uneven regional distribution. It enhances the capacity for stable regulation of water resources over a broader geographical area, ensuring the improvement and optimization of the water resource environment at a higher level, as well as the stable supply of water resources for economic and social development. China's northwestern region boasts vast territorial space, but severe water shortage has significantly constrained the region's development. If a water network connecting this region with others is established, facilitating "balanced distribution" and "stabilization" of water resources in this region, the ecological environment will undergo remarkable improvement and reversal. This would have immeasurable and far-reaching impacts on the region's industrial and agricultural development, urbanization, and the "Belt and Road" initiative. The "Hu Huanyong Line"[15] might eventually become a merely historical term as a result of the elimination of regional development parities.

The ever-normal granaries of important natural resource are not limited to those of land and freshwater. Ecological resources that are crucial to the national economy and people's livelihoods can form permanent reserve or a reserve-release mechanism through expanded protection, conservation, and restoration. For example, during the accelerated urbanization in China, to address a series of urban problems arising from the conflicts between population, resources and the environment, many regions of China increasingly incorporated the concept of "sponge city"[16]into goals of urban planning, construction and renovation. Essentially, a sponge city is

---

[15]The Hu Huanyong Line, also called the Heihe-Tengchong Line, or the Aihui-Tengchong Line (and internationally as the Hu line), is an imaginary line that divides the area of China into two parts with contrasting population densities. It stretches from the city of Heihe in the northeast to Tengchong in the south, diagonally across China. Chinese population geographer Hu Huanyong imagined the line in 1935 and called it a "geo-demographic demacaration line". This imaginary line divides the territory of China as follows (going by 1935 statistics): West of the line: 64% of the area, but only 4% of the population (1935); East of the line: 36% of the area, but 96% of the population (1935).

[16]The term "Sponge City" first arose in China, in a number of coordinated projects approved by the central government. A Sponge City is one that relies on the installation of additional green areas and replaces concrete with permeable surfaces. These surfaces absorb water during times of rainfall. Then, when hot weather predominates, the water evaporates and cools the city down. The concept of a "sponge city" is an innovative urban development model designed to enhance a city's ability to manage water resources sustainably and resiliently. Inspired by the natural water-absorbing properties of a sponge, this approach focuses on absorption, storage, infiltration, purification, and controlled release of rainwater to address urban challenges such as flooding, water scarcity, and pollution. By integrating green infrastructure—such as permeable pavements, green roofs, rain gardens, and wetlands—into urban planning, sponge cities aim to mimic natural hydrological processes. This model not only mitigates flood risks by improving water retention and drainage but also promotes water conservation through rainwater harvesting and reuse. Additionally, sponge cities contribute to ecological restoration, pollution reduction, and climate resilience, while enhancing the overall urban environment by increasing green spaces and improving air quality. In China, the sponge city initiative has gained significant traction as a solution to the water-related issues exacerbated by rapid urbanization, with cities like Beijing, Shanghai, and Wuhan implementing projects to transform their urban landscapes into more sustainable and livable spaces. In

an Ever-normal Granary of resources constructed for sustainable urban development, encompassing ecological elements such as water, land and air, as well as broader ecosystems including mountains, rivers, forests, fields, lakes, grasslands and deserts. These elements are integrated into a buffer regulation system characterized by "storage, infiltration, purification and release". In summary, given the prominent contradictions between resource constraints and sustainable development in China, the transition from "opening up the source and regulating the flow" to "regulating the source and the flow — recycling—sustainable utilization" in the development and utilization of various resources has become inevitable. The ever-normal granaries will undoubtedly play a key role in this transition.

The Grand Ever-normal Granary is a system involving multiple participants, and enterprises in the market are also one of the main entities in its construction. In the eyes of the most excellent entrepreneurs, maintaining a buffer stock is a necessary condition for ensuring business success. Konosuke Matsushita, in particular, emphasized that businesses, regardless of their size or industry, should adhere to the philosophy of "damstyle management"—a seemingly conservative yet proactive approach that emphasizes maintaining reserves. By reserving a certain amount of capital, production facilities, manpower, inventory, technology, planning and new product development, much like a dam, a company can remain largely unaffected even when external conditions change. Konosuke Matsushita believed that though the philosophy of damstyle management is easy to understand but difficult to be implemented, companies must pay this "insurance premium" for stable operations, decisively implement and vigorously promote it. The damstyle management is a crucial part of Konosuke Matsushita's management philosophy. Konosuke Matsushita fully understood the uncertainties of the world: in an environment filled with unpredictability, minimizing various types of inventory might make a company efficient and competitive in the short term, but in the long run it often becomes a trigger for crises. Therefore, companies must independently build their own ever-normal granaries to prepare for potential crises and seize possible opportunities.[17] By transplanting the concept of the Ever-normal Granary into the business management, Konosuke Matsushita not only transcended traditional business management thinking but also provided theoretical and practical foundations for market participants to engage in the construction of the Grand Ever-normal Granary based on

essence, a sponge city represents a holistic approach to urban development, balancing ecological health with human needs in the face of growing environmental challenges.

[17] Using Reserves to Address Potential Crises: Enterprises should not assume that favorable economic conditions will last indefinitely. They must consider the possibility of economic downturns and prepare various reserves during times of financial surplus. Using Reserves to Seize Potential Opportunities: Even if a company operates at only 80% to 90% of its production capacity, it can still generate profits. When market demand suddenly increases, the company can immediately ramp up production to meet the demand. Matsushita specifically pointed out that damstyle management involves intentional reserves, not surpluses resulting from poor decision-making. See: Matsushita, Konosuke. 1984. *The Complete Collection of Business Management, vol.5: Tap Water Management Philosophy*. Taibei: Celebrity Publishers. pp. 27–29.

long-term interests, thereby optimizing reserve structures and improving reserve efficiency.

Approaching the development and utilization of natural resources with a sense of reverence and fostering a sense of crisis and vigilance towards development are the foundational principles of the Ever-normal Granary. Based on China's national conditions, the Ever-normal Granary must be selectively constructed for various aspects, including population, resources, production capacity, and products. Through and coordinated planning across time and space, it aims to create a stable and integrated mechanism that harmonizes economic and social benefits, short-term and long-term objectives, overall and local interests, as well as government and market roles. This, in turn, will better safeguards national security and promote long-term sustainable development.

Although the operation of the Ever-normal Granary is based on the simple principle of buying and selling (*ditiao*), it requires considerable flexibility and adaptability in practical implementations. Otherwise, it may not stabilize the market but instead be manipulated, while excessive intervention might lead to the opposite effect of "ever-normal being abnormal". From this perspective, the buffer buying and selling requires a nuanced and timely judgment of priorities and an appropriate "degree", which goes beyond rigid and somewhat inflexible theoretical analysis. Some may worry that building a Grand Ever-normal Granary could result in huge expenditures and fiscal deficits. However, the (New) Functional Finance theory offers us the following insight: if fiscal spending is endogenously aligned with right choices that benefit the nation and its people, and if it focuses on the population, agricultural and industrial products, and basic natural resources that truly support sustainable economic and social development as the "real standard", then the resulting deficits are good deficits. These can create a positive feedback mechanism and ultimately contribute to ever-normal and stable development. Therefore, the construction of a Grand Ever-normal Granary should not be constrained by quantitative limits on fiscal spending. In fact, constraints related to population, resources, environment, productivity, and production relations may be more relevant as true fiscal constraints. The economic functions and public responsibilities of the Grand Ever-normal Granary should be evaluated dynamically and structurally in terms of "quality". In the traditional Chinese context, this "quality" is the relationship between heaven and humanity. The traditional macro-ethical appeal of "respecting Heaven" (*jing tian*) and "nourishing the people" (*yang min*) remains meaningful in today's socialist China.

Chapter 9

Conclusion: The Spirit of the Middle Way in Chinese Economic Tradition

> The sage knows the flaws of the mind's operation and perceives the misfortunes of blindness and being closed to the truth. This is why he is without desires and aversions, without beginnings and ends of things, without the remote or near, without broadness or shallowness, without antiquity or modernity. He lays out all the myriad things and causes himself to exactly match how each settles on the suspended balance.
> — *Xunzi*[1]

> What China should do most urgently in the future is not to follow the West, but to follow the spirit of independent innovation and self-reliance of the ancient Chinese.
> —*Qian M*[2]

In the chapter "conclusion" of *The Economic Principles of Confucius and His School*, Chen Huan-chang states, "If we take the whole history of China and compare it with the whole history of the West, the Chinese should not be ashamed."[3]He believes that China's ancient civilization was by no means inferior to that of the West, but "the great trouble has been that, when the Chinese government was at its worst, the modern nations, rising just a little earlier than China, entered into her door and interfered with her affairs."[4] Since the modern times, as Western influence spread eastward, China's development has been in a relatively weaker position compared to that of the Western world for more than a hundred years. Today, with its rapid economic rise, China is experiencing resurgence. Under the new development paradigm and circumstances, China has a new understanding of its own traditions at

[1] Knoblock, John. 1994. *Xunzi: A Translation and Study of the Complete Works*, Vol.3. Stanford: Stanford University Press. p. 103.

[2] Qian, Mu. 2001. *Research Methodology of Chinese History*. Beijing: SDX Joint Publishing Co. p.74.

[3] Chen, Huan-chang. 1911. *The Economic Principles of Confucius and His School*. New York: Columbia University Press. p.727.

[4] Chen, Huan-chang. 1911. *The Economic Principles of Confucius and His School*. New York: Columbia University Press. p.727.

W. Xian, *Chinese Food Security Strategy*, Research Series on the Chinese Dream and China's Development Path,
https://doi.org/10.1007/978-981-95-7964-8_9

a new starting point. Looking back at the history and assessing the present, the Chinese people have no reason to feel ashamed but instead should be filled with self-confidence.

The economic tradition of China is an organic whole that encompasses a fundamental way of thinking, along with the economic ideas, policies, and practices derived from it. Its formation, development, improvement and innovation over a long historical process demonstrate its unique and profound value and connotations. It is not only a treasure trove of immense richness but also a foundation for Chinese people today to articulate economic stances, propose economic solutions, and promote an economics with Chinese characteristics. Of course, this does not mean that we can make discoveries or inventions by simply delving into ancient texts. In the context of a contemporary world where both ancient and modern, as well as domestic and foreign perspectives converge, examining traditions through comparative methods, diverse approaches, and broad horizons not only enables us to gain deeper understanding but also opens up new discoveries. This means that such a treasure can only be unearthed with new methods and selected with fresh perspectives, enabling it to engage in equal communication and dialogue with modern economic theories and policy practices. In doing so, we can reconstruct the relationship between the two and further facilitate their modern transformation and reshaping in a modern context. Only in this way can the principle of "making the past serve the present" be truly implemented.

Taking the Ever-normal Granary as an example and entry point, we navigate through the research between ancient and modern, as well as Chinese and Western economic (intellectual) history, attempting to explore in this direction. By doing so, we aim to enable economic (intellectual) histories separated by millennia to discover and inspire each other through cross-temporal comparison. We find that the Ever-normal Granary system in ancient China and certain modern Western economic theories, policies, and practices all adhere to the common principle of buffer buying and selling. The latter, adapting to the needs of industrial society and market economy, continuously endows this economic principle with new meaning through the "revival" of the Ever-normal Granary. Rather than fading away due to the barriers of time and space, this economic tradition of China has continually transcended its historical context, prompting us to further inquire: How was it possible for ancient Chinese to make such an invention?

In its long history, China has already emerged as a unified country that exhibits a certain degree of "modernity". Ensuring the well-being of its people through economic management has long been a fundamental requirement of its governance philosophy rooted in "people-centric values" and "benevolent rule". The two-thousand-year tradition of the Ever-normal Granary indicates that China has long possessed macroeconomic thinking. From Wallace to Keynes, the "rediscovery" of the Ever-normal Granary further demonstrates that ancient Chinese had a profound understanding of the intrinsic "principles" of macroeconomics. Viewed in this light, the creation and development of the Ever-normal Granary hold an underlying logic that has been overlooked. From the "use" of the Ever-normal Granary to the "theory" of *qing* and *zhong* discussed in *Guanzi*, and then to the "essence" in dialectical moderation, we find that the Chinese concept of holding to the "mean" serves as the ontological source of the economic thinking behind the Ever-normal Granary system. Therefore, when we hope for the Chinese to achieve historical transcendence of the Ever-normal Granary once again, the primary task is to "return to the roots", for only then can we "open new paths".

Tracing back to the great era in which the pre-Qin philosophers lived, we find that within *Guanzi*, a text well-versed in economic analysis, the seemingly disorderly and unsystematic economic discourse actually conceals a complete "Dao" (way) of economics. The essence of this economic "Dao" lies in that "all things are born of the two, *Yin* and *Yang*, with reciprocal reference to each other, so that a third comes into being", while its principle is described as that "*qing* and *zhong* give birth to balance (*heng*)". In practical application, it is manifested through the four flexible A-B models. The discovery of the economic "Dao" in *Guanzi* through dialectical thinking signifies that the Chinese people achieved a pivotal and axial breakthrough in economic thought during the Axial Period of world civilization. The essence of this breakthrough, namely "maintaining balance through the mean", has largely shaped the Chinese people's economic way of thinking and worldview. Once formed, it inevitably transformed into an economic and cultural gene essential for our nation's survival and development, exerting a subtle yet pervasive influence on subsequent economic cognition and practice, akin to an "invisible hand". To this day, this economic "tradition" still lies hidden beneath the surface of "modernity". When the principle of "maintaining balance through the mean", which spans from ancient to modern times, is sorted out and clarified, it is most appropriate to summarize the historically transcendent A-B models as the "ever-normal principle".

The "ever-normal principle" and its logical elaboration provide us with a deeper and more concise understanding of Chinese economic traditions. The ever-normal principle reflects the "middle way spirit" of Chinese economic thought, which can be described as the "Ever-normal Granary of thought". It highlights the unique rationality inherent in Chinese economic thinking and serves as an important symbol of Chinese wisdom in economics. When discussing how to study Chinese economic history, Qian Mu, a prominent historian in China, keenly observed "the presence of a certain moderation in the historical process of China", which is characterized by "not taking extremes and not going too far".[5] The economic society is an inseparable organic whole, where seemingly contradictory economic affairs are actually interdependent and interconvertible. Recognizing and practicing these affairs in a one-sided, isolated, or fragmented manner ultimately harms both the recognition and practice themselves. This aligns with Confucius's admonition: "To delve into strange doctrines can bring only harm."[6] Rational or optimal economic

[5] Qian, Mu. 2001. *Research Methodology of Chinese History*. Beijing: SDX Joint Publishing Co. p.70.

[6] Watson, Burton. (trans.) 2007. *The Analects of Confucius*. New York: Columbia University Press. p.22

choices should involve "exploring it from end to end"[7] and dialectically employing the middle way (the mean). From this perspective, we can derive the following insights: among competitors, there exists a transcendent relationship called "partnership"; between gains and losses in games, there is a transcendent outcome known as "win-win"; and between economic booms and depressions, there is a transcendent state termed as "ever-normal". This implies that the seemingly simple adherence to "the mean" actually encompasses creative cognition and action. The original economic system of the "socialist market economy" is a typical example of grand dialectical application of Chinese economic wisdom in the era of reform and opening up. It strives to realize the ideal society pursued by the Chinese people, namely, the harmonious coordination and unity of moral integrity and material benefit. Within this logic, a market economy that is truly beneficial to the society requires modern states to play an active role in managing the market—coordinating all parties and dialectically employing the middle way—to lead the economic society down the ever-normal path.

"Maintaining balance through the mean" is the fundamental approach to keep the sustainable development of the Chinese economy. In the face of various new situations, new problems, and new contradictions, how can this excellent tradition be transformed into a conscious aspect of contemporary Chinese economic thought and practice? Or, how can the dialectical application of the ever-normal principle better realize its value under new historical conditions? Here, we propose several basic principles from both epistemological and methodological perspectives.

Firstly, civilization encompasses various paths, and China's economic development has its own unique characteristics and logic. Decades of practice have made it clear that China's development has not "followed" any particular model or path; rather, it has been based on national conditions, taking the road of reform and opening-up, and creating the Chinese miracle. The only reasonable explanation here is that China's economic development must be understood through the lens of the "Chinese Road" and "Chinese Path to Modernization". The Western historiographical community once proposed the influential concept of "China-centered Approach", which argues that one should not only examine Chinese history from a Chinese rather than Western perspective but also recognize that "although the context is increasingly influenced by the West, the internal history remains Chinese."[8]

[7] When Zhu Xi annotated the sentence from "The Analects: On Governance", he quoted Fan Zuyu's commentary: "Heterodox doctrines (non-Confucian) are not the teachings of the sages, but rather represent a different kind of thought." See: Zhu, Xi. 2016. *Collected Commentaries on the Four Books*. Beijing: Zhonghua Book Company. p. 57. The term "heterodox" (*yi duan*, literally meaning "other side") can be interpreted as "a different kind" (*yi duan*, literally meaning "one side"), which corresponds precisely with Confucius's epistemology of "exploring it from end to end" in *The Analects: Zi Han*: "The Master said, Do I have knowledge? I have no special knowledge. But if an uneducated fellow comes to me with a question, I attack it with all sincerity, exploring it from end to end until I've exhausted it." See: Watson, Burton. (trans.) 2007. *The Analects of Confucius*. New York: Columbia University Press. p.61.

[8] Cohen, Paul A. 1984. *Discovering History in China: American Historical Writings on the Recent Chinese Past*. New York: Columbia University Press. p.196.

However, the word "centered" inevitably conjures up a narrow sense of self-centeredness. Therefore, we use the "Chinese Road" here to illustrate the unique logic and practical approach of China's economy in the context of openness. It is important to emphasize that only by returning to the "Chinese Road" can we break free from the limitations of a monolithic development model, truly confront national conditions, and adopt a pragmatic attitude. This allows us to view China and the world from a broader perspective with an open and inclusive mindset, steadfastly embarking on the Chinese path to modernization. In Mao Zedong's poem "Reply to Mr. Liu Yazi", there is a line that goes as "try to take longer views in judging anything", implying that looking at the whole from a holistic perspective is far clearer, more accurate, and more profound than viewing the parts in isolation. More fundamentally, only by returning to and facing the differentiated whole can we find and apply the middle way (the mean), thus maintaining balance through the mean.

Secondly, returning to the "Chinese Road" necessitates viewing the "Chinese Road" as a continuous historical process. This involves abandoning the dichotomy that opposes tradition and modernity, as well as the syndromes of "historical amnesia" and "forgetfulness of traditions", thereby establishing a "historical view" for China's economic development and Chinese economics. Engels stated: "Political economy, therefore, cannot be the same for all countries and for all historical epochs….Political economy is therefore essentially a historical science."[9] If one can observe the entirety of a phenomenon within visible and accessible space, it is not difficult to understand the dialectical application of the mean in this context. However, achieving this over the span of historical time is a challenging task because people are prone to suffering from historical amnesia and even intentional forgetfulness. Nonetheless, practice has repeatedly proven that the notion and attempts to achieve development by severing ties with history and neglecting past experience will always end in failure. The Chinese Road and Chinese path to modernization should be viewed as integral parts embedded in the evolutionary process of Chinese civilization throughout history, rather than as inorganic equilibria based on logical time and desire atoms. In this way, we can truly face history and tradition. In addition, from an economic perspective, we can have history and tradition as "resource" and "capital", unearthing the treasures left by our predecessors and "investing" them in a dynamic and promising economic society at present time. As Friedrich List, a pioneer of the German Historical School said: "But between the individual and the whole human race there is the nation with its special language and literature, with its own origin and history, with its manners and habits, its laws and institutions; with its claims to existence, its independence, its progress, its duration…"[10] It seems that the so-called "whole" encompasses not only the spatial unfolding between the inside and the outside (global integration) but also the temporal extension between the past and the present (integration of past and present). Only by establishing con-

---

[9] Engels, Frederick. 1970. *Anti-Dühring: Herr Eugen Dühring's Revolution in Science*. trans. Emile Burns. New York: International Publishers. p.163.

[10] List, Frederick. 1856. *National System of Political Economy*. trans. G. A. Matile. Philadelphia: J. B. Lippincott & Co. p.263.

nections between the past and the present can we further plan for the future in the middle of time—by standing firmly on reality, we can look back as far into history as we can look forward into the future.

Thirdly, recognizing contradictions in economic and social issues and advocating for "the mean" does not mean adopting simplistic compromise, nor does it mean resorting to specious eclecticism. Instead, it involves the intersecting application of both synthesis and analysis, as well as their unification. The logic of "maintaining balance through the mean" has an inherent requirement for "harmony", which necessitates the use of synthetic methods. However, synthesis must also be grounded in analysis and integration. For example, the aforementioned two points illustrate that economic affairs must be analyzed from a holistic perspective of time and space, which means that both traditional Chinese economic thought and modern Western economic theories must have their own values. Then, how should the relationship between the two be handled in the process of constructing and developing the economic theory of socialism with Chinese characteristics? A reasonable approach would be roughly as follows: first, conduct independent analyses according to their respective unique logics, and then employ (cross-temporal) comparative methods to place them on an equal footing for reference. Through a mindset of mutual interpretation and integration — observing differences within similarities and seeking commonalities within differences — we can strive for consensus, learn from each other's strengths, and organically integrate the two, transforming them into an economic theory and policy system that is both Chinese and Western (coordinated and unified), neither purely Chinese nor purely Western (transcendent and creative), and inclusive and all-embracing. Thus, the intersecting application and unification of synthesis and analysis in the analytical approach can be termed "Chinese synthesis", with its intrinsic requirement being synthetic analysis and organic integration based on a holistic and systemic view.

Fourthly, the dialectal application of the mean is highly flexible; it adjusts and changes according to time and circumstances. As is stated in *zhongyong (The Doctrine of the Mean, or* Abiding in the Mean and the Constant*)*, "The noble person practices the mean and keeps to the constant because, as a noble person, he accords with circumstances to achieve the mean."[11] Zhu Xi comments, "The mean has no fixed form; its existence accords with circumstances", while "the noble person… is capable of according with circumstances in finding the perfect balance."[12] In the rapidly changing economic society, good institutions and policies that conformed to "the mean" in the past may have deviated from it over time. Therefore, the essence of "the mean" lies in innovation and transcendence. This involves evolving with the times, and employing the dynamic concept of "according with circumstances to achieve the mean" to forge a vibrant development path with countless "proper balance in the economy". In this way, we may shift from *Ji Ji* (Already Fulfilled) to *Wei*

[11] Gardner, Daniel K. 2019. Zhu Xi's commentarial work: Abiding in the Mean and the Constant. in *Zhu Xi: Selected Writings*. ed. Philip J. Ivanhoe. New York: Oxford University Press. p.195.

[12] Gardner, Daniel K. 2019. Zhu Xi's commentarial work: Abiding in the Mean and the Constant. in *Zhu Xi: Selected Writings*. ed. Philip J. Ivanhoe. New York: Oxford University Press. p.195.

Ji (Not Yet Fulfilled), and then from *Wei Ji* (Not Yet Fulfilled) back to *Ji Ji* (Already Fulfilled)...[13] In this process, it is necessary to adopt a continuous open attitude to embrace, understand, and learn from emerging new or even disruptive economic affairs, thereby continually expanding the overall boundaries and providing the necessary conditions for dynamically determining the "middle way" for balanced economic and social development. In this way, within the dynamic flow of time and the energy exchange of space, we endow the top-level design of reform and opening-up with another layer of meaning—reform and opening-up, at its core, is profound reflections and concise expressions of an ancient yet vibrant tradition based on the spirit of the mean in the contemporary era. Only by guiding ourselves with grand historical and cosmological perspectives of "change" (reform) and "solution" (opening-up) can we dynamically find and maintain the "middle way" for China's development with a conscious framework of a holistic view of time and space.

It is particularly important to point out that the flexibility, adaptability and progressiveness inherent in China's reform and opening-up policy, characterized by its ability to "advance with the times" and "keep pace with the world", implies a fundamental principle as follows: only by adhering to the notion of "The World Belongs to All (*tianxia weigong*)" and "Public Interests Serve the People" (*gong nai weimin*) as constraint and ultimate goal, can we transcend the narrow self-interest or group-interest, embracing a truly holistic view of time and space. This enables us to act effectively and fearlessly. In other words, by steadfastly upholding the "one" (for the public, or for the people), we can go through all changes while adhering to "the mean". This is perhaps the essence of the maxim, "Be discriminating, be undivided, that you may sincerely hold fast the Mean."[14]

In summary, better inheriting and promoting the spirit of "the mean" in China's economic traditions will help overcome many ingrained problems and break free from the rigid thinking patterns and discourse systems that are rooted in monism or binary opposition. By embracing the vigorous and unceasing progress symbolized by *Qian* (the creative, dynamic principle in the *I Ching*, symbolizing heaven and initiative for reform), and the nurturing and inclusive nature of *Kun* (the receptive,

---

[13] In the sixty-third hexagram of the *I Ching* (*Book of Changes*), *Ji Ji* (*Already Fulfilled*), the discrete Yin and Yang lines intermingle, with the lower trigram of *Li* (fire) and the upper trigram of *Kan* (water), signifying mutual assistance and harmony, where both the firm and the yielding are in correct places. The *Tuanshu* (Commentary on the Decision) states, "Because the firm and the yielding are in correct places, and respond to their proper ones" However, the pinnacle of development is but fleeting, as prosperity reaches its zenith before declining. The *Tuanshu* further explains, "Beginning: good fortune, for the yielding is in the central. End: disorder. There is no way out." Thus, matters transition into the final hexagram of the *I Ching*, the sixty-fourth hexagram, *Wei Ji* (Not Yet Fulfilled), which heralds the commencement of a new cycle of development. Hence, the *Xugua* (Sequence of Hexagrams) comments, "Things cannot be exhausted, and thus after *Ji Ji* (Already Fulfilled) comes *Wei Ji* (Not Yet Fulfilled), marking the end of the sixty-four hexagrams." It is merely the cyclical movement of the sixty-four hexagrams. See: Huang, Alfred. 1998. *The Complete I Ching*. Vermont: Inner Traditions. pp. 486–487.

[14] Legge, J. (trans.) 1865. *The Shoo King, or The Book of Historical Documents*, vol.1. London: Trübner & Co. pp.61–62.

yielding principle in the *I Ching*, symbolizing earth and openness and inclusiveness),[15] as well as adhering to the ideal that "people are my brothers and all things are my kinds"[16] and "all things between the Heaven and the Earth are one",[17] we can creatively develop an economic theory and practice system that is truly distinctive to China, constructive and vibrant.

An important aspect of the middle-way spirit in Chinese economic tradition is its deep-seated sense of potential crises. "The superior person contemplates the law of waxing and waning, and takes preventive measures against possible decline",[18] therefore "taking precautions against unforeseen events is the normal way to govern a state."[19] The unpredictable transitions between abundance and scarcity in

[15] *Qian* (The Heaven Symbol): One of the eight trigrams, it consists of three *yang* lines: ☰. It is also one of the 64 hexagrams when it consists of six *yang* lines: ䷀. According to scholars on *Book of Changes*, as the *qian* trigram is composed only of *yang* lines, it is purely *yang* and is thus used to symbolize all *yang* things or principles. The *qian* trigram symbolizes heaven, and in social terms, it symbolizes the social roles played by the male, the father, and the monarch, as well as decisive and vigorous ways of doing things. In this context, *qian* also means creating and leading all things under heaven.

See: http://www.chinesethought.cn/EN/shuyu_show.aspx?shuyu_id=2280.

Kun(The Earth Symbol): One of the eight trigrams, *kun* consists of three *yin* lines: ☷. It is also one of the 64 hexagrams when it consists of six *yin* lines. According to scholars on *Book of Changes*, as the *kun* trigram is composed only of *yin* lines, it is purely *yin* and is thus used to symbolize all *yin* things or principles. The *kun* trigram symbolizes earth, and when it comes to society, it symbolizes the social roles played the by the female, the mother, and the subjects of the ruler, as well as gentle, kind, and generous ways of doing things. In this context, *kun* also means creating and nourishing all things under heaven.

See: http://www.chinesethought.cn/EN/shuyu_show.aspx?shuyu_id=2273

In *I Ching (Book of Changes)*, there are following sentences: "Heaven acts with vitality and persistence. In correspondence with this, the superior person keeps himself vital without ceasing." "Earth's nature is to extend and respond. In correspondence with this, the superior person enriches her virtue, to sustain all beings." Huang, Alfred. 1998. *The Complete I Ching*. Vermont: Inner Traditions. p.24, pp.41–42.

[16] Zhang, Zai. 1978. Zhengmeng: Qian Cheng. in *Collected Works of Zhang Zai*. ed. Zhang, Xichen. Beijing: Zhonghua Book Company. p. 62.

[17] Cheng, Hao and Cheng Yi. 2004. *The Collected works of Cheng Hao and Cheng Yi*, vol.2. ed. Wang, Xiaoyu. Beijing: Zhonghua Book Company. p. 15. Humans and all things are one. The ancients believed that humans and all things were produced by heaven and earth, and that despite belonging to different categories, they ultimately followed the same fundamental principle and had a commonality or consistency, just like the parts of a person's body; humans must acknowledge this so they won't lose their pre-eminence over all things. In this way, Confucian scholars of the Song and Ming dynasties reinterpreted the concept of "benevolence," and also this is how the idea of eco-civilization is being explored today. This idea, like the concept that "all people are my brothers and sisters, and all things are my companions," transcends the limitations of human-oriented thinking and achieves a high degree of unity and harmony between our own selves and other human beings as well as between our own selves and everything else. See: http://www.chinesethought.cn/EN/shuyu_show.aspx?shuyu_id=4660

[18] Huang,Alfred. 1998. *The Complete I Ching*. Vermont: Inner Traditions. p.487.

[19] Wu, Jing. 2009. *Annotated Political Program of Zhenguan Period*, vol.2. ed. Xie, Baocheng. Beijing: Zhonghua Book Company. p.128.

agricultural production instilled a strong sense of crisis in ancient Chinese, leading to the establishment of ever-normal granaries to mitigate fluctuations. From a higher perspective, this sense of crisis developed into a unique development philosophy based on "the mean": "The superior person should not forget danger when the country is at peace, not forget defeat when the country exists, and not forget chaos when the country is well-governed." The best attitude to avoid extreme and uncontrolled economic and social development is to maintain an eternal sense of awe and veneration towards the world at all times, recognizing that a seemingly stable economic system actually encompasses uncertainties that cannot be described by probabilities. To a great extent, the transitions between security and danger, existence and extinction, governance and chaos arise because people forget the potential dangers, extinctions, and chaos, as well as the possible historical transformations between them. The deep-rooted tradition of crisis awareness and the practical demands of economic and social development require China to continue the Ever-normal Granary tradition and transcend it in the new era. Thus, we propose incorporating various resources essential for economic and social development into the "Grand Ever-normal Granary", establishing a mechanism that maintains ever-lasting security and ensures continuous stability, thereby better serving China's long-term development.

The Ever-normal Granary should not merely be viewed as a preventive policy. Due to its characteristic of cross-time resource allocation, the Ever-normal Granary, which "stores water to nourish fish", represents a beneficial and proactive strategic investment for the future. Although this investment incurs costs, the New Functional Finance suggests that if fiscal policy focuses on people, prioritizes human welfare, and aims at stable development with core resource elements as the benchmark, then deficit spending will yield a positive feedback through cyclical accumulation. From this perspective, could the saying in *The Great Learning*, "the accumulation of wealth is the way to scatter the people; and the letting it be scattered among them is the way to collect the people", be seen as a simple expression of Functional Finance by ancient Chinese people?

The excellent economic traditions are still alive, but we need to further promote and transcend them, leveraging this time-transcending tool more effectively by transforming it into a conscious effort in economic cognition and policy implementation on a larger scale and to a greater extent. This requires us to uphold the spirit of "the mean" and to perceive the economic society and the entire world through the concept that "all things are nourished together without their injuring one another. The courses of the seasons, and of the sun and moon, are pursued without any collision among them."[20] Not only are government, market and society a unified whole, but also heaven and humanity, China and the foreign world, and the ancient and the modern. By not severing the ties between heaven and humanity, between people and self, between objects and self, or between time and space, and by not neglecting or underestimating any aspect, our vision will naturally remain unobscured, and our

[20] Legge, J. (trans.) 1960. *The Chinese Classics: Confucian Analects; The Great Learning; The Doctrine of the Mean.* Hong Kong: Hong Kong University Press. p.427.

analytical capabilities will not be constrained. This should be the desirable method and path for inheriting Chinese economic traditions, transforming foreign economic traditions, and unifying and transcending them for the use of China in the new era.

Xue Fucheng, an essayist, diplomat and one of the main leaders of the Westernization Movement[21] in late Qing dynasty, who served as an envoy to four Western countries and navigated between Chinese and Western cultures, offered a penetrating analysis as follows long ago:

> I have heard Westerners say that the Chinese value the old, while Westerners value the new. They pride themselves on their ability to create new methods to achieve prosperity and strength, while subtly mocking China for its reluctance to change. Yet little do they know that only by not forgetting the old can one innovate, and only by being able to innovate can one restore the old…The problem of China lies not only in its inability to innovate but also in its inability to preserve the old… It is precisely because they are too quick to forget the old that their daily progress is hindered. After carefully observing the current situation and deliberating on the best course of action, I conclude with the two principles: "We should examine the old, but not disdain it; we should understand the new, but not blindly chase after it."[22]

Facing the unprecedented changes of the time, Xue Fucheng earnestly advised the Chinese people not to cling to outdated ways or to blindly embrace the new while forgetting their roots, which would lead to the two pitfalls of restoration of ancient ways and blind admiration for the West. This is because "the new" and "the old" are inherently a whole: "inability to preserve the old" leads to "inability to innovate", and those who "forget the old" would find that "their daily progress is hindered". He hoped that the Chinese people would "restore the old" with the stance to "innovate", and "innovate" with the attitude of "not forgetting the old", thereby harmonizing and transcending both and achieving a creative transformation between the new and the old. Only in this way could they independently forge a balanced path to prosperity and stability that suits the national conditions. This is precisely the adaptation and application of the enduring tradition of "the mean" in context of openness and even globalization.

To seek transcendence, one must firstly attain understanding, and then adhere to "the mean", balancing entry and exit with moderation. The enduring spirit of "the mean", which has persisted through millennia, reveals the core essence of China's economic traditions. It embodies dialectical Eastern wisdom, a practical art of

---

[21] The Westernization Movement, also known as the "self-salvation movement of the late Qing dynasty", was a movement that emerged from the 1860s to1890s. Advocates of the movement imported military equipment, machinery production means, and scientific technologies to maintain feudal ruling, Slogans during the early and late periods of the movement included "achieve self-reliance" and "seek prosperity". The Westernization Movement introduced advanced Western scientific technologies and brought forth the emergence of the first modern enterprises in China. These first enterprises have since promoted China's development, especially China's national capitalism. See: https://www.cnkeywords.net/vocabulary/toVocabulary/4c2e0bdd19e111e7a7ac4ccc6a5d5f99/vocabulary.html

[22] Ding, Fenglin and Wang Xinzhi ed. 1987. *Selected Works of Xue Fucheng*. Shanghai: Shanghai People's Publishing House. p. 424.

adhering without being conservative, learning from the ancients without reviving the past, and adapting flexibly to changes in time and space. Under its nourishment, Chinese civilization has taken deep root and continues to thrive.

With the spirit of "the mean" in mind, we find their practical applications. In the new era of converging opportunities and challenges, the development and innovation of economic theory and practice with Chinese characteristics cannot be separated from this wisdom. The economic path of Chinese civilization embodies its unique logic.

References

1. “An-Shi Rebellion”, Encyclopedia of China. https://www.zgbk.com/ecph/words?SiteID=1&ID=390056
2. “Harmony Begets New Things”. https://www.chinesethought.cn/EN/shuyu_show.aspx7shuyu_idw4475
3. “Junshufa, Balanced-delivery Law”. https://www.chinaknowledge.de/History/Terms/junshufa.html
4. “Soil Conservation and Domestic Allotment Act (1936)”. https://nationalaglawcenter.org/wp-content/uploads/assets/farmbills/soilconserv1936.pdf
5. “Wang Anshi”, Encyclopedia of China. https://www.zgbk.com/ecph/words?SiteID=1&ID=390233&Type=bkztb&SubID=681
6. “Yin and Yang”, Key Concepts in Chinese Thought and Culture. https://www.chinesethought.cn/EN/shuyu_show.aspx?shuyu_id=2172
7. “zhongyong”, Key Concepts in Chinese Thought and Culture. https://www.chinesethought.cn/EN/shuyu_show.aspx7shuyu_idw2179
8. Agricultural Adjustment Act of 1933. https://nationalaglawcenter.org/farmbills/
9. Aizer, A. et al. 2020. Do Youth Employment Programs Work? Evidence from the New Deal. *NBER Working Paper No. 27103.*
10. Ames, Roger T., and David L. Hall. 2001. *Focusing the Familiar: A Translation and Philosophical Interpretation of the Zhongyong*. Honolulu: University of Hawai’i Press.
11. Arestis, P., and M. Sawyer. 2004. *Re-examining Monetary and Fiscal Policies in the Twenty-First Century*. Cheltenham: Edward Elgar.
12. Bai, Liping. 2013. Emperor Kangxi and the Construction of Community Granary: A Case Study of Zhili. *Social Sciences of Beijing* 5:42–46.
13. Bai, Liping. 2018. *Warehouse Transformation and Social Change in the Middle Reaches of the Yangtze River in the Late Qing Dynasty*. Beijing: China University of Political Science and Law Press.
14. Ban, Gu. 1962. *Book of Han*. Vol. 24. Beijing: Zhonghua Book Company.
15. Bell, S. 1999. *Functional Finance: What, Why, and How? Working Paper No. 287.* Levy Economics Institutes of Bard College.
16. Bell, S. 2000. Do Taxes Bonds Finance Government Spending? *Journal of Economic Issues* 34 (3): 603–620.
17. Beveridge, W. H. 1944. *Full Employment in a Free Society*. New York: W. W. Norton & Company, Inc.
18. Bloom, Irene, trans. 2009. *Mencius*. New York: Columbia University Press.

W. Xian, *Chinese Food Security Strategy*, Research Series on the Chinese Dream and China’s Development Path,
https://doi.org/10.1007/978-981-95-7964-8

19. Blum, J. M., ed. 1973. *The Price of Vision: The Diary of Henry A. Wallace 1942-1946*. Boston: Houghton Mifflin Company.
20. Bodde, D. 1946. Henry A. Wallace and the Ever Normal Granary. *The Far Eastern Quarterly* 5 (4): 411–426.
21. Cai, Fang. 2007. Why Doesn't Okun's Law Work in China: A Second Discussion of Relationship Between Economic Growth and Employment? *Macroeconomic Research* 1:11–14.
22. Chang, Jianhua. 2018. A Study of Civilian-Run Granary in the Period of Kangxi and Yongzheng. *Collected Papers of History Studies* 1:14–28.
23. Chen, Chunsheng. 1989. On the Ever-Normal Granary in Guangdong during the Qing Dynasty. *Journal of Chinese Historical Studies* 3:66–79.
24. Chen, Chunsheng. 1994. On the Rise of Charity Granary in Guangdong at the End of Qing Dynasty. *Journal of Chinese Social and Economic History* 1:50–66.
25. Chen, Chunsheng. 2020. *Market Mechanisms and Social Change: An Analysis of Rice Prices in Guangdong in the 18th Century (revised ed.)*. Beijing: Beijing Normal University Press.
26. Chen, Guanlong. 1991. On the Storage System for Famine Relief in the Ming Dynasty. *Seeker (Qiu Suo)*. 5:117–122.
27. Chen, Huan-Chang. 1911. *The Economic Principles of Confucius and His School*. New York: Columbia University Press.
28. Chen, Huan-Chang. 1913. *The Economic Principles of Confucius and His School* and Its Application in China. *The Confucian Association Monthly* 1 (1):
29. Chen, Huan-Chang. *The Economic Principles of Confucius and His School*. Trans. Hua Han. Beijing: The Commercial Press.
30. Chen, Lai. 2017. *Ancient Religion and Ethics: The Roots of Confucianism (revised ed.)*. Beijing: Peking University Press.
31. Chen, Mengjia. 1956. *Review of Yin Ruins Oracle Inscriptions*. Beijing: China Science Publishing and Media Ltd.
32. Chen, Wanxiong. 1997. *Origin and Development of May Fourth New Culture Movement*. Shanghai: SDX Joint Publishing Company.
33. Chen, Xu. 2010. A New Study on the Creation of the Preparedness Granary in the Ming Dynasty. *Agricultural Archaeology* 1:236–247.
34. Chen, Yao. 2017. *The Modes of Ditiao: The Grain Trade and Local Society in Xiangtan in the Qing Dynasty*. Xiamen: Xiamen University Press.
35. Chen, Zhiping. 2016. Zhu Xi's Design of Community Granary and Its Evolution. *Researches in Chinese Economic History* 6:18–31.
36. Cheng, Hao, and Cheng Yi. 2004. In *The Collected works of Cheng Hao and Cheng Yi*, ed. Wang Xiaoyu, vol. 2, 11. Beijing: Zhonghua Book Company.
37. Cheng, Yi. 2019. *The Yi River Commentary on the Book of Changes*. Trans. L. M. Harrington. New Haven and London: Yale University Press.
38. Cochrane, Willard W. 1993. *The Development of American Agriculture: A Historical Analysis*. 2nd ed. Minneapolis: University of Minnesota Press.
39. Cohen, Paul A. 1984. *Discovering History in China: American Historical Writings on the Recent Chinese Past*. New York: Columbia University Press.
40. Colander, D. 1984. Was Keynes a Keynesian or a Lernerian? *Journal of Economic Literature* 22 (4): 1572–1575.
41. Cui, Yun. 2004. On the Storage System for Famine Relief in the Ming Dynasty. *The Northern Forum* 5:81–83.
42. Davidson, P. 1982. Rational Expectation: A Fallacious Foundation for Studying Crucial Decision Making Processes. *Journal of Post Keynesian Economics* 5 (2): 182–198.
43. Davis, J. B. 1994. *Keynes S Philosophical Development*. Cambridge: Cambridge University Press.
44. Davis, J. S. 1938. The Economics of the Ever-normal Granary. *Journal of Farm Economics* 20 (1): 8–21.

45. De Bary, William Theodore, and Irene Bloom, eds. 1999. *Sources of Chinese Tradition*. Vol. 1. 2nd ed. New York: Columbia University Press.
46. Deng, Xiaoping. 1994. *Selected Works of Deng Xiaoping*. Vol. 3. Beijing: Foreign Languages Press.
47. Deng, Yibing. 2019. *Research on Government and Beijing Grain Market in Early Qing Dynasty*. Beijing: Social Sciences Academic Press.
48. Deng, Yunte. 1937. *A History of Famine Relief in China*. Beijing: Commercial Press.
49. Dimand, R., and M. A. Dimand. 1990. J. M. Keynes on Buffer Stocks and Commodity Price Stabilization. *History of Political Economy* 22 (1): 113–123.
50. Ding, Fenglin, and Wang Xinzhi, eds. 1987. *Selected Works of Xue Fucheng*. Shanghai: Shanghai People's Publishing House.
51. Dong, Wei. 2018. *A Book on Relieving Famine and Reviving the People*. Vol. 1, 2, 3. Beijing: China Bookstore.
52. Dunstan, Helen, and Wang Jiang. 2007. 1748 Re-examined: Raison D'Stat and Policy Change Towards the Ever-normal Granaries. *The Qing History Journal* 2:1–11.
53. Dunstan, Helen. 2006. *State or Merchant Political Economy and Political Process in 1740s China*. Massachusetts: The Harvard University Asia Center.
54. Elliott, J. E., and B. S. Clark. 1987. Keynes's "General Theory" and Social Justice. *Journal of Post Keynesian Economics* 9 (3): 381–394.
55. Engels, Frederick. 1970. *Anti-Duhring: Herr Eugen Duhring's Revolution in Science*. Trans. Emile Burns. New York: International Publishers.
56. Ezekiel, M. 1966. Henry A. Wallace, Agricultural Economist. *Journal of Farm Economics* 48 (4): 789–802.
57. Fan, Ye. 1965. *The Book of the Later Han*. Vol. 37, 39. Beijing: Zhonghua Book Company.
58. Fang, Guancheng. 2017. *Maps of the Charity Granaries in the Capital Area*. Ed. Cui Guangshe et al. Baoding: Hebei University Press.
59. Fang, Xiuqi, et al. 2019. *The Impact of Historical Climate Change on China's Society and Economy*. Beijing: China Science Publishing and Media Ltd.
60. Fantacci, L., and Rosselli, A. 2009. Stabilizing Commodities. Buffer Stock Plans by Keynes and Kahn. *ESHET 13th Conference Paper.*
61. Fantacci, L., et al. 2010. Speculation in Commodities: Keynes' "Practical Acquaintance" with Future Markets. *Journal of the History of Economic Thought* 32 (3): 397–418.
62. Fantacci, L., et al. 2012. Speculation and Buffer Stocks: The Legacy of Keynes and Kahn. *The European Journal of the History of Economic Thought* 19 (3): 453–473.
63. Feng, Liutang. 1934. *A History of Food Policy in Ancient China*. Beijing: Commercial Press.
64. Forstater, M. 1999. Functional Finance and Full Employment: Lesson from Lerner for Today. *Journal of Economic Issues* 33 (2): 475–482.
65. Ganzel, Bill. 2003. *CCC, Civilian Conservation Corps, 2003* [EB/OL]. http://www.livinghistoryfarm.org/farminginthe30s/water_12.html
66. Gao, Shi, and Yang Zhenzao. 1991. *Records of Changshu County*. Vol. 3. Nanjing: Jiangsu Ancient Books Publishing House.
67. Gao, Wangling. 2005. *Living Tradition: Economic Development and Government Policies in Eighteenth-Century China*. Beijing: Peking University Press.
68. Gardner, Daniel K. 2019. Zhu Xi's Commentarial Work: Abiding in the Mean and the Constant. In *Zhu Xi: Selected Writings*, ed. Philip J. Ivanhoe. New York: Oxford University Press.
69. Geng, Hu. 2002. Further Exploration of the Relationship Between *Hedi* and *Pingdi*. *Journal of Chinese Social and Economic History* 2:48–56.
70. Gordon, W. 1997. Job Assurance: The Job Guarantee Revisited. *Journal of Economic Issues* 31 (3): 826–834.
71. Graham, B. 1937. *Storage and Stability: A Modern Ever-normal Granary*. New York and London: McGraw-Hill Book Company, Inc.
72. Graham, B. 1944. *The World Commodities and World Currency*. New York and London: McGraw-Hill Book Company, Inc.

73. Graham, F. D. 1942. *Social Goals and Economic Institutions*. Princeton: Princeton University Press.
74. Graham, F. D. 1944. Keynes vs. Hayek on a Commodity Reserve Currency. *The Economic Journal* 54 (215/216): 422–429.
75. Gu, Ying. 1993. A Preliminary Exploration of the Problem of Grain Accumulation in the Preparedness Granaries in the Ming Dynasty. *Collected Papers of Historical Studies* 1:20–26.
76. Guanzi. 1985. *Guanzi: Political, Economic, and Philosophical Essays from Early China*. Vol. 1. Trans. Walter A. Rickett. Princeton: Princeton University Press.
77. Guanzi. 1998. *Political, Economic, and Philosophical Essays from Early China*. Vol. 2. Trans. Walter. A. Rickett. Princeton: Princeton University Press.
78. Guo, Moruo, et al. 1984. *The Complete Works of Guo Moruo: History*. Vol. 5. Beijing: People's Publishing House.
79. Guo, Moruo. 1954. A Study of the Chapter "on Extravagance in Spending". *Historical Research* 3:27–62.
80. Han, Hua. 1999. Chen Huan-zhang's Interpretation of Confucius' "Economical Principles" in the Modern Era. *Social Science Research* 1:87–92.
81. Harrod, R. F. 1969. *The Life of John Maynard Keynes*. New York: Augustus M. Kelley Publishers.
82. Harvey, P. 1989. *Securing the Right to Employment*. Princeton: Princeton University Press.
83. Hayek, F. A. 1943. A Commodity Reserve Currency. *The Economic Journal* 53 (210/211): 176–184.
84. He, Chunzhi. 2010. *A Compendium on Famine Relief.* ed. Chen, Zhe and Luo Xinglian. In *Collections of Chinese Books on Famine Administration*, ed. Wenhai Li et al., vol. 1, 115–152. Tianjin: Tianjin Ancient Books Publishing House.
85. He, Rong. 2014. The Development and Management of the Ever-Normal Granary in Xinjiang in the Qing Dynasty. *Journal of Xinjiang University (Philosophy, Humanities & Social Sciences)* 42 (2): 66–69.
86. Heisenberg, Werner. 1958. *Physics and Philosophy: The Revolution in Modern Science*. New York: Harper & Brothers Publishers.
87. Henry, J. F. 2001. Keynes' Economic Program, Social Institutions, Ideology, and Property Rights. *Journal of Economics Issues* 35 (3): 633–655.
88. Hirai, T. 2009. Aimed at the Stabilization of Commodity Prices- Keynes's Hopes Betrayed and the Transmutation Process of the International Control Scheme. *ESHET 13th Conference Paper.*
89. Hsiao, Kung-chuan. 1960. *Rural China: Imperial Control in the Nineteenth Century*. Seattle: University of Washington Press.
90. Hu, Bo. 2002. A Tentative Study on the Changes in the Grain Storage Scale of the Ever-Normal Granary in the Loess Plateau Region of Shaanxi During the Qing Dynasty. *Journal of Shaanxi Normal University (Philosophy and Social Sciences)* S1:157–159.
91. Hu, Huojin, and Zhang Hanyu. 2012, January 18. Elderly Administrators Overseeing the Granaries for Famine Relief in the Townships of the Ming Dynasty. *Chinese Social Sciences Today*. A05.
92. Hu, Jichuang. 1998. *History of Chinese Economic Thought*. Vol. 1. Shanghai: Shanghai University of Finance and Economics Press.
93. Huang, Boxuan. 1944. The Origin and Nature of Ever-Normal Granaries. *Economic Forum* 2 (2): 47–54.
94. Huang, Alfred. 1998. *The Complete I Ching*. Vermont: Inner Traditions.
95. Huang, Han. 1936. *Guanzi S Economic Thought*. Shanghai: Commercial Press.
96. Hucker, Charles O. 1988. *A Dictionary of Official Titles in Imperial China*. Taipei: Southern Materials Center, Inc.
97. Innes, A. M. 1913. What Is Money? *The Banking Law Journal* 30 (5): 377–408.
98. Innes, A. M. 1914. The Credit Theory of Money? *The Banking Law Journal* 31 (2): 151–168.

99. Novak, James L., et al. 2022. *Agricultural Policy in the United States: Evolution and Economics*. 2nd ed. London and New York: Routledge.
100. Jaspers, Karl. 1953. *The Origin and Goal of History*. New Haven and London: Yale University Press.
101. Jevons, W. S. 1981. Papers on Political Economy. In *Papers and Correspondence of William Stanley Jevons*, ed. R. D. Collison Black, vol. 7. London: Macmillan.
102. Jia, Genliang, and Liu Lin. 2011. Rare-earth Issues in China: A Perspective from Economic History and an Analysis of Evolutionary Economics. *Journal of Peking University (Philosophy and Social Science)* 4:138–146.
103. Jiang, Pu. 1986. *Explanations to the Classics and Histories for Imperial Review*, vol. 25. In *Complete Library in the Four Branches of Literature (Wenyuange Edition), Zi section*, vol. 723. Taibei: Commercial Press of Taiwan.
104. Jiang, Xidong. 1996. Merchants[5] Market Monopoly and Government's Anti-monopoly Measures in the Song Dynasty. *Researches in Chinese Economic History* 2:32–41.
105. Johnson, Elizabeth. 1973. John Maynard Keynes: Scientist or Politician? In *After Keynes: Papers Presented to Section F (Economics) at the 1972 Annual Meeting of the British Association for the Advancement of Science*, ed. Joan Robinson, 11–25. Oxford: Basil Blackwell.
106. Julio, Lopez G., and Michael Assous. 2010. *Michal Kalecki*. London and New York: Palgrave Macmillan.
107. Kadmos, G., and O' Hara P. A. 2000. The Taxes-Drive-Money and Employer of Last Resort Approach to Government Policy. *Journal of Economics and Social Policy* 5 (1): 1–18.
108. Kahn, R. F. 1931. The Relation of Home Investment to Unemployment. *Economic Journal* 41 (162): 173–198.
109. Kahn, R. F. 1984. *The Making of Keynes' General Theory*. London and New York: Cambridge University Press.
110. Kalecki, M. 1943. Political Aspects of Full Employment. *Political Quarterly* 14 (4): 322–331.
111. Kang, Peizhu. 1996. The Decline of Storage Systems and Famines in the Qing Dynasty. *Social Science Front* 3:186–191.
112. Kazuo, Inamori. 2015. *The Way to Work*. Trans. Cao Xiuyun. Beijing: Machinery Industry Press.
113. Keynes, J. M. 1937. The General Theory of Employment. *Quarterly Journal of Economics* 51 (2): 209–223.
114. Keynes, J. M. 1938. The Policy of Government Storage of Food-Stuffs and Raw Materials. *The Economics Journal* 48 (191): 449–460.
115. Keynes, J. M. 1943. The Objective of International Price Stability. *The Economic Journal* 53 (210/211): 185–187.
116. Keynes, J. M. 1999. *The General Theory of Employment, Interest and Money*. Trans. Gao Hongye. Beijing: The Commercial Press.
117. Keynes, J. M. 2013. Activities 1922-1929: The Return to Gold and Industrial Policy. In *The Collected Writings of John Maynard Keynes*, ed. D. Moggridge, vol. 19. New York: Cambridge University Press.
118. Keynes, J. M. 2013. Activities 1931-1939: World Crisis and Policies in Britain and America. In *The Collected Writings of John Maynard Keynes*, ed. D. Moggridge, vol. 21. New York: Cambridge University Press.
119. Keynes, J. M. 2013. Activities 1940-1944: Shaping the Post-war World: The Cleaning Union. In *The Collected Writings of John Maynard Keynes*, ed. D. Moggridge, vol. 25. New York: Cambridge University Press.
120. Keynes, J. M. 2013. Economic Articles and Correspondence: Investment and Editorial. In *The Collected Writings of John Maynard Keynes*, ed. D. Moggridge, vol. 12. New York: Cambridge University Press.
121. Keynes, J. M. 2013. Essays in Persuasion. In *The Collected Writings of John Maynard Keynes*, ed. D. Moggridge, vol. 9. New York: Cambridge University Press.

122. Keynes, J. M. 2013. The General Theory of Employment, Interest and Money. In *The Collected Writings of John Maynard Keynes*, ed. D. Moggridge, vol. 7. New York: Cambridge University Press.
123. Keynes, J. M. 1944. Note by Lord Keynes. *The Economic Journal* 54 (215/216): 429–430.
124. Keynes, J. M. 2013. A Treatise on Money: The Applied Theory of Money. In *The Collected Writings of John Maynard Keynes*, ed. D. Moggridge, vol. 6. New York: Cambridge University Press.
125. Keynes, J. M. 2013. Activities 1940-1946: Shaping the Post-war World: Employment and Commodities. In *The Collected Writings of John Maynard Keynes*, ed. D. Moggridge, vol. 27. New York: Cambridge University Press.
126. Knapp, G. F. 1924. *The State Theory of Money*. London: Macmillan.
127. Knoblock, John. 1994. *Xunzi: A Translation and Study of the Complete Works*. Vol. 3. Stanford: Stanford University Press.
128. Kong, Xiangjun. 2009. Research on Ever-Normal Granary in the Two Song Dynasties. *Journal of Nanjing Agricultural University (Social Sciences)* 9 (4): 102–108.
129. Kregel, J. A. 1993. Keynesian Stabilization Policy and Post-war Economic Performance. In *Explaining Economic Growth: Essays in Honour of Angus Maddison*, ed. E. Szimai et al., 429–445. Amsterdam: Elsevier Science Publishers B.V.
130. Kregel, J. A. 1996. The Theory of Value, Expectation and Chapter 17 of the General Theory. In *A Second Edition of the General Theory*, ed. G. C. Harcourt and P. Riach, 261–282. London: Routledge.
131. Kregel, J. A. 2010. Keynes's Influence on Modern Economics: Some Overlooked Contributions of Keynes's Theory of Finance and Economics Policy. In *The Return to Keynes*, ed. B. Bateman et al., 241–256. Harvard: Harvard University Press.
132. Lang, Xiaoqing. 1933. *A History of Food Supply in China*. Beijing: Commercial Press.
133. Laozi. 2001. *Dao De Jing: The Book of the Way*. Trans. Moss Roberts. Berkeley, Los Angeles and London: University of California Press.
134. Legge, J., trans. 1865. *The Shoo King, or The Book of Historical Documents*, vol. 1–2. London: Tuubner & Co.
135. Legge, J., trans. 1960. *The Chinese Classics: Confucian Analects; The Great Learning; The Doctrine of the Mean.* Hong Kong: Hong Kong University Press.
136. Legge, James, trans. 1885. *The Sacred Books of China: The Texts of Confucianism, Part 3–4, The Li Ki.* Oxford: Clarendon Press.
137. Lerner, A. P. 1943. Functional Finance and the Federal Debt. *Social Research* 10 (1): 38–51.
138. Lerner, A. P. 1946. Money. In *Encyclopedia Britannica: A New Survey of Universal Knowledge*, vol. 15, 14th ed., 693–698. London: Encyclopedia Britannica, Inc.
139. Lerner, A. P. 1947. Money as a Creature of the State. *The American Economic Review. Papers and Proceedings of the Fifty-ninth Annual Meeting of thse American Economic Association* 37 (2): 312–317.
140. Lerner, A. P. 1951. *Economics of Employment*. New York: McGraw-Hill.
141. Lerner, A. P. 1983. The Economic Steering Wheel. In *Selected Economic Writings of Abba P. Lerner*, ed. D. Colander, 271–277. New York: New York University Press.
142. Leuchtenburg, William E. 2009. *Frankin D. Roosevelt and the New Deal: 1932-1940*. New York: Harper Perennial.
143. Li, Chaomin. 2000. A Safeguard for the Prosperity of Modern American Agriculture: The Ever Normal Granary and the Agricultural Adjustment Act of 1938. *Journal of Finance and Economics* 12:56–62.
144. Li, Chaomin. 2000. The Ever-normal Granary: A Debate in the 1930s' U.S. *Journal of Shanghai University of Finance and Economics* 3:13–20.
145. Li, Chaomin. 2000. The Influence of the Idea of Ever Normal Granary on Henry A. Wallace and the Agricultural Adjustment Act in the New Deal. *Fudan Journal (Social Sciences)* 3:42–50.

146. Li, Chaomin. 2002. *Ever-normal Granary: A Chinese Idea in the American Systems.* Shanghai: Shanghai Far East Publishers.
147. Li, Chaomin. 2002. The Ever Normal Granary: Reflections on the Tracing of the Source of Contemporary Economic Stability Policy to China. *Fudan Journal (Social Sciences)* 2:70–76.
148. Li, Chaomin. 2004. The Practical Significance of Agricultural Legislation and the Ever-normal Granary Program in the United States Over the Past 70 Years. *Issues in Agricultural Economy* 4:73–77.
149. Li, Chaomin. 2014. *The Mystery of the Rise of the Great Nations: The Chinese Origin of the American Ever-normal Granary System.* Beijing: Central Compilation & Translation Press.
150. Li, Chaomin. 2002. On the Influence of Wang Anshi's Economic Thoughts on the Ever-normal Granary of the New Deal in the United States. *Journal of Southwest Normal University* 6:96–100.
151. Li, Dun J. 1967. *The Essence of Chinese Civilization.* Princeton: Van Nostrand.
152. Li, Fenyang. 2006. *Research on Storage Systems in the Qing Dynasty.* Taibei: Wenhai Press Company.
153. Li, Huarui. 2012. The Development and Changes of the Disaster Relief Storage System in the Song Dynasty. In *Jinan Historical Science*, ed. Mingda Ma, vol. 7, 497–531. Guilin: Guangxi Normal University Press.
154. Li, Huarui. 2012. The Registration System and Statistical Survey of Households Needing Disaster Relief in the Song Dynasty. *Historical Research* 6:30–42.
155. Li, Jing. 2015. A Preliminary Study of the Relief Granary During the Ming Dynasty: A Case Study of the Southern Zhili Region. *Journal of Chinese Architecture History* 1:330–363.
156. Li, Jinshui. 2007. *Researches on Wang Anshi's Economic Reform.* Fuzhou: Fujian People's Publishing House.
157. Li, Lillian M. 2007. *Fighting Famine in North China: State, Market, and Environmental Decline, 1690s-1990s.* Stanford: Stanford University Press.
158. Li, Linfu, et al. 1992. In *Six Institutions of Tang Dynasty*, ed. Zhongfu Chen, vol. 20. Beijing: Zhonghua Book Company.
159. Li, Tao. 2004. *Supplement to Historical Mirror to Aid in Government.* Vol. 33, 62, 175, 214, 231, 239, 245, 251, 256. Beijing: Zhonghua Book Company.
160. Li, Wenhai, et al., eds. 2010. *Collections of Chinese Books on Famine Administration.* Tianjin: Tianjin Ancient Books Publishing House.
161. Li, Xinchuan. 2000. *Miscellaneous Records of Historical Documents from Jianyan Period, Section 1.* Vol. 15. Beijing: Zhonghua Book Company.
162. Li, Yun. 2020, November 26. Five Archaeological Discoveries Make Xia Culture More Credible. *Guangming Daily*, p. 1.
163. Liang, Gengyao. 2005. Community Granary of Southern Song Dynasty. In *Economic Pulse*, ed. Chen Guodong et al., 136–163. Beijing: Encyclopedia of China Publishing House.
164. Liang, Qichao. 1989. *Thoughts from the Ice-Drinker s Studio.* Vol. 28. Beijing: Zhonghua Book Company.
165. Lin, Puchu. 1930. A Study of Granaries. *New Life* 3 (9): 76–88.
166. Lin, Xiyi. 1986. Sequel to the Eleven Drafts of *Lin Xiyi*, vol. 11. In *Complete Library in the Four Branches of Literature (Wenyuange Edition), Ji section*, vol. 1185. Taibei: Commercial Press of Taiwan.
167. List, Frederick. 1856. *National System of Political Economy.* Trans. G. A. Matile. Philadelphia: J. B. Lippincott & Co.
168. Liu, An. 2012. *The Essential Huainanzi.* Trans. J. S. Major, S. A. Queen, A. S. Meyer and H. D. Roth. New York: Columbia University Press.
169. Liu, Cuirong. 2005. Review of the Stability Function of the Qing Dynasty Warehousing System. In *Economic Pulse*, ed. Guodong Chen et al., 317–346. Beijing: Encyclopedia of China Publishing House.
170. Liu, Diyuan. 1997. *Review of Keynesian Economic Doctrine.* Wuhan: Wuhan University Press.

171. Liu, Jiapeng. 2010. *The Evolution of Thoughts on Grain Reserve Regulation System in Ancient China*. Beijing: Economic Press China.
172. Liu, Jinzao. 2000. *Sequel to Comprehensive Textual Research of Historical Documents of Qing Dynasty*. Vol. 60. Hangzhou: Zhejiang Ancient Books Publishing House.
173. Liu, Qiugen. 1989. The Operation of the Ever-Normal Granary in the Tang and Song Dynasties and the Implementation of the Green Sprouts Act. *Journal of Hebei University (Philosophy and Social Sciences)* 4:16–20.
174. Liu, Xu, et al., eds. 1975. *Old History of Tang Dynasty*. Vol. 44, 49, 123. Beijing: Zhonghua Book Company.
175. Liu, Xuyi, and Cunxun Li. 2002. *General History of the United States*. Vol. 5. Beijing: People's Publishing House.
176. Liu, Zai. 1986. Community Granary of Hu's Family in Nankang. *Collections of Liu Zai*, vol. 22. In *Complete Library in the Four Branches of Literature (Wenyuange Edition), Ji section*, vol. 1170. Taibei: Commercial Press of Taiwan.
177. Long, Wenbin. 1998. *Economic and Political Structures of Ming Dynasty*. Vol. 56. Beijing: Zhonghua Book Company.
178. Lu, Zengyu. Six Strategies After the Disaster. *Imperially Authorized Compendium of Disaster Relief*, vol. 4. ed. Zhao Li and Xu Na. In *Collections of Chinese Books on Famine Administration*, ed. Wenhai Li et al., vol. 3. Tianjin: Tianjin Ancient Books Publishing House.
179. Lu, Zengyu. Twenty Policies for Coping with Emergencies. *Imperially Authorized Compendium of Disaster Relief*, vol. 3. ed. Zhao Li and Xu Na. In *Collections of Chinese Books on Famine Administration*, ed. Wenhai Li et al. Tianjin: Tianjin Ancient Books Publishing House.
180. Luo, Jiangling. 2017. *Research on the Program of College Graduates as Village Officials and Relevant Problems*. Beijing: China Social Sciences Press.
181. Luo, Weidong, and Jiang Ziqiang. 1994. The Lange Model and the Theory of Socialist Market Economy: The Historical Origins of the Theory of Socialist Market Economy. *Academic Monthly* 5:41–46.
182. Lynn, R. J. 1994. *The Classic of Changes: A New Translation of the I Ching as Interpreted by Wang Bi*. New York: Columbia University Press.
183. Ma, Duanlin. *Comprehensive Textual Research of Historical Documents*. Beijing: Zhonghua Book Company.
184. Ma, Feibai. 1979. *New Interpretation of the Qing-Zhong Chapters in Guanzi*. Beijing: Zhonghua Book Company.
185. Ma, Li, and Fang Xiuqi. 2009. The Spatial Patterns of Grain Storage Quota in the Ever-Normal Granary in Qing Dynasty. *Journal of Chinese Historical Geography* 3:68–74.
186. Macdonald, D. 1948. *Henry Wallace: the Man and the Myth*. New York: The Vanguard Press.
187. Major, J. S. 1993. *Heavens and Earth in Early Han Thought: Chapters Three, Four and Five of the Huainanzi*. Albany: State University of New York Press.
188. Mandel, E. 1967. *An Introduction to Marxist Economic Theory*. New York: Pathfinder Press.
189. Marx, Karl, and Frederick Engels. 1986. *Karl Marx and Frederick Engels: Selected Works*. Vol. 3. Moscow: Progress Publishers.
190. Marx, Karl, and Frederick Engels. 2010. *Marx & Engels Collected Works*. Vol. 24. London: Lawrence & Wishart.
191. Marx, Karl. 1972. *Critique of the Gotha Program*. Beijing: Foreign Languages Press.
192. Marx, Karl. 1976. *Capital: A Critique of Political Economy*. Vol. 1. Trans. Ben Fowkes. London: Penguin Books.
193. Marx, Karl. 1981. *Capital: A Critique of Political Economy*. Vol. 3. Trans. David Fernbach. London: Penguin Books.
194. Matsushita, Konosuke. 1984. *The Complete Collection of Business Management, vol. 5: Tap Water Management Philosophy*. Taibei: Celebrity Publishers.
195. Mehrling, P. 2000. Modern Money: Fiat or Credit? *Journal of Post Keynesian Economics* 22 (3): 397–406.

196. Mencius. 2009. *Mencius*. Trans. Irene Bloom. New York: Columbia University Press.
197. Michell, W. F. 1998. The Buffer Stock Employment Model and the NAIRU: The Path to Full Employment. *Journal of Economics Issues* 32 (2): 547–555.
198. Milburn, Olivia. 2010. *The Glory of Yue: An Annotated Translation of the Yuejue Shu*. Leiden and Boston: Brill.
199. Milburn, Olivia, and trans. 2016. *The Spring and Autumn Annals of Master Yan*. Leiden and Boston: Brill.
200. Minsky, H. P. 2008. *John Maynard Keynes*. New York: McGraw-Hill.
201. Minsky, H. P. 2008. *Stabilizing an Unstable Economy*. New York: McGraw-Hill.
202. Mirabeau, V. D. R. 1968. *Francois Quesnay: The Economic Table, an Attempt Towards Ascertaining and Exhibiting the Source, Progress, and Employment of Riches with Explanations*. New York: Bergman Publishers.
203. Montes, L. 2003. Das Adam Smith Problem: Its Origins, the Stages of the Current Debate, and One Implication for Our Understanding of Sympathy. *Journal of the History of Economic Thought* 25 (1): 63–90.
204. Mosler, W. 1997–1998. Full Employment and Price Stability. *Journal of Post Keynesian Economics* 20 (2): 167–182.
205. Murong, Hao. 2004. Exploring Ever-Normal Granary in the Han Dynasty. *Inner Mongolia Social Science* 35 (3): 77–79.
206. Murray, M. J., and M. Forstater, eds. 2013. *Employment Guarantee Schemes*. New York: Palgrave Macmillan.
207. Needham, Joseph. 1959. *Science and Civilisation in China*. Vol. 3. Cambridge: Cambridge University Press.
208. Ni, Yuping. 2013. *Finance and Society During the Jiaqing and Daoguang Reigns of the Qing Dynasty*. Beijing: The Commercial Press.
209. Niu, Jingzhong. 1991. The Social Functions of the Ever-Normal Granary and Community Granary in the Qing Dynasty. *Journal of Inner Mongolia University (Humanities and Social Sciences)* 22 (1): 45–51.
210. Ouyang, Xiu, and Song Qi. 1975. *New History of Tang Dynasty*. Vol. 51, 54, 149. Beijing: Zhonghua Book Company.
211. Palma, G. 1994. Kahn on Buffer Stock. *Cambridge Journal of Economics* 18 (1): 117–127.
212. Pan, Xiaowei. 1984. On Charity Granary in Tang Dynasty. *Agricultural History of China* 4:18–23.
213. Pan, Xiaowei. 1998. Further Studies on Charity Granary in Tang Dynasty. *Agricultural History of China* 3:32–38.
214. Pang, Pu. 2009. *Studies on the Dialectics of Confucianism*. Beijing: Zhonghua Book Company.
215. Pierson, J. H. G. 1964. *Insuring Full Employment: A United States Policy for Domestic Prosperity and World Development*. New York: The Viking Press.
216. Pikett, T. 2014. *Capital in the Twenty-First Century*. Trans. Goldhammer, Arthur. Cambridge: Belknap Press.
217. Publicity Department of the CPC Central Committee ed. 2018. *Thirty Lectures on Xi Jinping Thought on Socialism with Chinese Characteristics for a New Era*. Beijing: Xuexi Chuban She (Learning Press).
218. Qian, Mu. 2001. *Research Methodology of Chinese History*. Beijing: SDX Joint Publishing Co.
219. Qing, Gui, Dong Gao, et al. 1985. *Factual Record of Qing Dynasty: Records of Emperor Gaozong*. Vol. 46, 50, 65, 189. Beijing: Zhonghua Book Company.
220. Qiu, Jun. 2012. *Supplement to Great Learning*. Vol. 14, 25, 27. Ed. Jing Liangnian. Shanghai: Shanghai Bookstore Publishing House.
221. Ramsay, T. 2002–2003. The Jobs Guarantee: A Post Keynesian Analysis. *Journal of Post Keynesian Economics* 25 (2): 273–291.

222. Rasmussen, W. D. et al. 1976. A short history of Agricultural Adjustment, 1933–75. *National Economic Analysis Division, Economic Service, U.S. Department of Agriculture, Agriculture Information Bulletin.* (391). https://ageconsearch.umn.edu/record/309186?v=pdf
223. Ren, Jiliang. 2005. *Research on Guanzi's Economic Thought: Historical Analysis of "Qing-Zhong Principles"*. Beijing: China Social Sciences Press.
224. Robinson, Joan. 1973. What Has Become of the Keynesian Revolution? In *After Keynes: Papers Presented to Section F (Economics) at the 1972 Annual Meeting of the British Association for the Advancement of Science*, ed. Joan Robinson, 1–10. Oxford: Basil Blackwell.
225. Roosevelt, Franklin D. 1938. *The Public Papers and Addresses of Franklin D. Roosevelt.* Vol. 2, 3, 4. Ed. Samuel I Roseman. New York: Random House.
226. Rowe, William T. 2001. *Saving the World: Chen Hongmou and Elite Consciousness in Eighteenth-Century China.* Stanford: Stanford University Press.
227. Ruan, Yuan, ed. 2009. *Annotations to the Thirteen Classics.* Beijing: Zhonghua Book Company.
228. Scheiber, H. N., et al. 1976. *American Economic History.* New York, Hagerstown, San Francisco, London: Harper & Row.
229. Schlebeker, John T. 1975. *Whereby We Thrive: A History of American Farming, 1607-1972.* Iowa: The Iowa University Press.
230. Scitovky, T. 1984. Lerner's Contribution to Economics. *Journal of Economic Literature* 22 (4): 1547–1571.
231. Sen, Amartya. 1981. *Poverty and Famine: An Essay on Entitlement and Deprivation.* Oxford: Clarendon Press.
232. Shanyou Academy of History and Culture. ed. *Xitai Collection (with Three Other Works).* Shanghai: Shanghai Ancient Books Publishing House.
233. She, Yu. 2013. *Minor Policies on "Village Officials", Grand Strategy for Talents: Evaluation of Program of College Graduates as Village Officials.* Beijing: China Development Press.
234. Shen, Defu. 1959. Ministry of Revenue. In *Anecdotes and Unofficial Stories During Emperor Wanli S Reign*, vol. 12. Beijing: Zhonghua Book Company.
235. Shen, Kuo. 2008. *Brush Talks from Dream Brook.* Vol. 1. Trans. Hong Wang, and Zhao Jing. Chengdu: Sichuan People's Publishing House.
236. Shen, Shixing, et al. 1995. *Code of Great Ming Dynasty,* vol. 22. In *Supplement to Complete Library in the Four Branches of Literature. ed. Committee for Compilation of Supplement to Complete Library in the Four Branches of Literature. Shi section,* vol. 789. Shanghai: Shanghai Ancient Books Publishing House.
237. Shen, Wenfu. 1944. On the Ever-Normal Granary Policy Advocated by Wallace in the United States. *Economic Forum* 2 (7–8): 21–26.
238. Shen, Wenfu. 1945. On the Ever-Normal Granary Policy Throughout History and Around the World. *Eastern Miscellany 41 (6)*: 20–30.
239. Shi, Su. 1986. Community granary. *Annals of Huiji.* vol. 13. In *Complete Library in the Four Branches of Literature (Wenyuange Edition), Ji section*, vol. 486. Taibei: Commercial Press of Taiwan.
240. Shi, Tao. 2010. *A Study of Natural Disasters and Governmental Management Systems in the Northern Song Dynasty.* Beijing: Social Sciences Academic Press.
241. Shi, Yang. 2023. Historical Predecessors of "*di*" and "*tiao*": The Usage of "糴" (*di*) in Unearthed Texts from the Warring States to the Western Jin Dynasty. *Journal of Chinese Historical Studies* 2:68–84.
242. Sima, Guang. 1956. *Comprehensive Mirror to Aid in Government.* Vol. 226. Beijing: Zhonghua Book Company.
243. Sima, Qian. 1982. *Records of the Grand Historian.* Vol. 30, 97, 129. Beijing: Zhonghua Book Company.
244. Sima, Qian. 1993. *Records of the Grand Historian: Han Dynasty.* Vol. 2. Trans. Burton Watson. Hong Kong and New York: Columbia University Press.

245. Skidelsky, Robert. 2003. *John Maynard Keynes: 1883-1946, Economist, Philosopher, Statesman*. New York: Penguin.
246. Smith, Adam. 1976. *The Theory of Moral Sentiments*. Oxford: Oxford University Press.
247. Sotiropoulos, D. P. 2011. Kalecki's Dilemma: Toward a Marxian Political Economy of Neoliberalism. *Rethinking Marxism* 23 (1): 100–116.
248. State Council Information Office of the People's Republic of China. 2019, October 14. *Food Security in China*. http://www.scio.gov.cn/zfbps/ndhf72019n/202207/t20220704_130642.html
249. Su, Shi. 1986. *The Collected Works of Su Shi*. Vol. 33, 35. Ed. Kong Fanli. Beijing: Zhonghua Book Company.
250. Su, Zhe. 1990. *Collections of Su Zhe*. Vol. 35. Eds. Chen, Hongtian and Gao Xiufang. Beijing: Zhonghua Book Company.
251. Swann, Nancy Lee, trans. 1950. *Food and Money in Ancient China: The Earliest Economic History of China to A.D. 25, Han Shu 24, with Related Texts, Han Shu 91 and Shih-Chi 129*. New Jersey: Princeton University Press.
252. Tang, Pin. Petition to Ban Pawning Grain in the Pawnshops. *Collection of Memorial to the Throne of Qing Dynasty*, vol. 45. In *Supplement to Complete Library in the Four Branches of Literature*. ed. Committee for Compilation of Supplement to Complete Library in the Four Branches of Literature. *Shi* section, vol. 473. Shanghai: Shanghai Ancient Books Publishing House.
253. Tcherneva, P. R. 2008. Keynes's Approach to Full Employment: Aggregate or Targeted Demand? *Working Paper No. 542*. https://www.econstor.eu/bitstream/10419/31663/1/585087695.pdf
254. Tcherneva, P. R. 2011. Fiscal Policy: Why Aggregate Demand Management Fail and What to Do About it. *Working Paper No.65O*. https://www.econstor.eu/bitstream/10419/57004/1/654831750.pdf
255. Tcherneva, P. R. 2012. Permanent on-the-Spot Job Creation-the Missing Keynes Plan for Full Employment and Economic Transformation. *Re^vie^w of Social Economy* 70 (1): 57–80.
256. Tcherneva, P. R. 2020. *The Case for a Job Guarantee*. Cambridge: Polity Press.
257. Tcherneva, P. R., and L. R. Wray 2005. Employer of Last Resort: A Case Study of Argentina's *Jefes* Program. *Working Paper No. 41, Center for Full Employment and Price Stability of the University qf Missour-Kansas City*. https://papers.ssrn.com/sol3/papers.cfm?abstract_id=1010145
258. Teng, Haijian. 2006. Origin and Status of Civilian Conservation Corps in the History of America. *Journal of Historical Science* 10:57–64.
259. Tian, Hua. 1992. Research on the Ever-Normal Granary in the Jin Dynasty. *Agricultural Archaeology* 9 (1): 256–261.
260. Tong, Weihua. 1984. Primitive Agricultural Remains from the Site of Magnetic Hill and Relevant Problems. *Agricultural Archaeology* 1:194–207.
261. Toqto'a, et al. 1985. *History of Song Dynasty*. Vol. 176, 324, 459. Beijing: Zhonghua Book Company.
262. Tsien, Tsuen-Hsuin. 1959. Asian Studies in America: A Historical Survey. In *Asian Studies and State Universities*, ed. Ssu-yu Teng, 108–121. Bloomington: Indiana University.
263. Waley, Arthur. 1960. *The Book of Songs, The Ancient Chinese Classic of Poetry*. New York: Grove Press.
264. Wan, Junren. 2000. On the Moral Dimension of the Market Economy. *Chinese Social Sciences* 2:4–13.
265. Wan, Junren. 2000. *The Dimension of Morality: An Introduction to Modern Economic Ethics*. Guangzhou: Guangdong People's Publishing House.
266. Wan, Weihan. 2010. Labor Relief. Miscellaneous Remarks on Famine Relief Policies. ed. Li, Wenhai. In *Collections of Chinese Books on Famine Administration*, ed. Wenhai Li et al. Tianjin: Tianjin Ancient Books Publishing House.
267. Wang, Anshi. 2017. *Complete Works of Wang Anshi*. Vol. 6. 7th ed. Wang, Shuizhao. Shanghai: Fudan University Press.

268. Wang, Fuzhi. 1996. *Complete Works of Wang Fuzhi*. Vol. 12. Changsha: Yuelu Publishing House.
269. Wang, Liqi, ed. 1992. *Discourses on Salt and Iron: Annotated and Commented*. Vol. 6. Beijing: Zhonghua Book Company.
270. Wang, Pizhi. 1981. *Fleeting Gossip by the River Sheng*. Ed. Youren Lu. Beijing: Zhonghua Book Company.
271. Wang, Qinruo, et al. 2006. *Prime Tortoise of the Record Bureau*. Vol. 106. Nanjing: Phoenix Publishing House.
272. Wang, Weiping, and Wang Hongxu. 2017. Evolution and Characteristics of the Preparedness Granary Policy in the Ming Dynasty. *Academics* 8:198–208.
273. Wang, Wendong. 2006. A Comparative Study of the Green Sprouts Act in the Song Dynasty and the Ever-Normal Granary System in the Tang and Song Dynasties. *Researches in Chinese Economic History* 3:29–36.
274. Wang, Wenjin, et al. *Comprehensive Institutions*. Vol. 12. Beijing: Zhonghua Book Company.
275. Wang, Xingya. 1993. The Pros and Cons of Implementing the Elderly Administration System in the Ming Dynasty. *Journal of Zhengzhou University (Philosophy and Social Sciences Edition)* 2:22–28.
276. Watson, Burton, trans. 2007. *The Analects of Confucius*. New York: Columbia University Press.
277. Wei, Shou. 1974. *History of Wei*. Vol. 62. Beijing: Zhonghua Book Company.
278. Wei, Tian'an. 2007. Some Issues Concerning the Ever-Normal Granary System. In *The Song History Research Forum*, ed. Xidong Jiang et al., vol. 8, 45–59. Hebei University Press.
279. Wei, Xi. 2010. Solution to Problems. *The Strategies of Famine Relief*. In *Collections of Chinese Books on Famine Administration*, ed. Wenhai Li et al., vol. 2. Tianjin: Tianjin Ancient Books Publishing House.
280. Wei, Zheng, ed. 1973. *The Book of Sui*. Vol. 24. Beijing: Zhonghua Book Company.
281. Wen, Yibo. 1943. *A History of Grain Administration in China*. Chongqing: Cheng Chung Book Company.
282. White, Jonathan B. 2002. *Saving Adam Smith: a Tale of Wealth, Transformation, and Virtue*. Upper Saddle River: Prentice Hall.
283. Will, Pierre-Etienne, and R. Bin Wong, eds. 1991. *Nourish the People: The State Civilian Granary System in China, 1650-1850*. Ann Arbor: University of Michigan Press.
284. Will, Pierre-Etienne. 1990. *Bureaucracy and Famine in Eighteenth-century China*. Trans. Elborg Forster. Stanford: Stanford University Press.
285. Wong, R. Bin. 1997. *China Transformed: Historical Change and the Limits of European Experience*. Ithaca and London: Cornell University Press.
286. Wray, L. R. 1998. *Understanding Modern Money: A Key to Full Employment and Price Stability*. Northampton: Edward Edgar.
287. Wray, L. R. 1998. Zero Unemployment and Stable Price. *Journal of Economics Issues* 32 (2): 539–545.
288. Wu, Baosan. 1989. *Research on Guanzi's Economic Thought*. Beijing: China Social Sciences Press.
289. Wu, Jing. 2009. *Annotated Political Program of Zhenguan Period*. Vol. 2, 8. Ed. Baocheng Xie. Beijing: Zhonghua Book Company.
290. Wu, Siwu. 2018. Differentiation of the Concepts of Charity Granary and Community Granary. *Collected Essays on Qing History* 2:287–300.
291. Wu, Siwu. 2018. *Institutional Dilemmas of Granary and Its Disaster Relief Practices in the Qing Dynasty*. Beijing: Social Sciences Academic Press.
292. Wu, Tao. 1996. A Preliminary Study of the Granary System in the Suzhou-Songjiang Region During the Ming Dynasty. *Agricultural History of China* 3:53–61.
293. Wu, Tao. 1997. On the Storage System in the Suzhou-Songjiang Region During the Early Qing Dynasty. *Agricultural History of China* 2:40–49.
294. Wu, Zeng. 1985. *Nenggaizhai Studio's Random Records*. Vol. 2. Beijing: Zhonghua Book Company.

295. Xi, Jinping. 2017. *Secure a Decisive Victory in Building a Moderately Prosperous Society in All Respects and Strive for the Great Success of Socialism with Chinese Characteristics for a New Era: Report to the 19th National Congress of the Communist Party of China*. Beijing: People's Publishing House.
296. Xi, Jinping. 2022. *Hold High the Great Banner of Socialism with Chinese Characteristics and Strive in Unity to Build a Modern Socialist Country in All Respects: Report to the 20th National Congress of the Communist Party of China*. Beijing: People's Publishing House.
297. Xi, Yufu, and Shen Shixu. 1974. *Classified Anthologies of Imperial Regulations*. Vol. 153. Taibei: Wenhai Press Company.
298. Xian, Wen, and Feng Xiaoying. 2012. Loan-Created Deposits and Endogenous Supply of Money: From the Perspective of the Nature of Money. *Journal of Finance and Economics* 1:14–23.
299. Xian, Wen, and Li Dawei. 2016. The Development Strategy of Late-Developing Countries: From Comparative Advantage to Appropriate Catch-up. *Social Sciences in Ningxia* 5:76–83.
300. Xian, Wen. 2017. The View of "Three *yi*" and Dialectical Reasoning: A Brief Exploration of the Economic Theory of *qing* and *zhong* in *Guanzi*. *The Ideological Front (Yunnan University's Journal of Social Sciences)* 43 (4): 98–107.
301. Xie, Fuzhan. 2019. Accelerating the Construction of a Discipline System, Academic System, and Discourse System for Philosophy and Social Sciences with Chinese Characteristics. *Chinese Social Science* 5:4–22.
302. Xu, Gengsheng. 2007. *American Agricultural Policies*. Beijing: Economy and Management Publishing House.
303. Xu, Jianqing. 1987. Examining the Accumulation in China's Feudal Society and Its Role in Social Reproduction from the Perspective of Granary Storage. *Researches in Chinese Economic History*31–48.
304. Xu, Song, ed. *Draft for the Collected Statutes of Song Dynasty*. Shanghai: Shanghai Ancient Books Publishing House.
305. Xu, Xueju. 1996. *Collection of Canons of the Ming Dynasty*. Vol. 101. Beijing: Bibliography and Document Publishing House.
306. Yan, Sisheng. 2004. On the Interconnection Between Community Granaries and Bao-Jia System. In *The Complete Works of Wei Yuan, vol. 15. ed. Editing Committee of The Complete Works of Wei Yuan. in Collected Essays on Statecraft of Qing Dynasty, vol. 40*, ed. Changling He and Wei Yuan, 286–288. Changsha: Yuelu Publishing House.
307. Yang, Guanqing. 1986. Attaching Importance of Paper Money, *keting leigao*. vol. 9. In *Complete Library in the Four Branches of Literature (Wenyuange Edition), Ji section*, vol. 1165. Taibei: Commercial Press of Taiwan.
308. Yang, Guo, and Zhao Zhile. 2014. The Countermeasures Against Famine by Different Scholar-Officials in Song Dynasty. *Wuhan University Journal (Philosophy & Social Science)* 2:47–55.
309. Yang, Jingren. 2010. On Construction. *Compilations for Relief and Aid*, vol. 13. ed. Hao, Bingjian. In *Collections of Chinese Books on Famine Administration*, ed. Wenhai Li et al., vol. 5, 3196–3198. Tianjin: Tianjin Ancient Books Publishing House.
310. Yang, Lien-sheng. 1961. *Studies in Chinese Institutional History*. Cambridge: Harvard University Press.
311. Yang, Shi. 1986. *Collection of Yang Shi*, vol. 12. In *Complete Library in the Four Branches of Literature (Wenyuange Edition), Ji section*, vol. 1125. Taibei: Commercial Press of Taiwan.
312. Yang, Shiqi, et al. 1962. Veritable Records of Emperor Taizong in Ming Dynasty. ed. Institute of History and Philosophy. *Academia Sinica*.
313. Yao, Jianping. 2005. Internal and External Functions: The Purchase and Sales of Grain from the Ever-Normal Granary in the Hubei-Hunan Regions During the Qing Dynasty. *Social Science Journal* 4:122–127.
314. Ye, Shi. 2010. A petition to Emperor Ningzong. In *The Collected Works of Ye Shi*, ed. Liu Gongchun et al., vol. 1, 2. Beijing: Zhonghua Book Company.

315. Ye, Shichang. 1965. On *qing-zhong* Principles in Guanzi. *Economic Research Journal* 1:56–61.
316. Ye, Tan. 1990. A Survey of Theories on Paper money in Song Dynasty. *Researches in CHINESE Economic History* 4:133–145.
317. Yu, Dunkang. 2016. *The Past and Present of Philosophy of Changes*. Beijing: China Renmin University Press.
318. Yu, Jinghui, and Lei Bo. 2016. The Green Shoots Lending policy in Xining Period of Northern Song Dynasty and the Debate on the Meaning of the Classics. *Historical Research* 2:20–39.
319. Yu, Jinghui. 2014. "Rites of Zhou Dynasty: Treasurer of Taxes" and Market Exchange Law in Xining Years: An In-depth Reading of the Article and Wang Anshi's Practical Philosophy. *Journal of Capital Normal University* 4:23–33.
320. Yu, Shude. 1921. Preventive Measures Against Agricultural Famines in Ancient China - Ever-Normal Granaries, Charity Granaries and Community Granaries (Part1). *Eastern Miscellany 8* (14): 18–30.
321. Yu, Shude. 1921. Preventive Measures Against Agricultural Famines in Ancient China - Ever-Normal Granaries, Charity Granaries and Community Granaries (Part 2). *Eastern Miscellany* 18 (15): 17–33.
322. Yu, Yingshi. 2014.*On. Heaven and Man: An Exploration of the Origins of Ancient Chinese Thought*. Beijing: Zhonghua Book Company.
323. Yu, Youyu. 1948. 』*Study of China's Warehousing System*. Shanghai: Cheng Chung Book Company.
324. Yuan, Mei. 1993. Reply to Governor-general of Jiangnan Province and Jiangxi Province on Matters of Revitalization and Reform. In *Collected Works of Yuanmei (xiao cangshanfang wenji), vol. 15. in Complete Works of Yuan Mei*, ed. Wang Yingzhi, vol. 2. Nanjing: Jiangsu Ancient Books Publishing House.
325. Yuan, Xie. 1986. Community Granaries of Hongdu Prefecture. *Collected Works of Yuan Xie (qiezhai ji)*, vol. 10. In *Complete Library in the Four Branches of Literature (Wenyuange Edition), Ji section*, vol. 1157. Taibei: Commercial Press of Taiwan.
326. Jiangyue, Zhai, trans. 2005. *Guanzi*, vol. 1. Nanning: Guangxi Normal University Press.
327. Zhang, Gong. 1986. *A Preliminary Exploration of Granary System in the Tang Dynasty*. Beijing: Zhonghua Book Company.
328. Zhang, Lin, and Bi Zhi. 2010. Impact of Institutionalists on "New Deal". In *Research Reports on Foreign Economics and China*, ed. Enfu Cheng et al., 251–255. Beijing: Social Sciences Academic Press.
329. Zhang, Tingyu, et al. 2000. *Comprehensive Textual Research of Historical Documents of Qing Dynasty*. Vol. 32, 34, 35, 36. Hangzhou: Zhejiang Ancient Books Publishing House.
330. Zhang, Wen. 2001. *Study of Social Relief in the Song Dynasty*. Chongqing: Southwest Normal University Press.
331. Zhang, Yan. 1993. A Preliminary Study on the Ever-Normal Granary System in the Qing Dynasty. *The Qing History Journal* 4:28–39.
332. Zhang, Yan. 1993. Charity Granary of Salt in the Qing Dynasty. *Salt Industry History Research* 3:50–58.
333. Zhang, Yan. 1998. On the Relationship Between Ever-Normal Granaries and Relevant Granaries in the Qing Dynasty. *The Journal of Chinese Social and Economic History* 4:52–58.
334. Zhang, Zai. 1978. *Collected Works of Zhang Zai*. Ed. Zhang Xichen. Beijing: Zhonghua Book Company.
335. Zhang, Zhaoyu. 2016. Study on Labor Relief in the Ming Dynasty. *Historical Research in Anhui* 6:21–28.
336. Ruyu, Zhao, ed. *Memorials Submitted to the Throne in the Song Dynasty*. Vol. 107. Shanghai: Shanghai Ancient Books Publishing House.
337. Zhao, Erxun. 1977. *Food and Money, II. Draft of Qing Dynasty*. Vol. 121, 3557. Beijing: Zhonghua Book Company.

338. Zhao, Jing. 2002. *A Comprehensive History of Chinese Economic Thought*. Vol. 1. Beijing: Peking University Press.
339. Zhao, Lisha. 2014. Patronized Art Project in the New Deal. *Public Art* 4:5–9.
340. Zhao, Shuzheng. 1989. *Research on Guanzi's Economic Thought*. Shanghai: Shanghai Classics Publishing House.
341. Zhen, Dexiu. 1937. Memorial to Set Up Community Granaries in Twelve Counties. In *Collected Works of Zhen Dexiu*, vol. 10. Changsha: Commercial Press.
342. Zhong, Yongning. 1990. The Ever-Normal Granary and Rice Exportation in Hunan During the Early Qing Dynasty. *Seeker (Qiu Suo)* 1:107–110.
343. Zhou, Qiong. 2011. Research on Relief Systems in the Qianlong Period *Providing Jobs Instead of Reliefs*. *Journal of Tsinghua University (Philosophy and Social Sciences)* 4:66–79.
344. Zhou, Zhiyuan. 2014. Re-exploration of Preparedness Granary in the Ming Dynasty. In *Studies on the Institutional Systems of the Ming Dynasty*, ed. Yanhong Wu, 262–279. Hangzhou: Zhejiang University Press.
345. Zhu, Hu. 2014. Food as the Heaven for the People: Policy Evolution and Structural Transformation of Disaster Preparedness Storage in the Qing Dynasty. *Journal of Historical Science* 4:20–25.
346. Zhu, Xi. 2002. *Complete Book of Zhu Xi*. Ed. Zhu Jieren, et al. Vol. 20, 24, 25. Shanghai and Hefei: Shanghai Ancient Books Publishing House: Anhui Education Publishing House.
347. Zhu, Xi. 2016. *Collected Commentaries on the Four Books*. Beijing: Zhonghua Book Company.
348. Zhu, Xi. 2020. *The Original Meaning of the Yijing: Commentary on the Scripture of Change*. Trans. Joseph A. Adler. New York: Columbia University Press.
349. Zou, Jinwen, and Huang Ailan. 2010. Monetary Policies in Ancient China: An Exposition on Adjusting Paper Money's Value. *Journal of Central China Normal University* 5:56–61.
350. Zuo, Qiuming. 2016. *Zuo Tradition / Zuozhuan: Commentary on the "Spring and Autumn Annals"*. Trans. Stephen Durrant, Wai-yee Li, and David Schaberg. Seattle and London: University of Washington Press.

MIX
Papier aus verantwortungsvollen Quellen
Paper from responsible sources
FSC® C105338

If you have any concerns about our products,
you can contact us on
ProductSafety@springernature.com

In case Publisher is established outside the EU,
the EU authorized representative is:
Springer Nature Customer Service Center GmbH
Europaplatz 3, 69115 Heidelberg, Germany

Printed by Libri Plureos GmbH
in Hamburg, Germany